Macromedia® FLASH™ MX

ActionScript
FOR FUN & GAMES

Updated for Flash MX with 12 new games!

- CASINO AND CARD GAMES
- ARCADE GAMES
- BRAIN TEASERS
- HUNT AND CLICK GAMES
- TOYS AND GADGETS
- TRIVIA AND WORD GAMES
- BALL AND PADDLE GAMES
- PICTURE PUZZLES
- CONSTRUCTION TOYS

Gary Rosenzweig

que®

```
function moveFox() {
foxBounds = determi
// if ground under fox, the
right now, tom ve and
n ne
b   hi
if (Ta ) checkFa
// if no ground
// lef left if
under fox
if (Key.isDown(Key.LEFT)) {
then start falling
if (foxSpeed < foxBounds.l
foxPos.x -= foxSpeed;
jump animation
```

Macromedia® Flash™ MX ActionScript for Fun & Games

International Standard Book Number: 0-7897-2799-4

Library of Congress Catalog Card Number: 2002105211

Printed in the United States of America

First Printing: July 2002

05   04   03   02   4   3   2

Trademarks

Warning and Disclaimer

EXECUTIVE EDITOR
Candace Hall

ACQUISITIONS EDITOR
Laura Norman

DEVELOPMENT EDITORS
Laura Norman
Sean Dixon

MANAGING EDITOR
Thomas F. Hayes

PROJECT EDITOR
Tonya Simpson

COPY EDITOR
Margo Catts

INDEXER
Chris Barrick

PROOFREADER
Plan-It Publishing

TECHNICAL EDITOR
Doug Scamahorn

TEAM COORDINATOR
Cindy Teeters

MULTIMEDIA DEVELOPER
Michael Hunter

INTERIOR DESIGNER
Trina Wurst

COVER DESIGNER
Anne Jones

ILLUSTRATIONS
William Follett

Overview

Contents

About the Author

Gary Rosenzweig is a game designer, programmer, entrepreneur, and the author of eight other books on Macromedia Director and Flash. He owns and operates CleverMedia, a Shockwave game development company that runs four game sites on the Internet: `http://clevermedia.com`, `http://gamescene.com`, `http://gamespark.com`, and `http://flasharcade.com`.

Since founding CleverMedia in 1996, the company has produced more than 200 games. The games on the four sites that make up the "CleverMedia Network" are all free for Web surfers to play. Many of the games have also been licensed to other Web sites.

Rosenzweig started in the multimedia business by obtaining a bachelor's degree in computer science from Drexel University in Philadelphia. His interest in newspapers took him to the University of North Carolina in Chapel Hill, where he earned a master's degree in journalism and mass communication.

Rosenzweig wrote his first book in 1995 on Macromedia Director Lingo and distributed it free on the Internet. In 1996, *The Comprehensive Guide to Lingo* was published by Ventana, followed the next year by *The Director 6 Book*. In 1999, *Special Edition Using Director 7* was published by Que. That was followed by *Special Edition Using Director 8* and then 8.5. After *Macromedia Flash 5 ActionScript for Fun & Games*, Gary wrote *Sams Teach Yourself ActionScript in 24 Hours*. Gary has also spoken at many Macromedia user conferences and the Game Developers Conference.

Gary reads a lot of classic science fiction books, likes to go to the movies, and enjoys travel. Gary's wife, Debby, owns and runs The Attic Bookstore (`http://www.atticbookstore.com/`), a used-book store. Gary and Debby live in Denver, Colorado, with their cat, Lucy, and dog, Natasha.

Dedication

I dedicated my third book, Special Edition Using Director 7, to my fiancée, Debby Thomsen. I'd like to dedicate this book, my ninth, to my wife, Debby Rosenzweig.

After writing so many books, she is used to what I say when I am finished with a book. Usually it is something like "That was too much stress. I'm never writing another book again!" Another thing she is used to is what I say a few weeks later, which is usually something like "Guess what, I just agreed to write another book!"

Debby is as much a part of this book as I am, even though she didn't write a word. I couldn't have written this book without her constant love and support. I love her more than anything.

Acknowledgments

Thanks to my wife, Debby, who enjoys challenging me to board games on our front porch and likes to test out the latest games at CleverMedia.

Thanks to my mom and dad, Jacqueline and Jerry, who always had a closet full of games while I was growing up and never complained that I was playing the Atari too much.

Thanks to my brother, Larry, who played games with me while we were growing up, even though he was several years younger and I always won.

Thanks to my grandmom, Rebecca Jacob, who bought me my first computer. A week later I had written my first game.

Thanks to my aunt and uncle, Barbara and Richard Shifrin, who collected chess sets and taught me how to win at Risk.

Thanks to William Follett, Brian Robbins, and Jay Shaffer, my friends and co-workers at CleverMedia. When you work with these guys, you realize that the only thing more fun than playing games is making them.

Thanks to my in-laws, Tage and Anne Thomsen, and Andrea Thomsen for their support while I wrote this book.

Thanks to all the people at Que who helped put this book together: Candy Hall, Laura Norman, Tom Hayes, Tonya Simpson, Margo Catts, Chris Barrick, Doug Scamahorn, Cindy Teeters, Michael Hunter, Trina Wurst, Anne Jones, and William Follett.

We Want to Hear from You!

As the reader of this book, *you* are our most important critic and commentator. We value your opinion and want to know what we're doing right, what we could do better, what areas you'd like to see us publish in, and any other words of wisdom you're willing to pass our way.

As an executive editor for Que, I welcome your comments. You can email or write me directly to let me know what you did or didn't like about this book—as well as what we can do to make our books better.

Please note that I cannot help you with technical problems related to the *topic* of this book. We do have a User Services group, however, where I will forward specific technical questions related to the book.

When you write, please be sure to include this book's title and author as well as your name, email address, and phone number. I will carefully review your comments and share them with the author and editors who worked on the book.

Email: feedback@quepublishing.com

Mail: Candy Hall
           Que Publishing
           201 West 103rd Street
           Indianapolis, IN 46290 USA

For more information about this book or another Que title, visit our Web site at www.quepublishing.com. Type the ISBN (excluding hyphens) or the title of a book in the Search field to find the page you're looking for.

Introduction

This is the second edition of *Macromedia Flash ActionScript for Fun & Games*. Here you will find all the material covered in the first edition, plus updates and 12 new games.

This book looks at ActionScript by presenting many complete programs. Each program contains a lot of ActionScript code that you can look at, learn from, and alter. Better still, these programs are toys, gadgets, and games.

This second edition is for Flash MX, also known as Flash 6. Although many of the book's first edition games will still work with Flash 5, you should be using Flash MX if you plan to use this book to learn ActionScript.

Although Flash 5 was the first version of Flash deep enough to allow us to make good Web-based games, Flash MX is even better. Most notably, Flash MX is much faster than its predecessors. This means that our games will run more smoothly on a larger number of user computers. In addition, we can now attempt some more complex games that are only possible with this better performance.

The first edition of this book was so well received that I didn't want to mess with it too much. So instead of changing the book, I simply added to it. Chapters 5 through 16 each have a new game, matching the theme of the rest of the chapter and usually building on what was taught in the earlier games of the chapter.

I've also updated several games to take advantage of some of Flash MX's new capabilities. For instance, the drawing program in Chapter 7, "Construction Toys," now uses Flash MX drawing commands instead of duplicating movie clips. In other cases, where performance in an older game would not have changed, I've left the ActionScript with code that works in both Flash 5 and MX.

What Is in This Book?

Although Flash has just recently come of age as a programming environment, it long ago established itself as an entertainment medium. Flash is used for everything from Web site window dressing to long-playing animated features.

With ActionScript, there is another side to Flash that still deals with entertainment: games. The contents of this book deal primarily with teaching you how to make games with Flash.

I start off by reviewing some Flash basics in Chapter 1, "Flash Elements Used to Make Games and Toys," by focusing on how different elements of Flash can be used to make interactive applications. Chapter 2, "An Introduction to ActionScript," will come in handy for someone who has used Flash a lot but hasn't done much programming before. It also will help people who have programmed in other languages, but never before in Flash.

Chapter 3, "ActionScript Elements Used to Make Games and Toys," looks at different ActionScript elements and techniques and shows you how they can be used to create games and other things. This chapter gives you the background you need for the rest of the book. In Chapter 4, "The Game-Creation Process," you learn about game planning and programming.

The rest of the book, except for the last chapter, contains many example programs with all the source code. Chapter 5, "ActionScript Design Effects," Chapter 6, "Toys and Gadgets," and Chapter 7, "Construction Toys," describe toys and gadgets that are fun, but not necessarily games. Then, starting with Chapter 8, "Hunt and Click Games," all the way through to Chapter 16, "Arcade Games," the rest are all about games.

Each section in Chapters 5 to 16 starts by describing the game to be built. Then it describes my approach to building the game. Next, the elements needed to make the game are reviewed. Finally, the code for each game is revealed, with descriptions about what each part of the code does. Each section ends with some comments about how the game can be taken even further.

The book ends with Chapter 17, "Advanced Techniques," in which you learn some special techniques, such as high score boards and preloading screens. Finally, don't miss the comprehensive list of Web resources in Appendix A, "Internet Resources for the Flash Developer."

The bottom line is that this book contains lots of ActionScript code! There are far more lines of code in this book than in any other I've ever seen on Flash. There are about 37 games here, with all the source code printed in the book and available to you on the CD-ROM.

Who Is This Book For?

This is a hands-on guide to learning ActionScript; it's not a book for dummies or idiots. What this means is that I don't hold the reader's hand through every step of every project in every chapter. If a technique is covered in an earlier chapter, I might not explain it all over again. Instead, I take that project deeper and explain a new technique so that you can continue to learn new things.

This book requires you to learn and think. If you don't understand something the first time, read over the text again, try the example on the CD-ROM, and play with the technique in Flash before moving on. You'll benefit in the long run with a deeper understanding of how ActionScript works and how to use it in projects beyond the scope of this book.

This book can be used by a variety of people. If this book has caught your eye in a bookstore, an online bookseller, or you are looking at a friend's copy, then chances are you fall into one of these groups.

Animators

As an animator, you already use Flash to create linear animation. Perhaps you know how to make a button or two as well. This book takes you beyond that into the wonders of ActionScripting. You'll learn how to put your animated characters and scenes inside toys and games.

Illustrators

If you are a graphic designer, chances are that you have worked in Flash or another vector-drawing program. By using the tutorials that come with Flash MX, you can learn how to draw in Flash. Then you can use this book to make your drawings interact with the users in toys and games.

Programmers

Perhaps you are a programmer who has worked in another language such as Java, C++, or Lingo. This book teaches you how to use your programming skills in Flash. You can get a good overview of ActionScript in Chapters 1 to 3, or just dive right into source code starting with Chapter 5.

Flash 3 and Flash 4 Programmers

This book is also good for Flash 3 or Flash 4 programmers looking for a guide to help them take the leap to Flash MX. The difference between programming Flash MX or Flash 5 and earlier versions is quite large. The environment and commands are almost completely different. To really use the power of Flash MX, you'll have to forget about many techniques used in earlier versions and start learning again from scratch.

Readers of the First Edition of This Book

If you have used the Flash 5 version of this book, you are probably wondering whether this book is worth buying. I thought a lot about readers of the original book while adding the new material. I wanted to be sure there would be plenty of new stuff to learn. Each chapter, from 6 through 16, includes a new game. In most cases, this new game builds on the games from the first edition and presents an even more complex example. Think of this book as "Volume II," but with all the material from the first book so you don't have to keep two books on your desk.

Web Home Page Owners

Maybe you are not a computer professional, but just someone who has a home page and some spare time to improve your skills. Flash MX is a fairly inexpensive development program for you to use to improve your site. With this book, you can immediately grab a game that you like, maybe alter the graphics a bit, and post your own game. Don't expect miracles without putting in the time to learn Flash basics and the material in Chapters 1 through 4, but a smart, hands-on learner should be able to get going quickly.

Professional Web Site Developers

If you are a professional Web site developer, you might be expected to have many skills under your belt. You'll need to know HTML, style sheets, JavaScript, Perl, and several programs such as PhotoShop or Fireworks, Dreamweaver, and so on. Flash is also quickly gaining status as one of the tools that every Web site developer should know.

But knowing the basics probably isn't enough. You'll eventually need to create something. Although other books teach you the basics and leave it up to you to figure out how to put the pieces together to create full programs, this book shows you how to create these programs. You can learn from this to create your own programs from scratch, or use one of the games here as a jump-start to quickly create your own version.

Students

Flash is being taught in many colleges and universities today. This trend will continue as Flash continues to gain popularity. This book could be used as a hands-on text for students wanting to learn ActionScript. Some classes might only teach Flash basics, and you can use this book to place you ahead of everyone else. Other classes might be more advanced and use this book as a text for hands-on learning.

What Should You Already Know?

This book is obviously not meant to be a general reference book for Flash MX. Instead, it is a hands-on learning resource for Flash MX ActionScript. The book already assumes that you are somewhat familiar with Flash's interface and operation.

This does not mean that you need to be an expert graphic artist. I'm not. Many people associate Flash only with graphic talent. This was true when graphics were all that early versions of Flash could do, but now it is a programming environment as well. This book can be used by expert illustrators and programmers alike.

What you should know is how to use the basics of Flash. You should be familiar with all the ideas in the tutorials that come with Flash MX. You should know how to work with the main timeline to add frames and label them. You should know how to create movie clips, buttons, and graphics. They don't have to look great; you just need to know the procedure for creating them in Flash.

On the other hand, some people will be able to use this book even if they have never used Flash before. If you are a patient, hands-on learner, willing to spend the time to immerse yourself into a new subject until you learn it, you can use this book to jump right past beginner Flash techniques and into expert ActionScript programming.

What Can You Do with This Book?

So now that you've determined that you are one of the types of people who can use this book, the next question is, "What can this book do for you?"

Learn ActionScript

There are several ways to use this book—the first is to use it to learn ActionScript. This book goes way beyond a simple beginner's guide, teaching you how to use ActionScript for complex things.

You'll learn about a wide variety of commands, functions, and techniques used in games and other applications. You'll not only learn what these things do, but see them inside real programs so that you can better understand how they work.

Learn How to Create Games in Flash

All the programs in this book can be considered some type of game or something that can be used as part of a game. Even if you already know ActionScript, this book can teach you how to use that knowledge to create games. In Chapter 4, I will go into detail about how games are made. The rest of the book is packed with examples.

Stealing These Games

Of course, you can buy this book, take the source code, and make your own games. You can take the source code as it is and post the games on your Web site; however, you will probably want to give them your own graphic style first.

Keep in mind, however, that the book and source code are written for those interested in learning about ActionScript. Don't expect to be able to jump right to Chapter 16 and start tinkering with code. Although some people might be able to do this, others will have difficulty without the information in Chapters 1 to 15.

Chapter 4 goes into some detail about how to take the games in this book and customize them to make your own. Then, a section in each chapter after that gives suggestions on what you might do to the games to make them your own.

The CD-ROM

A book like this would not be very useful if you had to type in every source code listing yourself. The way Flash movies are put together makes this even harder, because so many different elements, such as movie clips, buttons, and graphics, need to be placed in just the right spot.

To make the process of understanding the programs easier, you should always refer to the source code files on the CD-ROM.

While you go through each project, always remember to open the example movie on the CD-ROM to see the real program in action. Then use this source file to make modifications or test out new code.

You'll see a line like this to tell you which file to use:

Example file: Example.fla

Although typing in the source code and trying to re-create the examples is probably a good exercise, even the most precise developer will find it hard to re-create complete, complex programs from the pages in a book.

Conventions

There are several conventions in this book to help you understand what you are reading. Any words that you see in *italics* are real commands, functions, or other pieces of syntax that are part of ActionScript. You can look up any of these in the Flash MX documentation. For instance, *gotoAndPlay()*, *stop()*, and *_x*.

On the other hand, if you see something in quotes, such as "myVariable," then it is a user-defined piece of syntax. These are usually variable names or user-defined function names.

While you are looking through the code, you will often see two slashes together like this: "//." This is Flash's way of saying that the text after the slashes is a comment. This often happens at the beginning of lines, so that the entire line is a comment. If you typed in the code without any of my comments at all, it would still work in the same way. The comments are just my way of letting you know what is happening in the code. You should adopt the practice of commenting your code as well. Commenting your code can help you or your co-workers alter your games in the future.

Updates and Communication

While writing this book, I took a lot of care to be sure no errors or omissions exist. I write as carefully as I can, and several editors look over the text before publication. However, there is only a limited about of time to produce a book like this. If I took all

Flash Elements Used to Make Games and Toys

- The Flash Interface
- Creating Buttons
- Creating Text
- Importing Media into Flash
- Organizing your Movie
- Finishing Your Movie

Before learning how to make games in Flash, let's look at the basics of Flash from the viewpoint of the ActionScript programmer. Because this is not a beginner's book, it won't spend too much time on the basics, as that is a job better left to the tutorials that come with Flash MX. Instead, this book reviews many of the elements in Flash MX and shows you how they will be useful in building toys, gadgets, and games with ActionScript.

The purpose of the first four chapters of this book is to prepare you for the rest of the chapters that will present specific ActionScript examples. These first four chapters will help you build your skills so you are ready to take on these examples.

The Flash Interface

To create complex programs with ActionScript in Flash, you should first become an expert at using the Flash interface. The interface is the collection of windows, panels, and menus that make up Flash MX.

The Main Flash Window

The Flash interface is centered around the main window. Its main feature is the Stage, which can be seen in Figure 1.1 with a large tree and a fox holding a basket.

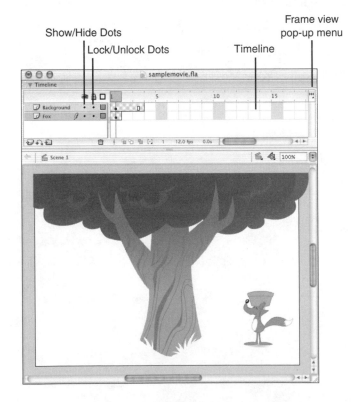

Figure 1.1
Flash's main window is the centerpiece of the Flash interface.

Some features of the main window are more useful than others for the ActionScript programmer. The timeline is at the top of the window. You can see frames going across, with the numbers 1, 5, 10, and 15 marking some of the frames. Down the side of the timeline are layers. There are two layers in this case: "Background" and "Fox."

You might notice that the frames in the timeline seem a lot wider than what you might be used to seeing because the Frame view has been expanded. You can expand the view by using the Frame view pop-up menu, indicated in Figure 1.1. There are several other options, such as shortening the height of each layer, which you can investigate as well.

The Stage area in the main window can show a lot more than just the Stage. In fact, it will show you whatever element in your movie you want: the Stage, a graphic, a button, or even a movie clip.

The image shown on the Stage portion of the main window can be enlarged and shrunk. The Scale pop-up menu at the upper-right corner of the main window is hardly worth noting, because the shortcut keys to control the scale are much more useful. You can use Command+2 on the Mac and Ctrl+2 in Windows to scale the Stage area in the main window to fit the space available. Command+3 on the Mac and Ctrl+3 in Windows scale the work area so that all the drawn items, whether on the Stage or off, fit the space available. Likewise, Command+1 on the Mac and Ctrl+1 in Windows quickly return the Stage to 100%. Using the Mac Command key or the Windows Ctrl key and the + or - keys zoom you in and out as well. After you master these keys, you'll never need to use the pop-up menu.

The last things to point out in the main window are the Show/Hide and Lock/Unlock dots displayed to the right of the layer name. These are incredibly useful for enabling you to see layers by themselves or with only a few other layers visible. Locking layers also enables you to select items without items in other layers getting in the way of your cursor. Of course, it also prevents you from making changes on the Stage to the elements in that layer.

Panels

Although the Flash main window is your canvas, it actually shows you very little precise information about your movie and its elements. The details are all in the small panel windows that appear below and to the right of the main window in the default layout, but can be moved anywhere.

These panels can be customized in all sorts of ways. Panel windows house the panels, and can hold several panels at once. For instance, Figure 1.2 shows a panel window that contains the Color Mixer, Color Swatches, Components, and Answers panels. Only the Color Swatches panel has been expanded for use.

Figure 1.2
*This panel window
contains four
panels.*

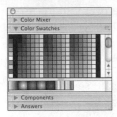

Panels can be rearranged in panel windows, and new panel windows can be created as well. This is all done by clicking and dragging the rough-textured area at the left side of the title bar of each panel. It takes some practice to get used to moving the panels about, but you can always reset them by choosing Window, Panel Sets, Default Layout.

TIP

Just because you can move panels from panel window to panel window doesn't mean you should. I find the default layout to be the best and I stick to it. This will also help you work on other computers if you need to, because you won't have become used to some nonstandard arrangement. Flash MX features several different default panel arrangements, all found under Window, Panel Sets. You can choose one that best fits your work process.

The Info panel, which you can get by choosing Window, Info, is useful for the precise placement of items on the Stage. If you select an item, you can type in values for the position of the item (X and Y) and the width and height of the item (W and H).

The Transform panel can be accessed by choosing Window, Transform. This panel, shown in Figure 1.3, enables you to scale and rotate an item that you have selected.

Figure 1.3
*The Transform
panel enables you
to scale and rotate
items.*

Another panel that the ActionScript programmer uses all the time is the Property inspector. This panel shows information about the currently selected item if the item is a graphic, button, or movie clip. The Property inspector is shown in Figure 1.4. You can use the Property inspector to name frames when a frame is selected, or to name movie clips and other symbols when they are selected. You can also change many properties of a movie clip by using the Property inspector.

Figure 1.4
*The Property
inspector lets you
name movie clips.*

As mentioned, the Property inspector lets you name frames. The funny thing about naming frames is that you can do it in any layer you want. So you can name the first frame by selecting the first frame in the top layer, and then name the second frame by selecting the second frame in another layer. Sound confusing? It is. I recommend always using just one layer to label all the frames.

Perhaps the most important window besides the Stage for both the ActionScript programmer and the graphic artist is the Library window. Figure 1.5 shows this panel with a button, a folder, a graphic and a movie clip.

Figure 1.5
*The Library panel
shows you what ele-
ments are in your
movie.*

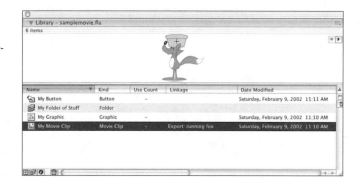

The Library panel shows you a list of all the different types of elements in your movie. What is listed and what is not might seem arbitrary at first. For example, graphics drawn directly on the screen, even after they have been grouped together, are not shown. Make them into a graphic symbol, and they appear.

Think of it this way: The library stores reusable items for you. Any symbol, whether it is a movie clip, graphic, or button, can be used in one or more places throughout your movie. However, a series of lines and fills drawn directly on the Stage can only be used in the frame or series of frames where it is located in the timeline.

Just because a symbol is in the library doesn't mean that it will be exported with the movie. For instance, you can import a bitmap or sound and then never place it on the Stage or in the timeline. Or, you can create a movie clip and then never use it. In that case, Flash is smart enough not to include the item in the final compressed Flash file. This will make the file smaller for users to download.

What if the library element never appears on the Stage but your code uses the library element? Flash won't know about this, and that element won't be included in the final file. To tell Flash to include a library element, even if it doesn't seem to need it, you must set the linkage of the item in the Symbol Properties dialog box, shown in Figure 1.6. Selecting the Options pop-up menu seen in the upper-right corner of Figure 1.5 opens this dialog box. If you do not see the Linkage Properties area of the Symbol Properties dialog box, try pressing the button labeled Advanced. The rest of the window expands to show the linkage properties, and the Advanced button toggles to become labeled Basic.

Figure 1.6

The Symbol Properties dialog box lets you force Flash to include items in the library for export to ActionScript.

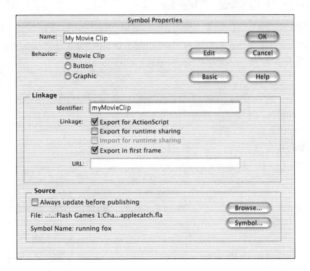

Menu Items

Like panels, the menu item choices in Flash are plentiful. However, only a handful of them are used by ActionScript programmers on a regular basis. For the common menu choices, the ActionScript programmer should know where to find them, as well as their keyboard shortcuts.

File Menu

The File menu contains the standard set of commands that all Macintosh and Windows programmers should be familiar with. Along with Open, Save, and Save As, there is also the Import command, which lets you import bitmap and vector graphics and sounds.

The most important command in the File menu is the simple Save command, with the keyboard shortcut Command+S on the Mac and Ctrl+S in Windows. Use this often. If you work on a file for hours without saving, and then Flash or your computer crashes, you'll be sorry if you didn't remember to hit the Save keyboard shortcut every five minutes or so.

TIP

Flash MX can occasionally crash, and you will lose all your work since your last save. This is an unfortunate fact. Macromedia is under a lot of pressure to deliver timely new releases of Flash with new features demanded by developers. The downside of the rapid growth of Flash is that it is not the most stable program. However, if you remember to save often, these crashes will be only a minor annoyance.

The File menu is also where you find the Publish and Publish Settings commands. You'll learn more about these commands at the end of this chapter.

Edit Menu

The Edit menu contains the usual commands: Copy, Cut, and Paste. The Undo command is particularly useful in Flash because you can undo up to 100 actions. This enables you to back up quite a bit. You can set the number of Undo levels in Flash's preferences.

The Preferences dialog box is shown in Figure 1.7. In addition to setting the number of undo levels, you can also set a number of preferences arranged in five different tabs. I prefer to stick with the defaults, but it is good to know that the options are there.

Figure 1.7

Reaching the Preferences dialog box is done using the main menu bar, but its location depends on your operating system.

View Menu

In the View menu, you can change the magnification of the Stage, choose how much graphic detail you want shown on the Stage while working with your movie in Flash, and work with the grid and guides.

The grid is useful for quickly lining up elements on the Stage when you are more interested in ActionScripting than in tweaking the positions of various graphics. Figure 1.8 shows the Grid dialog box that you get by choosing View, Grid, Edit Grid. You can set the size of the grid as well as its color, whether it is visible, and whether items snap to it.

If you use the Grid dialog box rather than the Show Grid and Snap To Grid commands, you can turn both those options on and off at the same time more quickly.

Figure 1.8

The Grid dialog box lets you set the color and level of activity of the grid.

The View menu also contains an item called Hide Panels. This quickly hides and shows all the panels, including the Tools palette. An even easier way to do this is to use the Tab key. This is handy when some of the panels are covering the Stage and you need to get to them, but don't want to lose the positions of your panels on the screen.

Insert Menu

The Insert menu has two useful functions for ActionScript programmers. The first is the Convert to Symbol command. This takes whatever elements you have selected on the Stage, and quickly converts them to a graphic, movie clip, or button. The new symbol is placed in the library, but it also remains on the Stage in exactly the same position as the original elements.

When you use this command, you are immediately presented with a simple Symbol Properties dialog box that forces you to choose the type of symbol and name it (see Figure 1.9).

Figure 1.9

The Symbol Properties dialog box appears when you choose Insert, Convert to Symbol. It is the same dialog box that appears if you want to change the symbol properties.

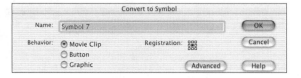

The Convert to Symbol command enables you to create all your graphics, movie clips, and buttons directly on the Stage, and then add them to the library afterward. You can also nest this command to create symbols inside symbols. For instance, you could create a button-looking item, use Convert to Symbol to turn it into a button, and then use Convert to Symbol again to place the button inside a movie clip.

The other important functionality of the Insert menu is the series of commands that enables you to insert frames in the main timeline. You can use Insert, Frame to insert a new frame, stretching the current keyframe. Or you can use Insert, Keyframe or Insert, Blank Keyframe to insert a new keyframe into the timeline. Using Insert, Keyframe makes a copy of the current keyframe, whereas Insert, Blank Keyframe creates a new keyframe with no items on the Stage in that layer. You can also use Insert, Remove Frames to delete the frames selected in a layer, or Insert, Clear Keyframe to remove a keyframe without deleting actual frames in the layer.

TIP

The difference between a frame and a keyframe is that a keyframe defines a point in the timeline where all the items in that layer are set to exact positions on the Stage. Until the next keyframe, they won't move. However, animators can choose to tween movement between keyframes so that the items on the Stage move gradually from the position specified in one keyframe to the position specified in another keyframe. Try the animation lesson that comes with Flash MX to learn more about keyframes.

These commands might seem a bit confusing to someone who has not done any animation work in Flash before. The best way to learn them is to use them. Create a movie and try to insert and remove frames and keyframes. You'll begin to understand the way these commands work.

Modify Menu

The Modify menu gives you a few other ways to quickly access panels. The Modify, Document command opens the dialog box shown in Figure 1.10. The Document Properties dialog box allows you to change the dimensions of your movie, the speed at which the movie runs, and its background color.

Figure 1.10
The Document Properties dialog box allows you to set some of the most important properties of your movie.

Document Properties	
Dimensions:	550 px (width) x 400 px (height)
Match:	Printer Contents Default
Background Color:	
Frame Rate:	12 fps
Ruler Units:	Pixels
Help Make Default	Cancel OK

The set of commands under the Modify, Transform menu item should be mentioned as well. These commands allow you to scale, rotate, and flip graphics on the Stage. You'll be learning how to do these sorts of things in ActionScript throughout the book, but these commands can be used on items that are not controlled by ActionScript to modify graphics and symbols.

The Modify, Group command should also be mentioned. When graphics are drawn on the Stage, they are drawn on top of each other and remove previous lines and fills under them. For instance, if you draw a big blue circle, then draw a small red circle in the middle of it, and then remove the red circle, you get a hole in the middle of the blue circle where the red one used to be. However, if you group the blue circle before drawing the red one, then the blue circle is not partially erased by the red one. Instead, the blue circle exists as it originally was drawn, under the red circle. Grouping is covered in detail in the "Drawing" lesson that comes with Flash MX.

Text Menu

These commands give you quick access to properties in the Text panels. You'll learn more about working with text in the "Creating Text" section later in this chapter.

Control Menu

The Control menu contains a command that you will be using constantly as an ActionScript programmer: Test Movie. This command, which has the keyboard shortcut of Command+Return on the Macintosh and Ctrl+Enter in Windows, takes your current movie, makes a final compressed Flash file from it, and then runs that movie in a preview window.

When this movie runs, it is running just as it would be in the Flash player, or in the user's Web browser. This is different from the Play command in the Control menu, which does *not* use any complex ActionScript code at all. Play is completely useless for the ActionScript programmer, whereas Test Movie is invaluable.

Window Menu

The Window menu is where you have access to open all your panels as well as assorted other windows. It is important that you master some of the keyboard shortcuts here so you can have quick access to your most useful tools.

Table 1.1   Mac and Windows Shortcuts for the Window Menu

To Access...	Press This on Mac	Press This in Windows
Properties Panel	Command+F3	Ctrl+F3
Info Panel	Command+I	Ctrl+I
Library	Command+L	Ctrl+L
Reference Panel	Shift+F1	Shift+F1
Actions Panel	Command+F9	Ctrl+F9

Reference Panel

The Reference Panel gives you access to Flash's ActionScript Dictionary. Even the best ActionScript programmer won't know all the parameters, uses, and idiosyncrasies of all the Flash syntax. This instant help can quickly get you the information you need on a particular command or function.

Creating Buttons

There are three types of symbols in Flash: graphics, buttons, and movie clips. Both buttons and movie clips can have scripts attached to them. Graphics, on the other hand, cannot. Because the ActionScript programmer needs to create and use a lot of buttons and movie clips, let's look at each, starting with buttons, to see how they are made.

The Button Timeline

You can create a button by either choosing Insert, New Symbol, or selecting a set of items on the Stage and choosing Insert, Convert to Symbol. When you do this, make sure you set the symbol type to "Button" in the dialog box. You can also open the Library window and use the pop-up menu at the top and choose New Symbol.

After you have a button, you can double-click it on the Stage to edit it while still seeing it in the context of the Stage. Or you can double-click its name in the Library window to edit it by itself in the Flash main window.

Either way, you will see a special type of timeline at the top of the Flash main window. As shown in Figure 1.11, this special timeline defines the four images needed to define a button: Up, Down, Over, and Hit.

Figure 1.11

The timeline above a button presents a predefined set of four frames.

Although you can add as many layers as you want to a button, only the first four frames shown in Figure 1.11 are used. Here is what they are used for:

- **Up**—The image of the button that is normally shown.
- **Over**—The image of the button shown when the user moves the cursor over it.
- **Down**—The image of the button shown when the user has pressed the button, but not yet released it.
- **Hit**—The shape of the area that is used to determine when the cursor is over the button or when the button is clicked.

Typically, you would focus your button-creation efforts on the Up frame. Then, you would create variations of that frame for the Over and Down frames. The Over frame might highlight the button in some way, whereas the Down frame might show the button depressed or highlighted in some other way. In the next section, you'll see some examples of button design.

TIP

You can create a button that only has an Up frame. If you leave the other three frames blank, without even a keyframe there, then the Up frame is used for all four states of the button.

The Hit frame is special in that it is never seen. It also doesn't care about the color or type of graphics in it. You can choose not to create a Hit frame, as well as an Over or Down frame. In that case, the Up frame will be used for each of these.

Think of the Hit frame as an invisible shape under the button that defines the clickable area of the button. You can therefore create a clickable area that is larger or smaller than the visible graphic of the button.

TIP

You can actually create an invisible button by placing nothing in the Up, Over, or Down frames, but something in the Hit frame. When you do this, the button is shown on the Flash main window as a light blue shape. However, when you run the movie, that button will not be visible at all. It can be clicked, however, and the script in it will be executed. Users can still tell it is a button because their cursors change when they roll over it. In addition, they may already know it is a clickable area because of your design.

Button Example

Example file: Samplebuttons.fla

Let's take a look at an example of a button. Figure 1.11 showed a labeled button with a rectangular shape. It was drawn directly on the Stage with the Rectangle tool, and then converted to a button by choosing Insert, Convert to Symbol. You can see this button in the file Samplebuttons.fla on the CD-ROM in the folder for this chapter.

This button was created by first selecting the Rectangle tool. If you double-click that tool, you get to set the corner radius for the curved corner of the rectangle. The corner radius for this example button is 2. The color for the stroke of the rectangle was set to black and the fill color to blue. After drawing the rectangle, I selected the Text tool and typed "PRESS ME!" After the text was centered, the result is the image you see in Figure 1.11.

When I used Convert to Symbol, I named the button "My Button." This new symbol appears in the library, and remains on the Stage at the location of the original elements.

If you double-click the symbol in the library, you can edit the button by itself on the Stage. The four prelabeled frames appear at the top of the Flash main window. However, only the Up frame contains anything. The Over, Down, and Hit frames are all blank. The Press Me! button will work just fine, but it will use the same image for the Up, Over, and Down states, and the shape of that image for the Hit state.

To continue to develop this button, the first thing to do is create a keyframe for each of the four preset frames. You do this by selecting the frame in the timeline and using the F6 key three times to create three more keyframes. Then, go back to the Over and Down states and alter them in some way. In the case of this sample button, I changed the color of the fill on each of these frames. For the Hit frame, there is no need for the text, because only the shape of the image in the Hit frame matters.

Creating Text

There are three different types of text boxes in Flash MX. The first, static text, is little more than text-shaped graphics as far as the ActionScript programmer is concerned. The other two, dynamic text and input text, can be accessed and changed by ActionScript.

Text Properties

Use the Property inspector to control all the text properties. When you select a piece of text, the Property inspector changes to show various pieces of information about the text. You can see the Property inspector in Figure 1.12.

Figure 1.12
The Property inspector allows you to change the font properties of text.

The most important setting for text fields is in the upper-left corner of the Property inspector. Figure 1.12 shows Static Text as the type for this text field. You can change this to Dynamic Text or Input Text.

Dynamic Text

If you change the text field type to Dynamic Text, you get a slightly different-looking Property inspector. Figure 1.13 shows this version of the panel.

Figure 1.13

The Property inspector now shows the properties for a dynamic text field.

A pop-up menu lets you choose whether you want the text to be Single Line, Multiline or Multiline No Wrap. The other three options that you can see as little buttons are Selectable, Render Text as HTML, and Show Border Around. The HTML option lets you use some basic HTML tags such as <B> in your text. The Border option places a thin border around the text and makes its box opaque. The Selectable option enables users to highlight portions of the text as they would in a word processor.

The most important option in this panel for the ActionScript programmer is the Var field. You can enter a name of a variable here. When the movie runs, the variable and this dynamic text box will be linked. When the value of one changes, so does the other. This enables you to set a variable with code, and have the user see it on the screen.

On the right end of the panel is a button labeled Character. This brings up a dialog box that lets you specify which character shapes you want Flash to save in the final Flash file so they can be used in the text box. For instance, if the text box will only contain numbers, you might want to specify that rather than making Flash save a complete character set with the movie. On the other hand, you could choose to not save any character shapes at all, which will force the text area to be drawn with the fonts installed on the user's machine.

TIP

Flash is smart enough that it never includes more than one copy of each character shape with the final compressed Flash movie. So if you specify two dynamic text areas that use all the characters in the font Arial, then this font will be saved only once and shared with both text areas. It's useful, therefore, to choose a primary font for each movie and specify that this font be used with every dynamic text area you create.

Input Text

The third option for a text box is Input Text. The Property inspector looks pretty much the same as it does in Figure 1.13.

With input text boxes, there is a fourth option in addition to Single Line, Multiline, and Multiline No Wrap. This fourth option is for a Password text box. As you might guess, this type of text box does not show the characters typed, but shows dots instead.

The new Maximum Characters setting limits the number of characters typed. Setting this to 0 allows unlimited characters to be typed in.

TIP

Flash has a great feature associated with single-line input text. When the user types beyond the size of the text box, the text automatically scrolls to the right. The user can still use the arrow keys to move the cursor back. This allows for large pieces of text to be entered without having to worry about creating large text areas in which the user can type.

Importing Media into Flash

Although Flash has a vector drawing tool at its heart, it can also use a variety of other media, such as bitmap graphics and sounds. However, it isn't capable of editing these forms of media, just displaying them.

To create bitmaps and sounds, you need to use other programs. For instance, you might use Adobe Photoshop to create bitmaps and Sound Forge to create sounds. Let's take a brief look at these two types of media and how ActionScript can use them.

Bitmaps

To get bitmaps into Flash, choose File, Import. You can import a wide variety of image file formats, including JPEG, GIF, PICT, and BMP formats. When you import a file, the media is added to your library.

After you have a bitmap image in the library, there's not much you can do with it with ActionScript. You can certainly place this bitmap inside a movie clip or button and use it that way, however.

You can do only a few things with a bitmap after it is in Flash. Figure 1.14 shows the Bitmap Properties dialog box that you get when you double-click the bitmap in the library.

Figure 1.14
*The Bitmap
Properties dialog
box allows you to
set the compression
level for the bitmap,
turn smoothing on
and off, and re-
import the bitmap
with the Update
button.*

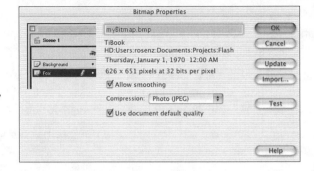

You can also convert bitmaps to vector graphics by selecting the bitmap on the Stage
and then choosing Modify, Trace Bitmap. The dialog box that appears is shown in
Figure 1.15.

Figure 1.15
*The Trace Bitmap
dialog box allows
you to convert a
bitmap to a vector
drawing.*

The Trace Bitmap function replaces the bitmap on the Stage with a set of filled vector
areas. In many cases, this results in a drawing that looks worse than the original bitmap,
but at least it can be scaled as vector graphics can.

TIP

Many graphic artists convert bitmaps to vector graphics at some point during produc-
tion. For instance, the artist might draw something on paper, scan it in, and then trace
the resulting bitmap to create a vector graphic. However, many of these artists use
another program, such as Abode Streamline, to do the conversion, not Flash. Then,
the graphic is imported into Flash. The graphic artist also does a lot of work on the
vector graphic afterward to get it to look the way it was originally intended.

Sounds

You import sounds into Flash the same way that you import bitmaps. Flash can import
standard sound formats such as AIFF, MP3, Sun AU, and Wave.

After a sound is in Flash, you can double-click its entry in the library to get the Sound
Properties dialog box shown in Figure 1.16.

Figure 1.16

The Sound Properties dialog box enables you to set the compression rate used when the sound is included in the final Flash movie.

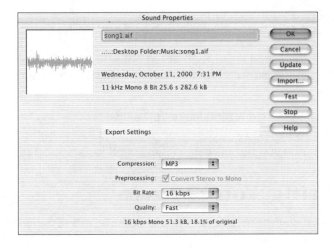

TIP

The sound compression settings in the Sound Properties dialog box are important if you value the quality of the sound in your final movie. For instance, using MP3 compression at 16KBps (kilobytes per second) yields a sound of moderate quality that is good for special effects and such. However, if you are using some nice music, you might want to go with 32KBps or even 64KBps. Experiment with different settings to find one that fits the sound, while keeping the compression setting as low as possible to save file space. You can also set a default setting for all the sounds in the movie when you publish.

Sound elements are typically dragged to the timeline and placed in a keyframe. This means that the sound is triggered when this keyframe is reached. You can dictate how the sound plays by selecting the keyframe with the sound attached and then opening the Properties panel.

Shown in Figure 1.17, the Properties panel lets you set the way the sound is triggered, decide whether it loops or not, and even apply an effect such as a fade. However, this is not how you will be using sound in this book, so I won't go into detail about how to control this type of sound usage.

Figure 1.17

The Properties Panel allows you to control a sound that appears in the timeline.

Instead, you will use sound triggered by ActionScript commands. You can control when and how any sound plays with ActionScript.

However, if the sound is not used in the timeline at all, Flash does not include it when the final Flash file is made. Then, when your ActionScript attempts to use the sound, it isn't there.

To make sure a sound is included with the final movie, you need to set its linkage properties (refer to Figure 1.6). The name you give a sound in the Linkage Properties dialog box is the name you use to refer to that sound in ActionScript.

Organizing Your Movie

Organization is even more important to ActionScript programmers than it is to Flash animators. Symbols in the library should be thoughtfully named. They should be organized in folders if needed. The layers in the timeline should make it easy for the programmer to access different elements on the Stage.

The Library

You can organize the library by creating folders inside the Library window. Folders work just like folders or directories in your operating system. You can create folders and store various library elements in them. For instance, if you have 52 graphics to represent the 52 cards of a deck, you could place them all in a folder called "cards." This means that all 52 cards will be shown as one item in the library. That item can then be expanded to show the 52 graphics inside it.

To create a folder, open the Library window and choose New Folder from the pop-up menu at the upper right. When something is in a folder, it can be used just as easily as if it were not. You don't have to refer to the folder's name in either the animation tools or your ActionScript code.

The Library window also includes several other tools that help you organize. For instance, you can sort by any of the criteria listed at the top as column headings. Figure 1.18 shows a fully-expanded Library window. If you want to sort by the Date Modified column, just click the column title. The little button with a pyramid-shaped icon on it just to the right of the column headings allows you to switch from ascending to descending order and back again.

With this view, you can see what items are used and how often. Of course, this does not take into account usage by your ActionScript code.

Figure 1.18
This Library window includes a folder that has been expanded to show its contents.

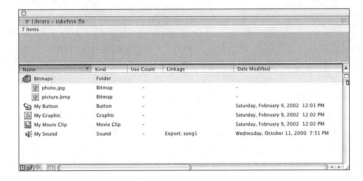

Frames

Labeling keyframes in your movie should not be an option for ActionScript programmers. In your code, you can tell the movie to jump from one frame to another in a nonlinear fashion. To do that, you need to name the frames. You can do this by using the Properties panel.

Although you can reference frames by their number in ActionScript, you shouldn't. Why? Well, suppose you write code that jumps from frame 7 to frame 13 to frame 8. Then, you decide to insert a frame before frame 1. Now, what used to be frames 7, 13, and 8 are frames 8, 14, and 9. You'll have to change your code in all three places.

If you name frames with recognizable names, you can refer to them by name in your code. No matter how many frames you insert or delete, you can always rely on a keyframe to keep the same name.

Layers

Although layers don't actually come into play for most ActionScripting, they are valuable organizational tools. You can and should have layers for labels, timeline-based ActionScript code, and graphics. Figure 1.19 shows a layer setup that organizes things well.

Figure 1.19
This timeline setup includes a layer just for labels, one for ActionScript, and others for graphics.

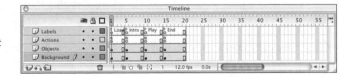

You can also double-click the little icon to the left of each layer name to bring up the Layer Properties dialog box shown in Figure 1.20. You can choose to show the layer as an outline or use it as a guide layer. This means that the layer appears to you in Flash, but is not used in the final movie.

Figure 1.20
The Layer Properties dialog box lets you define a layer's type.

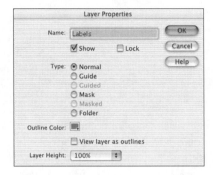

Remember to not only use layer organization in your main timeline, but also in movie clips, graphics, and buttons.

Scenes

A higher level of organization in Flash involves scenes. Each Flash movie is made up of one or more scenes. Many of the examples in this book use only one scene and you could easily forget that scenes even exist.

However, scenes can also be great organizational tools. Think of them as combining movies, one after the other, in a single movie. Each scene has its own main timeline. Figure 1.21 shows the Scene panel with three scenes. They are played in the exact order shown, although ActionScript can override this and play the scenes in any order, or even jump from one frame in one scene to one frame in another scene.

Figure 1.21
The Scene panel allows you to create and rearrange scenes in your movie.

Off-Stage Area

One part of Flash that is very useful for ActionScript programmers, but is rarely mentioned in books such as this, is the off-Stage area. If you look back at Figure 1.1, you can see that the Stage is in the middle of the window, but there is a gray area outside the Stage rectangle as well. You can place elements in this off-Stage area. When the movie is played back in the user's browser or in the Flash player, the user will not see this area.

WARNING

Actually, there is a way that the user can see the off-Stage area. If the Flash movie is scaled in the Flash player, the Flash preview window, or in a browser, the Flash movie usually tries to hold its proportions. This means that some area at the top or bottom might show. However, if the movie is placed in a Web page with the proper tags, this will not happen.

For example, one way you will use the off-Stage area in this book is to place a small movie clip that will have some ActionScript attached to it. Although ActionScript in the main timeline executes once, you can make ActionScript attached to movie clips execute once every frame. So, by placing a small movie clip off the Stage where it is not visible, you can write ActionScript that performs repetitive actions such as animation and user-controlled movement.

Finishing Your Movie

When you are finished with your movie, whether it is a simple animation or a complex application, you need to export it as a compressed Flash file, also known as a .swf file. You can do this with the File, Publish command.

However, before you do that, you need to check your movie over for a few things, and then use File, Publish Settings to make sure the .swf is created exactly as you want it.

Final Checklist

Before publishing your movie, here's a handy checklist of things to look over to avoid easy-to-solve problems:

- **Movie Clip Instance Names**—Make sure all the movie clips you placed on the Stage are named what your code expects them to be named.
- **Linkage Properties**—If you have movie clips that are not used on the Stage, but your code needs them, make sure to set the linkage properties of these movie clips in the library so that they export with the movie. Also be sure to set the linkage name so it matches your code. The same is true for sounds in the library.
- **Dynamic Text Links**—If you are using any dynamic text on the Stage that links to an ActionScript variable, be sure its name is what your code expects.

- **Fonts**—In any dynamic text or input text, make sure you have set the text box to include any characters you might need from the font. Otherwise, the movie might look very different on a machine that does not have the same fonts as yours.

- **Stops**—The basic ActionScript command *stop()* needs to be placed on any frame that has some interaction with the user. Without *stop()*, the frame is no more than a single frame in an animation. This is also true for movie clips in your movie. If they are controlled by ActionScript, they need a *stop()* on the first frame. You'll learn more about *stop()* in Chapter 2, "An Introduction to ActionScript."

Publishing

Before using the File, Publish command, you'll want to check the Publish Settings dialog box by choosing File, Publish Settings (see Figure 1.22). This large dialog box has three panels. The Formats panel allows you to select the different formats that can be exported. However, formats such as GIF, JPEG, and PNG are just still images. Formats such as QuickTime Movie and RealPlayer do not support Flash 5 or MX ActionScript. This leaves the .swf format, as well as Projectors, as your only real options. You can also choose to export an HTML page that can be used with the .swf file.

Figure 1.22
The Publish Settings dialog box allows you to export Flash movies as one of several formats.

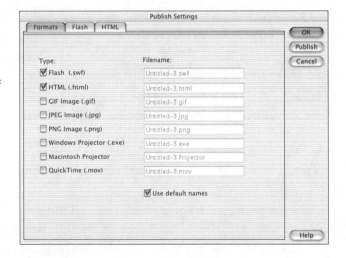

The Flash panel allows you to control several settings of the final .swf file (see Figure 1.23). The Generate Size Report option places a rundown of the contents of the .swf file in the Flash Output window for you to see. This allows you to track down file-size hogs, such as large sounds that can be trimmed.

Figure 1.23

The Flash panel of the Publish Settings dialog box allows you to change some important settings for making a .swf file.

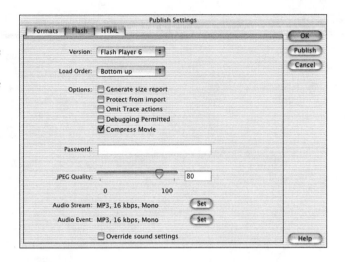

The Omit Trace Actions option allows you to turn off the messages sent by ActionScript *trace* commands. These aren't used in .swf files shown in browsers anyway, however.

The Protect from Import option should stop anyone, including yourself, from importing the .swf file back into Flash.

The Debugging Permitted option allows you to debug your movie when it is running. We will learn more about debugging in Chapter 4, "The Game-Creation Process."

The next group of settings enables you to set the default compression for images and sounds. You can even check the Override Sound Settings option to force all sounds to be compressed by these defaults, even if one or more is set to some custom compression level.

The Version setting at the top of the window seems as if it could work miracles. It claims that you can save the movie as a Flash 1, 2, 3, 4, 5 or MX movie. So you can make movies with complex ActionScripting that will work with Flash 3 players? Wrong. If you have any ActionScripting at all, chances are that the movie needs to be exported as Flash 5 or MX. If you use the newer Flash MX commands, then MX is your only option.

In the last panel of the Publish Settings dialog box, seen in Figure 1.24, you can determine what the HTML file exported with the .swf file will be like.

All the properties shown in Figure 1.24 seem to control the .swf file, right? Nope. They actually only set the tags of the HTML page. The next section looks at these tags.

Figure 1.24
The HTML panel of the Publish Settings dialog box enables you to control the HTML file that gets exported with the .swf file.

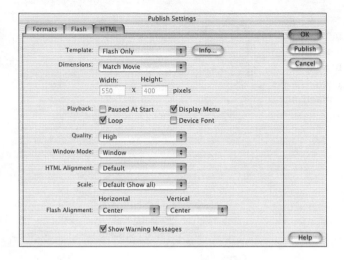

Putting Flash on the Web

If you want to put your movies on the Web, they should be embedded into HTML pages. Sure, you can place them on the Web as just raw .swf files, but then they will attempt to scale to the size of the browser window, which is probably not what you want.

Instead, by using two tags, you can place the .swf files into a Web page for both Internet Explorer and Netscape browsers. Better yet, you can specify a lot of custom settings for how the movie appears. Flash can do most of this automatically when you publish. You can use the Publish Settings dialog box shown in Figure 1.24 to set most of the options. However, it might be useful for you to know what the tags are really like. If you are like me, you would rather build your own HTML than use a template generated by a program such as Flash.

The following object tag embeds a 550×400 Flash movie named Sample.swf. The movie starts by playing immediately, the quality level is high, it uses device fonts, and the background color of the movie is white.

```
<OBJECT classid="clsid:D27CDB6E-AE6D-11cf-96B8-444553540000"
codebase="http://download.macromedia.com/pub/shockwave/
cabs/flash/swflash.cab#version=6,0,0,0"

WIDTH=550 HEIGHT=400>
<PARAM NAME=movie VALUE="sample.swf">
<PARAM NAME=play VALUE=true>
<PARAM NAME=quality VALUE=high>
<PARAM NAME=devicefont VALUE=true>
<PARAM NAME=bgcolor VALUE=#FFFFFF>
</OBJECT>
```

The long string of characters starting with "classid" is the designation for Flash that Internet Explorer understands. The part that starts with "codebase" tells Internet Explorer to go and get Flash if the user doesn't already have it.

Netscape doesn't understand the OBJECT tag because OBJECT tags are used to designate ActiveX controls. ActiveX is a technology used to embed media into Internet Explorer. Flash is an ActiveX control as far as Internet Explorer is concerned. For Netscape, you need an EMBED tag that tells the browser to use the Flash plug-in to run the Flash movie.

```
<EMBED src="sample.swf"
play=false
quality=high
devicefont=true
bgcolor=#FFFFFF
WIDTH=550 HEIGHT=400
TYPE="application/x-shockwave-flash"
PLUGINSPAGE="http://www.macromedia.com/go/getflashplayer">
</EMBED>
```

You can see that these tags are pretty similar. The TYPE parameter tells Netscape that this is a Flash movie, and the PLUGINSPAGE tells Netscape where to send the user if it turns out that the user doesn't have Flash.

WARNING

Although the OBJECT tag includes the number of the version of Flash needed to play your movie, the EMBED tag does not. This means that if someone has Flash 5 in Netscape, and he plays your Flash MX movie, the browser will attempt to do it, even though his version of Flash can't understand your Flash 5 ActionScript commands. The result is that your movie will appear not to work properly. You can include a message on the Web page, such as "Requires Flash 6 Player," to warn users. Also check with the sites listed in Appendix A, "Internet Resources for the Flash Developer," for the latest JavaScript techniques for determining which version of Flash the user has.

So you need to include both the OBJECT and EMBED tags, right? Yes. But it's more complex than that. You see, Internet Explorer can also use the EMBED tag to show media with plug-ins. So it is possible that someone with Internet Explorer could have both the Flash ActiveX control and the Flash plug-in. In that case, they would see your Flash movie twice on the same page.

There is an easy way to prevent this, fortunately. If you place the EMBED tag inside the OBJECT tag, Internet Explorer ignores it. So the final version looks like this:

```
<OBJECT classid="clsid:D27CDB6E-AE6D-11cf-96B8-444553540000"
codebase="http://download.macromedia.com/pub/shockwave/cabs/
flash/swflash.cab#version=6,0,0,0"
```

```
WIDTH=550 HEIGHT=400>
<PARAM NAME=movie VALUE="sample.swf">
<PARAM NAME=play VALUE=true>
<PARAM NAME=quality VALUE=high>
<PARAM NAME=devicefont VALUE=true>
<PARAM NAME=bgcolor VALUE=#FFFFFF>
<EMBED src="sample.swf"
play=false
quality=high
devicefont=true
bgcolor=#FFFFFF
WIDTH=550 HEIGHT=400
TYPE="application/x-shockwave-flash"
PLUGINSPAGE="http://www.macromedia.com/go/getflashplayer">
</EMBED>
</OBJECT>
```

This code works well, but it poses one problem: Almost every parameter is repeated twice, once for the OBJECT tag and once for the EMBED tag. If you make a change, you need to remember to make it in both places.

Now that you know how the basics of Flash relate to ActionScript programming, you're ready to learn how to be an ActionScript programmer. The next chapter gets you started using ActionScript.

2

An Introduction to ActionScript

Programming in ActionScript can be done by people experienced in other programming languages, or by people who have no programming experience but know how to use Flash to create graphics and animation.

This chapter starts by defining the basic elements of ActionScript, and then moves to some hands-on examples. You'll learn how to program in ActionScript in 24 *easy* lessons. This chapter contains the first 14 lessons, which show you the most basic ActionScript commands. Chapter 3, "ActionScript Elements Used to Make Games and Toys," continues with the final 10 lessons.

Lesson 1: What Is ActionScript and Where Does It Go?

ActionScript is the programming language inside Flash MX. It allows you to provide more than just linear animation instructions as you can do with the main timeline. With ActionScript, your Flash movie can react to events, such as user choices or random chances. ActionScript can take control of what the user sees, so that instead of plain animation, you can show nonlinear presentations, interactive applications, or games.

NOTE

ActionScript in Flash MX is derived from two sources. The first is the set of macro commands that existed in all the previous versions of Flash, particularly Flash 4, where a similar, but very basic programming language was used. The other influence on Flash MX ActionScript is JavaScript. This is the language used to write short programs that appear in HTML pages for Internet Explorer and Netscape browsers. It has become popular with Web developers who are the primary audience for Flash MX. To make it easier for Web developers to learn ActionScript, many of the new commands, functions, and other syntax have been made to look like JavaScript.

ActionScript programs are lists of instructions for Flash to follow. They can be put in several places in your Flash movie. Knowing where to put a script is half the battle. Let's look at some of the places where scripts go and when Flash uses these scripts.

Frame Scripts

You can place scripts on keyframes in the main timeline of your movie. To do this, just select the keyframe in the main timeline and press F9. The Actions panel appears, with "Actions—Frame" in the title bar at the top of the panel. (You'll be examining the Actions panel in the next section.)

Frame scripts can contain two different script elements. The first is a list of commands that are executed as soon as the keyframe is reached while the movie is playing. These commands are followed, one after the other, until the script is done.

The second type of script element that can be included in frame scripts is called a function. Functions are reusable pieces of code that can be used by commands in the frame script as well as by other scripts throughout the movie.

Button Scripts

You can also attach scripts to buttons that appear on the Stage. First, you have to create the button as a library element. Then, drag it to the Stage if a copy of the button is not already there. With the button selected on the Stage, press F9 to bring up the Actions panel. If the Actions panel is already on the screen, just selecting the button will focus the Actions panel on the script attached to the button.

The Actions panel is now titled "Actions—Button." The button uses any script you enter here. However, you can't just enter a series of commands. Instead, you must tell the button how it should react to different button events, such as being pressed, having the cursor roll over it, and so on. The code that handles an event is called a handler. Button scripts are a series of one or more handlers.

Movie Clip Scripts

You can also attach a script to a movie clip. To do this, first create a movie clip so that it appears in the library. Then place an instance of the movie clip on the Stage. Now you can open the Actions panel, with the movie clip instance selected, just as you can with buttons.

The Actions panel is titled "Actions—Movie Clip." As with buttons, you can't enter a series of commands as you would with frame scripts. Instead, you must place your commands inside handlers that react to events that occur to movie clips. However, movie clips react to a whole different set of events than buttons do.

In the next few sections, you'll be looking at examples of frame scripts, button scripts, and movie clip scripts.

Lesson 2: Using the Actions Panel

To program in ActionScript, you need to use the Actions panel. This window has two modes: normal and expert. In normal mode, the window acts like the Flash 4 Actions window. You can select commands, functions, operators, and other syntax from the list to the left, and the item is automatically placed in the ActionScript program to the right.

Figure 2.1 shows the Actions panel in normal mode. A one-line program containing the command *gotoAndPlay* was placed there by finding the command in the list on the left and double-clicking it to place it in the program to the right. When this command is selected in the program to the right, information about it appears at the bottom of the Actions panel. You can change this information by using the pop-up menus and text fields there. For instance, Frame Label has been selected as the type and My Frame Name as the frame. The command in the window will change to reflect these choices.

Figure 2.1
The Actions panel in normal mode enables you to select commands and customize them.

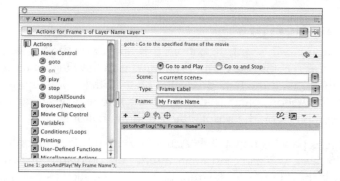

All the programming I do uses the Actions window expert mode. This name is a little misleading, as it implies that the Actions window is harder to use. In fact, the opposite is true. Expert mode makes the Actions window little more than a simple text editor where you actually type in the code rather than select it from a list. The Actions window becomes easier to use, but it's also easier to create code that won't work.

To switch between normal and expert mode, you can use the Actions window properties pop-up menu that is brought up by the little arrow button at the upper-right corner of the Actions window (refer to Figure 2.1). You can also use the keyboard shortcuts, Shift+Command+N and Shift+Command+E on the Mac and Shift+Ctrl+N and Shift+Ctrl+E in Windows. However, make sure that the Actions window is in focus when you use these shortcuts, because when it isn't, these commands perform entirely differ- ent tasks.

Figure 2.2 shows the Actions window in expert mode. The editable properties of the *gotoAndPlay* command are no longer at the bottom of the screen. The list of com- mands on the left is still there, however, and you can double-click them to add com- mands to the program on the right. However, you can also just type the commands straight in, something you cannot do when the Actions window is in normal mode.

Figure 2.2
The Actions win- dow in expert mode allows you to type directly into the program listing.

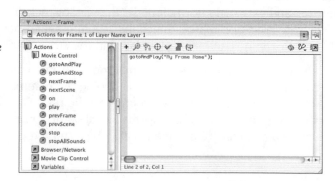

Deciding which mode of the ActionScript window to use is not hard. To write anything but basic programs, you need to use the expert mode. The normal mode does not let you easily enter the types of syntax needed for real programming.

On the other hand, the normal mode of the Actions window can be a great learning tool. Instead of requiring you to guess at the syntax of each command, or use the documentation to look up each one, the normal mode spells it out for you. This can help you quickly learn your way around commands such as *gotoAndPlay*.

Lesson 3: Your First ActionScript Program

The first ActionScript command you should learn is called *trace*. The *trace* command writes some information to the Flash Output window. The Output window is a little text window that can appear when you preview your movie in Flash. It is typically used to send debugging messages while you develop your program.

Although this example will not be anything you can use in a real Flash movie, it is the quickest way to show that you can write ActionScript that can actually make Flash do something.

To create this example, open a new Flash movie. The timeline automatically contains a single layer with a single keyframe in it. Select this keyframe and press F9 to bring up the Actions panel. Then switch the Actions panel to expert mode by using the pop-up menu at the upper-right corner of the window.

Now you can click in the empty program listing area on the right side of the Actions window. Type this single line of code:

```
trace("Hello World!");
```

NOTE ·
A semicolon is used at the end of each complete Flash command that appears on a single line, as is the case at the end of the *trace* example.

The *trace* command is a built-in Flash function. Functions use parentheses to enclose parameters. Parameters are bits of information given to the function so it can complete its task. The *trace* command requires exactly one parameter: the text to be placed in the Output window. Some functions require more than one parameter, whereas others require none.

Your screen should now look something like Figure 2.3. Here you can see the single layer and keyframe in the timeline. The Actions window is titled "Actions—Frame" to indicate that it is holding ActionScript that pertains to the currently selected keyframe. The *trace* command is the only thing in the program listing.

Figure 2.3

The "Hello World" program is attached to the first and only keyframe.

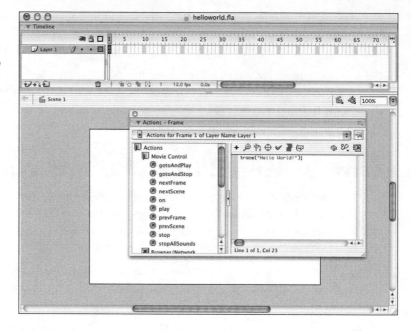

Try to create this movie from scratch. However, if you need it, the movie is also included as Helloworld.fla on the CD-ROM in the folder for this chapter.

To run this program, choose Control, Test Movie. Flash might take a second to create the .swf file, and then the file opens in the preview window. This window remains blank because there are no graphics in the movie. However, the Output window also opens, showing the words "Hello World!" (see Figure 2.4).

Figure 2.4

The Flash Output window contains the results of the simple trace program.

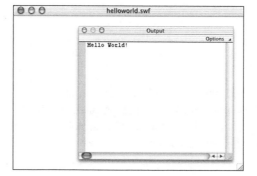

This is a significant step in becoming an ActionScript programmer. You have given Flash a command. In return, Flash has indicated that it understands you and will obey!

> **NOTE**
> The "Hello World" program is a tradition that dates back to the earliest programming languages. It is seen as the most basic program there is, and is thus usually the first lesson taught, whether the language is assembly language on an ancient hulking mainframe computer, BASIC, Pascal, C, Java, or ActionScript. You have just followed in the footsteps of millions of computer programmers when they started to learn their trade.

Lesson 4: Controlling Flash Playback

In "Lesson 2: Using the Actions Window," you caught a glimpse of the ActionScript command *gotoAndPlay*. This command tells Flash to forget about playing the next frame in the timeline, but instead to jump to a completely different frame. By using *gotoAndPlay*, you can control the playback of a Flash movie.

Create a new Flash movie. This time, you'll add several keyframes to it. Create a series of four keyframes and name them "part1" to "part4." These keyframes represent four parts of an animation. In addition to naming these four keyframes, also place a piece of static text on each so that users can tell which part they are seeing on the screen. In the example movie Gotoandplay.fla, static text "PART 1" to "PART 4" has been placed on each of the keyframes. So the text "PART 1" appears on the keyframe "part1," the text "PART 2" appears on the keyframe "part2," and so on.

The keyframes have also been separated by several frames so that the labels can be read in the main timeline. Figure 2.5 shows the main timeline, where you can see the four labels. The second keyframe is selected and you can see the text "PART 2" on the Stage.

Open the Actions window with the second keyframe selected. Now, type this command in the Actions window:

```
gotoAndPlay("part4");
```

Notice that after you add some ActionScript to a keyframe, it contains a little "a" in the timeline.

This is the only ActionScript in the movie. When you test this movie, here's what should happen: The movie starts off at the keyframe "part1" and shows the text "PART 1" on the screen. It then advances along the timeline until it hits the keyframe "part2." This is where the ActionScript is located. Flash then follows the command and jumps to keyframe "part4." It does this before it even has a chance to display the "PART 2" text on the "part2" keyframe. The movie is now at "part4," and the text "PART 4" is displayed. The movie then continues to move down the timeline until it hits the end. At this point, the movie loops back to the first frame and displays "PART 1" again. The whole process repeats endlessly.

Figure 2.5

This movie contains four keyframes and a script placed in the second keyframe. The second keyframe is selected and the Actions window shows the script in it.

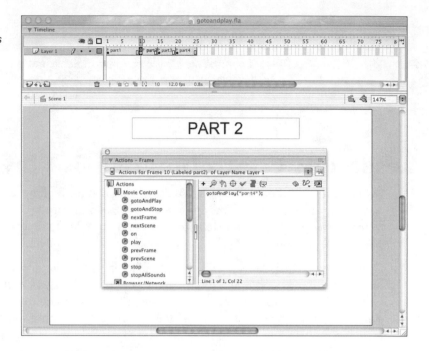

You have used ActionScript to make Flash do something other than play a straight animation. The movie could have proceeded from "part1" to "part2" to "part3" to "part4," but because of your script, it skipped "part2" and "part3" altogether. You have learned how to control the movement of a Flash movie with ActionScript.

Example file: Nonlinear.fla

Let's look at another example. Using the same basic movie setup, you'll create little keyframes at the end of each part of the movie. You'll be placing scripts that run after a part is over, rather than when one begins.

Figure 2.6 shows this setup. There are four labeled keyframes just like in the previous example, but also four other keyframes that come after each part of the movie. It is these unlabeled keyframes that contain the code.

The keyframe that comes after "part1" contains this code:

```
gotoAndPlay("part3");
```

The keyframe that comes after "part2" contains this code:

```
gotoAndPlay("part4");
```

The keyframe that comes after "part3" contains this code:

```
gotoAndPlay("part2");
```

The keyframe that comes after "part4" contains this code:

```
gotoAndPlay("part1");
```

Figure 2.6
This movie has four parts. Each part starts with a labeled keyframe and ends with an unlabeled keyframe that contains a small script.

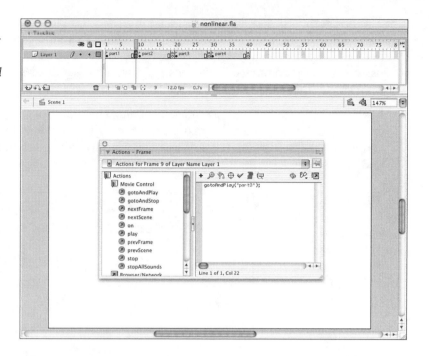

When you run this movie, found on the CD-ROM as Nonlinear.fla, the movie starts by showing "PART 1." Then, instead of continuing to the frame "part2," it is forced by the ActionScript to jump to "part3." So the movie goes from "PART 1" to "PART 3." Then, at the end of "part3," the movie is told to jump back to "part2." At the end of "part2," the movie is told to jump ahead to "part4." The sequence, therefore, is "PART 1," "PART 3," "PART 2," and then "PART 4." It then repeats.

By using ActionScript, you've completely circumvented the normal animation sequence of the movie and replaced it with your own.

Although these two examples create predictable results, you can use the *gotoAndPlay* command in other ways, in conjunction with buttons and such, to give the user control over which part of the Flash movie gets played next.

Lesson 5: Creating Buttons to Give the User Control

Example files: Stop.fla, Navigation.fla

In the previous example, ActionScript controlled the playback of the movie without any user interaction. Let's add some buttons that will allow the user to tell the Flash movie what part to play next.

The first step in giving the user some control over the playback of the movie is to take away some of the control from Flash. Flash wants to animate. It starts with frame 1 and pushes forward to the next frame and the next. You can tell Flash to cut that out by using the *stop()* command. This halts the animation and leaves the Flash movie sitting on a single frame.

Figure 2.7 shows the example movie Stop.fla. There are four keyframes, each with a label in the timeline and some text on the Stage. The first keyframe includes a short script with the *stop()* command. When you run this movie, the movie stops at frame 1 and never advances past it.

Figure 2.7

This movie contains a sequence of keyframes, but the stop() command in the first frame halts the movie there.

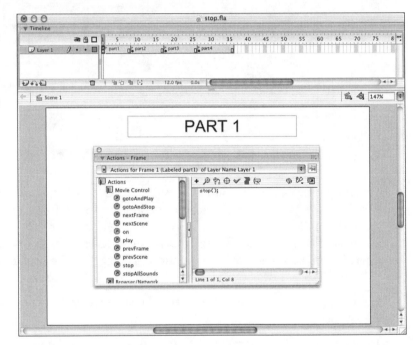

Now that you have taken control of the movie away from Flash, you can give the user some control. Create a simple button symbol and place it on the Stage. It doesn't have to be anything fancy. In the example movie, a small circle is used as a button.

Next, I created a new layer with only one keyframe, so that the same items appear throughout the movie. I placed four different instances of the same button from the library in this layer. You can see the result in Figure 2.8.

You'll use the same *stop()* command placed on the first keyframe of this movie. This halts the movie as soon at it begins. The four buttons are visible at the bottom of the screen. You'll attach a script to each one of these buttons.

Figure 2.8
This movie has two layers. The first is divided into four parts with four keyframes, although the second contains a single keyframe that stretches across the whole movie.

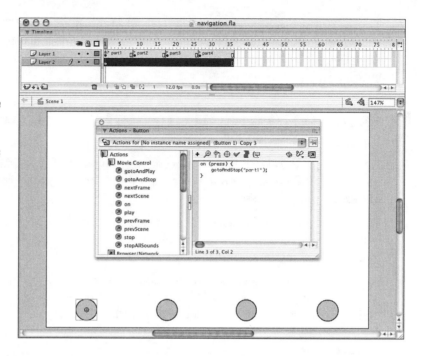

The first script can be seen in Figure 2.8. The first button is selected so the Actions window displays its script. Here it is again:

```
on (press) {
    gotoAndStop("part1");
}
```

This is what a typical button script looks like. It uses handlers to define what should be done during different button actions. In this case, the action is *press*. The syntax *on* is used to define the beginning of a handler like this. Then the bracket symbols { and } are used to contain the commands that should be executed when the event occurs.

In this case, a *gotoAndStop* command is issued. This is the sibling of *gotoAndPlay*. The difference is that the first command jumps to a new frame and halts, whereas the second command jumps to a new frame and immediately begins animating through to the next frame.

In addition to attaching this script to this button, also attach three similar scripts to the other three buttons. The only difference should be that the other buttons should jump to frames "part2," "part3," and "part4."

Example file: Navigation.fla

When you run this movie using Control, Test Movie, it begins with the movie stopped at the first frame. From there, the user can press any one of the four buttons to jump to any one of the other four frames. Try the example movie, Navigation.fla, to see how it works.

This is your first usable Flash movie. Instead of the simple "PART 1" to "PART 4" text shown on each keyframe, you can place a presentation similar to one seen in PowerPoint or other presentation software. This creates a whole other use for Flash beyond simple animation.

Lesson 6: Animating with ActionScript

Example file: Animate.fla

Next, you need to learn how to move items around the Stage with ActionScript. To do this, you'll place a script on a movie clip in the same way you placed a script on a button in the previous lesson.

Start by creating a new movie. Then, place a movie clip on the Stage. A movie clip that contains the image of a fox was placed on the Stage for the Animate.fla example movie. You can do something simpler if you want, such as make a circle.

After you have the movie clip in the library, you can place an instance of it on the Stage. At this point, you should have a movie with a single layer and single frame in it, and it should be on the Stage (see Figure 2.9).

Figure 2.9

This movie contains just one movie clip with a script attached to it.

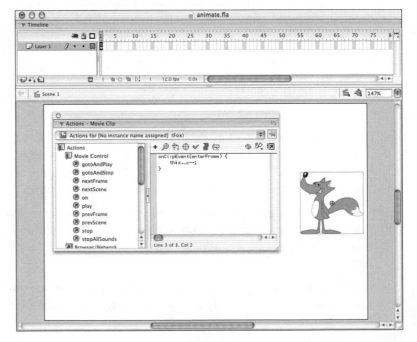

The script attached to the movie clip uses a handler just like the button script in the previous lesson. Instead of using *on* to define the handler, you need to use *onClipEvent* to define events that affect movie clips. In this case the event is *enterFrame*. This is an event that happens automatically, several times a second. If the movie is set to run at 12fps, then the *enterFrame* event should be sent to the handler 12 times per second.

Just as with the *on(press)* handler in the button script, the *onClipEvent(enterFrame)* handler uses { and } brackets to contain the commands that will be executed when the event occurs.

There is only one command here, which moves the movie clip 1 pixel to the left. Let's look at the script, and then the explanation of how it moves the movie clip to the left follows.

```
onClipEvent(enterFrame) {
    this._x--;
}
```

The command *this._x--* probably seems like Greek to anyone not familiar with programming languages, so I'll break it down, piece by piece.

The *this* means it's used when code in a movie clip refers to itself. So, in this case, *this* is a way to refer to the movie clip to which the script is attached.

After *this* is a period, usually called a dot. A dot after an object such as *this* means that you want to access a property of the object. The property in this case is _x, which refers to the horizontal position of the movie clip.

So *this._x* refers to the horizontal position of the movie clip. The -- is a decrement command. It takes the value of what is before it and reduces it by exactly 1. The command *this._x--* then takes the horizontal position of the movie clip and subtracts 1, thus moving the movie clip to the left.

If you wanted to move the move clip to the right, you could use ++, called the increment command. Likewise, if you wanted to move the movie clip several pixels at a time, you could have used += or -=, like this:

```
onClipEvent(enterFrame) {
    this._x -= 5;
}
```

The preceding code would move the movie clip 5 pixels at a time.

Lesson 7: Letting the User Control Movie Clips

Example file: Usercontrol.fla

Instead of moving the movie clip to the left or right as in the last example, let's make it follow the user's cursor.

The last lesson showed you how you can access the horizontal position of a movie clip. You can access the vertical position just as easily with the $_y$ property. Now all you need to learn is how to set a movie clip's position to the cursor location.

The cursor location is stored in two properties: _xmouse and _ymouse. These are the horizontal and vertical positions of the cursor. The question is, what are these properties *of*?

Well, they can be properties of any movie clip or of the movie itself. For instance, *this._xmouse* returns the horizontal location of the mouse as it relates to the center of the current movie clip.

What you need is the position of the movie clip in relation to the Stage. To get the properties of the Stage, you need to use the _root object rather than *this*. So _root._xmouse is the horizontal location of the mouse relative to the upper-left corner of the Stage.

To set the movie clip's position to the position of the cursor, you need to set both the $_x$ and $_y$ properties of the movie clip to the _xmouse and _ymouse properties of the Stage. Here is how the code should look:

```
onClipEvent(enterFrame) {
    this._x = _root._xmouse;
    this._y = _root._ymouse;
}
```

Figure 2.10 shows how the example movie Usercontrol.fla is put together. There is a single frame with a *stop()* command placed on it. The movie clip has the script from the preceding code placed on it. That is all that is required. When you run this movie, the movie clip with the fox will follow the cursor.

Now that you know how to control both the movie playback and the placement of movie clips, let's look into some of the basic elements of programming.

Figure 2.10
The script attached to this movie clip causes it to follow the cursor.

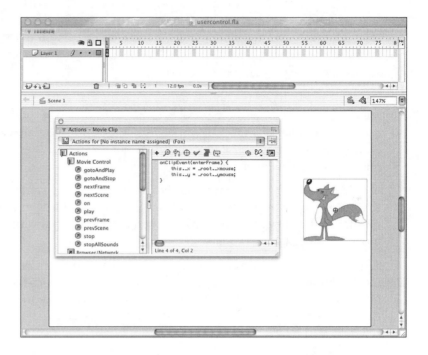

Lesson 8: Using Variables

Variables are little storage units in which you can put numbers and strings of characters. For instance, you can create a variable and place the number 5 in it. You can then add 2 to that variable and it will then hold the number 7. Here's how that would look in ActionScript:

```
myVariable = 5;
myVariable += 2;
```

In this case, the term "myVariable" refers to a variable that you, the programmer, created. To create a variable in Flash, all you need to do is to use it for the first time. Flash automatically creates a variable of that name. In this case, it did that, and placed the value 5 in it.

The next line uses this variable, adding 2 to it. The variable "myVariable" now contains the number 7.

TIP

Deciding what to name your variables is important. A variable's name should reflect its purpose. For instance, if a variable is to store the user's name, it should be something like "userName." When you look at your code later, there will be no confusion as to what that variable is for.

You can also place strings into variables. A string is a sequence of characters such as "Hello World". You can store strings in variables by using the = symbol just as you would if you were assigning a number to the variable.

```
myVariable = "Hello World";
```

Variables in Flash are not typed. Variable typing is a restriction used in other programming languages that allows a variable to be set to only one type of data. So if a variable is created to store a number, it can be used to store only numbers, never a string. However, because Flash ActionScript does not have this restriction, you can store either numbers or strings in any variable.

Variables can also hold other things besides numbers and strings. You can hold a pointer to a movie clip, for instance. Remember how you used *this* in the previous two lessons to refer to the current movie clip? You can assign *this* to a variable and then refer to the movie clip through this variable.

Although this might not be that useful when all you need to do to refer to the current movie clip is use *this*, it comes in handy when there is more than one movie clip that needs to be controlled. You'll be dealing with situations like that often in the games in the book. For now, it is enough to know that variables can hold numbers, strings, and references to movie clips.

TIP

All the variables used in these lessons and the rest of this book are global variables. This means that after you set their contents, they persist and are accessible though the main timeline or movie clip where they are contained. You can also use the *var* keyword to define local variables. Local variables are thrown away after the function or code segment in which they are defined is over. They cannot be accessed by other functions.

Lesson 9: Performing Operations

After you have variables storing information, you might want to change that information in some way. You've already seen that you can use ++ or += to change the value of a variable. You can also use a wide array of other operations on variables.

Let's start by looking at variables that contain numbers. You can perform a wide variety of mathematical operations on numerical variables with the +, -, /, and * symbols. Consider some examples.

If you create the variables "a" and "b," you can add them together and place the result in "c."

```
a = 7;
b = 5;
c = a + b;
```

In this example, "c" would end up holding the number 12. Here are some similar examples:

```
c = a - b;
c = a * b;
c = a / b;
```

The variable "c" will hold the value 2 after the first line, 35 after the second line, and 1.4 after the third line.

You can also perform more complex math operations by using a set of mathematical functions built into Flash. All these functions are prefaced with the term *Math* followed by a dot, and then the function name. For instance, you can get the square root of a number by using the *Math.sqrt* function:

```
a = 9;
b = Math.sqrt(a);
```

The value of "b" is 3, which is the square root of 9.

One of the most crucial elements of a computer language that allows programmers to make games with it is a random number generator. Without random numbers, many games would be completely predictable and unchallenging.

Flash can create random numbers by using the *Math.random()* function. This function produces a random decimal value between 0.0 and 1.0. You can produce more useful numbers by multiplying this by a larger integer, and then using the *int* function to convert it to an integer. For instance, the following gives you a random number from 0 to 9:

```
myRandomNumber = int(Math.random()*10);
```

You'll be seeing other mathematical functions throughout this book as the examples need them.

Strings can also have functions performed on them. For instance, to combine two strings, you can use the + symbol:

```
a = "Hello";
b = "World";
c = a + b;
```

The value of "c" after this will be "HelloWorld". Notice that there is no space between the two words. You have to tell Flash to put a space there. The following code does that to give you "Hello World" as a result:

```
a = "Hello";
b = "World";
c = a + " " + b;
```

An easier way to concatenate one string on to the end of another is to can use the +=
syntax:

```
a = "Hello";
a += "World";
```

Now that you know a little more about variables and how to use them, look at how
ActionScript can be used to make decisions.

Lesson 10: Conditional Statements

In "Lesson 5: Creating Buttons to Give the User Control," you learned how to use
buttons to allow the user to jump from one frame to the other. The user decides what
part of the movie he wants to see next, presses a button, and the script attached to the
button moves the movie to that frame.

ActionScript can also make decisions. To do this, it needs to base these decisions on the
comparison of values. This is done with the *if* statement. For instance, two values can
be compared. If both values are equal, then the program does something in reaction to
that fact.

Here is a program that compares a variable against a value. If this condition is met, then
the code inside the { and } brackets is executed. Otherwise, it is skipped.

```
if (a == 7) {
    gotoAndPlay("special frame");
}
```

The == symbol is used to compare two values to see whether they are equal. If they are,
then the condition is true. If not, then the condition is false. The job of the *if* statement
is to examine the condition and test to see whether it's true. If it is, the code in the
brackets is used.

You can extend the *if* statement to also perform actions if the condition is not met. By
using an *else* after the *if* statement, you can include another set of brackets that tells
Flash what to do if the condition is not met:

```
if (a == 7) {
    gotoAndPlay("special frame");
} else {
    gotoAndPlay("another frame");
}
```

You can also have a longer *if* statement that makes several conditional tests. The code
that comes after the first condition that is true is used. If none of the conditions are true,
then the code in the *else* portion of the statement is used instead.

```
if (a == 7) {
    gotoAndPlay("special frame");
} else if (a == 12) {
    gotoAndPlay("very special frame");
} else if (a == 15) {
    gotoAndPlay("extremely special frame");
} else {
    gotoAndPlay("a not so special frame");
}
```

You can also use the == symbol to compare two strings. For instance, to see whether the variable "username" contains the string "Gary", you could use this line of code:

```
if (username == "Gary") {
```

In addition to ==, you can use < to determine whether a number is less than another number, > to determine whether a number is greater than another number, or <= and >= to determine whether a number is less than or equal to or greater than or equal to another number. You can use these symbols for strings as well, in which case they compare the strings and determine whether one comes before the other alphabetically.

You can also make more than one comparison at a time. For instance, you can test to see whether both "a" is equal to a number and "username" is equal to a string:

```
if ((a == 7) and (username == "Gary")) {
```

The previous line is true only if both conditions are met. On the other hand, you can use an *or* to see whether either one or the other condition is met:

```
if ((a == 7) or (username == "Gary")) {
```

These *if* statements are the fundamental building blocks of all programs. You can use them to change variables, branch to other frames, or decide whether a player is winning or losing a game. Loops are another important part of programs, as you'll see in the next section.

Lesson 11: Loops

Conditional statements are a necessary element of programming; however, you couldn't do much without loops, either.

Computers excel at doing repetitive tasks. Loops are your way of making Flash do repetitive tasks. The most common type of loop is called the *for* loop. It enables you to perform a task an exact number of times. Here is a simple *for* loop:

```
for(i=0;i<10;i++) {
    trace(i);
}
```

NOTE

It has become traditional for programmers to use "i" as a generic program loop counter. In these cases, "i" stands for "increment." It is always a good idea to name your variables something that hints at what they are used for. However, in *for* loops, using "i" in a quick little loop is common.

The *for* loop looks cryptic at first. It is composed of three parts, all separated by semicolons. The first part lets you set a variable to a specific value. In this case, the variable "i" is set to 0.

The second part of the *for* syntax is a conditional statement, just like what would be used after *if*. In this case, the condition is false as long as "i" is less than 10.

The third part of the *for* syntax shows how the variable should be altered every time through the loop. In this case, "i" is incremented by 1 every time.

The result is that "i" starts at 0, gets 1 added to it every loop, and then the loop ends when "i" is no longer less than 10. So, "i" goes from 0 to 9 in 10 steps. If you run the previous code, you will see the numbers 0 through 9 placed in the Output window.

TIP

for loops should be used to process data inside programs, but not to animate objects on the screen. While a loop is in progress, the Flash screen is essentially frozen until the loop is complete. Short loops like the previous example run so quickly that they hardly affect the movie at all. However, long loops cause the movie to pause for seconds or longer.

Here's a more useful example of a *for* loop. Suppose you had 10 movie clips named "fox1" through "fox10" and you wanted to move them all 1 pixel to the left. This loop does that for you:

```
for(i=1;i<=10;i++) {
    _root["fox"+i]._x++;
}
```

The *for* loop takes "i" from 1 to 10. It uses the *_root* object introduced in "Lesson 7: Letting the User Control Movie Clips." You can refer to any movie clip in the main timeline by using *_root[]* with the name of the movie clip inside the brackets. In this case, the code builds a string by combining the word "fox" with the number "i."

There are two other ways to create loops in ActionScript. The first is to use the *while* loop. Instead of having an incremental counter, such as "i," a *while* loop continues to loop as long as a condition at the beginning of the *while* statement is true. A *do* loop is the opposite, placing the condition at the end of the loop. Neither of these types of loops are used much by beginners, but you should be aware of them.

Lesson 12: Text and Strings

Using numbers in ActionScript is pretty straightforward. You can add, subtract, and perform other operations to wind up with another number. A lot of different things can be done with string values, however. Learning how to manipulate strings is an important step in learning how to program.

One of the simplest things you can do with strings is combine them. You learned how to do this in "Lesson 9: Performing Operations." In "Lesson 10: Conditional Statements," you saw how you can compare strings to determine whether they are equal to each other, or come before or after each other alphabetically.

Now, let's look at some more string functions. For instance, suppose you want to find out whether one string is contained inside the other. To do this, you can use the *indexOf* command. This command returns the position of the second string inside the first. If the second string is not found, it returns a -1. For instance, the following code finds the string "World" at character position 6 of "Hello World." If you try to search for "Earth" instead, you get a value of -1 because "Earth" is not in "Hello World."

```
myString = "Hello World.";
myPosition = myString.indexOf("World");
```

TIP

When ActionScript refers to character positions, it begins counting at 0. So the first character of a string is character 0. The string "Hello" would be found at character 0 of the "Hello World." string.

You can also find the number of characters in a string by using *length*:

```
myString = "Hello World.";
myStringLength = myString.length;
```

Sometimes it's useful to get a specific piece of a string. Two ActionScript commands can do this. The first is *substring*, which gets a piece of a string from one character position to another. In this example, the variable "mySubstring" ends up containing the text "lo Wo":

```
myString = "Hello World.";
mySubstring = myString.substring(3,8);
```

You can also use the *substr* function to perform the same task. Rather than get the string from one position to the next, it gets a string starting at one position and continuing for a specified number of characters. So the following code gets the string starting at character 3 and extending for 5 characters:

```
myString = "Hello World.";
mySubstring = myString.substr(3,5);
```

If you have two functions that perform basically the same task, then why not three? The *slice* function is identical to the *substring* function.

Eventually, you will want to display text information to the user. Doing so is easy. In Chapter 1, "Flash Elements Used to Make Games and Toys," you learned about the dynamic text box. When you use the Property inspector to make a text box dynamic, you can also set it to be linked to an ActionScript variable.

Figure 2.11 shows the Property inspector with a text box that is now linked to the variable "mySubstring". The panel will now display the contents of "mySubstring" as long as the variable and the text box are at the same Flash level. It won't link the two if they are at different levels—for example, if one is inside a movie clip.

Figure 2.11
The Property inspector can be used to link a text box to an ActionScript variable.

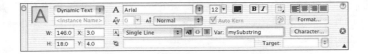

You can also link a variable to a text box that is set to be input text. In this case, the text box reacts to changes in the variable, but the variable also reacts to changes made when the user types in the input box.

In the next lesson, you'll learn about functions, and also see an example of a dynamic text box.

Lesson 13: Creating Functions

A function is a piece of code that can be used over and over again. You can pass values into it and receive one value from it. For example, you can have a function that returns the sum of two numbers. Here's how that would look in ActionScript:

```
function sum(a,b) {
    c = a + b;
    return c;
}
```

Generally, you place functions in frame scripts of the main timeline. You define a function by using the *function* keyword. Then you include the name of the function. That is followed by parentheses and then an open bracket }. Inside the parentheses, you can place nothing at all, or a comma-delimited list of variables that will be set when the function is called. These variables are called the function's parameters. For instance, the preceding function can be called like this:

```
trace(sum(7,12));
```

The result of this call would be the number 19, which would be placed in the Output window by the *trace* command. When "sum" is called, the value 7 is passed into the function in the variable "a" and the value 12 is passed in as the variable "b." When the function is finished, the *return* command sends the value of "c" back to the place where "sum" was called. So the result of "sum(7,12)" is 19, which the *trace* command uses to perform its duty.

You would use a function for two reasons. The first is to break your program into smaller pieces. If you have a 30-line program that performs three different tasks, you could instead have three 10-line functions that each perform a single task. This makes it easier to work with your code.

The other reason to use functions is they are reusable. You can call a function as many times as you like in the rest of your program. So if you have a piece of code that needs to be used several times, you can place it into its own function and just call that function repeatedly. You can call it with different parameters.

Example file: Framelabeler.fla

Here's a function that takes the name of a frame label as a parameter. It then performs two tasks. First, it places this name into a text variable called "frameLabelText." This text box is visible throughout the movie, so it acts as a sort of position indicator to tell the user where she is in the movie. The second task for the function is to *gotoAndStop* at the frame.

```
function gotoFrame(frameLabel) {
    frameLabelText = frameLabel;
    gotoAndStop(frameLabel);
}
```

This function gets placed in the first frame of the main timeline. Along with that function is one regular command line that uses this function to make the movie jump to the "introduction" frame. Because it's already there, the *gotoAndStop* command in the function has the effect of a *stop* command, but the variable assignment works just as well.

```
gotoFrame("introduction");
```

The Framelabeler.fla example movie contains this function in the first frame, as well as four other labeled keyframes. Five buttons along the bottom take the user to each of the five frames. Instead of each button having its own *gotoAndStop* command, they all call "gotoFrame".

Figure 2.12 shows the example movie. You can see the dynamic text area in the upper-left corner of the Stage. It contains the temporary contents "frame label." This will be immediately replaced by "introduction" when the first call of "gotoFrame" is made.

Figure 2.12

This movie has five frames and five buttons to take the user to each frame. The text box displays the name of the current frame label.

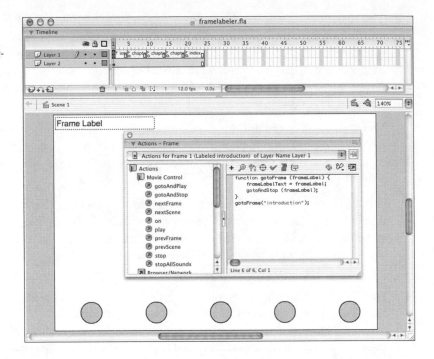

The usefulness of having one function control all the navigation is more than just saving some keystrokes while programming. Suppose you have 100 calls to "gotoFrame" by the time you are finished with your program. Then, you decide to take out the "frameLabelText" box or display the frame label somewhat differently. If you didn't use a function, you would have to go through your program and remove or change code in 100 places. But because all your navigation buttons use "gotoFrame," you can just change "gotoFrame" and all the navigation buttons will perform differently.

Lesson 14: Arrays

No introduction to any programming language would be complete without discussing arrays. Although a lot of simple work can be done without ever using arrays, a programmer cannot be considered anything but a novice unless she can use arrays.

Arrays are another type of variable. The variables you have been using so far can contain a single value: a number or a string. An array can contain zero, one, or more values. Here's what an array looks like:

```
myArray = ["Apple", "Orange", "Peach", "Plum"];
```

You can then use some special syntax to access one item out of the array:

```
myItem = myArray[1];
```

The value of "myItem" is "Orange" because arrays, like strings, begin counting positions with 0.

As you might guess, arrays are useful for storing lists of data. Several special functions exist for dealing with arrays. First, let's look at how to build them. There are several approaches to building an array. So far, you've seen the all-at-once approach. The entire array is declared all at once. You can also create an empty array and add items to it:

```
myArray = new Array();
myArray.push("Apple");
myArray.push("Orange");
myArray.push("Peach");
myArray.push("Plum");
```

The first line in the preceding code creates an empty array. Each of the next four lines adds one item to the array by using the *push* command. Although this seems more complex than the all-in-one-line approach, building an array like this is necessary if you don't know what all the elements will be right away. For instance, you might want to allow the user to enter data and then add it to an array.

You can get the length of an array just as you can get the length of a string:

```
myLength = myArray.length;
```

You've already seen how to extract a single item from an array by using bracket syntax. You can also use the *pop* command to remove the last item of an array and return it. The following piece of code adds four items to an array, and then uses a *while* loop to remove each item from the end of the array and send it to the Output window:

```
myArray = new Array();
myArray.push("Apple");
myArray.push("Orange");
myArray.push("Peach");
myArray.push("Plum");

while (myArray.length>0) {
    trace(myArray.pop());
}
```

In the Output window, the first line is "Plum" and the last "Apple," because *pop* takes the item from the end of the array.

You can also sort arrays. If the items in the array are numbers, Flash sorts them in numerical order. If they are strings, Flash sorts them in alphabetical order:

```
myArray = new Array();
myArray.push("Peach");
myArray.push("Orange");
myArray.push("Plum");
```

```
myArray.push("Apple");
myArray.sort();
trace(myArray.toString());
```

Notice that the last line of the previous code uses a *toString* function to convert the array to something that can be shown in the Output window. This can be useful when you want to make sure the array is what you expected it to be.

Finally, the *splice* array function allows you to remove one or more elements from an array:

```
myArray = ["Apple", "Orange", "Peach", "Plum"];
myArray.splice(2,1);
```

The *splice* function can work in several ways. In this example, it uses two parameters. The first is the item position at which to start deleting items. The second parameter is the number of items to delete. In this case, "Peach" will be deleted, being the item at position 2. You could delete both "Peach" and "Plum" by changing the second parameter to 2. If you remove the second parameter altogether, you can delete all the items in the rest of the array.

You can also use *splice* to insert items. By including a third parameter, you can specify what to insert:

```
myArray = ["Apple", "Orange", "Peach", "Plum"];
myArray.splice(2,1,"Pear");
```

In this case, "Peach" is removed, and "Pear" is inserted into that position. You could include a fourth parameter to insert a second item, and even more parameters to insert more items. You could also use a 0 as the second parameter, which would mean that no items are deleted, but some are inserted at that position.

Now that you've had a sampling of all the basics of ActionScript, it's time to start applying that knowledge to build useful pieces of Flash movies. In the next chapter, you'll build some of these pieces, and then starting with Chapter 5, "ActionScript Design Effects," you'll build complete programs.

3

ActionScript Elements Used to Make Games and Toys

Now that you have learned the basics of ActionScript, let's look at some more advanced examples. The following 10 lessons show you some techniques that will be used in the games later in this book.

Lesson 15: Controlling the Playback of a Movie Clip

 Example file: Mcplayback.fla

Movie clips are like extra little Flash movies inside your main Flash movie. They contain a complete timeline with layers and most of the elements of your main Flash movie. You can control your main Flash movie with commands such as *play()* and *stop()*. You can also control a movie clip with these commands.

On the CD, in a file named Mcplayback.fla, you'll see a movie clip named MyMovieClip in the library. This movie clip contains 10 frames labeled with some text so that you know which frame of the movie clip is being shown at which time.

By dragging that movie clip from the library to the Stage, you are creating an instance of that movie clip. You can and should name these instances. To do this, use the Property inspector. In Figure 3.1, you can see the Property inspector used to name the instance myMovieClip.

Figure 3.1

The Property inspector allows you to name movie clip instances.

> **TIP**
>
> You might have noticed that the movie clip instance is named the same as the movie clip in the library. This is commonly done when you are creating exactly one instance of a movie clip and have no plans to create more. The name of the instance is easier to remember when it is the same as the library item.

The example movie also has five buttons in the library. These have been placed on the Stage just under the movie clip instance. You don't need to name the button instances—in fact, you can't. Unfortunately, buttons by themselves cannot be referenced by code in any way, so there is no need for a name.

After the movie clip and the five buttons are on the Stage, you should get something that looks like Figure 3.2. The buttons look like video tape recorder controls, and that's exactly how they will be used.

Figure 3.2

The buttons allow you to control the playback of the movie clip above them.

The five buttons have complete control over the movie clip. The play button starts the movie clip moving forward. The clip continues to move forward, looping around to the beginning when it reaches the end. The stop button halts the movie clip at its current frame. The rewind button takes the movie clip back to frame one and stops it. The previous and next buttons advance the movie clip one step and stop it there.

Before the movie turns over control of the movie clip to the user, it must tell the movie clip to stop moving. Movie clips naturally want to start going as soon as they appear on the Stage. To prevent this, the following frame script was placed on the first frame of the main timeline. It stops the movie clip from animating, and also tells the main movie to stop.

```
myMovieClip.stop();
stop();
```

By using the dot-syntax, the first line tells the movie clip instance named "myMovieClip" to obey the *stop()* command. The second line has no instance name before it, so the command is issued to the same place where the script is located—in this case, the main timeline.

The button scripts use the same dot-syntax to send their commands to the movie clip. Here is the play button's script, which tells the movie clip to *play()*:

```
on (press) {
    myMovieClip.play();
}
```

The stop button sends the *stop()* command to the movie clip.

```
on (press) {
    myMovieClip.stop();
}
```

The rewind button needs to tell the movie clip to return to the first frame and stop there. The *gotoAndStop()* command with the parameter 1 does just that.

```
on (press) {
    myMovieClip.gotoAndStop(1);
}
```

The previous and next buttons move the movie clip backward or forward one frame. The *prevFrame()* and *nextFrame()* commands can be used for this. Here are both scripts:

```
on (press) {
    myMovieClip.prevFrame();
}

on (press) {
    myMovieClip.nextFrame();
}
```

Although the purpose of this lesson is to teach you how to control the playback of movie clips, you can actually use the method in this example as a way to play back an animation or even a slideshow with Flash.

Lesson 16: Controlling the Properties of a Movie Clip

Example file: Mcproperties.fla

In addition to controlling the insides of a movie clip, you can also control its external properties. For instance, you can control a movie clip's position, its rotation, and its scale.

The example movie Mcproperties.fla contains a sample movie clip of a fox in the middle of the screen. Both the library fox and the movie clip instance are named "fox."

In addition, there are eight buttons around the box. Each of these buttons sets a movie clip property of the fox. You can see how this screen appears in Figure 3.3. The first three are labeled "Left," "Middle," and "Right."

Figure 3.3

The fox movie clip in the center can be repositioned, scaled, and rotated by the buttons around it.

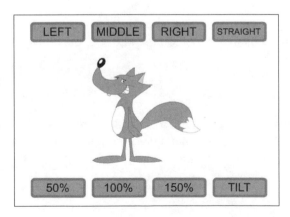

In "Lesson 6: Animating with ActionScript," in Chapter 2, you saw that the _x property of a movie clip can be used to set its horizontal location on the Stage. This is what the "Left," "Middle," and "Right" buttons will use. They could also use the _y property to set the vertical location of the movie clip, but that isn't needed in this example. Here is the code from the "Left" button. It sets the horizontal location of the fox to 200, which is slightly to the left of center, considering that the movie is 550 pixels wide. The "Middle" and "Right" buttons only differ in the value to which the _x property is set.

```
on (press) {
    fox._x = 200;
}
```

To scale a movie clip, you need to use the _xscale and _yscale properties. If these are set to the same value, they provide a way to uniformly scale a movie clip. A value of 100 stands for 100% scale.

TIP

You can also change only _xscale or _yscale individually, or set them to different values to make a movie clip thinner or flatter.

Here is the button script for the "50%" button. The other two scaling buttons use the same code, but with a different value.

```
on (press) {
    fox._xscale = 50;
    fox._yscale = 50;
}
```

To rotate a movie clip, you need to use the _rotation property. It takes a value in degrees, so 0 is the same as 360. You can go higher than 360 or lower than 0, but Flash just interprets that into a reading between 0 and 360.

Here is the script for the "Tilt" button. It rotates the movie clip 30° clockwise. The "Straight" button just sets the rotation back to 0.

```
on (press) {
    fox._rotation = 30;
}
```

By using these properties in more complex code to come later in this book, you'll be able to move movie clips around the Stage to create all sorts of games.

Lesson 17: Dragging and Dropping Movie Clips

Example file: Dragsimple.fla

An important part of many interfaces, whether they are games or applications, is the ability to drag elements around on the screen. This can be done several ways in Flash. Let's look at three of them.

The *startDrag* command tells Flash to make a movie clip automatically follow the cursor. The example movie Dragsimple.fla demonstrates how to use this command in the most basic way.

A movie clip with a circle drawn in it has been placed on the Stage and named "circle." As soon as the movie runs, the following command starts the circle following the cursor. It also tells the main timeline to stop animating so the movie doesn't continue past this frame.

```
startDrag("circle",true);
stop();
```

The *startDrag* command is using two parameters in this case. The first is the name of the movie clip to drag. The second is the keyword *true,* which in this case tells *startDrag* to lock the object's center to the cursor. If you used a *false* in this second parameter, the distance between the cursor and the center of the movie clip would remain the same as when the *startDrag* command was issued.

NOTE

The keywords *true* and *false* are called Boolean expressions. They can be used in cases in which an attribute is either on or off. They are also the results of comparisons, such as "a == b."

The example movie Dragsimple.fla forces the movie clip "circle" to follow the cursor. However, a more typical use of dragging is to have the user click an item to start dragging it, and then release the mouse to drop it.

Example file: Dragcomplex.fla

The drag and release behavior can be done by making a movie clip that contains a button inside it. In Dragcomplex.fla, an invisible button has been placed in the same circle movie clip. The button was made invisible by placing content on only the "Hit" frame inside the button.

So, the "circle" movie clip contains the same graphic as in Dragsimple.fla, but also a button. The following script has been attached to this button. It executes the *startDrag* command when the user presses down, and a *stopDrag* when the user lifts up the mouse button.

```
on (press) {
    startDrag("",false);
}

on (release) {
    stopDrag();
}
```

The empty quotes inside the *startDrag* command tell Flash that you want the current movie clip to be dragged. Because the button is inside the "circle" movie clip, that particular clip can be dragged. The *false* as the second parameter means that the movie clip will not lock its center to the cursor, but instead maintain the original distance between the cursor and the movie clip center. This makes it appear as if the cursor has grabbed a part of the circle and is dragging the circle by that point.

The *stopDrag* command needs no parameters. Only one movie clip can be dragged at a time, so all it needs to do is stop the current dragging action, which will return the movie clip to its immobile state.

One of the problems with the *startDrag* command is that only one movie clip can be dragged at a time. In addition, the dragging is happening automatically, which makes it hard for you to monitor the movie clip's progress as it is dragged. For these reasons, it is useful to know how to drag a movie clip without using the *startDrag* command.

Example file: Dragbetter.fla

The example movie Dragbetter.fla contains some code that does this. The movie is set up the same way as Dragcomplex.fla, with a movie clip that has an invisible button inside it. The script attached to this button, however, is different. All it does is set a variable called "drag" to *true* when the user presses down on the button, and *false* when the mouse button is lifted.

```
on (press) {
    drag = true;
}

on (release) {
    drag = false;
}
```

The "drag" variable becomes a global variable, which is shared by all the code associated with the movie clip. Therefore, the script attached to the movie clip can tell the value of "drag" and use it to determine whether or not the movie clip should follow the cursor.

The script attached to the movie clip sets the _x and _y properties of the movie clip to the _xmouse and _ymouse properties of the main timeline. These last two properties give you the mouse location relative to the Stage.

```
onClipEvent (enterFrame) {
    if (drag) {
        this._x = _root._xmouse;
        this._y = _root._ymouse;
    }
}
```

The *this* keyword is used to indicate that the object being referred to is the current one. The script is attached to the "circle" movie clip, so *this* refers to that clip. In the next section, you'll look at different ways of referring to movie clips at different levels.

Lesson 18: Movie Clips and Levels

The beginning ActionScript programmer might find it difficult to understand how movie clips and levels work. It helps to think of a movie clip as a Flash movie inside your main Flash movie. Although your main Flash movie has variables and properties, the movie clip inside it has its own world of variables and properties that are separate from the main Flash movie.

Whenever you place a movie clip on the Stage, you are creating a new world, also called an object. The main Flash movie is an object and the movie clip is an object inside that object.

Think of the Flash movie as a toy box full of toys. If you paint the toy box blue, it doesn't make all the toys inside it blue. Each toy maintains its original color. On the other hand, if you move the toy box across the room, all the toys come with it. However, they maintain their own properties, such as color and position inside the toy box.

Assuming the toy box is closed and you have told someone in the room to get the toy truck, that person might have a difficult time if she hasn't been told that the toy truck is inside the toy box. "Get the toy truck," isn't enough. You would have to say, "Get the toy truck that is inside the toy box."

Movie clips work the same way. If you have a movie clip that is at the main level of the Flash movie, you can refer to it by name, such as "toyTruck." However, if you have a movie clip "toyTruck" that is inside another movie clip called "toyBox," then you'll have to refer to it as "the toy truck inside the toy box," or "toyBox.toyTruck."

Example file: Levels.fla

Figure 3.4 shows a situation like this. The source for this movie can be found as the file Levels.fla on the CD.

Figure 3.4

The movie clip "secondMC" is inside the movie clip "firstMC," which is on the Stage.

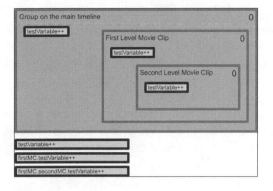

There are two movie clips in Levels.fla. However, only the movie clip called "firstMC" is on the Stage. The movie clip "secondMC" is actually inside "firstMC." A text box on the Stage and in each movie clip is linked to the variable "testVariable." These text boxes show you, at any time, the value of "testVariable" on the Stage in "firstMC" and in "secondMC."

The Stage and each movie clip contain a button that will increase the value of "testVariable." Here is the code inside each of these buttons:

```
on (press) {
    testVariable++;
}
```

The button changes the value of the variable "testVariable" found at the level of the button. So the button on the Stage changes the variable "testVariable" at the main level. The button in "firstMC" changes the variable "testVariable" in "firstMC." The button in "secondMC" changes the variable "testVariable" in "secondMC."

It is important to realize that these three variables named "testVariable" are actually three different variables. Because they are at different levels, they have no relationship to each other.

If you run this movie, you can see that pressing one of these small buttons changes the value of "testVariable" at only the level where the button is located.

You can also change the value of variables at levels other than the level where the code is located. By using ActionScript dot-syntax, you can force Flash to modify variables at different levels. The three larger buttons at the bottom of the screen show some examples.

All three of these buttons are on the Stage, not inside any movie clip. The first button changes the value of "testVariable" without specifying a movie clip. This results in the "testVariable" on the Stage being changed.

The second button specifies the variable "testVariable" inside the movie clip "firstMC." The code looks like this:

```
on (press) {
    firstMC.testVariable++;
}
```

The result is that the variable in the "firstMC" movie clip is changed. To change the variable inside "secondMC," you need to remember that "secondMC" is inside "firstMC." To get to this variable, tell Flash to look at the "secondMC" that is inside "firstMC."

```
on (press) {
    firstMC.secondMC.testVariable++;
}
```

These three buttons are similar to saying, "paint the room blue," then "paint the toy box blue," and then "paint the toy truck inside the toy box blue."

In all the previous examples, the name of the movie clip instance has been used directly in the code. There is another way that you can refer to movie clips. You can use the _root property of the Flash movie to refer to a movie clip like this:

```
_root["firstMC"].testVariable++;
```

This comes in handy if you have a space in the name of the movie clip instance, because you can't use the other method with spaces in the name. This alternative method will also come in handy when you need to use more complex code to construct the name of a movie clip as a string, rather than having it hard-coded into the program. You'll see one use of that in the next section.

Lesson 19: Duplicating Movie Clips

Being able to manipulate movie clips is an important part of building games. However, you'll also need to be able to create movie clips. Although this is easy enough to do in Flash, you might want your code to be able to create the movie clips after the movie has started running.

Think about a game in which enemy spaceships are attacking the player. One ship comes, and then another, and then another, and so on. Instead of having to create dozens or hundreds of movie clips ready for the game to use, you can have the code create them as necessary.

There are two ways to create movie clips. One is to duplicate a movie clip that already exists. Another is to create a movie clip from a symbol in the library.

To duplicate a movie clip, you need to use the *duplicateMovieClip* command. This command creates a carbon copy of an existing movie clip. Here is an example:

```
firstclip.duplicateMovieClip("newclip",0);
```

The command *duplicateMovieClip* must be triggered by the movie clip to be duplicated. So it starts with the name of that movie clip, in this case "firstclip." There are also two parameters. The first parameter is the name of the new movie clip instance. The second parameter is the level of this new movie clip.

This is where it can get a bit confusing. The *duplicateMovieClip* command uses the term "level" to describe the order in which movie clips are drawn. This is different than the use of the term "level" in the last section, when it was used to describe which movie clips were inside other movie clips.

If a movie clip is drawn at level 0, like in the previous one-line code example, then it is drawn under a movie clip at level 1. Level 1 is drawn under level 2, and so on.

You don't have to worry about two movie clips being at the same level because they can't be. Flash won't let two movie clips be created at the same level. So with every use of *duplicateMovieClip*, you need to use a different level number.

Example file: DuplicateMovieClip.fla

In DuplicateMovieClip.fla, the first and only frame of the main timeline contains the variable "level," which is set to 0. On the Stage is a button labeled "New MC." There is also a movie clip with the name "firstclip." Each time the button is pressed, the following code is executed:

```
on (press) {
    // duplicate first clip
    firstclip.duplicateMovieClip("newclip"+level,level);

    // set a random position
    _root["newclip"+level]._x = int(Math.random()*550);
    _root["newclip"+level]._y = int(Math.random()*400);

    // increase level
    level++;
}
```

> **NOTE**
>
> Notice that for the first time, I've used comments in the ActionScript code. These comments start with two slashes. Everything else on a line after the two slashes is ignored by Flash and is there only to make it easier for you to understand what the code is doing. As the blocks of code in this book get longer and longer, you'll see comments to help you read through them. You should also use comments in your code to make it easier to edit later, or for a co-worker to be able to understand it more easily.

The variable "level" is used in many ways in this handler. First, it is used to compose a name for the new movie clip. The first time the variable is used, the movie clip will be named "newclip0." The variable is also used as the level for the movie clip.

At the end of the handler, "level" is incremented by one. So the next movie clip created will be "level1" at level number 1.

This handler also sets the horizontal and vertical location of this new movie clip to a random spot on the Stage. Notice that the *_root[]* syntax is used to indicate which movie clip is being referred to.

Another way to create new movie clips is to use the *attachMovie* command. This command does not require that the movie clip already be on the Stage. Instead, it just needs to be in the library. However, if a movie clip is in the library and not used on the Stage, Flash automatically won't include it in the final .swf file. To force it to include this movie clip, you need to select it in the library and use the Options menu to set the Symbol Linkage Properties. You can see this dialog box in Figure 3.5.

Figure 3.5

The Symbol Linkage Properties dialog box lets you include a movie clip in the .swf even if it isn't used on the Stage.

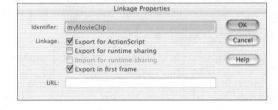

The Symbol Linkage Properties needs to be set to Export This Symbol. Then, you have to come up with a name for the symbol that the code will use to refer to it. I usually use the symbol's name as it appears in the library.

Example file: AttachMovie.fla

The *attachMovie* command uses the name in the Symbol Linkage Properties dialog box as the first parameter. The second parameter is the name of the instance of the movie clip on the Stage, and the third parameter is its level. The code for this button, found in the movie AttachMovie.fla, is almost the same as the code for the DuplicateMovieClip.fla movie, with the exception of one line.

```
on (press) {

    // duplicate first clip
    attachMovie("myMovieClip","newclip"+level,level);

    // set a random position
    _root["newclip"+level]._x = int(Math.random()*550);
    _root["newclip"+level]._y = int(Math.random()*400);

    // increase level
    level++;
}
```

Example file: RemoveMovieClip.fla

You can also remove movie clips from the Stage by using the *removeMovieClip* command. For instance, the following code, found in RemoveMovieClip.fla, removes the previous movie clip before creating a new one:

```
on (press) {
    // remove previous movie clip
    _root["newclip"+(level-1)].removeMovieClip();

    // duplicate first clip
    attachMovie("myMovieClip","newclip"+level,level);

    // set a random position
    _root["newclip"+level]._x = int(Math.random()*550);
    _root["newclip"+level]._y = int(Math.random()*400);

    // increase level
    level++;
}
```

These techniques mean that your games and applications can create their own movie clips, adding them and removing them from the Stage as necessary.

Lesson 20: Controlling Multiple Movie Clips

Now that you know how to create a bunch of movie clips with ActionScript, let's look at how to control them. You know that you can control one movie clip with code attached to it, but what if you have several movie clips that need to be controlled? What if these movie clips all need to behave in the same way?

If you place those movie clips on the Stage, you can copy and paste code from one movie clip on to the others. This has several disadvantages. First, there's the copying and pasting. Then, if you decide to change the code, you need to change it in all the instances of the movie clip.

Creating an "Actions" Movie Clip

One way to control several movie clips is to place code in one spot that controls all these clips. For instance, if you have 10 movie clips, you can place code on the first clip that controls all 10.

But rather than place the burden of control on one out of many clips, why not create a movie clip for the express purpose of controlling other clips? This common technique makes it easy to remember where you put your code. I call it the "actions movie clip."

Start by using the text tool to create a small text box on the Stage and type the word "actions" in it. (This is just so it can be identified easily.) Then, with this text box selected, choose Insert, Convert To Symbol, and turn it into a movie clip named "actions." Move it to the gray area off the Stage, so the word "actions" isn't visible to the user.

This movie clip is used to attach a script that will control all sorts of things in the movie. For instance, suppose you want to have a movie that creates 10 movie clip instances from a library symbol, and then rotates them all a little each turn.

Example file: actionsMC.fla

First, create the symbol. Set its linkage properties in the symbol's Properties dialog box to Export for ActionScript with a name "sample." You can see this in the example movie ActionsMC.fla.

The only code needed will be attached to the movie clip "actions." There will be two parts to this code, each inside an *onClipEvent* handler. The first such handler will react to a *load* event. The *load* event occurs when the movie clip first appears. The code in it will be executed once at this time. In this case, take the opportunity to create 10 new movie clips:

```
onClipEvent (load) {

    // create 10 movie clips
    for(i=0;i<10;i++) {
        _root.attachMovie("sample","sample"+i,i);

        // set the location
        _root["sample"+i]._x = i*50+50;
        _root["sample"+i]._y = 100;
    }
}
```

Not only are the movie clips created, but their locations are set. The vertical location is set to 100, but the horizontal location is set to different locations starting at 50 and continuing to 500. You can see what this looks like in Figure 3.6.

Figure 3.6
These 10 movie clips were created by ActionScript from a library symbol.

The second part of the code is inside an *onClipEvent(enterFrame)* handler. The code here executes every time the "actions" movie clip loops. If the movie is set to run at 12 frames per second, then the code should run 12 times a second.

```
onClipEvent (enterFrame) {

    // loop through and rotate each movie clip
    for(i=0;i<10;i++) {
        _root["sample"+i]._rotation += 5;
    }
}
```

This code loops through all the movie clips and rotates each one by 5°. The result is that there will be 10 movie clips on the Stage and all 10 will be rotating.

Example file: Gears.fla

I've also created a more advanced version of this movie that is set up in exactly the same way, except for the code. In Gears.fla, the movie clips are placed close together so that the cogs on the gears touch. To make them act like gears, each movie clip starts rotated 15° more than the previous one. Because the cogs are 30° apart, it makes the cogs of one gear interlock with the cogs of the previous one. Then, instead of each gear rotating in the same direction, each gear rotates in the opposite direction of the one before it. Here is this code:

```
onClipEvent (load) {
    initialRotation = 0;

    // create 10 movie clips
    for(i=0;i<10;i++) {

        // attach the movie clip
        _root.attachMovie("sample","sample"+i,i);

        // set its position
        _root["sample"+i]._x = i*37;
        _root["sample"+i]._y = 100;

        // set initial rotation so each new one is off by 15 degrees
        _root["sample"+i]._rotation = initialRotation;
        initialRotation += 15;
    }
}

onClipEvent (enterFrame) {
    // loop through every other movie clip
    for(i=0;i<10;i+=2) {
```

```
        // make this one rotate clockwise
        _root["sample"+i]._rotation += 5;

        // make next one rotate counterclockwise
        _root["sample"+(i+1)]._rotation -= 5;
    }
 }
```

To further understand how this code works, open the Gears.fla movie and play around with it. This code, like more code to come in this book, can be explained only so far with text. You need to open Flash and poke around at the examples to gain a full understanding of how they work.

Event Handlers

The only way to trap events such as "enterFrame" in Flash 5 was to use *onClipEvent* attached to a movie clip. However, in Flash MX there is an alternative. You can tell Flash to run a specific function when an event such as "enterFrame" occurs. Better still, you can do this in the main timeline, without creating an "Actions" movie clip.

Here is a simple example. This script, when placed in the main timeline, sends text to the Output window every frame.

```
 _root.onEnterFrame = function() {
     trace("enterFrame Event");
 }
```

Instead of the *trace* command, you can insert the same sort of commands used earlier in this lesson. You can also define a separate named function to handle the event. Here is another way of writing the previous example:

```
 _root.onEnterFrame = myFunction;
 function myFunction() {
     trace("enterFrame Event");
 }
```

You can use this technique to get all sorts of events, such as *onMouseUp*, *onKeyup,* and *onLoad*. You can check out the documentation for a full list and descriptions of what triggers each event.

You can find this technique used in several games, starting with the Find the Picture game in Chapter 13.

Lesson 21: Detecting Collisions

In games, things collide, usually with disastrous results for one or both objects colliding. You need to be able to write code that detects whether two objects collide, or whether the cursor location collides with an object.

In Flash, the primary way to determine whether two objects collide, or an object is covering a certain point on the screen, is to use the *hitTest* function. You can feed the *hitTest* function either the location of a point or another movie clip.

Let's start with testing for collision with a point. Suppose you have a movie clip on the screen and you want to determine whether the user's cursor is over it. You can attach this code to the movie clip:

```
onClipEvent (enterFrame) {
    if (this.hitTest(_root._xmouse,_root._ymouse,true)) {
        this._x = int(Math.random()*550);
        this._y = int(Math.random()*400);
    }
}
```

By using *this.hitTest()*, you are asking for the function *hitTest* to be used on the current movie clip. The three parameters passed into it are the horizontal location of the mouse, the vertical location of the mouse, and a *true*. This last parameter determines whether Flash uses the bounding box around the movie clip as the area for collision detection, or whether only the exact shape of the object is used. This code uses the latter parameter option by indicating *true*.

Example file: Runaway.fla

You can see this code in action in the sample movie Runaway.fla. When you move the cursor over the movie clip, it jumps to a random spot on the screen.

Example file: Collision.fla

To determine whether two movie clips intersect, you can instead use a single parameter—a pointer to the second movie clip—to see whether they both collide. In the movie Collision.fla, two movie clips are on the Stage. The larger is named "target" and the smaller is named "bullet." There is also an "actions" movie clip just off the Stage. The following code is attached to it:

```
onClipEvent (enterFrame) {

    // see if the bullet hit the target
    if (_root["target"].hitTest(_root["bullet"])) {

        // collision, so target grows
        _root["target"]._xscale += 5;
        _root["target"]._yscale += 5;

        // bullet resets
        _root["bullet"]._x = 350;

    } else {
```

```
        // no collision, continue to move bullet
        _root["bullet"]._x -= 5;
    }
  }
```

This code moves the bullet to the left 5 pixels at a time. When the two movie clips collide, the target grows slightly by having its scale increased by 5%. The bullet's horizontal position is reset so it can begin its approach again.

So far, you have learned how to scale a movie clip and change its position. Next, you'll learn how to change a movie clip's appearance in a more drastic way.

Lesson 22: Using Movie Clips to Change What Is on the Screen

Unfortunately, in Flash you can't swap one movie clip for another on the Stage. One way to make up for this is to remove one movie clip and create another in its place. But when you have a single movie clip that needs to change its image often, you need a quicker way to do it.

Another method is to create a movie clip that contains all the different states of that object. For instance, if the object is a spaceship, I might have frames in that movie that represent the spaceship without any engines on, the spaceship with the main engine on, the spaceship with the left engine on, the spaceship with the right engine on, and a series of frames that make up an animation of the spaceship exploding.

Example file: Changingimages.fla

In Changingimages.fla, there are buttons on the left that allow you to select which part of the "ship" movie clip will be shown. Figure 3.7 shows you what this movie looks like.

Figure 3.7
Changingimages.fla
lets you play with a single movie clip to have it show different views of the same object.

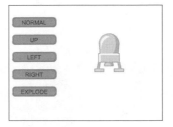

Each of the buttons in Changingimages.fla takes the movie clip to a different frame. For instance, this is the script on the up button:

```
on (press) {
    ship.gotoAndStop("up");
}
```

The code on the Explode button is different from all the rest because it uses *gotoAndPlay* so that the movie clip jumps to the "explode" frame and continues to animate.

```
on (press) {
    ship.gotoAndPlay("explode");
}
```

The movie clip contains an eight-frame sequence starting with "explode" that shows the explosion. The last frame of this sequence has a *stop()* command placed on it so that when the explosion is done, the movie clip waits on that last frame, which is blank, instead of looping back around to the first frame of the movie clip.

Check out Changingimages.fla from the CD and pay special attention to the timeline inside the "ship" movie clip. This is where the frames are labeled so that the code can use frame names rather than numbers.

Lesson 23: Accepting Keyboard Input

The previous example used five buttons to allow you to test the five different portions of the movie clip. Although buttons are a primary source of input into Flash movies, in the world of games, you'll eventually want to accept input directly from the keyboard.

There are two ways to get keyboard input from the user. The first involves a special way to use buttons. The second method uses only code to test whether keys are pressed at any given time.

To use the button method, create a normal Flash button. It doesn't have to be anything special because you'll be hiding it off the Stage. The following sample code can be attached to that button to have it accept the "r" key and use it to move a movie clip:

```
on (keyPress "r") {
    circle._x++;
}
```

TIP

Note that *keyPress* actions attached to buttons are case sensitive. This means that if you are looking for the "r" key to be pressed, the button will not respond to Shift+R.

Example file: Keyboardbutton.fla

For movement, it is often better to look for the arrow keys to be pressed rather than letters. To do this, you can use some special syntax. Here is a longer script that enables the user to move the movie clip in all four directions. You can find this script in the Keyboardbutton.fla movie on the CD.

```
on (keyPress "<Right>") {
    circle._x++;
}

on (keyPress "<Left>") {
    circle._x--;
}

on (keyPress "<Up>") {
    circle._y--;
}

on (keyPress "<Down>") {
    circle._y++;
}
```

Although using buttons allows ActionScript to capture individual keypresses, it does not work well in situations where you want fast and fluid movement. In these situations, the *Key* code object allows you to test the state of any key to see whether it is currently being pressed.

> **TIP**
>
> If you use a button to detect keypresses, you'll notice that the user can hold a key down and the action takes place repeatedly. Most computers are set to repeat keys if the user holds down the key. The delay between the first and second time the key is activated, and the delay between each successive key, is determined by the user's system keyboard settings. You should not rely on this keyboard functionality for games in which you want the user to be able to hold down a key to repeat an action. Instead, use the *Key.isDown()* function described in this section.

The *Key.isDown()*function allows you to test a key. For instance, if you want to see whether the "r" key is pressed, you can do this:

```
if (Key.isDown("r")) {
    circle._x++;
}
```

Example file: Keyisdown.fla

This code does not have to be and should not be attached to a button. Instead, it should be attached to an "action" movie clip, as is the case in the movie Keyisdown.fla. The code is inside an *onClipEvent(enterFrame)* handler so that the keyboard is checked every frame. The code looks for the arrow keys again, which are signified by special constants, such as *Key.RIGHT*.

```
onClipEvent(enterFrame) {
    if (Key.isDown(Key.RIGHT)) {
        _root.circle._x++;
    }

    if (Key.isDown(Key.LEFT)) {
        _root.circle._x--;
    }

    if (Key.isDown(Key.UP)) {
        _root.circle._y--;
    }

    if (Key.isDown(Key.DOWN)) {
        _root.circle._y++;
    }
}
```

If you run this example movie, you'll see that the circle behaves in a much more fluid way. The frame rate of the movie has been increased to 120fps to take advantage of as many frames per second as the computer can handle.

So when is it a good idea to use a button to accept keystrokes and when is it a good idea to use the *Key* object? If you are looking for a single keypress to trigger an event, then use a button. This reacts to the keypress 100% of the time. The *Key.isDown()* function sees the key pressed only if the key happens to be down when the function is called. So if the user presses down and then lifts up quickly, the keypress could be missed. This can easily happen on slow computers.

The *Key.isDown()* function, on the other hand, is good for when you want the player to control movement. In this case, you want fluid movement that will continue at a constant rate as long as the player holds down the key. By using *Key.isDown()*, you can also test for more than one key being pressed at a time, whereas a button reacts to a single keystroke only.

Lesson 24: Playing Sounds

To conclude the ActionScript tutorial part of this book, you'll see how to use sounds. Flash has the capability to play sounds by placing them in the timeline of the movie, or placing them in a movie clip in the timeline. However, you can also trigger sounds by using ActionScript commands.

Unfortunately, triggering a sound from the library is not as simple as one command. First, you have to make sure that the sound is included in the final .swf file. Do this by setting its Symbol Linkage Properties. The "Lesson 20: Creating an 'Actions' Movie Clip" section showed you how to do this. For this example, let's assume that the sound is linked with the name "beep."

You still have to use several lines of code to get the sound to play. First, you need to create a variable that is of type *Sound*. Next, you have to tell this variable that "beep" is the sound to play. Then, you have to trigger that sound. Here's how the code looks inside a button script:

```
on (press) {
    mySound = new Sound();
    mySound.attachSound("beep");
    mySound.start();
}
```

NOTE

The *start* command for sounds can also use two parameters. The first is the number of seconds into the sound before it should start. So if you want to skip the first 3 seconds, use a 3. For normal playback, use 0. The second argument is the number of times the sound is to loop. So to get 10 "beeps" in a row, use 10.

You can also do many tricks with sound. The most useful is setting the volume of the sound. This way, if you have a sound that is too loud, you can adjust the volume in your ActionScript rather than having to remake the sound.

To adjust the volume, use the *setVolume* command. This takes a value from 0 to 100. Here's the same code, but with the volume cut in half:

```
on (press) {
    mySound = new Sound();
    mySound.attachSound("beep");
    mySound.setVolume(50);
    mySound.start();
}
```

Another trick worth noting is the *setPan* command. This takes a value of −100 to 100. For stereo sounds, it works like a balance control with −100 being all left speaker and 100 being all right speaker. For monaural sounds, it forces the sound more from one speaker than the other. Here's a script that plays the sound from only the left speaker:

```
on (press) {
    mySound = new Sound();
    mySound.attachSound("beep");
    mySound.setPan(-100);
```

```
    mySound.setVolume(100);
    mySound.start();
}
```

One very frustrating thing about sounds is that when you set the volume or pan, it remains set, even when you want to play a completely different sound later. So if you use *setPan* or *setVolume* just once, get into the habit of setting them every single time. Otherwise, the previous setting is used for the new sound.

Example file: Sound.fla

The example movie Sound.fla has four buttons. The large middle one plays the sound normally. The large buttons to the left and right play the sound only from the left or right speaker. The smaller button in the middle plays the sound at 50% volume.

You can learn even more about sounds in Chapter 6, "Toys and Gadgets," in the section called "Jukebox." You can also learn more in Chapter 7, "Construction Toys," in the section called "Music Mixer."

This concludes the two-chapter tutorial that takes you through your first steps in ActionScript. In the next chapter, you'll learn about programming techniques such as planning, debugging, and testing. Then, beginning with Chapter 5, "ActionScript Design Effects," you'll begin to work through larger examples of programs.

The Game-Creation Process

Just knowing some ActionScript commands is not enough to enable you to make complete programs, such as games. You must learn some basic programming practices first, as well as some general information about how games are made. Let's start by considering how Flash measures up as a game-development environment.

Flash and Games

Flash did not start off as a program that you could use to make games. The initial uses for Flash were to make animations and Web site interfaces. Only with the addition of today's robust ActionScript can real games be created with Flash.

Weaknesses

Certainly Flash is far from an ideal game-development environment. Following are some reasons Flash makes it difficult to program games:

- **Timeline-based**—Flashmovies are built around a timeline. Although Flash is ideal for animation, to make games you have to write code that actually fights Flash's normal state of moving forward through the timeline to get to the next frame.

- **Slow**—Flash is slow, there's no doubt about that. Compared to its older brother, Macromedia Director, it can be frustratingly slow for developers who use both. This limits Flash to turn-based games and arcade games with a small number of simple elements.

- **Flat**—Flash has no is real capability to do any 3D graphics. Although some third-party programs claim to add 3D to Flash, they are only talking about 2D graphics that are rendered from 3D models. Most major games today are 3D, even if they don't need to be. 3D has become the accepted standard for graphics in games. The good news is that this standard is usually not applied to Web-based games, for which Flash is usually used.

- **Limited feature set**—Suppose is you want to add some functionality to your game and you determine that Flash doesn't have the capability to handle it. If you were programming in a lower-level language, such as C++ or Java, you could alter your game engine to include that new function. However, Flash is what it is. Only Macromedia can add new features to Flash. This means you have to make some compromises when you are building your game, especially if your game pushes the limit of what Flash can do.

Strengths

Flash also has many advantages over other game-development environments. Although programming in lower-level languages, such as C++ or Java, offers you a lot of power, it can't beat Flash in these areas:

- **Rapid development**—Flash allows you to work very quickly to create a game from start to finish. You can create simple games in a matter of days or even hours.

- **Multimedia**—Flash allows you to import and use all sorts of different graphics and sound formats. You can work with artists and sound designers to quickly create your games without worrying about converting files or otherwise adjusting them to get them to work in your game.

- **Easy to use**—Flash is very easy to use. Features such as drag and drop, menus of ActionScript commands, and the panels and dialog boxes let you quickly add and modify elements while you spend minimal time on tedious tasks.

- **Delivery**—Flash's greatest strength, without a doubt, is how you can deliver your content. Thanks to the Flash browser plug-in, almost all Web surfers can view your content directly on a Web page. In addition, you can make standalone Flash projectors that allow you to deliver content to almost any Mac or PC.

It is almost more important to understand Flash's weaknesses than its strengths. Realize that you won't be able to create the next *Quake* or *Age of Empires*. However, also realize that you can create content that can be used by a much wider audience and can be distributed much more easily than those big-budget games.

Parts of a Game

Although each game is a little different, some parts of Flash games seem to be common to them all. Consider adding each of these parts when planning a game.

Loading Screen

Flash movies stream into the user's browser. This means they begin playing when only the first portion of the movie has arrived, on the assumption that the next portion of the movie will have been downloaded by the time it's needed. This happens automatically, whether you want it to or not.

Although streaming is great for animation, it is not always a good thing for games. In most cases, ActionScript controls the appearance of items on the Stage, not the animation timeline. Flash isn't smart enough to know which items you need first, so sometimes those items aren't there when streaming is still going on.

For this reason, avoid streaming for most games. Instead, make the first frame or scene in a movie the loading screen. The loading screen displays a message to the user and waits until the entire movie has been downloaded before proceeding to the next screen. This gives you complete control over what the user sees, rather than leaving it up to which items have arrived and which have not. Figure 4.1 shows a loading screen.

Figure 4.1

The loading screen can be as simple as the game title and a message telling the user that the game is loading.

Chapter 17, "Advanced Techniques," goes into detail about how to build these loading screens.

Splash Screen

A splash screen, sometimes called a title screen, is a cool-looking screen that introduces the game to the user. I sometimes like to let my illustrators go wild on this screen, creating embellished views of the game play.

Think of those old arcade machines from the '80s. Although the graphics in the game itself might have been only blocky pixels, the artwork on the outside of the box was usually detailed and colorful. That's one way to do a splash screen.

Another method involves taking some of the graphics and movie clips that are already in the game and arranging them in an artistic way around the title. This is how Figure 4.2 was made. Using the graphics that are already in the game prevents you from having to make the file size of the game even bigger.

Figure 4.2

This splash screen also doubles as the instructions.

Instructions

Having game instructions is important. Most games should be easy for people to play without ever reading the instructions, but some people like instructions, so you should always provide them.

In some cases, such as Figure 4.2 shown previously, you can combine the splash screen and the instructions. Other games might have them on a separate screen. If the game is complex enough, you might want to stretch the instructions across several screens in a tutorial of some sort.

Another option for instructions is to not include them in the game at all. Some of my games feature instructions on a separate HTML page of the Web site. This allows users to open it in a separate window to view at the same time they are playing the game. It also allows you to easily provide instructions in other languages.

Backgrounds

Some games have graphics that cover the entire screen. Other games take up only a portion of the screen at a time. This leaves room for you to create a colorful backdrop for the game.

For example, Figure 4.3 shows a game in which you have to click the spaceships before they abduct the bunnies. The only active elements in the game are the ships and the bunnies. However, the interesting moonscape-and-stars background makes the game far more appealing.

Figure 4.3
The background for this game fits the game play very well.

Most of the games in this book involve a cartoon fox and his friends. To further accommodate the use of the fox, background images such as forests and trees are used. This helps create the setting for the game as much as the fox himself.

Game Over Screen

When the game is done, the player is usually taken to the "game over" screen. The words "game over" don't have to be there as long as there is some indicator to the player that he is finished.

Sometimes, there is a screen for when a player wins a game, and another for when he loses. Of course, not all games have a win or lose option, because some are just played until the player runs out of ammunition, lives, or time.

Sometimes the "game over" screen includes a list of high scores and perhaps gives the player the ability to submit a high score. Chapter 17 shows you how to set up a high score board.

How to Program

If you've already read Chapters 2, "An Introduction to ActionScript," and 3, "ActionScript Elements Used to Make Games and Toys," you might think you already know how to program. But there is a difference between knowing how to write some ActionScript and having learned the skill of programming.

Programming is hard for most people; it is easy for me. But I have a college degree in computer science and have been programming for 18 years. Don't expect programming to be as easy for you unless you have similar experience.

Here are some guidelines to help you learn to program. As with other skills, programming is something that takes time to learn. You'll find that the more programming you do, the easier it becomes.

Breaking Down Problems

Programming is not something you do all at once; it is a process. A large program can be broken down into parts. These parts can be broken into still smaller parts, and so on. To write a program, you must look at the problem in front of you and break it into the smallest pieces to solve it.

For example, suppose you want to make a Space Invaders game. That's a big problem to solve. But if you break it down into smaller pieces, you'll find that it isn't so hard.

First, you would figure that there are several different elements in the game: the player's ship, the invaders, the bullets the ship is firing, and the bullets the invaders are firing.

Next, take one of those parts and break it down further. The player's ship moves horizontally across the screen, controlled by the arrow keys. This is a little more manageable problem.

You can break it down even further: How do you recognize when the user has pressed the left-arrow key? How do you move the ship to the left? How about the right-arrow key and moving the ship to the right? Solve these little problems and soon you'll have the bigger problem of moving a ship solved. Then, move on to the next part of the program.

This process takes patience. That is a necessary part of programming. You must also be patient with yourself. Unless you are an expert at ActionScript, you might have to pause while writing a program to look up a command or examine some materials so that you can learn more before proceeding. You can't expect to be able to write a complex program without hitting some gaps in your knowledge.

TIP

Remember: The most important thing to realize is that if a problem seems too big to handle, then it probably is. Break it down into smaller problems and you'll have your solution.

Good Programming Practices

While learning to program, it's a good idea to get used to some practices that will make your life easier. These are practices used by programmers all over the world in every programming language:

- **Comments**—Get in the habit of adding comments throughout your code. Even passages that seem self-explanatory now might become confusing when you return to them a few months later.

- **Variable names**—Use variable names that describe what the variable is used for. This can complement your comments to help clarify your code when you return to it later.

- **Function names**—The same is true for function names. They should describe what the function does.

- **Smaller is better**—There is no limit on the length of functions in Flash. However, if you write a 100-line function, you'll find it hard to modify later. Instead, break down the function into tasks and place each task into a different function.

- **Reusable is better**—While you are programming, always think about how a function can be used for a similar, if not exactly the same, task somewhere else in your program. For instance, if you have a function that adds one point to the user's score, make it so that the number of points added is taken from a parameter, allowing that function to be used to add 1 or any other number of points to the score.

- **Hard-coding is bad**—Hard-coding is the practice of including specific numbers in your code. For instance, if you place the number 550 in your code to describe the right side of the Stage, then 550 is said to be hard-coded into the program. If you decide to stretch the Stage to 600 pixels wide, you have to track down every instance of 550 in your code and change it to 600. Instead, set a variable called "screenRightSide" to 550 at the start, and use that variable throughout the program.

- **Organization is good**—Half of being a good programmer is being a good organizer. For instance, don't place functions in all sorts of different frames, but in one frame of your movie. Even then, try to group functions according to their tasks.

Debugging

All programmers need to do some debugging. It is impossible to write a complex program and have it work perfectly the first time you run it. To be a good programmer, you must be good at debugging.

Debugging doesn't always mean using the Flash ActionScript debugger either. You can debug in many ways. When you test a movie, you might get some error messages in the Output window. Usually, these messages are enough to point you to some problems in your program.

You can also use the *trace* command to place information about your program into the Output window. This command was introduced in Lesson 3 of Chapter 2. The *trace* command helps you keep track of when your program hits certain points, and what the values of some variables are at these points.

If you do want to use the debugger, check out the information in the Flash MX help documents. The debugger is a simple tool that allows you to see the values of variables as the Flash movie runs. It doesn't work magic, however. It is still up to your understanding of your own program to determine what is wrong.

Testing

Another stage of debugging deals with having other people test your games. Testing is important, especially if you are developing these games for professional purposes. As the programmer, you have a uniquely skewed view of how your program works and how it should work.

You might be surprised when someone who has never seen the game before sits down to play it for the first time. He might click things you never thought people would try to click. He might drag items off the Stage or place items in places they don't belong.

Often there are two stages of testing before a game is released to the general public. The first stage is called "alpha testing." In this stage, the game is tested by co-workers or people in some sort of private network. Then, in "beta testing," the game is tested by people from outside your company or network. In both stages, you should have people report problems to you and then you should post updates of the game as you fix problems.

Bugs in a game can be more than just error messages. Playability issues and missing features can also be considered bugs. Try to make the game the best you can before declaring it done.

Games and Legal Issues

So now that you know some ActionScript, you plan to recreate your favorite game from the 1980s, right? Ever consider that it might be protected with a copyright?

After you place something on your Web site, or your company's Web site, you are now a publisher. In the world of publishing, people can protect works they have created from being copied by another. If you re-create an existing game and publish it on a Web site, you could be sued for copyright infringement.

I'm not a lawyer, but I do know that there is a lot of legal gray area in the realm of games and copyrights. Some companies are claiming to own the very ideas to which popular genres of computer games are based on. Other companies don't seem to care whether their games are copied even if they have exactly the same name as the original.

If you feel that your game is close to one that has been previously published, you should to consult a lawyer. In my experience, lawyers give one of two responses. The first response is to explain to you that there is no simple answer and that you have to be careful. This response is of little help. The other response that lawyers give is that you should play it safe and not publish your game at all. This response makes sense, because you are asking the lawyer how to stay out of trouble, and she is telling you how. However, the response doesn't help you much if you want to create any games at all.

One thing you should do is familiarize yourself with the game you are creating. For instance, the game Othello is made by a toy manufacturer who probably wouldn't appreciate it if you made a game of the same name. However, the game Reversi is the same game. Reversi is considered an "old standard" game, like chess and checkers. Other games are more obvious: Scrabble is certainly off-limits unless you have a license from the owner. However, backgammon is considered to be in the public domain. Another case is that of Yahtzee, which is a game owned by Milton Bradley, although the similar games poker dice and yacht predate that one and are listed in many old game books as standards.

The purpose of this section is to make you aware of these issues. However, I can't offer any solutions other than to recommend that you consult with a lawyer.

NOTE
Keep in mind that the games in this book are meant for you to use and alter for use on your Web sites and other projects. All these games are generic concepts, such as jigsaw puzzles and trivia games.

Altering the Games in This Book

One very good reason to buy this book is so that you can take these games and make your own. To this end, you will probably want to alter the games somewhat so that they fit your needs better and reflect your style.

Changing the Graphics

The easiest way to use the games in this book on your Web site is to just change the graphics. You can go in to the different symbols in the library and redraw graphics, or copy images from other Flash movies you have made. If you keep the code the same, it is possible to make usable games without doing any programming.

Altering the ActionScript

At the end of most examples in this book, you'll find suggestions on how the project can be improved. Think of these as exercises for you as you learn to program with ActionScript. Of course you can also come up with your own ideas for altering the games.

Be warned, however, that adding features or changing the game requires intermediate to advanced ActionScript programming. If you can't figure out how to make a change that you want, take the time to learn more about ActionScript before proceeding. Otherwise, changing the games can be frustrating.

Combining Games

A common technique for game programmers is to try to combine two games to make a new one. You can do this with the games in this book. However, such a task requires advanced programming skill, so don't get frustrated if you don't succeed immediately.

The next section will help anyone who wants to alter the games avoid some common problems.

Top Pitfalls

Whether you are altering a game from this book or creating your own, you'll occasionally hit pitfalls. These are usually little annoyances that are quickly discovered and corrected. Here are some that I have come across while creating games in Flash.

Movie Clip Names

Every movie clip on the Stage has two names. The name by which it is called in the library makes no difference to your ActionScript code. However, the instance name applied to it by the instance of the movie clip on the Stage is all important. However, it is easy to forget to name movie clip instances altogether.

Linkage Properties

To confuse things even further, if you want to use the *attachMovie* command to create instances of a movie clip, you need to set the symbol's Linkage Properties and include a name. So there are three possible places to name a movie clip: in the library, in instances on the Stage, and in the Linkage Properties dialog box.

Movie Clip Levels

Another pitfall is forgetting where variables are located. For example, if a variable is in a script attached to a movie clip, it is at the level of that movie clip and not at the level of the main timeline. You can use dot syntax to access all the variables in your movie, but it's easy to forget where they are located.

Forgetting the Underscore

A minor annoyance is forgetting that most built-in Flash properties need the underscore (_) before them. If you have a movie clip named "myMovieClip," then "myMovieClip._x" is its horizontal position, but "myMovieClip.x" is just a variable called "x" inside "myMovieClip."

Splice and Slice

Another minor annoyance that can haunt you is accidentally using the *slice* function on an array—rather than the *splice* function—to delete an element from an array. That missing "p" can easily elude your eyes and the difference in functionality can create some puzzling bugs in your program.

Global and Local Variables

Remember that unless you use the keyword *var* before the first use of a variable in a function, the variable is a global variable. If you use this same variable name somewhere else, you might be stepping on the toes of the earlier variable. For instance, if you use "i" in a *for* loop, and then call another function inside the loop, and that function uses "i" for its own *for* loop, the two "i" variables overwrite each other's values. To avoid this, use different variable names or the *var* syntax.

You have learned a lot about ActionScript in Chapters 2 and 3, and general programming techniques in this chapter. You are now ready to move on to Chapter 5, "ActionScript Design Effects," and beyond, where you will find complete examples of ActionScript programs.

ActionScript Design Effects

- Expanding Buttons
- Color Cycling Rotating Spiral
- Randomness and the Old Film Effect
- Letter Movement
- Cursor Trail
- 3D Illusions

Most of the chapters in this book deal with toys, gadgets, and games. Although toys, gadgets, and games all include some level of interactivity, I want to first talk about Flash movies that have little or no interaction. These non-interactive movies are similar to plain Flash animations, but are created with the use of ActionScript.

This chapter provides you with a few simple examples of ActionScript at work. Although many great effects can be created with Flash animation techniques only, ActionScript can also be used for design effects.

In this chapter, you will learn how to manipulate graphics and colors, change text, and move items around the Stage.

Expanding Buttons

Example Movie: Expandingbuttons.fla

Many sites use Flash as a way to navigate from page to page. Even a simple Flash movie with just one button can be an improvement to a static Web page. With ActionScript, you can make these buttons even more animated.

Project Goal

The goal is to create buttons that do more than just change colors when the user rolls the cursor over them. Instead, they expand and then return to normal when the cursor leaves. Figure 5.1 shows five of these buttons with the cursor over the second.

Figure 5.1

Each button expands as the cursor moves over it.

From the figure, you might think that when the cursor rolls over the button, it suddenly enlarges. However, the effect is more complex than that. Instead of just enlarging instantly, the button grows gradually, which is a much more pleasing visual effect. You can check out Expandingbuttons.fla on the CD-ROM to see it in action.

Approach

Each button is to react when the cursor rolls over it and when the cursor leaves. In either case, the script reacts by changing the value of a variable, which is the target scale for the button to reach.

For example, when the button starts, its scale is 100%. When the user rolls the cursor over it, the target scale is then 150%.

Then a script acts *every* frame to change the current scale to the target scale. So, the button goes from 100% to 150% in intervals of 10%.

When the user rolls the cursor off the button, the opposite occurs as the target scale is set to 100%. The button shrinks 10% every frame until it reaches that target.

Preparing the Movie

The example movie contains several buttons. Each button is actually a movie clip with a button inside it. I had just one button in the library, but created five different movie clips. Then I placed the button in each movie clip along with a different piece of text to lay over the button. The result is five movie clips, all with different text but the same button.

The button can be any sort of shape or color. I used a conservative style just to demonstrate the scripts at work.

Writing the Code

Two types of scripts are used in this movie: those attached to buttons, and those attached to movie clips. The first button script is attached to the button inside the movie clip. A script attached to a button can detect mouse events that occur to only that particular button. These are called event actions and they are defined by the word *on*.

In the button script, there are three different event actions, two of which are *on(rollOver)* and *on(rollOut)*. These event actions both set a variable called "newscale" to the target scale for the button to enlarge or shrink to.

Here is what this script looks like for the button in the "Home" movie clip:

```
on (rollOver) {
    // set up for grow
    newscale = 150;
}
on (rollOut) {
    // set up for shrink
    newscale = 100;
}
on (release) {
    // do something
    trace("Home");
}
```

NOTE

The *on* declaration is used in button scripts to contain segments of code that should be executed when certain events concerning the button occur. Possible events are *press*, *release*, *releaseOutside*, *rollOver*, *rollOut*, *dragOver*, *dragOut*, and *keyPress*.

Each of the three event actions in the previous code segment contains a single line of code that runs when a specific event occurs to the button. For instance, when the user clicks and releases the button, the *trace* command executes. This places the word "Home" in the Output window. In reality, you would probably use a *getURL* command to make the browser jump to a new page. *trace* is used here as a placeholder just for this demonstration.

The "newscale" variable is a custom variable created to store the value of what the scale of the movie clip should be. When the user rolls over the button, the new scale should be 150%. When the cursor leaves the button, it should be 100%. This variable is set here so that the movie clip script can use it.

The movie clip script is placed one level up on the overall movie clip in the main timeline of the movie. You can see a diagram that shows the main timeline, the movie clip, and the button inside it along with the two scripts in Figure 5.2.

Figure 5.2

This diagram shows where the two ActionScripts are located relative to the main timeline, the movie clip, and the button.

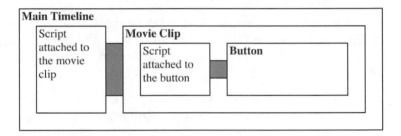

The movie clip script begins by setting the "newscale" variable to 100. Then, for each frame, the script checks this variable against the *_xscale* property of the movie clip. If they don't match, the *_xscale* is moved 10 closer to the "newscale" value. The *_yscale* property is also changed by the same amount.

```
onClipEvent(load) {
    // set initial scale to 100
    newscale = 100;
}

onClipEvent(enterFrame) {
    if (this._xscale > newscale) {
        // shrink
        this._xscale -= 10;
        this._yscale -= 10;
    } else if (this._xscale < newscale) {
        // grow
        this._xscale += 10;
        this._yscale += 10;
    }
}
```

NOTE

The *onClipEvent* declaration is used in scripts assigned to movie clips. It reacts to events like an event action, but to events happening to the whole movie, not just that single movie clip. The *enterFrame* event occurs every time a frame advances, or loops back, in the movie. A *mouseDown* event happens every time the user presses the mouse button, even if the cursor is not over that particular movie clip. Other events are *load*, *unload*, *mouseMove*, *mouseUp*, *keyDown*, *keyUp*, and *data*.

When the movie starts running, "newscale" is 100 and the *_xscale* property is also 100. On every *enterFrame* event, nothing happens. Then, when the user moves the cursor over the movie clip, and thus over the button inside the movie clip, the button's script changes "newscale" to 150.

NOTE

The *_xscale* and *_yscale* properties of a movie clip correspond to their horizontal and vertical size. A value of 100 for either of these means that the size is exactly equal to the original size of the movie clip instance. You can test and set these properties in ActionScript to stretch or shrink the movie clip. You can even use negative numbers, which would result in the movie clip image being flipped either horizontally, vertically, or both.

Now on every *enterFrame*, the value of *_xscale* and *_yscale* are less than "newscale." As a result, the scale is increased by 10. The button grows in size. When *_xscale* reaches 150, the growth stops as "newscale" and *_xscale* are once again the same. A similar process happens when the user moves the cursor off the sprite and "newscale" is set back to 100.

Loose Ends

To make a complete button bar, you must duplicate the movie clip several times. Inside each movie clip, you must alter the *on (release)* script to do something else, such as go to a different page from the other buttons. You also need to modify the text in the movie clip so that all the buttons look like they do in Figure 5.1.

Each movie clip must have an exact copy of the same ActionScript. This is unfortunate because a single change to this script means that you need to change it in all the buttons.

TIP

To avoid copying and pasting the same script into all the buttons, use an *#include* command to have Flash read the script from an external file each time the movie is compiled. This way, you can change the script in the external file, and all the buttons will instantly use the new script. However, you still need to copy and paste the *#include* command onto each movie clip instance.

When complete, there should be as many movie clips in the library as there are buttons, but only one actual button is needed in the library. Each button inside each movie clip should have a slightly different script attached to it, whereas each movie clip on the main timeline has a copy of the same movie clip script attached.

Take a look at Expandingbuttons.fla to see how all the pieces fit together.

Other Possibilities

You don't need to adjust both the _xscale and _yscale properties of the movie clip. You could do just one or the other to get a different effect. You also don't have to stick to my numbers. You could have the buttons expand to a larger size or shrink to a smaller one.

With a little more coding, you could make the buttons pulse instead of enlarge and hold their scale. Just check for when the scale expands to the maximum size, and then set the "newscale" variable back to 100. The result is that the buttons expand and contract quickly as the user rolls over them.

Color Cycling Rotating Spiral

Example Movies: colorchange.fla, colortransform.fla, gradualchange.fla, spiral.fla

A movie clip's scale is not the only thing that you can alter with ActionScript. Just about every aspect of a movie clip can be changed. Scale is an easy example. To change something like the movie clip's color is a little more difficult. In this section, you learn how to change a movie clip's color and rotate it.

Project Goal

The goal is to build a movie that features a rotating spiral that gradually changes colors. In doing so, you will learn about the Color object and the _rotation property.

Approach

You can use ActionScript to change most properties of movie clips on the Stage. In some cases, you just change the property directly. In other cases, you need to use functions to effect a change. This is the case when it comes to colors.

The Color Object

The Color object is what you use to change the color of a movie clip. Think of the color object as a set of commands that allows you to learn about and control the color of a movie clip.

To use a Color object, you must first create one related to the movie clip you want to affect. You do that like this:

```
myColorObject = new Color("myMovieClipName");
```

There are a two ways to inspect and affect the color object. One is to look at the color directly. You can inspect the color of a movie clip with just two lines of code. First, create a new Flash movie and place one movie clip on the Stage. Name the instance "myMovieClip." Then, in the main timeline, place the following script:

```
myColorObject = new Color("myMovieClip");
trace((myColorObject.getRGB()).toString());
```

When you test this movie, you will see that the Output window automatically opens and the value "0" is placed in it. This is the *trace* command telling you that the color value of your movie clip is 0.

For a more interesting result, try changing the color of the movie clip. You can do this by selecting the movie clip and selecting "advanced" under the Color drop-down menu in the Property inspector. Then change the R, G, and B fields to 128 as shown in Figure 5.3.

Figure 5.3
The Effect panel allows you to change the color of a movie clip.

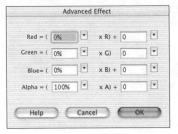

Now if you test the movie, you get the value of 8421504 placed in the output window. This corresponds to R, G, and B values of 128. With a slight tweak to the *toString* function, you can get a hexadecimal value rather than a decimal one. This means that it will look like the RGB values that Web designers use to define colors.

```
myColorObject = new Color("myMovieClip");
trace((myColorObject.getRGB()).toString(16));
```

NOTE

The *new* declaration allows you to create new instances of objects such as the Color object. You can also use it to create new arrays or sounds, as well as your own object constructs. If this seems confusing at this point, don't worry. A thorough understanding of how *new* works is not needed to be able to use it.

The output is now "808080," which is a hexadecimal number representing middle gray, or red, green, and blue values of 128—halfway between 0 and 255. The value of 16 tells it to convert numerical values into hexadecimal, as it did here.

Now that you know how to get the RGB value of a movie clip, the next step is to change it. This is done, not surprisingly, with the *setRGB* function. It accepts one parameter: the hexadecimal color you want to use. Here is an example that uses the same movie as the previous example, but with two new lines of code:

```
myColorObject = new Color("myMovieClip");
myColorObject.setRGB(0xFF0000);
```

The "0x in front of the number tells Flash that what follows is a hexadecimal number. This number, "FF0000," is red. The movie clip, regardless of its starting color, changes to red when the movie runs. A sample movie on the CD-ROM named Colorchange.fla demonstrates these two lines of code in action.

Transforming Colors

Using the color transformation object is another way to change the color of a movie clip and it has more versatility. This is sort of like an object inside an object. A transformation includes separate numerical values for red, green, and blue, as well as numerical values for the brightness of each of these colors. Figure 5.3 showed all six of these values, plus two values for the alpha channel, or transparency, of the image.

A color transformation object can include new values for each of these eight items. You define a color transformation object by creating a new variable. In this variable, you can place up to eight values as a single object. Here is an example:

```
myColorTransform = {rb:255, bb:0, gb:0};
```

This color transformation object can be used to tell any color object to change to red. It uses only three properties: the red, green, and blue color offsets. In addition to these properties, you can also set the red, green, and blue brightness with the "ra," "ga," and "ba" properties. To round off the properties, "aa" and "ab" are the alpha channel brightness and offset.

When it comes to colors in Flash, both the brightness and offset of the red, green, and blue colors are used to compute the final color. This means there are many ways to combine values to create the same color. In Figure 5.3, shown previously, you can see an example of how these numbers can be set.

After you have a color object and a color transform object, you can use them to change a movie clip's color. These three lines change a movie clip to red:

```
myColor = new Color("myMovieClip");
myColorTransform = {rb:255, bb:0, gb:0};
myColor.setTransform(mycolorTransform);
```

This example does essentially the same thing as the previous example, just in a different way. You can examine the sample movie named Colortransform.fla on the CD-ROM to see it in action.

The advantage of the *setTransform* function over the *setRGB* function is that you have more control over the color values. For instance, the numbers can be ActionScript variables rather than hard-coded numbers. You can then change these values over a period of time, thus changing the color over time.

The following movie clip script takes the red value of the movie clip from 0 to 255 and beyond. The result is that the clip starts as a black oval, and then gradually changes to red. The "load" event is used to set up the color object and the color transform object. The variable "n" is created there too. The "enterFrame" event is then used to set the color transformation, apply it to the color, and then increment the variable "n."

```
onClipEvent(load) {
    myColor = new Color(this);
    myColorTransform = {rb:255, bb:0, gb:0};
    n = 0;
}
```

```
onClipEvent(enterFrame) {
    myColorTransform.rb = n;
    myColor.setTransform(myColorTransform);
    n++;
}
```

NOTE
The operator "++" increments any variable by one. So, if "n" is equal to 7, and Flash encounters a "n++" line, then "n" increases to 8. You can also use "−−" to decrease a variable by one.

In this example, the value of "n," and thus the value of the color red, is taken from 0 to 255 and beyond. When it is greater than 255, then value of red is at its maximum and doesn't change. You can see this script in action on the CD-ROM by viewing the Gradualtransform.fla movie.

Although all this information about colors and transformations is interesting, it has yet to give you a useable special effect. So let's try something a little more mesmerizing.

The main example in this section makes a movie clip cycle through most of the colors of the rainbow. To do this, you need to change the red, green, and blue color components. The same *setTransform* function is used, but the way that the values change has to be more complex than in the previous example.

The values of red, green, and blue all start at 255 and work like this:

1. Red is decreased until it hits 0.
2. Blue is decreased until it hits 0.
3. Red is increased until it hits 255.
4. Green is decreased until it hits 0.
5. Blue is increased until it hits 255.
6. Green is increased until it hits 255.

This sequence takes the colors from black to cyan, cyan to green, green to yellow, yellow to red, red to magenta, and magenta to black. This hits all the colors except pure blue. This is how to make the color cycling spiral.

Preparing the Movie

The only element that you need in this movie is a spiral shape. Place that on the Stage in the middle. To take the color transformations well, the spiral should be black, and the background color of the Stage should be black.

Color Cycling and Rotation

There is just one script in this movie, which is attached to the spiral movie clip.

This script has a variable "n" that contains the mode of the color change. Its number corresponds to the number in the previous list. So, for instance, when "n" is 3, then the change occurring is that red is increasing.

The variable "n" starts at 1 and goes through 6 and then repeats. Here is a code segment that shows the long *if...then* sequence that uses "n" and changes the color transform object.

```
if (n == 1) {
    colorTransform.rb -= 5;
    if (colorTransform.rb == 0) n = 2;
} else if (n == 2) {
    colorTransform.bb -= 5;
    if (colorTransform.bb == 0) n = 3;
} else if (n == 3) {
    colorTransform.rb += 5;
    if (colorTransform.rb == 255) n = 4;
} else if (n == 4) {
    colorTransform.gb -= 5;
    if (colorTransform.gb == 0) n = 5;
} else if (n == 5) {
    colorTransform.bb += 5;
    if (colorTransform.bb == 255) n = 6;
} else if (n == 6) {
    colorTransform.gb += 5;
    if (colorTransform.gb == 255) n = 1;
}
```

NOTE

The operator "+=" takes a variable and adds a certain number to it. So "n += 5" adds 5 to n. This is the same as coding "n = n + 5." You can also use "-=" to subtract a certain number from a variable.

In each part of the *if...then* statement, the value of "n" is checked. According to which line it matches, one of the three color components of the "colorTransform" object is changed. If the change is complete, then "n" itself is changed to the next value.

The full program is a simple movie clip ActionScript with both an *onClipEvent(load)* and *onClipEvent(enterFrame)* function. The first sets up the color and transformation objects and the second performs the color cycling, step by step.

As an added bonus, you can also make the movie clip rotate. This is done by increasing the *_rotation* property of the movie clip each time the *onClipEvent* handler runs.

```
onClipEvent(load) {
    // create the color object and transform
    spiralColor = new Color(this);
    colorTransform = {rb:255, bb:255, gb:255};

    // start in mode 1
    n = 1;
}

onClipEvent(enterFrame) {
    // depending on which mode we are in, alter the transformation
    if (n == 1) {
        colorTransform.rb -= 5;
        if (colorTransform.rb == 0) n = 2;
    } else if (n == 2) {
        colorTransform.bb -= 5;
        if (colorTransform.bb == 0) n = 3;
    } else if (n == 3) {
        colorTransform.rb += 5;
        if (colorTransform.rb == 255) n = 4;
    } else if (n == 4) {
        colorTransform.gb -= 5;
        if (colorTransform.gb == 0) n = 5;
    } else if (n == 5) {
        colorTransform.bb += 5;
        if (colorTransform.bb == 255) n = 6;
    } else if (n == 6) {
        colorTransform.gb += 5;
        if (colorTransform.gb == 255) n = 1;
    }

    // set the new color
    spiralColor.setTransform(colorTransform);

    // rotate the spiral too
    this._rotation = this._rotation += 5;
```

NOTE

The *this* object allows a movie clip to refer to itself. Because this script is attached to a movie clip, using *this* inside the movie clip means that the command affects the movie clip itself, as opposed to another movie clip or the movie in general.

NOTE
The _rotation_ property of a movie clip can be used to turn the movie clip a number of degrees. You can use both positive and negative numbers. If you exceed 360, Flash wraps the values around; so, for instance, 370 is the same as 10.

Figure 5.4 shows a screen grab of the CD-ROM sample movie Spiral.fla in action. The spiral cycles through the colors and spins at the same time.

Figure 5.4
The spiral changes colors and spins.

The importance of this example is not the result itself, which can also be done with animation techniques, but the fact that it is all done with ActionScript. This makes the result much easier to achieve.

Loose Ends

The frame rate of this movie determines how fast the spiral rotates and changes colors. In Flash MX, you can go up to 120 frames per second. However, a slow computer might not be able to keep up with a fast frame rate, resulting in different speeds between fast and slow computers.

Other Possibilities

You can make the spiral rotate in the opposite direction by changing the "+=" to a "-=" in the last line of code. You can also change the way in which the colors shift by changing the red, green, and blue values in the code.

Randomness and the Old Film Effect

Example Movies: randomlocation.fla, randommovement.fla, oldfilm.fla

When you use Flash purely as an animation tool, you can create some amazing effects. However, the animation plays back exactly the same way each time. With ActionScript, you can use random numbers to vary what goes on in the movie.

Project Goal

The goal in this section is to learn about using random numbers to create visual effects. You eventually will use this to create an "old film effect" that puts random scratches and dots on top of any Flash movie.

Approach

There are two ways to generate random numbers in Flash 5. The old Flash 4 method is to use the *Random* function. This returns a value from 0 to one less than the number passed in. So *Random(5)* returns a value from 0 to 4.

In Flash 5, the new *Math.random()* function is recommended by Macromedia. It is possible that the old *Random* function will disappear in future versions of Flash. *Math.random()* returns a floating point number from 0.0 to 1.0.

The way to use *Math.random()* is to multiply the result by a larger number. For instance, multiplying the result by 500 gives you a result between 0.0 and 500.0. Using the *int* function rounds the result down and gives you an integer value from 0 to 499. Here is an example:

```
n = int(Math.random()*500);
```

The following short function takes a movie clip and repositions it anywhere on a 550×400 screen.

```
onClipEvent(load) {
    this._x = Math.random()*550;
    this._y = Math.random()*400;
}
```

The movie Randomlocation.fla on the CD-ROM demonstrates the use of the previous function. Try running it several times to see how the oval moves to a different location each time.

The next step in using random numbers is to record their values and use them to affect movie clips over a period of time, rather than in just one instant.

The following short movie clip script moves a movie clip in a random direction. It sets the value of "dx" and "dy" to a number from -5 to 5 and then changes the _x and _y properties of that movie clip by those amounts. In addition, 10% of the time the values of "dx" and "dy" are changed to new random values.

```
onClipEvent(load) {
    dx = Math.random()*10-5;
    dy = Math.random()*10-5;
}
```

```
onClipEvent(enterFrame) {
    this._x += dx;
    this._y += dy;

    if (Math.random() > .9) {
        dx = Math.random()*10-5;
        dy = Math.random()*10-5;
    }
}
```

The movie Randommovement.fla shows this script in action. The oval moves around in a random manner. It might even actually leave the Stage area because nothing has been placed in the code to make sure that it does not exceed these bounds.

Preparing the Movie

As an example of using random numbers, let's create a common Flash special effect: the look of old movie film. This is typically done with animation only. The animator places little nicks and marks on different frames of the movie, as well as a line that moves from side to side, representing a scratch in the film.

You can create all these effects more easily with ActionScript. First, the moving scratch can be accomplished by placing a vertical white line down the side of the movie.

To take this knowledge of random numbers and apply it to a movie to make an "old film effect," you first need some old film. By that, I mean that it helps to have an image that you can place the scratches and spots on top of.

Figure 5.5 shows such an image. It is not static either: The propeller on the plane is rotating and the eyes of the fox are blinking. Your movies will probably have even more animation in them.

Figure 5.5
A simple animated movie that could use some random spots and scratches to make it look more authentic.

In addition to this background art, you need a scratch and a spot movie clip to place on top. In the example movie, Oldfilm.fla, the scratch is a simple vertical line inside a movie clip. The spot is a small oval inside another movie clip.

Writing the Code

First, you need to write the code for the scratch. Place the scratch movie clip on the Stage and attach this ActionScript to the movie clip instance:

```
onClipEvent(load) {
    wanderAmount = 300;
    leftLimit = 10;
    rightLimit = 540;
    chanceOfJump = 50;
    xPosition = 275;
    speed = 10;
    chanceOfChange = 0;
}

onClipEvent(enterFrame) {
    xPosition += speed;
    this._x = xPosition;
    chanceOfChange++;
    if ((Math.random()*wanderAmount < chanceOfChange) or (xPosition < leftLimit)
        or (xPosition > rightLimit)) {
        speed = -speed;
        chanceOfChange = 0;
    }
    if (Math.random()*chanceOfJump == 1) {
        xPosition = Math.random()*(rightLimit-leftLimit)+leftLimit;
    }
}
```

NOTE

When you use math functions on numbers, Flash calculates the result with a specific precedence for operations: Multiplication and division are done before addition and subtraction. So 2×3+4 equals 10. If you want to force a different order of operations, you must use parentheses. For example, 2×(3+4) equals 14.

The first part of the script sets up some variables. The "leftLimit" and "rightLimit" variables are the horizontal boundaries of the line. The code won't let it go beyond these values. The "speed" variable is used to determine how much the line moves each frame. The rest of the variables are amounts that are used to determine changes during the animation.

Every time the frame loops, the horizontal position, "xPosition," of the movie clip is changed by the "speed" variable, which moves it left or right 10 pixels. The "chanceOfChange" is incremented, and then used to determine whether a change should occur. When "chanceOfChange" is 1, there is a 1 in 300 chance that there will be a change in that instant. By the time "chanceOfChange" equals 150, there is a 150 in 300, or 50% chance that there will be a change in that instant. This is a good way to manage the change so that it rarely happens right away, and also rarely waits a long time to happen.

In this case, "a change" is a reversal of direction. This is done by changing "speed" from a positive to negative number, or vice versa. This change also happens if the line hits the left or right horizontal limit.

Another type of change is determined by the "chanceOfJump" variable. This change actually repositions the line to a new location entirely. The reason for this is that real film scratches behave in this way. So, it more closely simulates reality.

The movie Oldfilm.fla shows this line effect, as well as the random spot effect you will look at next. Figure 5.6 shows what this looks like. You can see the random spots and the line over the image.

Figure 5.6
The old film effect is the line and two dots on top of a normal Flash animation.

The spots on the image are two movie clips that are constantly changing position. Basically, they use the same technique as the random location movie from earlier in this chapter. However, it's good to throw in a random chance of the scratch appearing at all. This chance builds from 0% to 100% just like the chances in the previous script.

```
onClipEvent(load) {
    chanceOfAppearing = 10;
    chance = 0;
}
```

```
onClipEvent(enterFrame) {
    chance++;
    if (Random(chanceOfAppearing) < chance) {
        this._x = Random(550);
        this._y = Random(400);
        chance = 0;
    } else {
        this._x = -100;
    }
}
```

When the movie clip starts, it has a 1 in 10 chance of appearing at a random spot on the Stage. If it doesn't, it has a 2 in 10 chance next time. This continues until it appears.

Loose Ends

Both of the spots and the line are best put off the Stage to the right, out of the visible area, so they are not seen when the movie starts. Then they will appear at random times and places.

Make sure the scripts are in the right places. Remember that you don't have to rely on re-creating the entire movie from the text in the book. You also have the example on the CD-ROM. With all the different elements in the Flash movie, such as the movie clip instance, script locations, and object names, I recommend that you use the example on the CD-ROM before you try to create your own example from scratch.

The end result of this exercise is a pair of movie clips and ActionScripts that you can place in any Flash animation to give that old film effect.

Other Possibilities

You can have more spots on the screen by duplicating the spot movie clip, making sure that both copies have the same ActionScript attached to them. This means there can be as many spots on the Stage at once as you want.

You can also have two scratches on the screen. Different segments of your animation can have different numbers of scratches and spots to represent better or worse portions of film.

Letter Movement

Example movie: textfly.fla

There seem to be a lot of Flash movies out there that include text flying around in all sorts of different ways. There are many ways to accomplish such effects, and each example on the Web probably does it a different way.

Project Goal

In this section, you will make a movie that takes a text phrase and creates a bunch of independent letters in random positions on the screen. Then, those letters fly across the screen to join together to make that phrase.

Figure 5.7 shows four screen shots of the example movie on the CD-ROM in action. The letters come down from the top, all scrambled, and then assemble at the bottom in the correct order.

Figure 5.7

These four screen-shots show how the ActionScript animation progresses.

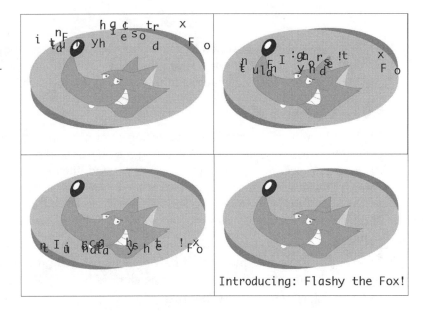

Check out the Textfly.fla example movie on the CD-ROM. In this case, it's helpful to see exactly where the following scripts belong, and how the whole movie is put together.

Approach

The approach here will be to divide the text into individual letters, each in its own movie clip. Then, these movie clips will be moved from a random location on the screen to a location that matches its position in the original text.

Preparing the Movie

The example movie includes a graphic in the middle of the screen that is completely independent of the text effect.

There is a single movie clip with the letter "A" inside it. This movie clip was created by first making a small text field. This field is set to Dynamic Text in the Properties panel, and is assigned the variable name "letterText" in the same panel (see Figure 5.8).

Figure 5.8

In the Property inspector, you can set a text area to Dynamic Text and assign it a variable name. This allows ActionScript to control the contents of the text.

Then the text field is converted to its own movie clip by choosing Insert, Convert To Symbol. This symbol instance is given the name "letter0" and positioned where the first letter in the phase should end up—in this case, in the lower-left corner.

Writing the Code

This program works by creating a collection of movie clips from a single movie clip. The collection is made by looping and creating a new movie clip for each letter with *duplicateMovieClip*. As each movie clip is created, the custom variables "endx" and "endy" are set in the movie clips. This is the location where the letters need to end up at the end of the animation. The "endy" variable is set to the *_y* location of the "Letter0" movie clip, whereas the "endx" is set to an increasing number from left to right.

The script creates new movie clips for only letters 1 and greater. The first letter, letter 0, uses the already existing "Letter0" movie clip.

```
text = "Introducing: Flashy the Fox!";
for (i=0;i<text.length;i++) {
    if (i > 0) duplicateMovieClip("Letter0","letter"+i,i);
    this["letter"+i].letterText = text.charAt(i);
    this["letter"+i].endx = this["Letter0"]._x + i*19;
    this["letter"+i].endy = this["Letter0"]._y;
}
```

NOTE

The *charAt* function returns the character at a specific spot in a string. The first character in a string is character 0. You can also use *substr* to get a range of characters.

NOTE

The *for* command creates a short loop. The code inside the loop executes a set number of times. The first parameter after the *for* command is used to set a variable. The second parameter is the test that should be performed before every loop to determine whether the loop should continue. The third and last parameter is a command to execute every time through the loop. For instance, "for (i=0; i<text.length; i++)" means that the variable "i" should start at 0, it should increase by one every loop, and the looping should continue while "i" is less than the length of "text."

The number 19 appears at the end of the fifth line to indicate that the letters are spaced 19 pixels apart. You have to adjust this if you are using a different font or font size.

TIP

This type of effect works best when you use a monospaced font, which is a font in which each letter is the same width. Monaco, Courier, and Courier New are good examples of such fonts. If you use a variable-width font, letters such as "w" and "l" can vary greatly in width. In that case, a fixed width in your code, such as the 19 in the previous code, can cause the text to fit together strangely.

The other part of this movie is the ActionScript attached to the "Letter0" movie clip. This script starts the movie clip at a random position at the top of the screen, and gradually moves the letter to its final position a little each frame.

Because the script is attached to "Letter0," every time the preceding script duplicates this movie clip, a duplicate of the script comes along with it. So each movie clip has a copy of the same code.

The first part of this script sets "startx" and "starty" variables to a random location just above the top of the Stage area. It then sets the location of the movie clip itself to these values. Remember that "endx" and "endy" were set by the main timeline script when it created each of these movie clips. So the movie clips now have a random starting point in "startx" and "starty," as well as a fixed end point in "endx" and "endy."

The variable "n" counts from 0 to 100 in steps of 5. This corresponds to the percent of the letter's journey that is complete. At 0, "n" signifies that the letter's position is at 0% of the end point and 100% of the start point. At 5, "n" signifies that the letter is at 5% of the end point and 95% of the start point. With each jump of 5, the letter gets 5% closer to the goal. The location is updated only if "n" is less than or equal to 100.

```
onClipEvent(load) {
    startx = Math.random()*550;
    starty = -Math.random()*100;
    this._x = startx;
```

```
        this._y = starty;
        n = 0;
    }

    onClipEvent(enterFrame) {
        n += 5;
        if (n <= 100) {
            this._x = endx*n/100 + startx*(100-n)/100;
            this._y = endy*n/100 + starty*(100-n)/100;
        }
    }
```

Loose Ends

The position of the "letter0" movie clip determines the position of the first letter of the final text, so place it carefully and experiment with its positioning. You should also alter the font with care, noting that using a variable-width font could cause trouble with some letters being wider than others.

Other Possibilities

You easily can vary this script in many ways. You can have the letters start from other areas of the screen, increment "n" more slowly or quickly, or even have the letters stack vertically rather than horizontally.

Cursor Trail

Example Movie: cursortrail.fla

Here's a special effect that is impossible without ActionScript. In the following example, when the user moves the cursor around, a series of movie clips appears to follow the cursor. This creates a trail of movie clips left behind the cursor.

Figure 5.9 shows the result of this effect. Each circle indicates a previous position of the cursor. The further back in time, the smaller and lighter the circle.

Figure 5.9
Placing new movie clips in the cursor's previous locations is the way to create this cursor trail.

Project Goal

The idea is to special have a fading trail of circles behind the cursor. As the user moves the mouse, the cursor will seem to paint this trail.

Each circle starts at its largest size and is fully opaque. It begins to fade as time goes by. Eventually it will become a very small circle, almost completely blended with the background. It will then disappear altogether.

There will be dozens of these circles on the screen at any one time, always shrinking and fading as new circles replace the old ones at the current cursor location.

Approach

The circles are movie clips that are created and disposed of as needed. The code stores all existing movie clips in an array. With each frame that passes, the code moves through the array, shrinking and fading each circle a little. When a circle is completely transparent, and thus no longer visible, it is removed. The reference to it in the array is also removed.

Preparing the Movie

The first thing special you need is a simple movie clip with a circle in it. It should be the size and color that you want the circles to appear when they are first created. In the example movie, it is a shade of blue, and about 20 pixels in diameter.

This movie clip should be named "cursor trail" and its linkage properties set so that it exports with the movie. Its linkage name will be "cursor trail" as well. You can set this up by selecting the movie clip in the Library and choosing Linkage in the Library panel's menu.

Now create a second movie clip. This will be just a dummy movie clip that is positioned off screen. In the example movie, I put a static text field with the word "Actions" on the stage and then converted it to a movie clip. You could also use a simple shape or anything you want.

The purpose of this "actions" movie clip is to hold a simple script that controls the rest of the movie. It is where the code is placed.

Writing the Code

This "actions" special movie clip has two *onClipEvent* handlers. The first runs at the start of the movie and creates an empty array to hold references to the trail movie clips. It also sets a counter, "trailNum," to 0. This variable keeps track of the number of the next movie clip to be created.

The "speed" variable is used in the rest of the script to determine how fast the trail movie clips shrink and fade.

```
onClipEvent(load) {
    // create array
    trail = new Array();
    trailNum = 0;

    // smaller numbers are slower
    speed = 2;
}
```

The next handler starts off by creating a new movie clip from the one in the Library. The handler gives it a unique name based on "trailNum," and also uses "trailNum" to assign it a unique level.

```
onClipEvent(enterFrame) {
    // new trail
    var mc = _root.attachMovie("cursor trail","cursor trail"+trailNum,trailNum);
```

The new movie clip will be set to the current position of the cursor.

```
    // set position
    mc._x = _root._xmouse;
    mc._y = _root._ymouse;
```

A reference to this new movie clip is placed in the array "trail." Then "trailNum" is incremented for the next time.

```
    // add to array
    trail.push(mc);
    trailNum++;
```

The rest of the handler loops through all the movie clips stored in "trail." It shrinks and fades each one by "speed." If any end up with an _alpha_ property of less than 0, then they are removed from the screen and the array.

```
    // deal with existing trails
    for(var i=trail.length-1;i>=0;i--) {

        // reduce alpha and scale
        trail[i]._alpha -= speed;
        trail[i]._xscale -= speed;
        trail[i]._yscale -= speed;

        // if this is one invisible, remove it
        if (trail[i]._alpha <= 0) {
```

```
            // remove array
            trail.splice(0,1);

            // remove movie clip
            trail[i].removeMovieClip();
        }
    }
}
```

Notice that the code loops through the array backward. It does so because items are occasionally removed from the array. If it were to loop forward, then when an item was removed, it would mess up the loop's current position. For instance, if item 1 is removed, then item 2 becomes item 1. When the loop continues, it starts looping at item 2 next, which was the old item 3. The old item 2, which is the new item 1, is skipped.

Loose Ends

If you play with the "speed" setting, you can change the trail's length. This also affects performance, because a very small speed, such as 1, eventually leads to 100 movie clips changing every frame.

Other Possibilities

There is no reason why the movie clips can't be animated. You simply need to supply more than one frame in the "cursor trail" movie clip. If you draw these frames well, you can create things like blazing fires or smoke.

3D Illusions

Example Movies: 3dcubepoints.fla, 3dcube.fla, 3dspaceship.fla

Another common Flash special effect is to simulate a small 3D object. Some developers say that Flash is not capable of real 3D, but then again, neither is any computer program because computer monitors are only 2D.

All 3D computer graphics are just illusions. Although Flash and ActionScript don't have much that can help you create 3D illusions, some special effects are still possible. By using trigonometry, you can convert 3D coordinates to 2D screen coordinates and simulate simple objects such as cubes.

Project Goal

In this section, you learn how to convert 3D coordinates into 2D screen locations. You use this knowledge to make a simple 3D cube and then a more complex model. The user can manipulate these models to see that they are true 3D, and not just 2D drawings.

Approach

To learn how to use 3D coordinates, a little background in 3D mathematics is needed. This is one of the most complex sections in this book, so feel free to skip it and go on to the next chapter if learning some new math is not your idea of a good time.

Preparing the Movie

In each of the examples to follow, all that is needed are some dots and lines. Creating a dot is easy, but the line needs to fit certain specifications. More on that to follow.

Writing the Code

The following sections describe, step by step, one way to make 3D models come alive in Flash MX. The first starts with code to convert 3D coordinates to 2D screen locations.

Converting Coordinates

The location of objects on the Stage is represented by two coordinates: x and y. Objects in a 3D space, however, need to have x, y, and z coordinates. The "z" represents depth.

To draw these objects on the Stage, you must have a function that converts x, y, and z to just a screen x and y. In addition, you need to rotate and tilt the objects. So, the conversion function should take into account a base rotation and tilt.

Note that this is certainly the most complex script in the book so far, and it is probably one of the most complex in the entire book.

The math function *Math.atan* is used to convert coordinates to an angle, and the *Math.sin* and *Math.cos* functions are used to convert angles back to coordinates. In this way, the point is converted from an x, y, and z position to an angle and distance from the center of a plane. Then the point is rotated and converted back to coordinates. This is done once for rotation and once for tilt. The result gives you x and y coordinates that can be used on the computer screen.

The comments in the following code explain what each section does. A step-by-step explanation follows.

```
// take 3d coordinates and convert to screen location
function plotPoint(object) {
    // get coordinates from object
    x = object.x;
    y = object.y;
    z = object.z;

    // determine distance from center
    radius = Math.sqrt (x*x+y*y);
```

③➤
```
// compute first angle
if (x == 0) angle = Math.atan(1000000);
else angle = Math.atan(y/x);
if (x < 0) angle += Math.PI;
```

④➤
```
// add rotation
angle += rotation;
```

⑤➤
```
// compute new coordinates
realx = radius*Math.cos(angle);
realz = radius*Math.sin(angle);
realy = z;
```

⑥➤
```
// determine new distance from center
radius = Math.sqrt(realy*realy+realz*realz);
```

⑦➤
```
// compute second angle
if (realz == 0) angle = Math.atan(1000000);
else angle = Math.atan(realy/realz);
if (realz < 0) angle += Math.PI;
```

⑧➤
```
// add angle of plane
angle += plane;
```

⑨➤
```
// compute screen coordinates
screenx = realx;
screeny = radius*Math.sin(angle);
screenz = radius*Math.cos(angle);
```

⑩➤
```
// center on screen
screenx += 275;
screeny += 200;
```

⑪➤
```
// return object
return({x:screenx,y:screeny,z:screenz});
```

NOTE

The *Math.atan()* function converts a line to an angle, in radians. You need to feed it the vertical difference between the start and end points of the line, divided by the horizontal difference of the start and end points of a line. For instance, if a line goes from 200,200 to 275,250, then you use "Math.atan(75/50)" to get the angle. The result is .9828 radians, which is about 56°. Real-life use of the *Math.atan()* function is a little more complex, but this gives you the basic idea.

Here are the steps for creating the preceding code:

1. The 3D coordinates are placed in x, y, and z.
2. The distance from the center of the 3D world to the object on the xy plane is determined.
3. The angle on the xy plane is determined.
4. The amount of rotation is added to this angle.
5. A new x, y, and z are determined that take into account this angle change.
6. The distance from the center of the world to the object on the yz plane is determined.
7. The angle on the yz plane is determined.
8. The tilt of the plane is added to this angle.
9. A new x, y, and z are determined that take into account this tilt.
10. The new coordinates assume that 0,0 is the center of the screen. So, the actual center of the screen (275,200 in this case) is added to them to correct it.
11. The x and y coordinates can now be used to display the object on the screen. The z coordinate can also be used to fade the color of objects that are farther from the user.

The "plotPoint" object uses orthographic projection to convert points with 3D coordinates to points with 2D coordinates. This means that there is no sense of perspective, so objects that are farther away do not shrink. This works well for small objects and special effects like this one, but does not work well for large 3D scenes.

Cube Corners

Now it's time to create the eight corners of the cube. Each point is stored in its own small object with an x, y, and z property. The whole list of objects is stored in an array.

```
// create an array of the 8 points in a cube
function makePoints() {
    points = new Array();
    points[0] = {x: 30, y: 30, z: 30};
    points[1] = {x: -30, y: 30, z: 30};
    points[2] = {x: -30, y: -30, z: 30};
    points[3] = {x: 30, y: -30, z: 30};
    points[4] = {x: 30, y: -30, z: -30};
    points[5] = {x: 30, y: 30, z: -30};
    points[6] = {x: -30, y: 30, z: -30};
    points[7] = {x: -30, y: -30, z: -30};
```

```
// create eight movie clips for cube corners
for(i=0;i<points.length;i++) {
    attachMovie( "point", "point"+i, i )
}
}
```

This function also creates eight movie clips from a clip stored in the library. Each clip is named starting with the word "point" and ending with a number from 0 to 7. This number corresponds to the point in the array that the clip represents.

Now that you have the points and a function to convert them to screen display locations, all you need is a small function that loops through the points and plots each one. In addition to setting the _x and _y properties of each point's movie clip, the _alpha property is set so that points fade a little according to their depth into the screen.

```
// loop through points and set corners of cube
function drawPoints() {
    for(i=0;i<points.length;i++) {
        loc = plotPoint(points[i]);
        this["point"+i]._x = loc.x;
        this["point"+i]._y = loc.y;
        this["point"+i]._alpha = loc.z+100;
    }
}
```

All the previous functions should be placed into the main timeline. In addition, after the functions, the following lines set up the model and prepare the "rotation" variable.

```
// call initial functions and stop on this frame
rotation = 0;
makePoints();
stop();
```

Now, only the call to "drawPoints" remains. This is done from inside a small "reposition" function. It changes the "rotation" variable depending on whether the cursor is to the right or left side of the screen. The function also sets the "plane" variable according to how high or low the cursor is. The function then calls "drawPoints" to set the current position of each point.

```
// reposition cube every frame
function reposition() {
    rotation += (275-_xmouse)/1000;
    plane = -(200-_ymouse)/100;
    drawPoints();
}
```

The "reposition" function is called from inside another movie clip, once each frame. This movie clip is an off-stage clip that exists to run this piece of code as it loops.

```
onClipEvent(enterFrame) {
    _root.reposition();
}
```

Now the movie is somewhat complete. The eight points show a cube on the screen that rotates and angles itself according to mouse movement. Check out 3dcubepoints.fla on the CD-ROM to see it in action. Figure 5.10 shows what this looks like.

Figure 5.10

A 3D cube repre-sented by eight points on the screen. The illusion is far more com-plete while the movie is running, because the cube spins.

Adding Edges

Although the eight points of the cube create a nice illusion, you can go further. If you add a line for each edge of the cube, it begins to appear much more cube-like, even while not rotating.

In Flash, dynamic lines are created by making a library movie clip of a simple line. This line needs to start at the center of the movie clip and extend down and to the right. It also needs to be a hairline width, and it extends exactly 100 pixels horizontally and verti-cally. Figure 5.11 shows the main Flash window with such a line being created. Note that the grid is set to 50×50 pixels.

Figure 5.11

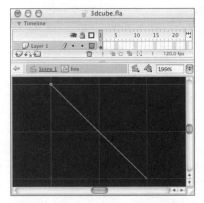

A simple line movie clip can be used to create dynamic lines on the Stage with ActionScript. The line extends exactly 100 pixels horizontally and vertically.

A cube has 12 edges, so you need 12 lines. Instead of specifying the x, y, and z coordinates of both ends of each line, you can use two of the points that are already in the "points" array. So each line has "p1" and "p2" properties.

```
/ create an array of the 12 lines in a cube
function makeLines() {
    lines = new Array();
    lines[0] = {p1: 0, p2: 1};
    lines[1] = {p1: 1, p2: 2};
    lines[2] = {p1: 2, p2: 3};
    lines[3] = {p1: 3, p2: 0};
    lines[4] = {p1: 4, p2: 5};
    lines[5] = {p1: 5, p2: 6};
    lines[6] = {p1: 6, p2: 7};
    lines[7] = {p1: 7, p2: 4};
    lines[8] = {p1: 0, p2: 5};
    lines[9] = {p1: 1, p2: 6};
    lines[10] = {p1: 2, p2: 7};
    lines[11] = {p1: 3, p2: 4};

    for(i=0;i<lines.length;i++) {
        attachMovie( "line", "line"+i, 50+i )
    }
}
```

The 12 movie clips are also created by this function. Each movie clip is named "linex," where "x" is the number that corresponds to the "lines" array.

In Flash, lines, are dynamically drawn by setting the location of the line to the first point, and setting the scale of the line to the second. Because the line inside the movie clip starts at the center of the movie clip, setting the location sets the upper-left corner of the line to the first point. Then, because the scale of the line determines the horizontal and vertical stretch of the line, setting the scale to the x and y difference between the second and first points positions the line perfectly.

For example, if you want a line that extends from 50,80 to 170,210, you first set the location of the line to 50,80. Then, you calculate that the horizontal difference for the line is 170–50=120. The vertical difference is 210–80=130. By setting the _xscale and _yscale to 120 and 130, respectively, you get a line from 50,80 to 170,210.

WARNING

It is crucial that the line movie clip be 100 pixels in width and height. This makes it so that a scale of 100% equals 100 pixels in width and height, a scale of 200% equals 200 pixels in width and height, and so on. The line also needs to be hairline width, so that the scaling never affects the width of the line. Any other line width, such as 1, is scaled as you use the _xscale and _yscale properties.

```
// loop through lines and set edges of cube
function drawLines() {
    for(i=0;i<lines.length;i++) {
        loc1 = plotPoint(points[lines[i].p1]);
        loc2 = plotPoint(points[lines[i].p2]);
        this["line"+i]._x = loc1.x;
        this["line"+i]._y = loc1.y;
        this["line"+i]._xscale = loc2.x-loc1.x;
        this["line"+i]._yscale = loc2.y-loc1.y;
        this["line"+i]._alpha = loc1.z+100;
    }
}
```

All that is left to do to add edges to the cube is to call the "makeLines" function when the movie starts, and call the "drawLines" function from inside the "reposition" function. Figure 5.12 shows the result. This can be found on the CD-ROM as 3dcube.fla.

Figure 5.12
*A 3D cube is shown
here with both
points and lines.*

Other Possibilities

You can create ,objects that are more complex than a cube, of course. Figure 5.13 shows a small model of a spaceship. This program, which can be found in 3Dspaceship.fla on the CD-ROM, dispenses with the "drawPoints" function altogether, although it still uses the "points" array to define each corner so that lines can be drawn between them.

Figure 5.13
*This is a simple 3D
model of a space-
ship; the ship
rotates in the actual
program.*

By playing with the lists of points and lines, you can create any number of different 3D models. You can give the user control of the rotation and tilt, or have the tilt fixed and the model rotating at a constant speed. You can even change the center point of the screen to give the illusion that the model is moving.

6

Toys and Gadgets

Before looking at full games, you should take a look at toys and gadgets. These are not quite games, because they don't have objectives or scores, but they are full applications that can stand alone.

First, you will look at two interactive gadgets: a magic crystal ball and a music jukebox. Then, you will look at two more complex but non-interactive movies: a clock and a lava lamp. Finally, we'll look at the mother of all computer toys: the Game of Life.

The Magic Crystal Ball

Example Movie: crystalball.fla

Random-answer prediction machines are perhaps the most common interactive gadget found on the Internet. They are usually called Magic Eight Balls, after the popular real-world Tyco toy.

Figure 6.1 shows how a gadget of this sort might look.

Figure 6.1
The fox answers your question after you click the crystal ball.

Project Goal

When the user clicks, the fox waves his hands and invokes the crystal ball to give an answer. The answer is taken at random from a list of text responses.

Approach

Most of the effort going into this movie is actually the drawing and animation itself. The ActionScript is simple.

Preparing the Movie

Take a look at the animation first. There are two stages to the movie. The first is a static frame that looks just like Figure 6.1. The movie is waiting for the user to click the crystal ball.

The only element needed to accomplish this is a simple *stop()* command placed in any layer. Figure 6.2 shows the main timeline for this movie. A little "a" in the first frame of the second "Text" layer shows that an ActionScript is attached to that frame. This is the *stop()* action.

Figure 6.2

The main timeline shows the complete crystal ball animation.

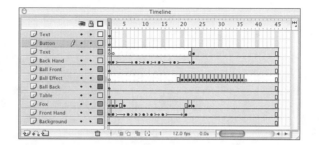

The way the main timeline is set up is completely at the discretion of the animator. In this case, the fox is broken into a main layer and one layer for each hand. The ball is broken into several layers as well.

It is important to note how the animation unfolds over time. The first frame is a static frame in which no animation takes place, but text is displayed and a button is present. The text is the same text you can see in Figure 6.1. The button is actually an invisible button placed over the crystal ball.

To create an invisible button, you create a new button member, use any colored area to create the button shape, and drop it onto the main timeline in a layer near the top. At this point, the button is visible, as it is in Figure 6.3.

Figure 6.3

The first frame of the crystal ball movie shows the central button over the crystal ball.

The desire is to have the button invisible to the user while at the same time making it an active button that can be clicked. To do this, go to the Property inspector, choose Alpha as the effect, and set it to 0%. Figure 6.4 shows this panel.

Figure 6.4
The Property inspector allows you to set the Alpha of an element to 0%, thus making it invisible.

NOTE

The Alpha effect relates to the term *alpha channel* when it comes to images. A graphic image is said to have four channels: red, green, blue, and alpha. The first three channels determine the color of a pixel. The last channel determines its transparency. When the alpha channel is 0, the pixel is completely transparent. Setting the Alpha of a Flash element to 0 makes that element completely transparent.

Even though the button is completely transparent, Flash still considers it to be on the Stage. Thus, the button is 100% active and responds to mouse clicks. This is one way to make an invisible button. Another way is detailed in the "Memory Game" in Chapter 14, "Brain Puzzles."

When the user clicks the button, the movie jumps to frame 2 and continues playing. This plays out the rest of the animation until the end of the movie.

If you look at the main timeline of the sample movie from frames 2 to 22 you can see that the hands animate with a little bit of tweening. At frame 20, the "Ball Effect" layer animates, creating a flash inside the ball. The actual movie can be seen on the CD-ROM in the file Crystalball.fla.

The most important change in the time span of the animation is the appearance of a second text area in frame 23. This is the text area that holds the answer to the user's question. The text in it is set when the button is first clicked, but the text does not become visible until frame 23.

So the movie consists of one frame at the beginning that waits for user input, and then a series of frames that animate, showing the text midway. When the animation is done, the movie loops back to the first frame to await the next question.

Writing the Code

The actual "magic" for this movie is all done in the ActionScript for the button. You've already learned that it jumps the movie to frame two and gets it animating. That's the last thing it actually does. Before that, it generates the answer and places it in the text area.

Because it is a button that activates the response, you need to place all the code in a button event. This always starts with *on* and then specifies the event. The most commonly used event is *release*.

First, the script creates an array and fills it with a list of responses. There are many ways to do this. One way would look like this:

```
responses = new Array("Yes", "No", "Ask again later","It is certain",
"Doubtful", "Probably", "The answer is unclear","Of course not!","Certainly!",
"It looks positive", "It looks negative");
```

This is the most compact way of declaring the array and filling it at the same time. However, it is a bit messy in that the text runs off the right side of the screen. Here is another way of doing it:

```
responses = new Array();
responses[0] = "Yes";
responses[1] = "No";
responses[2] = "Ask again later";
responses[3] = "It is certain";
responses[4] = "It is certain";
responses[5] = "Doubtful";
responses[6] = "Probably";
responses[7] = "The answer is unclear";
responses[8] = "Of course not!";
responses[9] = "Certainly!";
responses[10] = "It looks positive";
responses[11] = "It looks negative";
```

This way is a lot neater, because each answer is on its own line. It is much easier to see what is there. However, you have to individually enter each element number in the brackets. Make a mistake and you might miss a possible answer, or leave a space blank. But there is yet another way to do this, which is even better:

```
responses = new Array();
responses.push("Yes");
responses.push("No");
responses.push("Ask again later");
responses.push("It is certain");
responses.push("Doubtful");
responses.push("Probably");
responses.push("The answer is unclear");
responses.push("Of course not!");
responses.push("Certainly!");
responses.push("It looks positive");
responses.push("It looks negative");
```

If you use *push*, each answer is added to the array one after the other. It looks neat and is easy to see on the screen, plus it's easy to add new answers or remove answers.

NOTE

A quick and easy way to add an element to the end of an array is to use *push*. You can actually add more than one element by including more than one parameter to *push*. You can also use it as a function at the same time, because it returns the new length of the array. For instance, *newLengthOfArray = myArray.push("Gary", "Debby")*.

After an array has been filled with potential responses, all that is needed is to pick one at random. You can get the number of items in an array with an array's *length* property. Then, you can use the *Math.Random* function to choose a random number that fits a random element in the array. You can read more about the *Math.Random* function in the section "A Touch of Randomness" in Chapter 5, "ActionScript Design Effects."

After you have a random number, you can use it to set the text in a text area. Remember to set up the text area as Dynamic Text, with a variable name, in this case "fortune." You can see how the Property inspector should look in Figure 6.5.

Figure 6.5

This Property inspector specifies that the text area is dynamic and linked to the variable "fortune."

Here is the complete code for the button. After the text has been set, the movie jumps to frame 2, which begins the animation. The text area actually doesn't appear until frame 23.

```
on (release) {
    // make list of possible responses
    responses = new Array();
    responses.push("Yes");
    responses.push("No");
    responses.push("Ask again later");
    responses.push("It is certain");
    responses.push("Doubtful");
    responses.push("Probably");
    responses.push("The answer is unclear");
    responses.push("Of course not!");
```

```
responses.push("Certainly!");
responses.push("It looks positive");
responses.push("It looks negative");

// get number of responses
n = responses.length;

// pick random response
r = Int(Math.random()*n);

// place response in text area
fortune = responses[r];

// start animation
gotoAndPlay(2);
}
```

NOTE

The two commands that you will use to move around in a Flash movie are *gotoAndPlay* and *gotoAndStop*. The main difference is that the second command jumps the movie or movie clip to the specified frame or label, but it does not trigger any code in that frame, nor does it continue to advance any animation. The *gotoAndPlay* command, on the other hand, runs any code in that frame and keeps the animation going. If you want to run any code in that frame, but not advance to the next, then use *gotoAndPlay*, but include a *stop* command in that frame.

When the animation is complete, the text appears in the middle of the crystal ball. Figure 6.6 shows what the screen now looks like.

Figure 6.6

At the end of the animation, the answer appears for a few seconds before the movie loops back to the beginning.

Loose Ends

You might want to place a *stop()* at the end of the animation so that the movie does not loop. You could place another button there to allow the movie to jump back to frame 1 if the player wants to ask another question.

Other Possibilities

It is easy to go into the code and change the list of possible responses. You don't even have to follow the positive/negative/undecided model used here. Instead, you can customize it to a particular subject, such as whether the local sports team will win today or what the weather will be like.

Music Jukebox

Example Movie: jukebox.fla

Adding sound to Web pages has never been straightforward. Either you need to use obscure HTML tags that work on only one browser, or you need to use one of many plug-ins, none of which ever caught on as the standard. However, if you are using Flash anyway, you might as well leave all the sound playing up to Flash.

Project Goal

An obvious way to demonstrate Flash's music-playing capability is to build a jukebox. This is just a simple movie that plays some songs.

Figure 6.7 shows the jukebox. It contains up to 10 different songs that can be played by clicking its selection box.

Figure 6.7

The jukebox is reminiscent of the type found at each table in a diner from the 1950s.

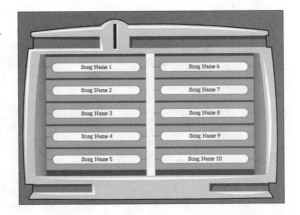

Approach

It's tempting, when building a movie like this, to create 10 different buttons, with 10 different pieces of code in each, to play the 10 different songs. This would work, but it would be hard to build and harder to modify.

A better way is to create 1 button and use it 10 times, once for each of the songs. Each "button" is actually a movie clip with a button inside it. There is only 1 movie clip and 1 button in the entire movie library. This 1 movie clip is placed on the Stage 10 times.

When the movie runs, the first thing that happens is that the text for each movie clip instance is changed. This is done with this piece of code:

```
// set the song names
this["1"].text = "Song Name 1";
this["2"].text = "Song Name 2";
this["3"].text = "Song Name 3";
this["4"].text = "Song Name 4";
this["5"].text = "Song Name 5";
this["6"].text = "Song Name 6";
this["7"].text = "Song Name 7";
this["8"].text = "Song Name 8";
this["9"].text = "Song Name 9";
this["10"].text = "Song Name 10";
```

The movie clips are all named "1" to "10" just to make things simple. After the above code runs, each movie clip instance displays a different song name. So even though there is one movie clip in the library, each instance now looks different.

Not only that, but the names of all 10 songs are in a single script. Had there been 1 song name in each movie clip, you would have to do quite a bit of work to open and close each movie clip to make 10 changes. This way, you can quickly change all 10 song names.

The other piece of code that helps keep the number of movie clips to 1 is the one attached to the button inside the movie clip.

```
on (release) {
    _root.playSong(this._name);
}
```

This one line of code takes the name of the movie clip, which could be anything from "1" to "10," and sends it to a "playSong" function at the root level. This same piece of code can be used in every movie clip because it uses the name of the movie clip instance, which is different in each case. As long as you remember to change the instance name every time you create a new instance of the movie clip, this code gets a different result for *this._name*.

The result of using this code is that you can make only one movie clip and use it as many times as you want in the movie. Now if changes are needed to the movie clip, either graphical or functional, you need to make those changes only one time. In addition, the final .swf file is smaller than one that has 10 copies of a similar movie clip in the library.

Preparing the Movie

After you have your 10 movie clips in place and your songs titled by the ActionScript of the first frame in the main timeline, you just need to add the sound.

Start by importing the 10 songs and naming those library items "song1" to "song10." After each is imported, you must change the Linkage property of each sound so that it is included when an .swf is made. You need to change it to Export this Symbol and include an identifier for each song. Figure 6.8 shows this dialog box. You can get to it by going to the Library window and choosing Linkage in its Options menu.

Figure 6.8
*The Symbol
Linkage Properties
dialog box allows
you to include
sounds with the
.swf file even when
they are not in any
timeline.*

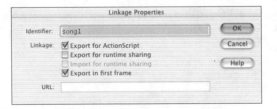

Unfortunately, there is no way to use true external sound files for the sounds. The only way to make a jukebox like this is to import all the songs and set their Linkage properties so that they are included with the .swf file. Perhaps in future versions of Flash, you will be able to access external files and play them.

Writing the Code

The code to play a sound is simple, but unfortunately not as simple as it should be. Instead of a single command to tell a sound to play, you need to have three lines. The first creates a sound object. The second associates a sound from the library with the object. The third tells the sound to play.

```
song = new Sound();
song.attachSound("song1");
song.start();
```

The "playSong" function must do a little more than this, however. First, it must tell any previous song to stop. The *stop* command does that. Assume that a previous song is playing and that it is still assigned to the global variable "song." Here is a simple version of the function:

```
function playSong(songnum) {
    // stop the previous song, if any
    song.stop();

    // play new sound
    song = new Sound();
    song.attachSound("song"+songnum);
    song.start();
}
```

One special effect to add is a light behind the selections on the jukebox. The selection movie clip is set up to have two frames: the first with the light off, and the second with the light on. You can see the light on in Figure 6.9.

Figure 6.9

The jukebox is playing song 2.

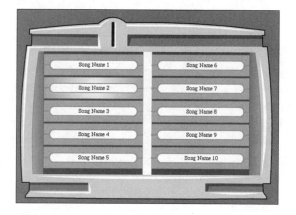

When each song begins, you should make sure that all the lights are off, and then turn on only the light behind the proper selection:

```
function playSong(songnum) {
    // stop the previous song, if any
    song.stop();

    // turn off all lights
    for(i=1;i<=10;i++) {
        this[i].gotoAndStop(1);
    }
```

```
// play new sound
song = new Sound();
song.attachSound("song"+songnum);
song.start();

// turn light on
this[songnum].gotoAndStop(2);
}
```

Check out jukebox.fla on the CD-ROM to see how all the pieces fit together.

Other Possibilities

The scripts in this section work pretty independently of the jukebox design. You could create something that looks like a floor model jukebox, or something that looks completely unlike a jukebox. You could even create a jukebox with multiple "screens" representing different song banks. Forward and Back buttons could be used to go from frame to frame where different songs are listed.

Analog Clock

Example Movies: simpleclock.fla, betterclock.fla

One of the things you can do with ActionScript is get the user's computer's time and date. This is done by using the Date object. Although there are many uses for this, you can tackle a simple one here by building an animated analog clock.

Project Goal

This clock should take the user's computer's time and display it like a wall clock or wristwatch. It should have hour, minute, and second hands. The hands can use any arrow-like movie clip, not just a simple line, so that odd and interesting clocks can be created.

Approach

To learn how to make a clock, you first need to learn how to use the Date object. This is where you get the current time to display.

Using the Date Object

Think of a Date object as a small array that holds several pieces of information about a moment in time. When you create a Date object, it captures the current time, according to the user's computer.

WARNING

Remember that relying on the date and time on a user's computer to be correct can be a bad idea. You would be surprised how many people have their clocks set to the wrong time. However, I usually don't hesitate to use their clock anyway, especially for gadgets and games. These people probably have bigger problems than your Flash movie showing the wrong time, such as all their email being sent with the wrong time stamp.

The elements in a Date object include the date, month, year, hour, minute, and second. To get any of these, all you need to do is use the proper function, such as *getDate()*. The following handler shows all the functions you can use to get information from a Date object:

```
on (release) {
    now = new Date();

    trace("toString:" + now.toString());

    trace("getDate:" + now.getDate());
    trace("getDay:" + now.getDay());
    trace("getFullYear:" + now.getFullYear());
    trace("getHours:" + now.getHours());
    trace("getMilliseconds:" + now.getMilliseconds());
    trace("getMinutes:" + now.getMinutes());
    trace("getMonth:" + now.getMonth());
    trace("getSeconds:" + now.getSeconds());
    trace("getTime:" + now.getTime());
    trace("getTimezoneOffset:" + now.getTimezoneOffset());
    trace("getYear:" + now.getYear());

    trace("getUTCDate:" + now.getUTCDate());
    trace("getUTCDay:" + now.getUTCDay());
    trace("getUTCFullYear:" + now.getUTCFullYear());
    trace("getUTCHours:" + now.getUTCHours());
    trace("getUTCMilliseconds:" + now.getUTCMilliseconds());
    trace("getUTCMinutes:" + now.getUTCMinutes());
    trace("getUTCMonth:" + now.getUTCMonth());
    trace("getUTCSeconds:" + now.getUTCSeconds());
}
```

There are a few things to note about the various functions. All the "UTC" functions rely on the user having his system properly configured with the correct time zone. Hours are added or subtracted from the local time on the user's computer to get universal time, depending on the user's time zone. Universal time will then be compatible from computer to computer, regardless of time zone. The *getTime* result is the number of milliseconds since January 1, 1970. The "day" is a number from 0 to 6 representing the day of the week. The month is a number from 0 to 11. However, the date is a number from 1 to 31. This might be hard to understand and remember, but it is not unique to Flash; other programming languages, such as C and JavaScript, use the same principles.

Here's the result of all these *trace* commands:

```
toString:Sat Oct 14 18:47:06 GMT-0600 2000
getDate:14
getDay:6
getFullYear:2000
getHours:18
getMilliseconds:0
getMinutes:44
getMonth:9
getSeconds:7
getTime:971570647000
getTimezoneOffset:360
getYear:100
getUTCDate:15
getUTCDay:0
getUTCFullYear:2000
getUTCHours:0
getUTCMilliseconds:0
getUTCMinutes:44
getUTCMonth:9
getUTCSeconds:7
```

You can also set any portion of a Date object. Each "get" function has a matching "set" function. So, for instance, to set the hour, use *setHour(newHour)*. Note that this changes the Date object only, but not the user's system clock. The next time you create a fresh Date object, it will match the system clock.

Preparing the Movie

One cool thing that can be created with the Date object is a clock. By translating the hour, minute, and second of the current time to degrees, you can set the *_rotation* property of three different movie clips to look just like the hands of a clock.

Figure 6.10 shows what this clock might look like. The shorter arm represents the hour, the longer arm represents the minute, and the tail is the second hand.

Figure 6.10
The clock shows 9:20 and 35 seconds.

What you can't see in Figure 6.10 is that the hands (and tail) of the clock move just like a real clock. This is accomplished in three steps. First the current time is read and placed into "hour," "minute," and "second" variables. Next, these numbers are converted into angles. Then, these angles are used to set the *_rotation* property of the three movie clips that represent the arms and tail.

Writing the Code

The code that does all this is an *onClipEvent (enterFrame)* script that is placed in an otherwise unused movie clip, as shown here. You can see exactly how that is set up by checking out Simpleclock.fla on the CD-ROM.

```
onClipEvent (enterFrame) {
    // get current time
    now = new Date();
    hour = now.getHours();
    minute = now.getMinutes();
    second = now.getSeconds();
    // convert to 12-hour clock
    if (hour > 12) {
        hour -= 12;
    }

    // determine angle of hands
    hourAngle = 360*hour/12;
    minuteAngle = 360*minute/60
    secondAngle = 360*second/60;

    // set angles of hands
    _root["hour hand"]._rotation = hourAngle;
    _root["minute hand"]._rotation = minuteAngle;
    _root["second hand"]._rotation = secondAngle;
}
```

You convert the time to angles by dividing it by the highest possible value and multiplying by 360. For instance, the minutes are divided by 60, giving a value between 0 and 1, and then multiplied by 360, giving a value between 0 and 360. Also note that 12 is subtracted from the hour so that it is a 12-hour clock rather than a 24-hour one.

The result of each operation is an angle from 0 to 360. 0 represents 0 (or 12) hours, 0 minutes, or 0 seconds. This corresponds to a hand on the clock being straight up, or at 0 degrees. This being the case, the three movie clips that represent the hands of the clock should be drawn pointing straight up, as in Figure 6.11. Then, when the _rotation is set, the hand points to the proper place.

Figure 6.11

The hands (and tail) of the clock should be drawn straight up to represent 12:00:00. Then, when the _rotation properties of the hands are set, they will point to the right place.

A problem with the code so far is that the clock does not operate completely like a normal clock or watch. For instance, the hour hand in Figure 6.10 is pointing at 9 o'clock. It will continue pointing at 9, even when it is 9:59, then it will instantly change to 10 at 10:00.

A real clock, however, moves the hour hand gradually throughout the hour, eventually getting to 10 at 10:00. You need to add a slight amount to the angle of the hour hand for each minute, and a slight amount to the angle of the minute hand for every second. Here is a piece of code that does this:

```
// add fractions of hour and minutes
hourAngle += minute/2;
minuteAngle += second/10;
```

The minute is divided by 2, which gives you 30 additional degrees for every hour. The second is divided by 10, which gives you 6 additional degrees for every second. Do the math: At 9:59, the angle is $9 \times 30 + 59/2 = 270 + 29.5 = 299.5$. At 10:00, the angle is $10 \times 30 + 0/2 = 300 + 0 = 300$.

Likewise, for the minute hand, at 20 minutes and 59 seconds, the angle is $20 \times 6 + 59/10 = 120 + 5.9 = 125.9$. After one more second, the angle is $21 \times 6 + 0/10 = 126 + 0 = 126$.

Figure 6.12 shows the clock with this piece of code inserted. Compare it carefully to Figure 6.10 to see that the hour and minute hands are a little more accurate.

Figure 6.12
This clock has new code to make the hour and minute hands more accurate.

The Betterclock.fla file has this extra bit of code in it to smooth out the hand movements. Note that you can actually see the minute hand move slightly as the time changes.

Other Possibilities

Of course, you can substitute anything you want for the clock hands. It can be as simple as lines or as complex as your own character. You can also color up the rest of the clock with numbers or background images.

One fun possibility would be to create a clock that runs backward. You can see this sort of novelty clock in stores and restaurants sometimes. You can also add a chime sound to be played when the hands strike the hour or every 15 minutes.

Lava Lamp

Example Movie: lavalamp.fla

This movie recreates the classic lava lamp. There are many lava lamp-like things on computers and the Web. Most of these are simply animations. You could make a great lava lamp animation with Flash and not need to have one piece of code.

However, that sort of defeats the purpose of a lava lamp. You are supposed to be able to stare at it for hours and never see the same pattern repeat. With an animated lava lamp, the pattern must repeat when the full length of the animation runs out.

Project Goal

In this section, you create a truly random lava lamp. This means that the code must decide when and where new bubbles appear. The result is a lava lamp that never repeats itself.

Approach

To create a truly random lava lamp, you need to use ActionScript. You need 20 movie clips that represent bubbles in the lava lamp. Then, you continuously call a function that moves the bubbles up and down the screen. Figure 6.13 shows what the lava lamp looks like.

Figure 6.13
The lava lamp is made up of a top and bottom, a transparent glass piece, and red bubbles.

Preparing the Movie

The graphics for the lava lamp movie need to be created with care. For instance, the bubbles themselves are filled circles with no stroke and a radial fill. The fill, however, is not a usual one. It is between a solid red and a transparent red. Setting the Alpha of the color to 0% creates the transparent red. Figure 6.14 shows the movie clip, plus the Fill and Mixer panels displaying the settings for the red to transparent red gradient.

Figure 6.14
The Fill panel shows a fill between a solid red and a transparent red. The Mixer panel shows the transparent red, which is obtained by setting the Alpha to 0%.

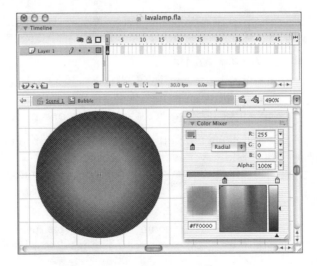

Writing the Code

The lava lamp uses 20 movie clips created from a single library clip. The *attachMovie* command is used to bring these instances into the movie. To read more about the *attachMovie* command, see the "3D Illusions" section in Chapter 5.

When the movie begins, the first and only frame in the timeline will execute the "initLamp" function. This will not only create the 20 bubble clips, but also an array full of objects that will represent the speed of each bubble.

In addition to the bubbles, the movie has an opaque top and bottom that hides the bubbles as they rise from the bottom or descend from the top. There is also a semitransparent glass graphic that should go on top of the bubbles.

This brings about a problem. When the *attachMovie* or *duplicateMovieClip* command is used, you must specify the level for the new movie clip. This level is used to determine which elements the clip is in front of and which elements the clip is behind. Because these are new movie clips, they are all in front of existing movie clips. This means the bubbles are in front of the top, bottom, and glass graphics. You can use the *duplicateMovieClip* command to create new instances of these three graphics that will be on top of all the bubbles.

Here is the "initLamp" function:

```
function initLamp () {
    // present and remember top and bottom
    top = 0;
    bottom = 300;

    // generate movie clips for bubbles
    numBubbles = 20;
    for (i=0; i<numBubbles; i++) {
        attachMovie("bubble", "Bubble"+i, i);
    }

    // duplicate top, bottom, and glass so they are above bubbles
    duplicateMovieClip("Glass", "Glass", i++);
    duplicateMovieClip("Top", "Top", i++);
    duplicateMovieClip("Bottom", "Bottom", i++);

    // generate objects for bubbles
    bubbles = new Array();
    for (i=0; i<numBubbles; i++) {
        bubbles[i] = {speed:0};
    }
}
```

> **NOTE**
> You can create quick little objects by just using brackets as shown in the last line of the "initLamp" function: "bubbles[i]= {speed:0}." You can then refer to the contents of this object with dot syntax such as "bubbles[0].speed." This makes your code more readable, and also allows you to have more than one piece of information as a single element in a variable or array. For instance, you could use "myObject = {speed: 6, weight: 40, clipname: "clip1"}" and then use syntax such as "myObject.speed" to get the values.

After all the elements are ready, the movie works off the principle that a function is called every so often to update the position of the bubbles and create new ones. An off-screen movie clip calls the "moveBubbles" function on every *enterFrame* clip event.

The "moveBubbles" function moves bubbles either up or down, stopping them at the top or bottom. It also, based on a 1 in 30 chance, calls "newBubble" to create a new bubble.

```
// move all existing bubbles
function moveBubbles () {
    for (i=0; i<numBubbles; i++) {
        // get current location
        y = _root["Bubble"+i]._y;
        // stop if at bottom
        if ((bubbles[i].speed > 0) and (y > bottom)) {
            bubbles[i].speed = 0;
        // stop if at top
        } else if ((bubbles[i].speed < 0) and (y < top)) {
            bubbles[i].speed = 0;
        // keep moving
        } else {
            // move
            _root["Bubble"+i]._y  = y+bubbles[i].speed;
            // shape
            height = _root["Bubble"+i]._yscale;
            width = _root["Bubble"+i]._xscale;
            if (height > width) height -= 1;
            _root["Bubble"+i]._yscale = height;
        }
    }

    // 1 in 30 chance of a new bubble
    if (Math.random()*30 <= 1) {
        newBubble();
    }
}
```

The "newBubble" function searches through the "bubbles" array to find a bubble that is not in use. It then starts the bubble from either the top or bottom. The size of the bubble is also set by a random number. It is always three times longer than it is wide. This difference slowly closes as the bubble moves.

```
function newBubble () {
    for (i=0; i<numBubbles; i++) {
        // find an unused bubble
        if (bubbles[i].speed == 0) {
            // start it at the top
            if (Math.random() < .5) {
                bubbles[i].speed = 1;
                _root["Bubble"+i]._y = -40;
            // start it at the bottom
            } else {
                bubbles[i].speed = -1;
                _root["Bubble"+i]._y = 340;
            }
            // shape it
            size = 40+ Math.random()*40;
            _root["Bubble"+i]._xscale = size;
            _root["Bubble"+i]._yscale = size*3;
            _root["Bubble"+i]._x = 10+Math.random()*80;
            // done
            break;
        }
    }
}
```

These three functions make up the heart of the lava lamp movie. To see how it all comes together, check out Lavalamp.fla on the CD-ROM.

Loose Ends

The glass graphic was created with alpha transparency in a similar fashion as the bubbles so that the bubbles show through. You might want to spruce up the exterior of the lava lamp with a label or logo to make it fit your site or project.

The Game of Life

Example movie: gameoflife.fla

"The Game of Life" sounds either like a profound experiment in artificial intelligence, or a cheesy board game. In fact, it is something in between.

The Game of Life was invented by mathematician John Conway and made famous in an article in Scientific American in 1970. Soon after, it was adopted by computer programmers as a classic programming experiment and pastime. Many long, sleepless nights have been spent by programmers playing with The Game of Life.

The idea is simple: a grid with dots. Each cell in the grid either has a dot or is empty. That's how it starts. During each "turn" of the game, a set of rules is applied to each cell. If a cell has a dot in it, and there are two or three dots in adjacent cells, then the dot stays. If there are less than two dots adjacent to it, then it dies (of loneliness!). If more than three dots are adjacent to it, then it dies (overcrowded). If a cell is empty, then a new dot can be born there if exactly three dots are adjacent to it.

Figure 6.15
*The Game of Life
follows the life and
death of little red
dots.*

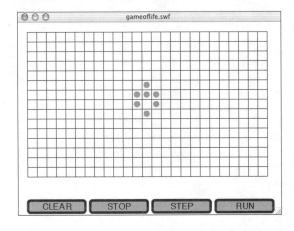

This simple set of rules is all you need. The results can be quite amazing. Try the example movie. Click to create a pattern like the one in Figure 6.15. Then press Run.

Project Goal

The program creates a grid of cells to fill the screen. Each cell can be either on or off. Cells that are on have dots in them. The user can click on a cell and change its value.

After the user finishes changing values, a press of a button starts the game. For each frame that passes, the set of rules is applied to each cell. Some cells change value.

The user can also press a button to stop the game. There is also a button to step through the game one turn at a time. The last button is for clearing the board.

Approach

The movie starts by creating the grid of movie clips. It also creates an array of arrays that stores the value of each cell. So the value is indicated by two values: which frame the movie clip is on and the value in the array. The reason for this is that ActionScript can access the value in an array much faster. We'll need to access these values quite a lot, so speed is important.

The main function of the movie is to loop through all the cells and compute whether the cell changes. Executing this function is one step, or turn, of the game. If the player presses the Run button, the movie continuously steps through the game. Pressing the Step button performs only one step.

Preparing the Movie

In addition to the four buttons seen in Figure 6.15, you need to create the cell movie clip. Call this movie clip "gridbox." It does not need to be on the Stage anywhere, but it should be linked as "gridbox" so you can create new ones with ActionScript.

The "gridbox" movie clip needs to have two frames: the first without a dot and the second with one. There should be a *stop()* in the first frame to prevent it from animating. There should be a button covering both frames that allows the user to click on the cell.

You also need a simple "actions" movie clip that is placed slightly off the Stage. This calls the main function once per frame and allows the game to continue after the user presses Run.

Writing the Code

This first function creates a 25×15 grid of cells. It also makes an array of arrays. Each array is a single row of cell values. So to access the value of the cell in the upper left corner, you would use "grid[0][0]." To access the value of the fifth cell from the left, seven down, you would use "grid[6][4]."

```
function createGrid() {
    // create movie clip and populate an array
    grid = new Array();
    for(y=0;y<15;y++) {
        var temp = new Array();
        for(x=0;x<25;x++) {
            mc = attachMovie("gridbox","gridbox "+x+" "+y,y*25+x);
            mc._x = x*20+30;
            mc._y = y*20+30;
            mc.x = x;
            mc.y = y;
            temp.push(false);
        }
        grid.push(temp);
    }
}
```

The "cycle" function is the heart of this program. It uses the rules to determine whether a cell has a dot in it.

One tricky thing that it does is to use a duplicate of the "grid" array. This is so that when the real "grid" is changing, those changes do not affect the other cells. Only the "baseGrid" array is examined.

```
function cycle() {
    // duplicate grid
    var baseGrid = duplicateGrid();

    // loop through all cells
    for(y=0;y<15;y++) {
        for(x=0;x<25;x++) {
            thisBox = baseGrid[y][x];
            mc = this["gridbox "+x+" "+y];

            // get number of live cells around this one
            n = 0;
            n += baseGrid[y-1][x-1];
            n += baseGrid[y-1][x];
            n += baseGrid[y-1][x+1];
            n += baseGrid[y][x-1];
            n += baseGrid[y][x+1];
            n += baseGrid[y+1][x-1];
            n += baseGrid[y+1][x];
            n += baseGrid[y+1][x+1];

            // dot stays if there was a dot before and
            // there are 2 or 3 dots around it.
            if (thisBox) {
                if ((n == 2) or (n == 3)) {
                    newValue = true;
                } else {
                    newValue = false;
                }

            // new dot born if no dot there before and
            // there are exactly 3 dots around it
            } else {
                if (n == 3) {
                    newValue = true;
                } else {
                    newValue = false;
                }
            }

            // go to correct frame of mc
            grid[y][x] = newValue;
```

```
            if (newValue) {
                mc.gotoAndStop(2);
            } else {
                mc.gotoAndStop(1);
            }
        }
    }
}
```

The "duplicateGrid" function makes a copy of the grid and returns it.

```
// make a copy of the grid
function duplicateGrid() {
    var newGrid = new Array();
    for(y=0;y<15;y++) {
        var temp = new Array();
        for(x=0;x<25;x++) {
            temp.push(grid[y][x]);
        }
        newGrid.push(temp);
    }
    return(newGrid);
}
```

So why couldn't we just have skipped the "duplicateGrid" function and set "baseGrid" equal to "grid"? Without the "duplicateGrid" function, we would not have made a copy of "grid." Instead, it would have linked both "grid" and "baseGrid" to the same array. The result would have been that a change to "grid" would appear in "baseGrid" as well.

The "actions" movie clip has an *onClipEvent (enterFrame)* handler that calls "runCycle" every frame. This function simply checks the "running" global and executes "cycle" if "running" is true.

```
function runCycle() {
    if (running) {
        cycle();
    }
}
```

Next are the scripts for the buttons. Each button has a simple *on (release)* script on it that calls one of these functions. This first one sets the "running" global to true.

```
function startCycle() {
    running = true;
}
```

If, instead of pressing Run, the user presses Step, then "cycle" is called once, but "running" is not changed.

```
function stepCycle() {
    cycle();
}
```

When the user presses Stop, all that is needed is for "running" to be set to false.

```
function stopCycle() {
    running = false;
}
```

The Clear button needs to do a little more work. It clears both the movie clips and the arrays.

```
function clear() {
    for(y=0;y<15;y++) {
        for(x=0;x<25;x++) {
            grid[y][x] = 0;
            this["gridbox "+x+" "+y].gotoAndStop(1);
        }
    }
    running = false;
}
```

The only other script in the movie is the button script on the button inside each "gridbox" movie clip. It toggles the value of the cell. Notice that back in "createGrid" we set "x" and "y" variables in each movie clip. This allows the movie clips to know to which cell they belong so that they can change the value in the "grid" array as well as change themselves.

```
on (release) {
    if (_currentframe == 1) {
        gotoAndStop(2);
        _parent.grid[y][x] = true;
    } else {
        gotoAndStop(1);
        _parent.grid[y][x] = false;
    }
}
```

Loose Ends

In addition to the functions in the frame script, you also have to have independent code to call the "createGrid" function and then issue a *stop()* command.

The other loose end is that the game needs some data to get going. If you just run it with no dots in the grid, then nothing happens. Try the pattern in Figure 6.15. It is called "small explosion." The programmers who originally built the first Game of Life program thought of names for some of the patterns.

There are many other patterns to choose from. You can try your own, or search the Web. A search for "game of life" will find many pages showing simple and complex patterns that do interesting things.

Other Possibilities

One thing you may want to add to this game is a set of buttons that pre-populate the grid with interesting patterns. After you pick out your favorite patterns you can have buttons that set the grid array and movie clip frames. Then, you can quickly access cool patterns without having to re-create them by hand each time you want to start.

Construction Toys

- Drag-and-Drop Make-a-Fox
- Click-And-Switch Make-A-Fox
- Sketchbook
- Music Mixer
- Dancing Fox

This chapter looks at Flash movies that allow users to create things. These types of toys appeal to the creative sides of users. There are no goals or score, just infinite possibilities.

First, you'll make a program that allows users to build an image from various parts. Making something like this as a computer program can be done in a number of ways. On the one hand, you can allow the user to drag and drop pieces onto a fixed body. Another way is to fix the position of the pieces, but allow the user to change the shape of each one.

Next, you'll make a program that allows the user to draw lines and shapes on a canvas. Then, switching from the visual to the aural, you'll make a program that allows the user to build a song from various music pieces. Finally, you'll allow the user to build a custom animation from a selection of sequences.

Drag-and-Drop Make-a-Fox

Example Movie: makeafox-drag.fla

Many computer toys and games have origins in pre-computer era toys. One of these old toys is the Mister Potato Head. This was a collection of plastic body parts that kids could stick on a potato and make a funny-looking person. Later, the potato was replaced with a plastic body.

Project Goal

The goal here is to create an application in which users can drag and drop pieces of a fox onto a fixed body to create their own foxes. The drag and drop must be very natural for anyone accustomed to using drag and drop in other computer programs.

Approach

The program needs to recognize when the mouse button is pressed and when it is released. It needs to decide which movie clip the cursor is over and allow that movie clip to be dragged throughout the duration of the mouse action.

This is not as easy as it sounds. To determine which movie clip the user clicked, you have to compare the location of the click with the area covered by each movie clip.

Preparing the Movie

To create a drag-and-drop construction toy, you first need to make various graphics pieces. Figure 7.1 shows the main body to the right, and various arms, legs, mouths, and eyes to the left.

Figure 7.1
The pieces on the left are moveable and can be dragged to the body on the right.

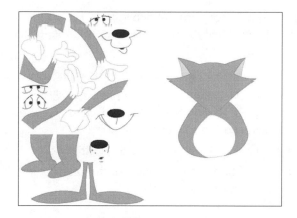

You can find the sample movie on the CD-ROM by looking at Makeafox-drag.fla. Click any piece to the left and you can drag it around the screen to any position.

Writing the Code

If you have done a little work with Flash before, you might recognize that this should be easy—just make the pieces movie clips and use the *startDrag* and *endDrag* commands, right? This actually makes things complex. I'm not a fan of the *startDrag* command, and do not use it here. One reason is that you cannot easily use it to click and drag something around the Stage.

If you make each piece a button, then you can place an *on(press)* function on it and issue a *startDrag* command. However, you cannot specify the button as a target of the *startDrag* command because it must be a movie clip for that. If you make it a movie clip, then you cannot have an *on(press)* function attached to it, as that is only for buttons. Instead, you must make each piece a movie clip with a button inside the movie clip. This can be a mess. Any time you want to add a new part to the movie, there are several steps to follow.

A better way to do this is to write the drag-and-drop code yourself. This will involve no code at all on the individual pieces, making them easy to create and add.

The only code needed is on a movie clip that exists only to hold this code. You can see it in the example movie as a clip beyond the upper-left corner of the movie with the text "Actions" placed in it.

This movie clip has an ActionScript attached to it that controls dragging for all the pieces. To control dragging, it needs to have several *onClipEvent* functions. Here is a run-down of what each must do:

- **load**—Set a variable to indicate that no dragging is going on yet.
- **mouseDown**—Identify which piece has been clicked and set a variable to indicate that this piece is now being dragged. Also, get the offset between the place the user clicked and the center of the piece.
- **mouseUp**—Reset the variable to indicate that no piece is being dragged.
- **enterFrame**—Change the position of the piece being dragged to correspond to the cursor position minus the offset.

Two things in the previous list might confuse nonprogrammers. The first is the recurring mention of a variable. This variable is called "dragPart" in the code and is set to 0 at the start. When it is set to 0, no dragging is taking place. However, when the user clicks a piece, "dragPart" is set to the number of that piece. When it is set to a number, dragging takes place. When the user drops that piece, the variable is set to 0 again.

The other complex feature of this code is the offset. When a user clicks a piece, he's unlikely to click the center of it. For example, the user might click the spot 10 pixels to the right and 5 pixels below the center. When the code starts repositioning the piece as the user drags, it attempts to set the position of the piece to the exact position of the cursor.

However, if the user does not click the center of the piece, the piece appears to immediately jump so that the center of the piece is directly under the cursor. But, if you subtract the 10 horizontal pixels and 5 vertical pixels from the position, then the piece does not jump at all. In fact, it appears as if the user has grabbed the piece at the exact spot that he clicked.

Now, take a look at each part of this ActionScript. First comes the *onClipEvent(load)*. This simply needs to initialize the "dragPart" variable.

```
// start with nothing dragging
onClipEvent (load) {
    dragPart = 0;
}
```

The *onClipEvent(mouseDown)* is the most complex piece of code. It loops through all 13 pieces and uses *hitTest* to determine which one the cursor is over. It then sets the "dragPart" variable as well as the "offsetx" and "offsety" variables.

Note that the movie clips that contain the pieces are named "Part1" to "Part13" to make this code simple.

```
// start drag
onClipEvent (mouseDown) {
    // get current location
    x = _root._xmouse;
    y = _root._ymouse;

    // find which, if any, part the cursor is over
    for(i=1;i<=13;i++) {
        if (_root["Part"+i].hitTest(x,y, true)) {
            // set to drag this part, remember offset
            dragPart = i;
             offsetx = _root["Part"+i]._x - x;
             offsety = _root["Part"+i]._y - y;
            break;
        }
    }
}
```

NOTE

Instead of getting the *_xmouse* and *_ymouse* properties, the preceding code uses *_root._xmouse* and *_root._ymouse* because the basic properties return the x and y position of the cursor relative to the movie clip, not the Stage. So, unless your movie clip happens to be at the exact upper-left corner, the values are not what you want. Adding *_root* before these properties forces ActionScript to give you the mouse position relative to the Stage.

When the user releases the mouse button, the "dragPart" variable is set back to 0.

```
// end drag
onClipEvent (mouseUp) {
    dragPart = 0;
}
```

The workhorse of this ActionScript is the *onClipEvent(enterFrame)* function. It tests "dragPart" to make sure it is not 0, and then resets the position of the part being dragged to the current mouse position plus the offset.

```
// if dragging, set new position
onClipEvent (enterFrame) {
    if (dragPart > 0) {
        _root["Part"+dragPart]._x = _root._xmouse + offsetx;
        _root["Part"+dragPart]._y = _root._ymouse + offsety;
    }
}
```

In the example movie, graphics, as opposed to movie clips, are used in the library. However, when each movable part is placed on the Stage, the behavior of each element is changed to "Movie Clip" and then named. Figure 7.2 shows the Property inspector with these settings. You can see that the library name is "Arm 1," but the instance name is "Part1." You can also see by the icon next to "Arm 1" that the library item is a graphic, but its behavior has been changed to that of a movie clip. With these settings, as far as the Flash movie is concerned, it is a movie clip named "Part1."

Figure 7.2

The Property inspector allows you to make Flash treat graphic elements as movie clips with names different from the names used in the library.

The layering of each element was adjusted appropriately as well. You can do this by choosing Modify, Arrange with an item selected. All the parts were made to float on top of the stationary head and body, except the legs, which attach behind them. This is the way the artist intended them to be used.

Figure 7.3 shows a sample use of this movie. A handful of items has been moved by the user from the left to the right to create one version of the fox.

Figure 7.3

The Make-A-Fox movie allows the user to drag fox parts around the screen.

Click-And-Switch Make-A-Fox

⟳ ▷⟨ Example Movie: makeafox-switch.fla

Another type of image construction program is one that keeps all the parts in the same position but allows the user to switch which graphic represents which part. This is a "Click-And-Switch" version of the previous example. No dragging is used at all, just clicks.

Project Goal

The image starts off complete, but the user can click a part and it swaps itself out with another version of that part. For instance, the user could click the eyes, and a different set of eyes would appear.

Approach

For this project to work, the movie library has to be arranged differently. Instead of individual graphics for each version of each part, there are movie clips. In each movie clip is every version of that part, one per frame. For instance, the "Eyes" movie clip has three frames, each with a different version of the eyes.

Writing the Code

Because no dragging and dropping are needed here, the script is a little simpler. It is just an *onClipEvent(mouseDown)* script placed on an "Actions" movie clip that is off the Stage. This script searches for the movie clip that was clicked in the same way that the Makeafox-drag.fla movie did, with *hitTest*.

However, rather than names such as "Part1" to "Part13" for the movie clips, names such as "Eyes" and "Head" are used. To make sure that the script checks all these movie clips, they are specified in a list and the code loops through each element in that list.

When the appropriate movie clip is found, the code advances it one frame. If this takes it beyond the number of frames available in the movie clip, it loops back to frame 1.

```
onClipEvent (mouseDown) {
    // get current location
    x = _root._xmouse;
    y = _root._ymouse;

    // see if this is over any parts
    list = ["Eyes", "Mouth", "Head", "Legs", "Left Arm", "Right Arm", "Body"];
    for(i=0;i<list.length;i++) {
        if (_root[list[i]].hitTest(x, y, true)) {
            // over a part
```

```
        with (_root[list[i]]) {
            // go to next frame or loop back to first frame
            if (_currentFrame == _totalframes) {
                gotoAndStop(1);
            } else {
                nextFrame();
            }
        }
        break;
    }
  }
}
```

NOTE

The *_currentFrame* and *_totalFrames* properties of a movie clip return the values you would expect. They are particularly useful in situations like this where there could be any number of frames in the movie clip and you want your code to handle all variations.

NOTE

The *with* action enables you to specify that you want all commands and functions inside the *with* structure to act as if they apply to a specific movie clip. This saves you from having to specify *_root[movieClip]* for each command or function.

The Makeafox-switch.fla movie on the CD-ROM shows this code in action. Figure 7.4 shows one possible outcome of the user's clicks. Note that no matter how many times and in what combination the user clicks, the fox always appears whole and intact.

Figure 7.4

The user can click any single part to change it.

Loose Ends

A few details about the Makeafox-switch.fla need attention to bring it together. First, there must be a *stop()* command in the first frame of *every* movie clip. This prevents it from just animating through all the variations when the movie is first run. There is also the matter of placing each movie clip on the Stage and naming each instance to match the items in the list in the script.

Other Possibilities

This type of program can be adapted for almost any object. For instance, you can have a car where the user can swap out tires and accessories. You can also just center in on the face to allow the player to swap eyes, noses, ears, mouths, hair, and so on. This could make a good cosmetics game.

Sketchbook

Example Movies: drawing-line.fla, drawing-fill.fla

Although the previous two examples allow for a lot of creativity, they do not enable the user to create just anything. Now, you'll see a drawing program that starts users with a blank canvas and enables them to draw anything they want.

Project Goal

The goal of this section is to create a program that enables users to draw as they would in a simple paint application. They should be able to paint lines and filled shapes. They should also be able to select from a variety of colors and print their creations.

Creating a Simple Drawing Program

Although the final movie enables the user to do a variety of things, you start out by just allowing the user to draw a continuous line.

This is done with Flash MX's new drawing commands. You can find these commands listed under Objects, Movie, Movie Clip, Drawing Methods in the ActionScript panel or the Reference panel.

The way that the drawing commands work is to simulate the movements of a person drawing with the mouse. You use *lineStyle* first to set the size and color of the line that is to be drawn. You use *moveTo* to move the invisible pointer to a location on the screen without drawing. Then you use *lineTo* to draw a line from the current location to a new one.

One element in the movie is a small off-screen movie clip named "actions." Its only purpose is to hold the movie clip script that facilitates drawing.

This script starts off by setting the "draw" variable to false. This variable is used to track whether the user is currently drawing. Then, the *lineStyle* command is used to set the size and color of the line.

NOTE

The third parameter of *lineStyle* is the opaqueness, or alpha, of the line. A value of 100 makes it opaque and a value of 50 makes it 50% transparent.

```
onClipEvent (load) {
    // drawing or not?
    draw = false;

    // 1-pixel line, black, opaque
    _root.lineStyle(1,0x000000,100);
}
```

When the user presses down on the mouse button, "draw" is set to true. Then the *moveTo* command places the invisible drawing pointer at the current location of the mouse. We need to use the *_root* values of *_xmouse* and *_ymouse* here because we want the location relative to the Stage, not relative to the "actions" movie clip.

```
onClipEvent (mouseDown) {
    // ok to draw
    draw = true;

    // move to starting location
    _root.moveTo(_root._xmouse, _root._ymouse);
}
```

When the user lifts up on the mouse button, the "draw" command is set to false. This signals that no more drawing should take place.

```
onClipEvent (mouseUp) {
    // stop drawing lines
    draw = false;
}
```

With each frame that passes, the "draw" variable is examined. If it is true, then a line is drawn from the mouse's previous location to the current location.

NOTE

The ActionScript constants *true* and *false* can be used by *if* and *for* commands to determine whether to execute code. You can also use them as values in your variables to represent on and off states.

```
onClipEvent (enterFrame) {
    if (draw) {
        _root.lineTo(_root._xmouse,_root._ymouse);
    }
}
```

NOTE

Notice that the drawing commands are all prefaced by *_root*. This makes the lines draw on the background of the root level, rather than the background of the "actions" movie clip. You could also have created a "canvas" movie clip and drawn on the background of that rather than the root level. When lines are drawn, they go on the background of the Stage or movie clip. This means that if there are other elements at that level, the lines will go behind them. So you usually want to draw in an empty level.

Figure 7.5 shows this movie after the user has clicked and dragged the mouse around a bit. Note that the drawing takes place only as fast as the frame rate of the movie, so you want to set it to a maximum of 120 frames per second to make the drawing as smooth as possible. You can see this movie on the CD-ROM as Drawing-line.fla.

Figure 7.5
The simple drawing program allows the user to draw a long black curve.

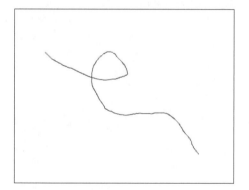

Creating a Complex Drawing Program

Although the previous program demonstrates some advanced ActionScript, it does not make a very exciting toy. Let's add the capability to change colors and fill areas. We'll also enable the user to print.

The *lineStyle* command accepts any color as its second parameter. The previous example used "0x000000" to represent black. The "0x" tells Flash that the color is a hexadecimal value like the ones that Web designers use in HTML. The other six digits represent the color.

You can also use a color value taken from a *getRGB* function. In the movie Drawing-fill.fla, I've set up several colored buttons. They are actually movie clips with a button inside each one.

Figure 7.6 shows the new movie, called Drawing-fill.fla. You can see a series of buttons on the left side of the screen that enable the user to select color.

Figure 7.6

The buttons on the left enable the user to select the color.

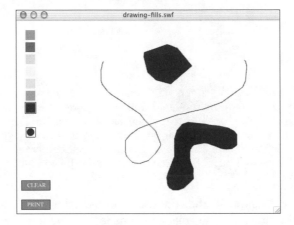

Each of the color buttons is made from a single movie clip. When the clip is placed on the Stage, the Property inspector's advanced color settings dialog is used to tint it. In addition, there is a button inside the movie clip that reacts to the user's clicks. Here is the code in that button. It takes the movie clip's color tint and stores it in the "brushColor" variable. It then sets the "lineColor" variable in the "actions" movie clip to this same value.

```
on (release) {
    // get color
    myColor = new Color(this);
    brushColor = myColor.getRGB();

    // set drawing color at root level
    _root.actions.lineColor = brushColor;

    // set the selection box
    _root["Color Selection"]._x = this._x;
    _root["Color Selection"]._y = this._y;
}
```

The button script also sets the "Color Selection" movie clip, a simple square box, to the location of the clip that was clicked. This causes the color button to be outlined the same way that the black color button is in Figure 7.6 (shown previously).

The little button with the circle in it that is under the color buttons allows users to decide whether they are creating filled shapes. This movie clip has two frames: one showing an empty circle and one showing a filled one. A button in the movie clip contains the following script that allows users to toggle between the two states. It also sets the variable "fill" in the "actions" movie clip.

```
on (release) {
    if (_currentFrame == 1) {
        gotoAndStop(2);
        _root.actions.fill = true;
    } else {
        gotoAndStop(1);
        _root.actions.fill = false;
    }
}
```

With the color buttons allowing the user to change the "lineColor" variable of "actions" and the fill button allowing the user to change the "fill" variable of "actions," the user can draw colored and filled shapes. The "actions" movie clip, as in the previous example, contains all the drawing code.

It starts by setting "draw" to false, "fill" to false, and "lineColor" to black. It also sets four variables that describe the limit of the drawing area. The user will not be allowed to draw outside this area.

```
onClipEvent (load) {
    // drawing or not?
    draw = false;

    // start not filling
    fill = false;

    // black is initial color
    lineColor = 0x000000;

    // set limits
    xmax = 550;
    xmin = 70;
    ymax = 400;
    ymin = 0;
}
```

When the user presses the mouse button, drawing begins. The mouse location is stored in "x" and "y." These values are checked against the limits of the drawing area, and drawing is started only if "x" and "y" are inside those limits.

The *lineStyle* command sets the color of the line to the current "lineColor." In addition, if "fill" is true, then a new array is initialized. This array holds the locations of all the points along the curve that the user is drawing. It starts by adding the location of the first point as a small variable object of the form {x: value, y: value}. You'll be using this array to create the filled area when the drawing is complete.

```
onClipEvent (mouseDown) {
    // move to starting location
    x = _root._xmouse;
    y = _root._ymouse;

    // start only if within limits
    if ((x>xmin) and (x<xmax) and (y>ymin) and (y<ymax)) {
        draw = true;

        // set up line and move to start
        _root.lineStyle(1,lineColor,100);
        _root.moveTo(x,y);

        // if filling, start off array
        if (fill) {
            fillArray = new Array();
            fillArray.push({x:x, y:y});
        }
    }
}
```

After "draw" is true, then drawing continues until the mouse is released. The new location of the mouse is placed in "x" and "y" of each frame. These values are tested against the limits of the drawing area and moved back into range if they are beyond those limits. Then the *lineTo* command is used to draw the current line segment. If "fill" is true, then a new item is added to the "fillArray."

```
onClipEvent (enterFrame) {
    if (draw) {
        // get current position
        x = _root._xmouse;
        y = _root._ymouse;

        // limit drawing area
        if (x < xmin) x = xmin;
        if (x > xmax) x = xmax;
        if (y < ymin) y = ymin;
        if (y > ymax) y = ymax;

        // draw line
        _root.lineTo(x,y);
```

```
          // if filling, remember point
          if (fill) {
              fillArray.push({x:x, y:y});
          }
      }
  }
```

When the user releases the mouse button, "draw" is set to false to end drawing. If the "fill" variable is true, then the "fillArray" is looped through and the entire shape is redrawn. The difference this time is that the *beginFill* and *endFill* commands surround the drawing. This results in Flash filling the shape with the "lineColor."

WARNING

Another way you might think to do this is to issue a *beginFill* before users start drawing and an *endFill* when they are finished, rather than re-creating each entire drawing a second time. But Flash doesn't like using fills from frame to frame. It terminates each fill with each frame, resulting in a mess. So if you record the steps in the drawing and re-create it within one handler, you can get a nice clean fill.

```
onClipEvent (mouseUp) {
    if (draw) {
        // stop drawing lines
        draw = false;

        // if fill, then redraw
        if (fill) {
            // start at first point
            _root.moveTo(fillArray[0].x,fillArray[0].y);

            // loop through points with fill turned on
            _root.beginFill(lineColor);
            for(var i=1;i<fillArray.length;i++) {
                _root.lineTo(fillArray[i].x,fillArray[i].y);
            }
            _root.endFill();
        }
    }
}
```

Adding Clear and Print Buttons

Clearing the drawing area is just a matter of drawing a filled box over the entire drawing area. This is done with the button script on the Clear button. This script sets the *lineStyle* to a line of size 0. It moves to the upper left corner of the drawing area, getting the limits of the drawing area from the variables in the "actions" movie clip. It then turns on fill and draws a box around the drawing area. The fill color is set to white so that anything in the area is overdrawn with white.

```
on (release) {
    // no line
    _root.lineStyle(0,0xFFFFFF,100);

    // move to upper left corner
    _root.moveTo(actions.xmin,actions.ymin);

    // make filled box with corners
    _root.beginFill(0xFFFFFF);
    _root.lineTo(actions.xmax,actions.ymin);
    _root.lineTo(actions.xmax,actions.ymax);
    _root.lineTo(actions.xmin,actions.ymax);
    _root.lineTo(actions.xmin,actions.ymin);
    _root.endFill();
}
```

The printing button is even easier. All you need to do is issue a *print* command. In addition, you need to assign the label "#p" to the only frame of the movie.

```
on (release) {
    // send a simple print instruction
    print(_root,"bframe");
}
```

NOTE

The *print* command sends the movie clip you specify to the user's operating system to be printed. You can specify *_root* to print the entire Stage. The second parameter defines the bounding box for the print area. See the manuals for more details on this.

Figure 7.7 shows the movie in use.

Loose Ends

Remember to place a *stop()* command on the first frame of the fill button movie clip. Otherwise, that movie clip will animate between frames 1 and 2. You can alter the colors of the color buttons by using the Property inspector and selecting tint from the color drop-down menu. You can use any color you like. You can also create many more buttons to provide more colors to the user.

Figure 7.7
The sketch program is shown after an artist has used it.

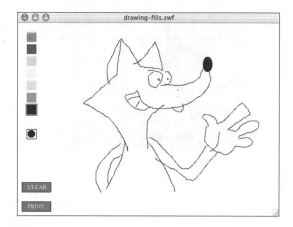

Other Possibilities

You could continue to expand this program, adding line sizes as well as colors. You could have buttons that set a "lineSize" variable in the "actions" movie clip. Then that movie clip could use that variable in a *lineStyle* command. You could also create an eraser by using a large line size and a white color.

> **NOTE**
>
> In the previous edition of this book, I used a completely different method to facilitate drawing. Instead of the drawing commands, which did not exist in Flash 5, I used a movie clip consisting of a hairline-thick line. This movie clip was duplicated over and over as the user moved the mouse. I then used circle and square movie clips to allow the user to create those shapes. If you are interested in this method, I have included these older files on the CD-ROM in a folder named `drawing alternatives`.

Music Mixer

Example Movie: musicmixer.fla

Graphics are not the only things that can be constructed with Flash. You can also play several sounds together to create a mix of music. You can allow users to choose which pieces of music they want to play and when.

Project Goal

This project creates a toy that enables users to mix various drum loops, bass loops, and single-instance sounds to create their own songs. The toy should make it easy to swap sound samples in and out of the program. It should also provide some feedback to the user about which samples are playing. Figure 7.8 shows what this application might look like.

Figure 7.8
This music mixer is made up of six drum loops, six bass loops, and six instance sounds.

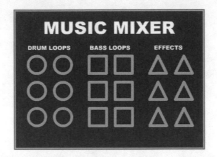

Approach

You will use six drum loops, six bass loops, and six single-instance sounds. Only one drum loop should be playing at a time, so when the user selects a second drum loop, it needs to turn off the first. Multiple bass loops can be played at the same time. Single-instance sounds do not loop, but simply play once when selected.

There are three different sets of switches. The first set represents the drum loops. Turn one on, and any one previously on automatically turns off. The second set represents bass loops; you can turn one, several, or all of them on at the same time. Pressing a button that represents a drum or bass loop when it is already on turns it off.

Buttons in the third set play single-instance sounds. They turn on for only a short period of time, while the sound plays. Whereas the drum and bass loops loop forever, single-instance sounds play only once per button press.

Preparing the Movie

The main element here is the 18 sounds needed. The example movie on the CD-ROM, Musicmixer.fla, used sounds created by a professional composer. You need to compose sounds for your project yourself, find a friend or co-worker to help, or license some music from elsewhere.

The drum and bass loops are short sounds that create perfect loops. They should be short enough that the file size does not become huge, but long enough so that the loop produces interesting sounds.

After you import all 18 sounds into Flash, you must set their Symbol Linkage Properties to Export This Symbol, and the identifier to something the code will understand. Figure 7.9 shows this dialog box.

Three different types of buttons need to be created. These are actually not buttons, but movie clips. So to avoid confusion, this book calls them "switches." Inside the movie clips are invisible buttons that react to mouse clicks. The movie clips themselves have at least two frames. The first represents the "off" state of the switch, whereas the rest of the frames are an animation representing the "on" state. Because the drum and bass sounds are loops, the animation loops in those two switches, although it plays once and then goes back to the "off" state in the instance sound switch. Check out the Musicmixer.fla movie on the CD-ROM to see what the animation sequences consist of.

Figure 7.9

The Symbol Linkage Properties of this sound have been set so the sound will be included with the Flash movie.

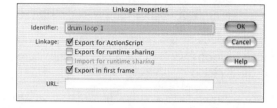

The buttons in the movie clips are just plain white shapes that are placed behind the other graphics in the movie clip so they are not visible. For the example movie, a small circular button was placed in the drum and bass switches, and a triangular one is used by the instance switches. Only two different types were used so they would be easier to hide behind the shape of the graphics for each one. Six copies of each of the switches are placed on the Stage. The arrangement can be anything you want. The arrangement was kept simple in the example movie, as you can see if you refer to Figure 7.8.

Writing the Code

All the code is attached to the buttons inside the switches. The first frame of every switch contains code to start the sound. In addition, this code advances the movie clip to the next frame. The button also appears in the rest of the frames of the movie clip. For the drum and bass loops, different scripts stop the sound.

The simplest ActionScript is the one in the instance sound switches. All these scripts need to do is start a sound playing and go to the next frame.

```
on (press) {
    // play the sound that matches
    // the name of this movie clip
    instanceSound = new Sound();
    instanceSound.attachSound(this._name);
    instanceSound.start();

    // start this movie clip animating
    gotoAndPlay(2);
}
```

Notice that the name of the sound is specified as *this._name*. This uses the name of the movie clip as the name of the sound. So if the movie clip is "instance 1," it attempts to play the sound "instance 1." The first "instance 1" is the name of a movie clip instance on the Stage; the second "instance 1" is the name of a linked sound in the library. This works as long as you take special care to make sure these names match exactly.

The advantage of doing it this way is that you can use the same movie clip many times on the Stage, with each one playing a different sound. The sound name is taken from the movie clip instance name, not from a hard-coded string inside the ActionScript.

When the movie clip advances to the next frame, an animation begins. At the end of the animation, the movie clip loops back to the first frame, where a *stop()* command prevents it from continuing to loop.

For the single-instance sounds, the same button appears across all frames, so the user can trigger another sound even if the animation is currently playing.

The bass loop switch movie clips are almost the same as the single-instance sounds. The main difference is that the sound must loop. Make this happen by adding two extra parameters to the *start* command. The first is the sound offset and the second is the number of loops. Because you don't want a sound offset, leave that at 0. But you do want the sound to loop, so set that to a very high number.

```
on (press) {
    // play the sound that matches
    // the name of this movie clip
    bassloop = new Sound();
    bassloop.attachSound(this._name);
    bassloop.start(0,9999);

    // start this movie clip animating
    gotoAndPlay(2);
}
```

The other difference between the single-instance sounds and the bass loops is that you can turn a bass loop off. To do this, you need a different ActionScript on the button inside the bass loop switch for frame 2 forward. This turns off the sound and sends the movie clip back to frame 1.

```
on (press) {
    // stop the sound with the
    // same name as this movie clip
    bassloop = new Sound();
    bassloop.stop(this._name);

    // turn this animation off
    gotoAndStop(1);
}
```

The button scripts for the drum loop are just a bit more complex. When you turn a drum loop on, it must make sure that all the other drum loops are off. To do this, it loops from "drum loop 1" to "drum loop 6" and turns each sound off. It also sets each switch movie clip back to frame 1. After that, it starts the new drum loop sound.

```
on (press) {
    // stop any other drum sound
    // and set any other drum switch to off
    drumloop = new Sound();
    for(i=1;i<=6;i++) {
        _root["drum loop "+i].gotoAndStop(1);
        drumloop.stop("drum loop "+i);
    }

    // play the sound that matches
    // the name of this movie clip
    drumloop.attachSound(this._name);
    drumloop.start(0,9999);

    // start this movie clip animating
    gotoAndPlay(2);
}
```

The other button code for a drum loop is the same as it was for a bass loop. It just turns off the sound and sends the movie clip back to frame 1.

```
on (press) {
    // stop the sound with the
    // same name as this movie clip
    drumloop = new Sound();
    drumloop.stop(this._name);

    // stop this animation
    gotoAndStop(1);
}
```

Loose Ends

Remember to name each of the 18 buttons something different and match the name to that of a linked sound in the library. Even if the sound is named in the library, you also have to have it in the Symbol Linkage Properties dialog box (refer to Figure 7.9).

The animations for each button type are up to you. In the example movie, I simply flash from white to black for the drum loops, use an expanding circle for the bass loops, and use three expanding lines for the single-instance sounds. The drum and bass loops need to have a *gotoAndPlay(2)* command in the last frame so that they will loop. The single-instance sounds can just be left to finish and return to frame 1. All these movie clips need to have a *stop()* command on frame 1 so they don't start animating when the movie is first loaded.

Other Possibilities

Swapping out the sounds in the example for your own is an easy modification, as long as you have sounds. Just delete the old sounds from the library and import your own. Remember to set the Symbol Linkage Properties.

You can also have more or fewer sounds. You might want to have fewer drum loops, but more single-instance sounds. As long as the instance names of the movie clips match the link names of the sounds in the library, you can have as few or as many sounds as you want.

The animation inside each switch can also be varied. If you have a lot of time to animate, you might want to abandon the idea of reusable movie clips and have a different clip for each switch. This will make it harder to modify the movie in the future, but will allow you to have an individual animation for each switch.

Dancing Fox

Example Movie: Dance.fla

So far you have seen how the user can create images and sound sequences. How about an animation sequence? This example is a movie where the user can make the fox dance. During a recording session, the user can select, in real-time, the dance moves that the fox makes. While this is happening, the time of each move is recorded. Then, the user can play back the dance sequence that he or she just created.

Figure 7.10 shows the example movie Dance.fla. The fox is in the middle of one of his moves.

Figure 7.10
Go Flashy, go!

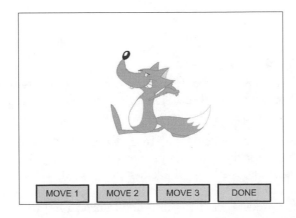

Project Goal

This program has two modes: record and playback. Users first use the record mode to control the fox in real-time. They can trigger one of three different dance moves. In between these moves, the fox returns to a base dance move.

When the user is finished recording, he or she can press the Done button to stop and return to the main menu. Another button triggers the playback mode. This re-creates the recorded sequence exactly.

Approach

At the heart of this movie is a "dance" movie clip. This contains all the fox's dancing sequences. You can control the fox by simply jumping to a named frame that represents the start of a sequence.

The recording is done by first noting the time that the recording session started. Then, when the user presses a button, the current time is recorded, along with the name of the move. This information is put into an array of objects of the format {time: value, move: value}.

The playback mode also starts by noting the current time. Then it constantly checks to see when it is time to tell the fox to do the first dance move, as indicated by the time of the first element in the array. When that time is reached, it starts looking for the second move's time, and so on.

A special dance move named "stop" is used to indicate the time at which the recording session ended. When the playback session gets to the "stop" command, it returns the movie to the main menu.

Preparing the Movie

The trick to this movie is getting the "dance" movie clip right. In the example movie, this is a sequence of 20 frames broken up into four 5-frame parts. Each part starts with a labeled frame such as "dance0." The last frame in each sequence is blank, but with a *gotoAndPlay("dance0")* command in it. Therefore, when each sequence is finished the fox returns to repeating the "dance0" sequence. The other three frame labels are "dance1," "dance2," and "dance3."

TIP

You'll notice that the last frame of each dance move sequence is totally blank except for the script. When you execute a *gotoAndPlay* command on a frame, that frame is never displayed. The command is obeyed immediately and the movie clip jumps to the new frame before it has a chance to display the current one.

At the root level of the movie, there need to be three frames. The first is the "menu" frame, which has a *stop()* command on it. The second is the "record" frame, and the third is the "playback" frame. The following section looks at the code for these three frames.

The "menu" frame has two buttons: Record and Playback. I've used the same button symbol throughout the example movie, but with a different piece of text on top of it. Each of these two buttons jumps to the appropriate frame.

The "record" frame has four buttons on it. The first three trigger one of the three dance moves. The fourth button stops the recording.

The "playback" frame has only one button. This button prematurely stops the playback of the dance sequence.

Writing the Code

All the recording code is on the "record" frame. It starts by initializing the array and getting the starting time.

```
// init array
danceArray = new Array();

// get starting time
startTime = getTimer();
```

The "danceButton" function is called by one of the three dance buttons at the bottom of the screen. It notes the time and the name of the dance move and adds it to the array. It also commands the movie clip instance, named "fox," to perform this move.

```
// user presses dance move button
function danceButton(moveName) {
    // calculate this time
    thisTime = getTimer() - startTime;

    // add time and move to array
    danceArray.push({time: thisTime, move: moveName});

    // show move
    fox.gotoAndPlay(moveName);
}
```

When the user presses the Done button, the "stop" move is recorded in the array and the movie returns to the "menu" frame.

```
// use presses stop button
function stopRecord() {
    // calculate this time
    thisTime = getTimer() - startTime;
```

```
    // add time and stop command to array
    danceArray.push({time: thisTime, move: "stop"});

    // return to main menu
    gotoAndStop("menu");
}
```

Most of the code for the "playback" frame is also in the main timeline. It starts by noting the start time and setting the variable "danceStep" to 0. This variable contains the number of the next dance move expected.

```
// get starting time
startTime = getTimer();

// start with step 0
danceStep = 0;
```

For each frame that passes, an "actions" movie clip that is off-screen calls "danceFrame" to check the status of the dance moves. This function calculates the current time and compares that to the time of the next dance move in the array.

If it is time for the next move, it first checks to see whether that movie is the "stop" command. If it is, then the sequence is over. Otherwise, the "fox" movie clip jumps to the correct frame and the "danceStep" variable is advanced.

```
// run every frame from "actions" mc
function danceFrame() {
    // calculate current time
    thisTime = getTimer() - startTime;

    // see if it is time for next move
    if (thisTime >= danceArray[danceStep].time) {

        // get move
        move = danceArray[danceStep].move;

        // if move is "stop" then return to menu
        if (move == "stop") {
            gotoAndStop("menu");

        } else {
            // otherwise, show move
            fox.gotoAndPlay(move);

            // advance to look for next step
            danceStep++;
        }
    }
}
```

Loose Ends

The three dance buttons on the "record" frame need scripts on them to call the "danceButton" function. Here is the first one:

```
on (press) {
    danceButton("dance1");
}
```

The Done button needs a similar script to call the "stopRecord" function.

```
on (press) {
    stopRecord();
}
```

The "actions" movie clip in the "playback" frame needs a small script that calls the "danceFrame" function each and every frame.

```
onClipEvent(enterFrame) {
    _root.danceFrame();
}
```

You also need simple *gotoAndStop* button scripts on the two menu buttons. That first frame should also have a *stop()* command on it to prevent the movie from animating when it runs.

Other Possibilities

In the example movie, when the fox does a dance move he does it once and then returns to "dance0." You could also have him repeat this move in an endless loop until another move is indicated. Just have each move sequence loop back to its own label rather than "dance0" each time. If you do that, you will probably also want to have a button on the "record" frame that allows users to indicate that they want to return to the "dance0" move.

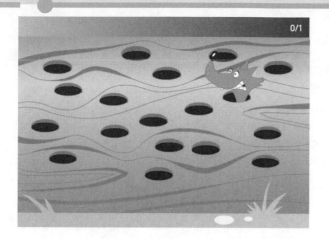

Hunt and Click Games

- Find-A-Fox
- Whack-A-Fox
- Shoot-A-Fox
- Hunt-A-Fox

Perhaps the simplest and most common game on the Web is the type in which a player is expected to click a target and score points. This type of game varies in difficulty depending upon how the target moves, if at all.

In this chapter, you will look at four major variations of the hunt-and-click game. The first is a game in which the targets don't move but are instead hidden in a complex picture. This is a little like the popular series of books *Where's Waldo?* Images of the fox are hidden in a drawing of trees and such.

In the second game, the foxes are not always on the screen. Instead they appear and disappear at random times. This is similar to the Whack-A-Mole game.

In the third game of this series, the foxes run, jump, duck, and hide in complex animations. Players must try much harder to hit the foxes. A game like this is usually called a shooting gallery.

The fourth game goes beyond the limits of the Flash stage and allows the user to scroll left or right in a panoramic view. You have to click on the foxes that appear momentarily behind trees and bushes.

The first three games are similar because the player's main action is to click a target. The only difference is how the target moves, if at all. However, this minor difference is enough to create games that seem to be completely different to the player. The fourth game is different in that the view can be changed. The panoramic scrolling technique in that game can be used for a variety of other purposes.

We'll start with the simplest game, which I've called Find-A-Fox.

Find-A-Fox

⟩⟨Example file: Findafox.fla

The Find-A-Fox game presents an image to the player and asks him to locate certain objects in it. In the case of the example movie, Findafox.fla, the scene is a forest and the objects the player is looking for are foxes.

This sounds like an easy game, but the idea is that the objects are supposed to be cleverly disguised and hidden. Figure 8.1 shows the example movie with seven foxes hidden in the forest.

Project Goal

When the player finds a fox in the picture, she should click it to select the fox. When this happens, there should be some feedback to let the player know that she's guessed right. There also needs to be a way to let the player know which foxes have been found.

Figure 8.1
*The forest scene
includes seven hid-
den foxes for the
player to find.*

When all seven foxes have been discovered, the game should automatically go to a new screen. This means that the program needs to keep track of what has been found and what has not.

Approach

It might seem that this game would be ridiculously simple to create. In fact, it would be nothing more than a few buttons if it weren't for two factors: You want feedback concerning which objects have been found, and you want the game to recognize when all the objects have been found.

The feedback feature can be accomplished by applying a color transformation to the object movie clips. If done with the correct color, the hidden foxes will stand out.

To determine whether all the foxes have been found, we use an array of true and false values. The array starts with seven false values, and each one changes to true as the player finds the foxes. When all seven values in the array are true, it means that the player has found all the foxes.

Instead of using buttons, we use movie clips plus an ActionScript control clip that looks for mouse clicks. When a mouse click is detected, the code loops through all the movie clips using *hitTest* to determine which one was clicked. This is similar to how the Make-A-Fox game in Chapter 7, "Construction Toys," determines which movie clip was clicked.

Preparing the Movie

Most of the effort to make this game actually involves drawing the background scene. In the example movie on the CD-ROM, nine layers of graphics make up the ground, trees, and other forest elements. Some of the graphics are on different layers to allow the foxes to be partially hidden behind trees and such.

Two movie clips are foxes. One uses thin lines so the fox can be hidden in tree bark. The other is a solid-shaped fox that can appear in the background. You can see these two movie clips in Figure 8.2. Each of these two clips are placed several times onto the Stage. They are in one of four different layers, positioned so they are behind some layers and in front of others.

Figure 8.2

Here are two movie clips used to hide foxes among the trees. The appropriate one is used depending on the background behind the fox.

In addition to the main frame where the game is played, we'll fill out this game with a start screen and an end screen. Both of these have a button to allow the player to start the game.

The code is all attached to a movie clip that is just off the Stage. This code assumes that the fox movie clips are named "fox0" to "fox6."

Writing the Code

When the movie clip loads, all the movie clip needs to do to start is set up the "found" array. The code fills the array with seven *false* values:

```
onClipEvent (load) {
    // create array to keep track of
    // which ones found
    found = [];
    for (i=0; i<7; i++) {
        found[i] = false;
    }
}
```

When the player clicks, the location is recorded in the variables "x" and "y." Then *hitTest* is used to check these values against the fox movie clips. When a match is found, the color of the movie clip is transformed to a red tint. This is enough to make the hidden foxes stand out from the background.

After every click, the "found" array is searched for a *false* value. This would indicate that there is at least one fox not yet found. However, if all the foxes have been found, then the movie is sent to another frame:

```
onClipEvent (mouseDown) {
    // record location of click
    x = _root._xmouse;
    y = _root._ymouse;

    // loop through all foxes to see if any hit
    for (i=0; i<7; i++) {
        if (_root["fox"+i].hitTest(x, y, false)) {
            // change color of fox
            myColor = new Color(_root["fox"+i]);
            myColor.setTransform({rb:128, bb:0, gb:0});
            // record that this one was found
            found[i] = true;
            break;
        }
    }

    // see if all foxes found
    gameover = true;
    for (i=0; i<7; i++) {
        if (found[i] == false) {
            // this fox not found, game not over
            gameover = false;
        }
    }

    // go to end frame if all foxes found
    if (gameover) {
        _root.gotoAndPlay("Game Over");
    }
}
```

NOTE

The *break* command can be used inside *for* loops and other types of loops to tell the code to break off the loop instantly. This comes in handy when there is more than one reason why the loop might end. In the previous code, the loop goes from 0 to 6, but it could also end if the *hitTest* returns *true*.

Loose Ends

The only other pieces of code in the game are the two "Play" buttons, one on the start screen and one on the end screen. In addition, there is a *stop()* command on all the frames so that the movie does not advance to the next frame.

The choice of the color transformation for the found foxes depends on your background. In this example, the background has a lot of greens, browns, and blues. I chose a medium red ({rb:128, bb:0, gb:0}) for the found foxes to contrast these colors.

Other Possibilities

The example described here is nothing more than a game for young children. However, the concept can be used for more sophisticated games.

For older children, you could have a math game in which they have to find certain types of numbers or words. For instance, they could have to pick the verbs out of an assortment of verbs, nouns, and adjectives. You could also do a geography quiz in which the player has to pick out certain countries or locations.

Whack-A-Fox

Example file: Whackafox.fla

One of the oldest arcade games is called Whack-A-Mole. This is a physical game, not a computerized one. There are holes in a platform through which appear little mole-like objects. You use a soft mallet, usually tied to the machine, to hit the moles. They appear in a random order at random times, so you have to be quick to hit them.

Whack-A-Mole games also appear in many forms on computers. They are very popular on the Web. Although they rarely look like a Whack-A-Mole game, the functionality is the same: Objects appear at random times and at random places and the player has to click them before they disappear.

In this example, found on the CD-ROM as Whackafox.fla, you'll look at a more traditional implementation of this game. Figure 8.3 shows the play area: a log with 18 holes. At different times, a fox pops up out of one of those holes and remains there for a second or so. Clicking the fox results in a "hit" animation and the player scores points.

Figure 8.3
The Whack-A-Fox game features a log with 18 holes. The fox could pop out from any one of them.

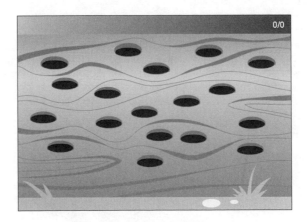

Project Goal

The game requires that the objects appear at random times and places. There are 18 holes through which a fox can pop out. After the fox appears, it quickly disappears again. This is an animation, part of which can be seen in Figure 8.4. However, while the fox is visible, the player can click it to "hit" it and score points.

Figure 8.4
One of the foxes has come out of a hole.

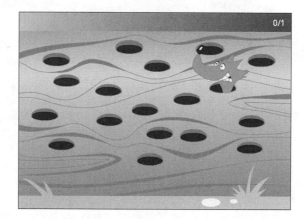

The game should run for a limited amount of time and keep track of how many objects the player has hit.

Approach

Each hole in the log is the instance of a movie clip. This clip can be just a hole at times, and can also show an animation of the fox popping up out of the hole.

Another movie clip, called "actions," signals the hole movie clips when it is their turn to act at regular time intervals. At first, the foxes pop up every 2 seconds. With each appearance, the time until the next fox appears decreases slightly.

When the player clicks the screen, the "actions" movie clip determines which fox was clicked. That movie clip is told to play another animation that shows the fox a bit dazed.

Every time a fox appears, a counter increases by one. Every time a player hits a fox, another counter increases by one. The score is then displayed as the number hit, then a "/", and then the number that have appeared. In other words, "5/12" means that the player has hit 5 out of 12 foxes.

Preparing the Movie

The 18 holes in the log are actually instances of a movie clip. The movie clip features a frame 1 that is just a hole. Later in that movie clip's timeline is an animation sequence that adds the fox popping out of the hole, hesitating, and then going back in. There is another sequence in the movie clip that shows the fox getting hit and then seeing stars. We'll use this one when the player gets the fox. You can see a part of it in Figure 8.5.

Figure 8.5
This fox has just been hit.

The 18 movie clip instances are named "fox 0" to "fox 17" so the code can identify them. There also needs to be a text area set to "Dynamic Text" and named "showScore." Figure 8.6 shows the Property inspector for this text area.

Figure 8.6
The Property inspector shows a text area set to be linked to the ActionScript variable "showScore."

Writing the Code

All the code for this game lies in the script attached to the "actions" movie clip that sits just off the Stage. It begins by initializing all the global variables. The time for the appearance of the first fox is set for 2 seconds, or 2000 milliseconds, from the start of the movie.

```
onClipEvent (load) {
    // how much time between fox appearances
    timeBetweenFoxes = 2000;

    // calculate time until next fox
    nextFox = getTimer() + timeBetweenFoxes;

    // init scores
    score = 0;
    numFoxes = 0;
}
```

NOTE

The *getTimer()* function returns the number of milliseconds since the Flash movie began. This clock constantly counts upward, so this is a good function to use to add time intervals to your games.

The task of the *onClipEvent(enterFrame)* function is to determine whether it's time for a new fox to appear. If so, a new hole is picked that is not already in use. The time gap between fox appearances is shortened by 10 milliseconds, causing the game to get faster and faster as time goes on. If the gap is less than 1,000 milliseconds, the game ends. This gives the player 100 opportunities to hit a fox, spread out over 150 seconds.

```
onClipEvent (enterFrame) {
    // see if it is time for the next fox
    if (getTimer() >= nextFox) {

        // shorter wait next time
        timeBetweenFoxes -= 10;

        // see if the game is over
        if (timeBetweenFoxes < 1000) {
            _root.gotoAndPlay("End");

        // new fox
        } else {

            // increase count and update score
            numFoxes++;
            _root.showScore = score + "/" + numFoxes;

            // loop until a fox is found that is
            // not in use
            while (true) {
                fox = Int(Math.Random()*18);
                if (_root["fox "+fox]._currentFrame == 1) break;
            }

            // tell fox to pop up
            _root["fox "+fox].gotoAndPlay("popup");

            // set time for next fox to appear
            nextFox = getTimer() + timeBetweenFoxes;
        }
    }
}
```

The next function handles the player's clicks. It uses the same technique as the Find-A-Fox game by looping through all the movie clips and using *hitTest* to determine the correct one.

The function also has to make sure that the fox is animating through the pop-up sequence at the time of the click. Frame 1 of the movie clip is the static frame of just a hole. Frames 2 through 24 are the animation of the fox getting hit. Frames 25 and on are the pop-up animation, which is the only time that the player should be able to click the fox. Therefore, if the frame number is more than 24, the click is allowed. Otherwise, it is ignored.

```
onClipEvent (mouseDown) {
    // get the location of the click
    x = _root._xmouse;
    y = _root._ymouse;

    // loop through all 18 foxes to see which was clicked
    for (i=0;i<18;i++) {

        // look only at clips that are doing the
        // pop up animation
        if (_root["fox "+i]._currentFrame > 24) {

            // see whether this was the one clicked
            if (_root["fox "+i].hitTest(x,y,false)) {

                // have the clip play the "whack" animation
                _root["fox "+i].gotoAndPlay("whack");

                // increase score and show it
                score++;
                _root.showScore = score + "/" + numFoxes;
            }
        }
    }
}
```

Loose Ends

As usual, you need a few extra scripts here and there. Small *stop()* commands need to be placed on the main game frame, as well as a start frame and end frame. In the example movie, these are in three different scenes.

Other Possibilities

Note that all the movie clip instances in this game do not have to use the same movie clip. The script only cares if there are "whack" and "popup" labels and that the pop-up animation starts after frame 24. You could conceivably make several different movie clips to use, each with a slightly different fox. Just make sure they are similar enough for the code to handle and that the movie clip instances are named properly when you place them on the Stage. This would add some variety to the game.

The end of the game can be determined in many different ways. The example movie waits until the time delay between foxes is less than a second. This corresponds to 100 foxes. You could, instead, use a fixed number of clicks by the player to determine the end of a game. You could also have levels. The player might need to get a certain number of hits in a level to be allowed to advance to the next.

Shoot-A-Fox

Example file: Shootafox.fla

Next comes the ultimate hunt-and-click game: the shooting gallery. Like the first game in this chapter, Find-A-Fox, the goal is to click objects on the screen. Like the second game, Whack-A-Fox, the objects appear on the screen at random times and places.

However, in this game the objects move. Rather than merely popping up out of a hole, the fox runs, swings, or peeks out from behind a tree. The player must have quick reflexes to catch a fox before he disappears again.

Figure 8.7 shows the scene, which is much like the scene for Find-A-Fox. However, this time the fox isn't standing still waiting for the player to discover him. The figure shows an animation in which the fox is dashing from side to side.

Figure 8.7

In the Shoot-A-Fox game, the fox moves around the screen, which makes him harder to hit.

Project Goal

This project builds on the Whack-A-Fox game. It features foxes that run through a whole animation sequence that could take them from one part of the screen to another. One animation shows the fox running from place to place, one shows him swinging from a tree, and one shows him peeking out from behind a tree. Each animation is used two or three times, for a total of seven possible sequences that can occur during the game.

Every two seconds or less, one of these animation sequences is triggered and the player has a chance to click and hit the fox. The animation sequence should continue, but there should be some indication of a hit, if there is one.

The game should keep track of how many shots were fired and how many hits there were, and then limit the player to a certain number of shots. The cursor should look like a gun crosshair rather than just a plain arrow cursor.

Approach

To create this game, I started with Whack-A-Fox, so a lot of this code should look familiar. However, there are some major improvements and feature additions.

The first change is the way that the movie clips are arranged. They need to animate to show movement, and also change to show that the fox has been hit. This calls for a movie clip inside a movie clip. The inner clip can be switched between not-hit and hit states. The outer clip dictates the fox's movement.

This game keeps track of both the shots taken and the hits. Both of these numbers are displayed on the screen for the player to see. When the player has used up all his shots, the game ends.

Another improvement in this game is the use of a custom cursor. We actually hide the computer's cursor when it is over the game, and replace it with a movie clip that floats above the scene. You can see this cursor as the crosshairs at the bottom of Figure 8.7.

Preparing the Movie

The trickiest part of creating this game is making the movie clips. Unfortunately, this is also difficult to explain here. I strongly recommend taking a look at the example movie, Shootafox.fla on the CD-ROM now.

In the library, you can see three movie clips: "Peeking Fox," "Running Fox," and "Swinging Fox." Each of these features either a single frame or short animation of the fox, followed by a short animation that has the fox looking surprised and outlined in yellow. The first part is for the normal animations, whereas the second part shows that the player has hit the fox. The second part starts with the frame label "hit."

There are also seven movie clips labeled "fox0" to "fox6." These clips contain one of the previous three movie clips, but are animated so that they move across the screen or peek out from behind a tree. The inner clips in each of these movie clips are all labeled "fox" so the code can address them. When the code needs to show that a fox has been hit, it tells the movie clip instance "fox" inside the movie clip instances "fox0" to "fox6" to go to frame "hit."

The layers in this movie play a big part. There are 15 layers that represent either scenery or foxes. This allows the foxes to appear behind some items and in front of others. There is also a layer for the "actions" movie clip and the "cursor" movie clip.

The cursor is a movie clip of some crosshairs. Beyond frame 1 is a short animation of a blast that plays whenever the player takes a shot. The movie clip loops back to frame 1, which has a *stop()* command.

Like the other two movies in this chapter, this one has a "start" scene, a "play" scene, and an "end" scene.

Writing the Code

The "actions" movie clip contains most of the code, as it did in the previous example. It starts with the *onClipEvent(load)* function. In addition to setting the score to 0, it also sets the "shotsLeft" to 50, giving the player 50 shots to hit as many foxes as he can. In addition to "showScore" being used to relay the score to the screen, a variable called "showShotsLeft" links to a text area to show the player how many shots remain.

The *onClipEvent(load)* code also hides the mouse with the *Mouse.hide()* command.

NOTE

The *Mouse* object allows you to control the visibility of the cursor while it is over the Flash movie Stage. You can use *Mouse.hide()* to make the cursor invisible, and *Mouse.show()* to make it visible again.

```
onClipEvent (load) {
    // how much time between fox appearances
    timeBetweenFoxes = 2000;

    // calculate time until next fox
    nextFox = getTimer()+timeBetweenFoxes;

    // init scores
    score = 0;
    shotsLeft = 50;
    _root.showScore = "Score:"+score;
    _root.showShotsLeft = "Shots Left:"+shotsLeft;

    // hide cursor
    Mouse.hide();
}
```

Because the real cursor is hidden, you need to replace it with something to indicate to the player where she is clicking. In this case, a movie clip called "cursor" is set to the mouse location.

In addition to this, the *onClipEvent(enterFrame)* function is the same as in the Whack-A-Fox game.

```
onClipEvent (enterFrame) {
    // set the cursor
    _root["cursor"]._x = _root._xmouse;
    _root["cursor"]._y = _root._ymouse;

    // see whether it is time for the next fox
    if (getTimer()>=nextFox) {

        // shorter wait next time
        timeBetweenFoxes -= 5;

        // see whether the game is over
        if (shotsLeft < 1) {
            _root.gotoAndPlay("End");

        // new fox
        } else {

            // loop until a fox is found that is
            // not in use
            while (true) {
                fox = int(Math.Random()*7);
                if (_root["fox"+fox]._currentFrame == 1) {
                    break;
                }
            }

            // tell fox to move
            _root["fox"+fox].gotoAndPlay(2);

            // set time for next fox to appear
            nextFox = getTimer()+timeBetweenFoxes;
        }
    }
}
```

The *onClipEvent(mouseDown)* function needs to take into account some of the improvements in the Shoot-A-Fox game over the Whack-A-Fox game. First, it uses the "cursor" movie clip location as the click spot, not the actual mouse location, which might have changed slightly since the frame was updated.

Then, it searches through the seven movie clips to find one that might have been hit. If one has, the "fox" movie clip inside that movie clip is told to play the "hit" animation.

The "score" variable is incremented if there is a hit, and the "shotsLeft" variable is decremented in either case.

The game ends when the *onClipEvent(enterFrame)* function attempts to move a new fox and discovers that the player is out of shots. This prevents the movie from ending the instant that the last shot is fired, but rather delays the end for about a second or so.

```
onClipEvent (mouseDown) {
    // show blast
    _root["cursor"].gotoAndPlay("blast");

    // get the location of the click
    x = _root._root["cursor"]._x;
    y = _root._root["cursor"]._y;

    // loop through all 18 foxes to see which was clicked
    for (i=0; i<7; i++) {

        // look only at clips that are doing the
        // pop up animation
        if (_root["fox"+i]["fox"]._currentFrame <= 1) {

            // see whether this was the one clicked
            if (_root["fox"+i].hitTest(x, y, false)) {

                // have the clip play the "hit" animation
                _root["fox"+i].fox.gotoAndPlay("hit");

                // increase score and show it
                score++;
            }
        }
    }

    // take away one shot
    shotsLeft--;

    // update score
    _root.showScore = "Score:"+score;
    _root.showShotsLeft = "Shots Left:"+shotsLeft;
}
```

This code also advances the cursor movie clip to the "blast" frame, which shows a yellow blast for a few frames and then returns to frame 1. Even if the player misses a fox, she at least has some feedback that a shot was fired.

A new function here, *onClipEvent(unload)*, runs when the movie clip is about to disappear from the Stage. This happens when the game is over. In this case, all it does is make the cursor visible again.

```
onClipEvent (unload) {
    // game over, so return cursor to normal
    Mouse.show();
}
```

Loose Ends

After all the code is in place, the movie clip instances need to be named "fox0" to "fox6" to match their library names exactly. The example movie is built so that all fox animations assume that the center of the movie clip is at the center of the Stage. This was done by adding the animation to the main timeline, selecting the animation sequence, choosing Edit, Copy Frames, and pasting these frames into a blank movie clip. Check the example movie Shootafox.fla on the CD-ROM to see how it all fits together.

Other Possibilities

The gameplay can be altered in many ways. There can be a timer, rather than a set number of shots. You can build levels that the player attains by getting a certain number of shots in a single round.

Note that in this game it is possible to score more than 50 points. How? Well, if you wait long enough, the foxes appear pretty rapidly. Soon, there is more than one on the screen at the same time. When two foxes cross each other's paths, it is possible to shoot once and hit two foxes. I consider this a game feature that rewards an experienced player. You might want to find a way to prevent this.

This game can also use some sound effects and maybe some background sounds. You might also want to add some distracting animation, such as a bird flying by or the wind blowing some branches.

Hunt-A-Fox

Example File: Huntafox.fla

One of the most popular computer games of all time is *Deer Hunter*. In this game, you sit and look at a panoramic image for hours while waiting for a deer to show up so you can blast it away. Even though this title sold millions of copies, it is a rather simple game. Something like it can easily be done in Flash.

Project Goal

The goal is to make a shooting game that allows the user to scroll left and right through a larger scene than can fit on the Stage at one time. Targets appear at random times and places, regardless of where the player is looking at the moment. The scrolling should give the player a sense of dimension by having nearby objects move faster than distant objects.

Approach

Building on the previous game, all you have to do is to allow the user to scroll a larger background image from side to side. But this is not as easy as it sounds. Some background elements are closer to the player than others. To give the proper feeling that the hunter is moving from left to right, closer objects should move faster than farther objects.

To do this, we break the background elements into four parts: trees that are close, bushes that are farther, the hills that are even farther, and the ground and sky. The ground and sky do not move at all. But the trees, bushes, and hills move according to how far they are from the player.

Foxes hide behind the trees and the bushes. This means that those foxes have to move along with those elements. Take a look at the example movie Huntafox.fla on the CD ROM to see what you're shooting for. If you move the cursor to the right side of the Stage, the scene pans to the right. See how the trees move faster than the bushes, which move faster than the hills? Also notice how the trees will, at times, obscure the bushes. A good player has to pan around quite a bit to hit as many foxes as possible. Figure 8.8 shows a case where a fox is almost completely hidden behind a tree because of the angle of view.

Figure 8.8

A fox is peeking out from behind a bush that is partially obscured by a tree.

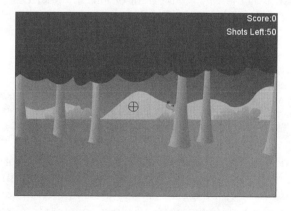

Preparing the Movie

The movie is similar to the previous example. The four layers—Background, Bushes, Hills, and Trees—are about 1200 pixels wide, centered on a normal 550 pixel-wide Stage. The Bushes, Hills, and Trees layers have a single movie clip in each—named "bushes," "hills," and "trees," respectively—that contain all the elements on that layer.

There are two layers with foxes. One layer contains foxes that are just behind the bushes, whereas another layer contains foxes that are just behind trees. The names of the fox movie clips are "fox0" through "fox6" for the foxes behind the trees and "fox7" through "fox9" for the three behind the bushes.

The fox movie clips are similar to the ones in the Shoot-A-Fox game, except the foxes stay visible much longer. To allow the foxes to fit behind narrow trees, I have used mask layers in each movie clip to hide the parts of the fox that are not supposed to be seen.

The fox graphic inside each fox movie clip is the same as the one used in the Shoot-A-Fox game. However, the last frame of the blast animation sends the parent movie clip back to its first frame. This means that when you hit a fox, it disappears as soon as the blast animation is done.

Writing the Code

Although the movie clips and layers are different than those in the Shoot-A-Fox game, the main script from that movie fits in well with this one. This is the script placed on the "actions" movie clip. Only two changes are needed, so I will not repeat all the code here. The first change is that there are now 10 foxes to choose from rather than 7, so the number inside the *Math.random* function should be 10.

The second change involves paying attention to the position of the cursor so the scene scrolls if the user is all the way to the right or left. In either case, a function named "moveScene" at the root level is called. It is passed either a -1 or 1, depending on the direction.

```
// pan left or right if needed
if (_root._xmouse < 50) {
    _root.moveScene(1);
} else if (_root._xmouse > 500) {
    _root.moveScene(-1);
}
```

The "moveScene" movie clip is in the main timeline. This script starts off by defining some variables. The "panAmount" keeps track of the amount that the user has panned left or right. For instance, if the user pans to the left, then the graphics move to the right, so the "panAmount" becomes 1. As they continue to move in that direction, the "panAmount" grows to 2, 3, and so on. If they move in the opposite direction, the "panAmount" goes to –1, –2, and so on.

Because we cannot draw a scene that is infinitely wide, we have to define pan limits. Two variables hold the maximum pan allowed to the left or right. I arrived at these values by trial and error. I started with 50 and saw that the player could pan past the end of the trees. Then I tried lower numbers until the player could no longer scroll off the end of the scene.

```
panLimitLeft = -30;
panLimitRight = 30;
panAmount = 0;
```

To pan the scene, first the future "panAmount" is checked against the limits. The function works only if the future value is within these limits.

Then the three movie clips—"trees," "bushes," and "hills"—are moved in the proper direction. The trees are moved by a factor of 10, the bushes by a factor of 5, and the hills by a factor of 4. I arrived at these values by trial and error. They seem to create a nice sense of depth.

The first seven foxes, being directly behind the trees, are moved along with the trees, by a factor of 10. The other three foxes are moved by a factor of 5, so that they stay behind the bushes.

```
function moveScene(d) {
    // check to see whether within pan limits
    if ((panAmount+d > panLimitLeft) and (panAmount+d < panLimitRight)) {
        // keep track of pan amount
        panAmount += d;

        // move three layers at different speeds
        trees._x += d*10;
        bushes._x += d*5
        hills._x += d*4;

        // foxes 0-6 track with trees
        for(i=0;i<7;i++) {
            _root["fox"+i]._x += d*10;
        }

        // foxes 7-9 track with bushes
        for(i=7;i<10;i++) {
            _root["fox"+i]._x += d*5;
        }
    }
}
```

I mentioned that there was a new script at the end of the "peeking fox" movie clip. The "peeking fox" is inside all three fox movie clips. It is the static image of the fox. It also contains a short blast animation that is shown when the fox is clicked on. At the end of this animation, I reset the "peeking fox" movie clip and also tell its parent movie clip to go to frame 1. This means that instead of playing out the entire show-wait-hide animation sequence, the fox jumps immediately back to the hidden state.

```
gotoAndStop(1);
_parent.gotoAndStop(1);
```

Loose Ends

All the standard parts of the previous games are still there. There is an introduction screen with a button on it. There are two text fields: score and shots left. The cursor is hidden and replaced with a crosshairs movie clip. These all use the same code as the Shoot-A-Fox game.

Other Possibilities

For a better game, I'd lengthen the amount of time between fox appearances. Right now it is 2 seconds, but it should be more like 2 minutes to be like *Deer Hunter*. You may want to make the length of time somewhat random to be even better.

Rather than have the viewpoint of the hunter shift from left to right, you could spin around in a circle instead. In some ways, this would be simpler. You would not need to bother with the layers of perspective like in this game. Instead, the background can be one solid piece. However, you also have to find a way to stitch together the right and left sides of the circular panorama. The easiest way to do this is to have the right side repeat a full Stage view of the left side. Then, when the player tries to scroll even farther to the right, you seamlessly jump all the way to the left. It takes a lot of patience and work to get it to happen smoothly, but it is possible.

Catch and Avoid Games

- Apple Catch
- Apple Letter Catch
- River Rafting Game
- Racing Game

Many games on the Web can be classified as catch-and-avoid games. They all share a few characteristics. The player controls an object or character that moves left and right across the bottom of the screen. Other objects fall from the top of the screen. The player must either catch or avoid these objects.

These games vary, however, in how the player's character is controlled, what the objects are, and other aspects. In this chapter, you will look at three different games. The first is a basic catch-the-objects game. The second builds on that and adds new features, such as some objects that are to be avoided rather than caught. The third game doesn't look like a catch-and-avoid game at all, but rather a movement-based game. However, it uses almost exactly the same code as the original game, just different graphics. The last game adds the illusion of depth by making the objects appear to come toward the player in a racing game.

Apple Catch

Example file: Applecatch.fla

In the first game, Apple Catch, the fox moves along the bottom of the screen and tries to catch apples that are falling from the tree. Figure 9.1 shows how the game will look. The game can be found on the CD-ROM as Applecatch.fla.

Figure 9.1
The Apple Catch game features a fox at the bottom of the screen and apples that fall from the top.

Project Goal

The fox is controlled by the left- and right-arrow keys. Rather than respond to a single key press, the fox should move as long as the player holds down one of those two arrow keys. The fox should stop automatically before going beyond the left or right side of the screen.

The apples should fall from a random place at the top of the screen. They should fall at random times, but not come too quickly. They should begin falling slowly, and then fall faster and faster as the game goes on.

After a certain number of apples have fallen, the game should end. The score should be equal to the number of apples that the fox has caught.

Approach

To move a fox, you use the Key object. This allows you to detect whether a key on the keyboard is being held down—in this case, the left-arrow key and the right-arrow key.

At the start of the game, no apples are present. You use *attachMovie* to create new apples. These apples are placed at random spots at the top of the screen, and then fall down until they're either caught by the fox or hit the bottom of the screen.

After an apple is created, a counter, "timeSinceLastApple," is reset to 0. This counter is then incremented once per frame. Only when the counter reaches 20 can another apple be created. This assures that an apple cannot be created until 20 frames have passed since the last apple was created.

The speed at which apples fall depends on an "appleSpeed" variable. Each time an apple is dropped, the "appleSpeed" variable is increased. So, as the game goes on, the apples fall faster and faster.

An apple clip is removed when it either hits the bottom of the screen or goes in the fox's basket. When an apple hits the fox's basket is determined by the position of the apple relative to the position of the basket. The fox movie clip is centered on the basket to make this calculation easier. Figure 9.2 shows the fox movie clip with the center marked by a cross.

Figure 9.2
The fox movie clip is centered on the basket.

When a certain number of apples have been dropped, the game ends. The number of apples caught is displayed in the upper-right corner and serves as the player's score.

Preparing the Movie

The background image in the example movie is complex, but that doesn't matter as far as the game is concerned. Only the apples and the fox matter. Both these movie clips are stored in the library, but no movie clip instances appear on the Stage. They are created by the code as needed.

The apple movie clip is just a static image of an apple. The fox, however, is a little more complex. The first frame, labeled "stand," is a drawing of the fox standing still. The second frame, "run," is the start of an animation that shows the fox's feet moving. It has a *gotoAndPlay* command in the last frame so that it loops back to the "run" frame. This provides two modes for the fox clip: The first has it just sitting on frame 1; the second has it animating in a loop through all the frames starting at frame 2.

Because neither the fox nor the apple clip appears in the movie until the code asks for it, you need to set the Linkage properties of both to "Export this symbol." The apple is given the identifier "apple" and the fox is given the identifier "running fox."

Writing the Code

As with most of our games, the trigger for all events occurs in an "actions" movie clip. You can find this clip just beyond the upper-left corner of the Stage in the example movie.

The ActionScript attached to this clip calls functions in the main timeline of the movie. This makes the code simpler because "_root" doesn't have to be placed in front of all the movie clip names.

The code calls the "initGame" function when the clip loads, and then calls three functions every frame.

```
onClipEvent (load) {
    _root.initGame();
}

onClipEvent (enterFrame) {
    _root.moveFox();
    _root.dropNewApple();
    _root.moveApples();
}
```

So all the work is really done in four functions declared in the main timeline. Let's look at them one at a time.

The first function, "initGame," sets up a whole bunch of variables at the start of the game. It also creates the fox movie clip. The reason the fox must be created by the code, rather than just put in place while the movie is built, is so the fox appears on top of the apples. If the fox is created as the movie is built, then each apple created by the code appears on top of the fox. When the fox is created by code, you can control the level at which the fox resides, relative to the level of the apples. You can see that the fox is assigned to level 999,999. The apples start at level 1 and so appear under the fox.

```
function initGame() {
    // the range of falling apple clips
    firstApple = 1;
    lastApple = 0;

    // init the score
    score = 0;

    // set the number of apples to fall
    totalApples = 20;

    // init the speed and time delay
    timeSinceLastApple = 0;
    appleSpeed = 5;

    // create the fox so that it is on top of the apples
    attachMovie( "running fox", "fox", 999999 );
    fox._x = 275;
    fox._y = 300;
}
```

To move the fox, you must use the *Key* object to examine the state of the keyboard. You use *Key.isDown(Key.RIGHT)* to see whether the right-arrow key is down, and *Key.isDown(Key.LEFT)* to see whether the left-arrow key is down. The variable "dx" is set to 10 or −10 to indicate how much and in what direction the fox should move.

NOTE

The *Key.isDown()* function allows you to determine whether a specific key is currently held down. This is particularly useful in arcade games that need keyboard control. To specify a key, you need to use its key code. In addition to numbers, such as 65 for the letter "A," you can also use constants such as *Key.UP* to specify special keys such as the up arrow. The ActionScript Reference Guide that comes with Flash MX lists all these codes in Appendix B.

As well as setting "dx," the function also sets the _xscale of the fox clip. The actual value of _xscale is kept the same, but sometimes it is negative and sometimes it is positive. This makes the movie clip flip horizontally so that the fox is facing the direction of movement.

After "dx" is set, the fox movie clip is moved by the value of "dx." Then, this new position is checked against the left and right limits of movement.

If there is movement going on, and the fox movie clip shows the fox standing still, then the clip is sent to the "run" frame so it appears as if the fox is running. On the other hand, if the fox isn't moving, but it isn't on frame 1, then the movie clip is sent there so the fox appears as if it is standing still.

```
function moveFox() {
    // check for arrow keys
    if (Key.isDown(Key.RIGHT)) {
        dx = 10;
        // fox faces right
        fox._xscale = -Math.abs(fox._xscale);
    } else if (Key.isDown(Key.LEFT)) {
        dx = -10;
        // fox faces left
        fox._xscale = Math.abs(fox._xscale);
    } else {
        // no movement
        dx = 0;
    }

    // move the fox and limit that movement
    fox._x += dx;
    if (fox._x < 30) fox._x = 30;
    if (fox._x > 520) fox._x = 520;

    // make the fox run or stand still
    if ((dx != 0) and (fox._currentFrame == 1)) {
        fox.gotoAndPlay("run");
    } else if ((dx == 0) and (fox._currentFrame != 1)) {
        fox.gotoAndPlay("stand");
    }
}
```

Once every frame, the "dropNewApple" function is called. A set of three nested *if* statements determine whether a new apple needs to be created.

First, the "timeSinceLastApple" variable is examined. The code continues only if the variable is greater than 20. This variable is incremented by 1 at the end of this function.

The next test is whether the number of apples dropped so far is less than the total number of apples to be dropped during the game.

Finally, the *Math.random()* function is used to give an apple a 10% chance of being dropped. This prevents the apples from being dropped at exact time intervals.

To create a new apple, the *attachMovie* function is used to create a new apple clip. The horizontal location of that clip is randomly chosen from between 30 and 520. Every time a new apple is created, the "appleSpeed" variable is increased slightly.

```
function dropNewApple() {
    // only drop if it has been long enough
    if (timeSinceLastApple > 20) {

        // only drop if there are more apples
        if (lastApple < totalApples) {

            // only drop 10% of the time
            if (Math.random() < .1) {

                // create next apple and set its locations
                lastApple++;
                attachMovie( "apple", "apple"+lastApple, lastApple );
                _root["apple"+lastApple]._x = Math.random()*490+30;
                _root["apple"+lastApple]._y = 0;

                // reset time delay for next apple
                timeSinceLastApple = 0;

                // increase apple speed
                if (appleSpeed < 10) appleSpeed += .5;
            }
        }
    }

    // even if no apple dropped, get closer to next drop
    timeSinceLastApple++;
}
```

The function to move the apples needs to do a lot more than just change the vertical location of the apples. It also needs to check whether the apple has hit the ground or landed in the basket.

To see whether the apple hit the ground, the function needs to determine only whether the position of the apple is below the bottom of the screen. Checking for a catch is a little harder, because the function has to find the difference from the position of the apple to the position of the fox, and see whether that falls in an acceptable range. If it is within 10 vertical pixels and 25 horizontal pixels of the fox, then the apple has been caught. Remember, the fox movie clip is centered on the basket, so the location of the fox is actually the location of the basket. Figure 9.3 shows the fox movie clip again, with a box representing the catch area.

Figure 9.3
*When the center of
an apple comes
within the 50×20
pixel box around
the center of the
basket, it has been
caught.*

NOTE

The *Math.abs()* function is useful for determining collisions between objects. If you take
the position of one object and subtract the position of another, you can get either a
positive or negative number. For instance, if the first object is 7 pixels to the right of
the second, then you get a 7, whereas if the first object is 7 pixels to the left you get a
−7. The *Math.abs()* function strips the sign so that you get a 7 in either case. This way,
you can test to see whether an object is a certain number of pixels away from another
object, regardless of which side it is on.

If a catch is made, or the apple hits the ground, the function "removeApple" is called. In
the case of the apple being caught, the score is also incremented.

```
function moveApples() {
    // loop through all existing apple clips
    for (i=firstApple;i<=lastApple;i++) {

        // get apple location
        x = _root["apple"+i]._x;
        y = _root["apple"+i]._y + appleSpeed;

        // see whether apple reached ground
        if (y > 400) {
            removeApple(i);

        // see whether apple hit basket
        } else if ((Math.abs(y-fox._y) < 10) and (Math.abs(x-fox._x) < 25)) {
            removeApple(i);
                score += 1;

        // continue to move apple
        } else {
            _root["apple"+i]._y = y;
        }
    }
}
```

The "removeApple" function uses *removeClip* to delete the apple clip. It also increments "firstApple" so that the "moveApples" function no longer needs to try to move that apple down.

If the apple is the last one, the movie jumps to the "game over" frame. The fox movie clip is also removed so that it does not remain on the screen.

```
function removeApple(n) {
    // take away apple movie clip
    _root["apple"+n].removeMovieClip();

    // reset range of apples to move
    firstApple = n+1;

    // see whether this was the last apple
    if (n == totalApples) {
        fox.removeMovieClip();
        gotoAndPlay("game over");
    }
}
```

Loose Ends

The previous code assumes that your Stage is 550×400, Flash MX's default size. You should adjust those numbers in the code if your Stage size is different. You can also adjust the margin on the left or right. The previous code limits the apples and fox to between 30 and 520, a 30-pixel margin. You can make that more or less.

The fox movie clip needs a *stop()* in the first frame to prevent it from automatically animating. Don't forget about the *gotoAndPlay* command in the last frame of that movie clip, either.

There is also a text area set to Dynamic Text and linked to the variable "score." This makes the display of the score effortless.

The complete game found in the example file Applecatch.fla on the CD-ROM contains three frames. The first is a start frame that has a *stop()* command on it. The button there takes the game to the "Play" frame where the action occurs. Then, of course, there is a "Game Over" frame after that. The frame arrangement is done differently from some of the previous games in this book that use different scenes for the frames. I kept the frames in the same scene so I could use a single instance of the background graphic across all three frames. However, parts of the game can also be arranged in separate scenes if you like that better.

Other Possibilities

This game can be adjusted in a number of ways. You can start the apples at a faster speed or adjust the delay between apples. You can easily change the number of apples that fall in the game.

You can also adjust the fox graphic and the *moveApples* function so that the player has a larger or smaller basket with which to catch the apples.

A clever programmer could also show the basket getting fuller and fuller as more apples are caught, and could possibly require the fox to go to a place on the screen to dump the apples from time to time.

The next section in this chapter builds on this game by adding bad apples to avoid.

Apple Letter Catch

⊳Example file: Applelettercatch.fla

The point of this next example is to add a "bad apple" to the previous game. This is actually simple to do. So, to add to that challenge, let's also introduce the idea of different good and bad apples so they don't all look alike. In fact, let's make the appearance of the apples important to the game.

Each apple that falls has a letter inside it. Depending on whether the letter is a vowel or a consonant, the apple is good or bad. The player tries to catch only the good ones.

Figure 9.4 shows this new game with a few apples in the air. The example on the CD-ROM is named Applelettercatch.fla.

Figure 9.4
The Apple Letter Catch game features apples with either vowels or consonants on them.

Project Goal

The goal here is to modify the Apple Catch game to allow for apples with different letters on them. Any apple with a vowel on it gives the player points, whereas any apple with a consonant on it gives the player negative points. The score should not be allowed to dip below 0, however.

Approach

In the Apple Catch game, a single library movie clip contains a single-frame static image of an apple. To accommodate different types of apples, you need two different movie clips: one for good apples and one for bad. In addition to that, each movie clip needs many frames, each representing a different apple. The good apple movie clip has 5 frames, each showing a vowel. The bad apple movie clip has 20 frames, each showing a consonant. (We'll leave the letter "y" out of this game.)

When it's time to drop a new apple, there is a chance that it is a good apple, and a chance it is a bad one. Regardless of which, the code displays a random frame from the appropriate apple movie clip.

Then, when the player catches an apple, the code determines which type it was and awards points accordingly.

Preparing the Movie

If you look at the example movie Applelettercatch.fla on the CD-ROM, you can see two apple movie clips in the library. The first is "bad apple" and it contains 20 frames. Each frame has the apple, plus a consonant over it. The other movie clip, "good apple," has 5 frames for the 5 vowels. Figure 9.5 shows the main Flash window open with the "bad apple" movie clip.

Figure 9.5
The "bad apple" movie clip has 20 frames. Each frame shows the apple and a different consonant.

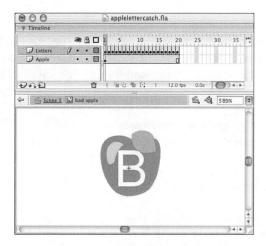

Both these movie clips need to be set to Export this Symbol in the Symbol Linkage Properties dialog box. They should be assigned the appropriate identifier: "good apple" and "bad apple."

Writing the Code

The "actions" movie clip code is the same as the code used for the Apple Catch game. Only the functions change.

The *initGame* function is the same, except that I have increased the number of apples that will fall to 50.

```
function initGame() {
    // the range of falling apple clips
    firstApple = 1;
    lastApple = 0;

    // init the score
    score = 0;

    // set the number of apples to fall
    totalApples = 50;

    // init the speed and time delay
    timeSinceLastApple = 0;
    appleSpeed = 5;

    // create the fox so that it is on top of the apples
    attachMovie( "running fox", "fox", 999999 );
    fox._x = 275;
    fox._y = 300;
}
```

The *moveFox* function is identical to the Apple Catch game, so there is no use repeating the code here. The *dropNewApple* function is different, however, because it needs to decide which type of apple to drop, and then pick a random frame in that movie clip to display.

```
function dropNewApple() {
    // drop only if it has been long enough
    if (timeSinceLastApple > 20) {

        // drop only if there are more apples
        if (lastApple < totalApples) {

            // drop only 10% of the time
            if (Math.random() < .1) {
```

```
                    // create next apple and set its locations
                    lastApple++;
                    if (Math.random() < .5) {
                        // 50% chance of a bad apple
                        attachMovie( "bad apple", "apple"+lastApple, lastApple );
                        _root["apple"+lastApple].type = "bad";
                    } else {
                        // 50% chance of a good apple
                        attachMovie( "good apple", "apple"+lastApple, lastApple );
                        _root["apple"+lastApple].type = "good";
                    }
                f = int(Math.Random()*_root["apple"+lastApple]._totalFrames) + 1;
                    trace(f);
                    _root["apple"+lastApple].gotoAndStop(f);
                    _root["apple"+lastApple]._x = Math.random()*490+30;
                    _root["apple"+lastApple]._y = 0;

                    // reset time delay for next apple
                    timeSinceLastApple = 0;

                    // increase apple speed
                    if (appleSpeed < 10) appleSpeed += .5;
                }
            }
        }

        // even if no apple dropped, get closer to next drop
        timeSinceLastApple++;
    }
```

The *dropNewApple* function also sets a "type" variable for each movie clip. Although no scripts are attached to these movie clips, they can still be given values for variables to be associated with the movie clip. So the "type" for a vowel is "good" and the "type" for a consonant is "bad." In the *moveApples* function, this variable is checked when the player makes a catch. This is how a good catch is differentiated from a bad one.

```
function moveApples() {
    // loop through all existing apple clips
    for (i=firstApple;i<=lastApple;i++) {

        // get apple location
        x = _root["apple"+i]._x;
        y = _root["apple"+i]._y + appleSpeed;

        // see whether apple reached ground
        if (y > 400) {
            removeApple(i);
```

```
            // see whether apple hit basket
        } else if ((Math.abs(y-fox._y) < 10) and (Math.abs(x-fox._x) < 25)) {
            if (_root["apple"+i].type == "good") {
                // good apple, get a point
                score += 1;
            } else {
                // bad apple, lose a point
                score -= 1;

                // don't go below 0
                if (score < 0) score = 0;
            }
            removeApple(i);

        // continue to move apple
        } else {
            _root["apple"+i]._y = y;
        }
    }
}
```

The *removeApple* function is identical to the same function in the Apple Catch game.

Loose Ends

Like the Apple Catch game, there are "start" and "game over" frames on either side of the "play" frame. Remember the "score" text area and the other factors mentioned in the "Loose Ends" part of the previous game as well.

Other Possibilities

Hey, this is an educational game! Unfortunately, it is only useful for small children who have not learned the alphabet yet. However, you can change the contents of each frame of the good and bad apples to have more advanced content. You might have to enlarge the apples to fit longer pieces of information on them.

For older kids, you could have verbs and nouns on the apples. Or, you could have odd and even numbers, numbers divisible by three, or fractions that can be reduced. Still older kids can pick out countries in a certain continent, or trees versus other plants. You could come up with any topic that can be broken into correct and incorrect answers.

River Rafting Game

Example file: Riverkayak.fla

This game uses the code from the previous two games to create a game that looks completely different from the other two. In this game, our hero fox travels down a river in a kayak, avoiding obstacles and trying to make good time.

The transformation of the previous games into this one takes surprisingly little effort. However, players will never think of the games as the same. Look at Figure 9.6 to see just how different this game looks from the Apple Catch games.

Figure 9.6
The River Kayak Adventure game features a kayak in the center of the screen while rocks and tree branches rush upward toward it.

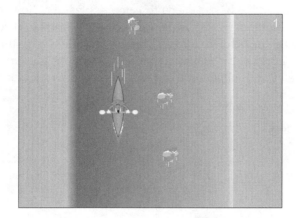

Project Goal

Part of the goal here is to create an illusion for the player. Although the kayak stays at the center of the screen as shown in Figure 9.6, the player should get the feeling that it is moving down the river. This is accomplished by having the objects move up the screen.

Most of the code in this game is borrowed from the two earlier games in this chapter. However, all, not just some, of the objects are to be avoided. Rather than catching objects to increase your score, the player is to avoid objects. Catches are thought of as spills. The game ends early if too many spills occur.

Approach

The first modification to the code is to make the objects move up rather than down. Then, any code that deals with collisions can be streamlined to account for the fact that all collisions are bad.

Much of the rest of the modifications are minor. The left and right margins need to be moved so the rocks appear in the river. The speed of the game can go much faster and more rocks can be on the screen at one time.

Rather than increase over time, the game's speed decreases to 0 when a rock is hit. This makes the player feel the impact. This slowdown also delays the end of the game.

Preparing the Movie

Instead of the "apples" movie clip, you need a "rocks" movie clip. In the example movie, Riverkayak.fla, the "rocks" movie clip has three frames. Each frame contains an animated graphic from another library element. Although each rock is in one frame of the movie clip, animation takes place in the graphic element. So if you try the example movie, you can see water running by each rock.

Rather than a fox with a basket ready to catch apples, the "fox" movie clip features a fox in a kayak. The first frame has the fox facing downstream with paddles out of the water. Then there are "left" and "right" frames with the kayak turned one way or the other and one paddle in the water. Figure 9.7 shows the fox turning right. After that, frame 4 starts a "spill" animation that plays when the kayak hits a rock.

Figure 9.7
The second frame of the fox movie clip shows the fox turning to the right.

The "rocks" and "fox" movie clips need to be linked, just like the "apples" and "fox" movie clips in the first game of this chapter, so that they are included with the movie.

Writing the Code

The script attached to the "actions" movie clip looks just like the one used in the first two games of this chapter. However, the names have been adjusted to apply to this game, rather than catching apples.

```
onClipEvent (load) {
    _root.initGame();
}

onClipEvent (enterFrame) {
    _root.moveFox();
    _root.newRock();
    _root.moveRocks();
}
```

The functions in the main timeline should look familiar to you at this point. Some sections of code are identical to the same functions earlier in this chapter. However, the variable names have been changed to make more sense for this game.

The "initGame" function starts the speed of the game at 0 this time. The location of the fox is placed right in the middle of the screen, rather than at the bottom.

```
function initGame() {
    // the range of rock clips
    firstRock = 1;
    lastRock = 0;

    // init the number of spills
    spills = 0;

    // set the number of rocks to pass
    totalRocks = 50;

    // init the speed and time delay
    timeSinceLastRock = 0;
    riverSpeed = 0;

    // create the fox so that it is on top of the rocks
    attachMovie( "kayaking fox", "fox", 999999 );
    fox._x = 275;
    fox._y = 200;
}
```

The "moveFox" function looks at the left- and right-arrow keys as before. In addition, it checks to see whether the kayak is performing a "spill" animation and ignores the keys if it is.

Instead of flipping the image as the Apple Catch game does, the code makes the "fox" go to frames labeled "left" or "right." The first frame is labeled "still" and shows the kayak going straight.

```
function moveFox() {
    if (fox._currentFrame > 4) {
        // if during a spill, don't look at keys
        dx = 0;
    } else if (Key.isDown(Key.RIGHT)) {
        // fox rows right
        dx = riverSpeed;
        fox.gotoAndStop("left");
    } else if (Key.isDown(Key.LEFT)) {
        // fox rows left
        dx = -riverSpeed;
        fox.gotoAndStop("right");
    } else {
        // no key
```

```
        dx = 0;
        fox.gotoAndStop("still");
    }


    // move the fox and limit that movement
    fox._x += dx;
    if (fox._x < 150) fox._x = 150;
    if (fox._x > 400) fox._x = 400;


    // go a little faster
    if (riverSpeed < 20) riverSpeed += .5;
}
```

The speed of the game is increased in the "moveFox" handler in this game to keep the kayak accelerating at a constant rate.

The "newRock" function is like the "dropNewApple" function of the previous game. However, it is simpler because it has only one movie clip to choose from.

```
function newRock() {
    // add new one only if it has been long enough
    if (timeSinceLastRock > 5) {

        // start only if there are more rocks
        if  (lastRock < totalRocks) {

            // add only 10% of the time
            if (Math.random() < .1) {

                // create next rock and set its location
                lastRock++;
                attachMovie( "rocks", "rock"+lastRock, lastRock );
                _root["rock"+lastRock]._x = Math.random()*250+150;
                _root["rock"+lastRock]._y = 450;

                // decide which frame to show
                f = int(Math.Random()*_root["rock"+lastRock]._totalFrames) + 1;
                _root["rock"+lastRock].gotoAndStop(f);

                // reset time delay for next rock
                timeSinceLastRock = 0;

                // init whether rock was hit
                _root["rock"+i].hit = false;
            }
        }
    }
```

```
    // even if no rock added, get closer to next rock
    timeSinceLastRock++;
}
```

Note that the variable "hit" is set to *false* for each new rock. This indicates that the kayak has never hit that rock. In the "moveRock" function, this is checked before a collision is allowed. When a collision happens, the "hit" variable of that movie clip is set to *true* so that it cannot be hit again as the boat passes over it.

Notice that the numbers for determining when a collision occurs are drastically different now that the fox has a kayak instead of a basket. The game looks for a collision within 60 pixels horizontally and 25 pixels vertically of the center. This approximates the shape of the kayak as shown in Figure 9.8.

Figure 9.8
The black box shows the area where a collision can occur. Because the collision occurs with the center of a rock, the edge of the rock can actually be much closer to the kayak than this box.

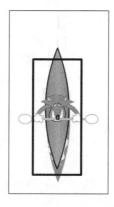

The number of hits is recorded in the "spills" variable. After the kayak has spilled six times, the game goes to a "lose" frame that declares the game over. Notice that this calls a new function, "removeAll," which is explained later.

```
function moveRocks() {
    // loop through all existing rock clips
    for (i=firstRock;i<=lastRock;i++) {

        // get rock location
        x = _root["rock"+i]._x;
        y = _root["rock"+i]._y - riverSpeed;

        // see whether rock reached past top
        if (y < -50) {
            removeRock(i);

        // to have a hit, rock must not have been hit before
        // and rock and boat are close enough
```

```
    } else if ((_root["rock"+i].hit == false) and (Math.abs(y-fox._y) < 60)
      and (Math.abs(x-fox._x) < 25)) {
        spills += 1;

        // note that rock was hit
        _root["rock"+i].hit = true;

        // turn boat over
        fox.gotoAndPlay("spill");

        // stop boat
        riverSpeed = 0;

        // is game over?
        if (spills > 5) {
            removeAll();
            gotoAndPlay("lose");
        }

    }
    // continue to move rock
    _root["rock"+i]._y = y;
    }
}
```

The "removeRock" function, like the "removeApple" function, looks to see whether this is the last rock. If so, the game goes to a frame labeled "win."

```
function removeRock(n) {
    // take away rock movie clip
    _root["rock"+n].removeMovieClip();

    // reset range of rocks to move
    firstRock = n+1;

    // see whether this was the last rock
    if (n == totalRocks) {
        removeAll();
        gotoAndPlay("win");
    }
}
```

In the previous code, you see two occasions in which the game ends. In both cases, the "removeAll" function is called. This function removes all the remaining rocks, if any, and the fox movie clip. This is needed because otherwise they stay on the screen even after the game is over.

```
function removeAll() {
    // take away all remaining rocks
    for (i=firstRock;i<=lastRock;i++) {
        _root["rock"+i].removeMovieClip();
    }
    fox.removeMovieClip();
}
```

Loose Ends

Instead of just one "game over" frame, this game features two. The first, labeled "lose," contains a message for players who hit too many rocks and did not complete the game. The second, "win," contains a message for players who made it past the rocks. The frames are essentially the same except for the message. They both have a "Play" button so the game can be restarted.

Other Possibilities

Because hitting a rock slows the player down, this game is an ideal candidate for a timer. You could mark the starting time of the game using the date object similar to the clock gadget in Chapter 6, "Toys and Gadgets." Then you could see how long it takes the player to finish the course. Not only will hitting a rock affect the speed of the kayak, but you can alter the code so that the kayak accelerates only when the boat is pointed straight ahead. This adds even more challenge to the game.

Another possibility for a different game would be to flip it around again so that the objects are moving down and change the kayak to a car or bike and the river to a road. This would make a good driving game.

Racing Game

▷✂ Example file: Racing.fla

To convert the kayak game to a racing game, you don't have to do anything except change the graphics. Swap the kayak for a car. Change the turn frames to show wheels turning rather than the kayak pointing in a different direction. Change the turn-over graphics to a car crash, and so on.

However, we can use similar techniques to create a different type of racing game. Instead of using a top-down view of the road, we can do a view from the driver's perspective. The road moves toward the player (see Figure 9.9).

Project Goal

The main goal of this game is to create the illusion of depth. Even though the screen is still 2D and no real 3D code is used, the player should still feel as if the road goes into the screen rather than simply scrolls down it.

Figure 9.9
In the racing game, the road comes toward the player.

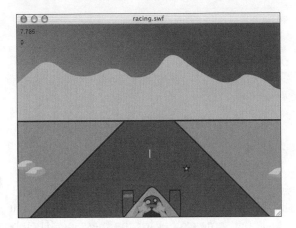

In addition, we'll make a simple set of rules. The road has marks on it that the player must hit to get points. The faster the player goes, the more potential points he can hit before time runs out. But the faster he goes, the more chance he has of not being able to catch the marks before they go past. In addition, if the player hits the side of the road, he slows down, thus reducing his potential score because there are fewer marks to hit.

Approach

The illusion of depth can be achieved with simple perspective tricks. Figure 9.9 showed the sides of the road drawn diagonally toward the bottom corners of the screen. Even though the road is assumed to be a constant width, the eye shows the road ahead to get smaller.

In addition to the lines, all the elements in the game should appear to approach from a distance. This means that they should travel not only down the screen, but also out to the sides. Play the game now to see how the rocks by the side of the road and the road marks that resemble stars act.

Three different elements move in the game: rocks by the side of the road, star-shaped "bonus" marks on the road, and the center line of the road. The rocks move down the screen according to the speed of the car. They also move out to the sides of the screen an equal amount.

The star marks are closer to the center of the screen, so they do not move out as much as they move down. Instead, they move out at half the speed. This matches the perspective suggested by the sides of the road. The center line of the road simply moves straight down.

All these elements are recycled throughout the game. For instance, as rocks reach a point off the bottom of the screen, they are reset to the horizon and come toward the user again.

In addition to moving the three elements of the game, we also scale them. So objects that are supposed to be far away look smaller, and they increase in size as they approach.

The goal here is not to create a pixel-perfect perspective, but to get close enough to allow the player's imagination to take over and make him feel like he is racing into the screen.

Preparing the Movie

The background and lines indicating the sides of the road are static elements. But you need movie clips for the rocks and the stars. The center line movie clip is a simple line, but it is positioned so that the center point of the movie clip is at the top of the line.

The car itself has just three frames: straight, left, and right. They are used to indicate whether the car is turning.

The rock and bonus movie clip should be placed off the bottom of the screen area. They should be named "sideObject" and "bonus." The car movie clip needs to be positioned at the bottom of the screen and named "car." In addition, a placeholder movie clip named "actions" should be placed off to the left. All four of these movie clips have scripts in them.

Two dynamic text fields need to be on the screen: "timeDisplay" and "score." They should both be linked to variables of that name.

In the example movie, I put an introductory frame as frame 1, so all the action takes place on frame 2. There is also a third frame labeled "game over."

Writing the Code

The main piece of code is attached to the car movie clip. It starts by setting the "speed" variable to 0. This variable should be at the root level because other movie clips will be accessing it.

```
onClipEvent(load) {
    // init speed
    _root.speed = 0;
}
```

The *onClipEvent(enterFrame)* handler first checks for all four arrow keys. The left- and right-arrow keys move the car to the left or right, and also make the car movie clip show the appropriate frame.

The up and down arrows change the speed of the car, by increments of .1. A check is made to make sure that the speed doesn't drop below 0.

If none of the arrow keys are pressed, then the car movie clip returns to the first frame.

The handler does two more checks. The first is to see whether the "bonus" movie clip is under the car. If so, then the player scores a point and the bonus movie clip is moved farther down off the screen to prevent the player from scoring on it again.

The last check determines whether the car is past the sides of the road. If so, the car is limited to the side and slowed down.

```
onClipEvent(enterFrame) {
    if (Key.isDown(Key.LEFT)) {
        // move left
        this._x -= 10;
        this.gotoAndStop("left");
    } else if (Key.isDown(Key.RIGHT)) {
        // move right
        this._x += 15;
        gotoAndStop("right");
    } else if (Key.isDown(Key.UP)) {
        // speed up
        _root.speed += .1;
    } else if (Key.isDown(Key.DOWN)) {
        // slow down
        _root.speed -= .1;
        // check for minimum speed
        if (_root.speed < 0) _root.speed = 0;
    } else {
        _root.car.gotoAndStop("straight");
    }

    // check for score
    if (this.hitTest(_root.bonus._x,_root.bonus._y)) {
        _root.score++;
        _root.bonus._y += 100;
    }

    // slow down if sides hit
    if (this._x < 80) {
        this._x = 80;
        _root.speed /= 2;
    } else if (this._x > 470) {
        this._x = 470;
        _root.speed /= 2;
    }
}
```

The sideObjects movie clip has a script attached to it that moves the object down and away from the center. For each frame that goes by, _y is increased and _x is changed. They both use "speed" as the magnitude of this change, but _x uses a "dx" modifier that is either 1 or –1. The first makes the object move to the right, and the second makes it move to the left.

When the object hits 600 _y, which is 200 pixels past the bottom of the screen, it is recycled back to 200 _y, which is the horizon line. Then a 50/50 chance determines whether it is placed on the left or right side of the road. The "dx" variable is set appropriately at this time.

Finally, the scale of the object is set according to the _y position of the object. This makes it grow larger as it approaches.

```
onClipEvent(enterFrame) {
    // move down
    this._y += _root.speed;

    // move out
    this._x += dx*_root.speed;

    // reset when at the bottom of the screen
    if (this._y > 600) {
        this._y = 200;
        if (Math.random() < .5) {
            // left side
            this._x = Math.random()*170;
            dx = -1;
        } else {
            // right side
            this._x = 550-Math.random()*170;
            dx = 1;
        }
    }

    // set scale according to vertical position
    this._xscale = this._y/4;
    this._yscale = this._y/4;


}
```

Notice that the sideObject movie clip doesn't interact with the car. Only the bonus object does that. But the side objects provide a visual guide for the player's eye to help the illusion of depth.

The center line of the road follows along with the rocks, but because it is in the center of the screen, it doesn't have to go to the left or right. It just moves down and scales.

```
onClipEvent(enterFrame) {

        // move down
        this._y += _root.speed;

        // recycle
        if (this._y > 400) {
            this._y = 200;
        }

        // set scaling
        this._xscale = this._y/4;
        this._yscale = this._y/4;

}
```

The bonus stars act more like the side objects. However, they don't just appear anywhere. They have a 50/50 chance of appearing in one of two spots on the road.

Then, when the bonus star moves down the screen, it moves to the side at only half the speed that it moves down the screen. This helps keep the perspective a little more accurate because the stars are closer to the center.

```
onClipEvent(enterFrame) {
    // move down
    this._y += _root.speed;
    this._x += dx*_root.speed;

    // reset when at the bottom of the screen
    if (this._y > 600) {
        this._y = 200;

        if (Math.random() < .5) {
            // come up left side
            this._x = 250;
            dx = -.5;
        } else {
            // come up right side
            this._x = 300;
            dx = .5;
        }
    }

    // set scale according to vertical position
    this._xscale = this._y/4;
    this._yscale = this._y/4;

}
```

The "actions" movie clip sits off the screen and handles the game clock. It notes the start time and counts down to 0. In the example movie, the game is a very short 15 seconds. You will probably want to lengthen that to a minute or two.

When the clock runs down to 0, the main timeline is sent to the "game over" frame. The "speed" is set to 0 so that the car freezes in place.

```
onClipEvent(load) {
    // calculate end time
    endTime = getTimer()+15000;
}


onClipEvent(enterFrame) {
    // calculate time left
    timeLeft = (endTime - getTimer())/1000;

    // game over
    if (timeLeft <= 0) {
        _root.speed = 0;
        _root.timeDisplay = "0";
        _root.gotoAndStop("game over");
    } else {
        // display time left
        _root.timeDisplay = timeLeft;
    }
}
```

11500

Beyond the *stop()* command on frames, the only other script is on the main game frame. It moves the car to the front of the screen, so that the center line and bonus stars appear to go under the car. In addition, a short loop copies the sideObject movie clip five times. Each copy is given a different _y value so that the rocks don't all appear at the same time.

```
// move car to front
car.swapDepths(999);

// create five rocks
for(i=0;i<5;i++) {
    mc = sideobject.duplicateMovieClip("side object"+i,i);
    mc._y = 400+Math.random()*200;
}
```

Loose Ends

The example movie includes an introductory frame and a button there to start the game. The third frame contains the text "Game Over" and omits the bonus movie clip, which is only on frame 2. This prevents the user from getting more points after the game is over. I've also added background scenery to the example movie.

Other Possibilities

The game is already pretty complex for a book example. However, there are many little features you can add to make it even more involved. For instance, you could change the background hills into a movie clip and have them scale up as the car races forward. This gives the illusion that the car is getting closer to the hills.

You could add more types of bonuses, worth different amounts of points. You could also cap the speed of the car, but have bonuses that allow the maximum speed to increase.

Aim and Shoot Games

- Move and Shoot the Balloons
- Aim and Shoot
- Balloon Invaders

Aim-and-shoot games are similar to catch-and-avoid games in two ways: The main character moves, and so do the other objects in the game. However, the new element introduced in this chapter is shooting. The character and objects never meet. Instead, the character shoots at the objects.

The first game you'll build in this chapter allows the player to move a character across the bottom of the screen and shoot directly up at objects overhead. In the second game, the character stands still, but is able to aim and shoot diagonally at the objects. In the third game, the objects move in a classic arcade pattern.

Move and Shoot the Balloons

Example file: Balloonshoot.fla

In this first game, there are three primary elements: the fox, the balloons, and the bullets. In this case, the bullets are just peas being shot from a straw. (That makes it suitable for all audiences.) Figure 10.1 shows the example game on the CD-ROM.

Figure 10.1

The Balloon Shoot game features a fox shooting peas through a straw at balloons passing by.

Project Goal

The goal is to build a game in which the fox moves left and right and can shoot bullets directly up from his position. The balloons float in from the left and right at random speeds and altitudes. After a fixed number of balloons float by, the game is over. The score is determined by how many balloons have been popped. Play the example movie, Balloonshoot.fla, on the CD-ROM to see how it works.

Approach

The fox's movement is similar to all the games in the last chapter. We'll even animate the fox as he moves and flip the movie clip horizontally so that he faces the proper direction.

The balloons are taken from a single movie clip that contains a light gray balloon. As well as a random altitude, speed, and direction, we will also assign a random color.

The bullets being shot from the fox's straw are another movie clip. We use a button that reacts to the spacebar to determine when the player fires. The new movie clip is created at the tip of the straw, and then moves upward from that moment on. We also set a timer and check it to make sure that the player can fire only once per second.

A balloon pops when a bullet gets too close to it. Instead of using *hitTest* to determine a collision, a mathematical formula determines when the bullet is close to the center of the balloon.

Preparing the Movie

In the example movie, Balloonshoot.fla on the CD-ROM, the fox is a movie clip with a "stand" frame and a "walk" animation sequence. It actually shows the fox walking to the left, as shown in Figure 10.2, but you can use ActionScript to flip the fox to make him appear to walk to the right when necessary. The position of the straw, however, should be at the same location in all frames, relative to the center point of the movie clip.

Figure 10.2
The fox walks to the left, but always keeps the straw pointed and ready to fire.

The balloon movie clip also has several frames. The first shows the normal balloon. The rest shows an animation of the balloon exploding. When the balloon is hit, it is told to play this short animation. Figure 10.3 shows the only frame of the animation for the example movie, but you might want to have a more elaborate explosion.

Figure 10.3
When a balloon is hit, this balloon explosion animation appears.

The balloon uses only shades of gray as coloring. When you create a new balloon movie clip in the code, you also color it in. This allows you to use one balloon movie clip, but have it appear to be different colors every time.

The bullet movie clip is a short line. Even though it is supposed to be a pea, a short vertical line helps give the illusion of upward movement.

Writing the Code

A small "actions" movie clip is positioned off the Stage and controls the action through calls to functions in the main timeline. It initializes the game when it loads, and then calls a series of functions every frame.

```
onClipEvent(load) {
    _root.initGame();
}

onClipEvent(enterFrame) {
    _root.newBalloon();
    _root.moveBalloons();
    _root.moveFox();
    _root.moveBullets();
}
```

The "initGame" function resets all the important variables used in the game.

```
function initGame() {
    // init balloon variables
    nextBalloonTime = 0;
    nextBalloon = 0;
    balloons = [];
    numBalloons = 10;

    // init bullet variables
    nextBulletTime = 0;
    nextBullet = 0;
    bullets = [];

    // init score
    score = 0;
}
```

For a new balloon to be created, it must pass three tests. The first test determines whether any more balloons are left in the game. The second test determines whether enough time has passed since the last balloon was created. The final test is actually a coin flip: a 50% chance that a new balloon will be created at this instant.

After all three tests have passed, the "newBalloon" function creates a new balloon that has a 50/50 chance of coming from the left or right side of the screen. The speed of the balloon is a random number from 3 to 5. This number is positive if the balloon is meant to float from the left to the right, and negative if it's meant to float from the right to the left.

The color of the new balloon movie clip is picked from a list of five colors. The *setTransform* command is used on a color object created from the new movie clip to set the color.

You keep track of the balloon movie clips by placing their names and speeds into an array called "balloons."

Finally, the "nextBalloon" and "nextBalloonTime" variables are set so that future calls to "newBalloon" can use them.

```
function newBalloon() {
    // more balloons?
    if (nextBalloon < numBalloons) {

        // time for next?
        if (getTimer() > nextBalloonTime) {

            // 50% chance of a new balloon
            if (Math.Random() < .5) {

                // create new balloon clip
                attachMovie("balloon", "balloon"+nextBalloon, nextBalloon);

                // choose which side to come from and random speed
                if (Math.Random() < .5) {
                    _root["balloon"+nextBalloon]._x = -30;
                    dx = int(Math.Random()*3)+3;
                } else {
                    _root["balloon"+nextBalloon]._x = 580;
                    dx = -int(Math.Random()*3)-3;
                }

                // choose height of balloon
                _root["balloon"+nextBalloon]._y = int(Math.Random()*100)+20;

                // choose color of balloon
                balloonColor = new Color("balloon"+nextBalloon);
                r = int(Math.Random()*5)+1;
                if (r == 1) {
                    balloonColor.setTransform({rb: 255});
```

```
            } else if (r == 2) {
                balloonColor.setTransform({gb: 255});
            } else if (r == 3) {
                balloonColor.setTransform({bb: 255});
            } else if (r == 4) {
                balloonColor.setTransform({rb: 255, gb: 255});
            } else if (r == 5) {
                balloonColor.setTransform({rb: 255, bb: 255});
            }

            // add balloon to array
            balloons.push({clip: "balloon"+nextBalloon, d: dx});

            // set things up for next balloon
            nextBalloon++;
            nextBalloonTime = getTimer() + 2000;
        }
    }
  }
}
```

NOTE

A quick way to determine a 50% change is to use the code *(Math.Random() < .5)*. Because *Math.Random()* returns a value from 0 to 1.0, but never exactly 1.0, testing for it to be less than .5 gives you a 50% chance.

After the balloons have been created, it is up to the "moveBalloons" function to keep them going. This function loops through the balloons and moves each movie clip the appropriate amount. It checks to see whether the balloon has reached the other side and removes the movie clip if it has. It also removes the item from the "balloons" array.

TIP

Note that the *for* loop in the "moveBalloons" function counts backward. It starts with the last movie clip in the "balloons" array and counts down to 0. This is done so that when a balloon is removed from the array, it does not change the positions of the other items in the array. For instance, imagine that item 3 of a 5-item array is removed. Then, item 4 becomes item 3 and item 5 becomes item 4. If you were counting up, you would skip the new item 3 and go right to the new item 4. However, if you count down, there is no such problem.

The "moveBalloons" function also checks to see whether all the balloons have been created in the first place, and that they have all since disappeared. This signals the end of the game.

```
function moveBalloons() {
    // loop through balloons in array
    for(i=balloons.length-1;i>=0;i--) {

        // get speed and clip
        dx = balloons[i].d;
        balloon = _root[balloons[i].clip];

        // move balloon
        balloon._x += dx;

        // balloon exit left
        if ((dx < 0) and (balloon._x < -20)) {
            balloon.removeMovieClip();
            balloons.splice(i,1);

        // balloon exit right
        } else if ((dx > 0) and (balloon._x > 570)) {
            balloon.removeMovieClip();
            balloons.splice(i,1);
        }
    }

    // see whether all balloons gone
    if ((nextBalloon >= numBalloons) and (balloons.length < 1)) {
        gotoAndStop("game over");
    }
}
```

The "moveFox" function checks the left- and right-arrow keys and moves the fox 10 pixels left or right. Like the games in Chapter 9, "Catch and Avoid Games," it uses the _xscale property to flip the fox movie clip to face the proper direction. It also sends the movie clip to its animated segment starting at frame 2 for walking, and to its standing-still segment at frame 1 for standing.

```
function moveFox() {
    // move fox to left, no flip
    if (Key.isDown(Key.LEFT)) {
        dx = -10;
        fox._xscale = Math.abs(fox._xscale);

    // move fox to right, flip
    } else if (Key.isDown(Key.RIGHT)) {
        dx = 10;
        fox._xscale = -Math.abs(fox._xscale);
```

```
    // stop moving
    } else {
        dx = 0;
    }

    // move fox
    fox._x += dx;

    if ((dx == 0) and (fox._currentFrame != 1)) {
        // set fox to stand
        fox.gotoAndStop(1);
    } else if ((dx != 0) and (fox._currentFrame == 1)) {
        // set fox to move
        fox.gotoAndPlay(2);
    }
}
```

To shoot a bullet, the player hits the spacebar. A button intercepts this keypress and the "shootBullet" function is called. Check the "Loose Ends" section at the end of this game description to see the code for the button.

The "shootBullet" function checks the current time to make sure enough time has passed since the last bullet was fired. This prevents the player from just shooting a shower of bullets that hits everything.

Like the balloons, each bullet is both a movie clip and an item in an array—in this case, the array "bullets." The array is used by "moveBullets" to keep the bullet going after it is fired.

Notice in the following code that the bullet movie clip starts off at the location of the fox, but 2 pixels to the right and 55 pixels above. This corresponds to the exact position of the tip of the fox's straw in relation to the center of the fox.

```
function shootBullet() {
    // see whether there has been enough time to reload
    if (getTimer() > nextBulletTime) {

        // create bullet clip
        attachMovie("bullet","bullet"+nextBullet,nextBullet+9999);

        // set location
        _root["bullet"+nextBullet]._x = fox._x+2;
        _root["bullet"+nextBullet]._y = fox._y-55;

        // add to array
        bullets.push(nextBullet);
```

```
        //get set for next bullet
        nextBullet++;
        nextBulletTime = getTimer()+1000;
    }
}
```

The "moveBullets" function works just like the "moveBalloons" function, except that it moves the bullets up rather than left or right. It checks to see whether the bullet has hit the top of the screen. It also checks to see whether the bullet has hit a balloon by calling "checkCollision." In either case, the bullet movie clip and array element are deleted.

```
function moveBullets() {
    // loop through all bullets
    for(i-bullets.length-1;i>=0;i--) {

        // get clip
        bullet = _root["bullet"+bullets[i]];

        // move clip
        bullet._y -= 10;

        // see whether it reached top
        if (bullet._y < 0) {
            bullet.removeMovieClip();
            bullets.splice(i,1);

        // see whether it hit a balloon
        } else {
            if (checkCollision(bullet)) {
                bullet.removeMovieClip();
                bullets.splice(i,1);
            }
        }
    }

}
```

The "checkCollision" function loops through all the balloons and determines whether any are close to this particular bullet. It uses a function called "distance" to get the distance from the center of the bullet to the center of the balloon. We'll look at that function next.

If the distance is less than 10 pixels, which is the approximate diameter of the balloon, then it is scored a hit. The balloon movie clip goes to frame 2, and a *true* is returned. This signals the "moveBullet" function shown previously to dispose of the bullet.

TIP

Why not use *hitTest* to determine when a bullet hits a balloon, rather than this "distance" function? Well, *hitTest* returns *true* if the bullet hits any part of the balloon. This includes the string hanging down from the balloon.

```
function checkCollision(bullet) {
    // loop through all balloons
    for(j=balloons.length-1;j>=0;j--) {
        balloon = _root[balloons[j].clip];

        // see whether the bullet is close to the balloon
        if (distance(bullet,balloon) < 10) {

            // go to "pop" frame of balloon
            balloon.gotoAndPlay(2);

            // remove balloon from array
            balloons.splice(j,1);

            // add to score
            score += 1;

            // return true, because there was a collision
            return(true);
        }
    }

    // return false, because there was a collision
    return(false);
}
```

The distance function uses a mathematical formula to determine the exact distance, in pixels, between two movie clips. First, it determines the horizontal and vertical difference between the two clips' locations. This is stored in "dx" and "dy." Then, it takes the square root of the sum of the squares of these numbers. This is the mathematical formula used to determine distance.

```
function distance(clip1, clip2) {
    // find distance between two movie clips
    dx = clip1._x - clip2._x;
    dy = clip1._y - clip2._y;
    return (Math.sqrt(dx*dx+dy*dy));
}
```

Loose Ends

To get the spacebar key press, we'll use a button. In the example movie, you can see this button as a piece of text, "button," just off the Stage to the upper left. This code is attached to it:

```
on (keyPress "<Space>") {
    _root.shootBullet();
}
```

According to the code, this button does not even react to a click. It wouldn't matter if the button did react, because the button is off the Stage. However, the program does look for and capture the spacebar. Then it calls the "shootBullet" function.

TIP

The reason we use this button to capture the spacebar press—and do not use a *Key.isDown* test in the "moveFox" function—is not easy to see at first. The *Key.isDown* test tests to see only whether a key is pressed during a certain instant. In this game, this happens once per frame. However, if a player presses the spacebar quickly, he could press it and release it between *Key.isDown* tests. Then the bullet wouldn't fire because the program didn't ever see it pressed. Using a button to capture a keystroke, however, guarantees that the keystroke is captured and used.

The example movie is set to run at 30 frames per second. I did this to make the animation smoother. If you want to change this, note that you need to change the movement amounts for the fox, balloons, and bullets to match. Otherwise, the game goes faster or slower than you might have intended.

Other Possibilities

The example movie can be made a little more interesting in a number of ways. Instead of being random, the colors can be linked to a certain number of points. For instance, red balloons can be worth 100 points, blue worth 50, and so on. Then, in turn, the colors can be linked to speeds and altitudes. Obviously, the higher and faster balloons should be worth more.

Next, you can move away from balloons altogether. This game is essentially similar to various anti-aircraft, "Sea Wolf," and alien invasion games. All you need to do is replace all the graphics.

Aim and Shoot
Example file: Aimandshoot.fla

What if, in the Balloon Shoot game, the character stood still instead of moving from side to side? Then, in addition, he could aim his straw to point anywhere on the screen, not just straight up. Also, what if the bullets obeyed the law of gravity and arced as they flew, eventually falling back to the ground?

Example movie Aimandshoot.fla shows how the game plays with these changes. Figure 10.4 shows the game in action, and you can see that the fox is in the middle, but bullets have been fired off at an angle. Now, let's look at how this is done.

Figure 10.4
The Aim and Shoot game is similar to the Balloon Shoot game, but with aiming and gravity.

Project Goal

The goal is to take the previous game, remove one element, and add two new ones. The element to be removed is the fox's left and right movement. In this game, the arrow keys have no effect and the fox stays in the center of the screen.

The two new elements are aiming and gravity. The player should be able to use the mouse to aim, and the straw points in the proper direction. Then, after the bullet leaves the straw, it gradually falls back to Earth.

Approach

To make the straw point in the proper direction, you first have to measure the horizontal and vertical distance from the cursor to the straw. Then you have to calculate the angle from this measurement.

This angle can easily be used to rotate the straw movie clip to point in the proper direction. However, you also have to use this angle to determine where the bullet starts and how many vertical and horizontal pixels it moves each frame.

Adding gravity is a little easier. When an object such as a bullet starts moving, gravity has no initial effect. However, each frame that goes by adds a little bit to the speed at which the bullet is falling. Because the bullet has a strong initial force upward, the bullet keeps moving upward, but at a slower and slower speed as gravity overcomes the initial push. Then, inevitably, the bullet begins to come down, faster and faster.

This downward movement is called "acceleration due to gravity," and it is approximately 32 feet per second per second (9.8 meters per second per second) in the real world. In the game world, we can use whatever number seems to create the right feeling for the player.

Preparing the Movie

The biggest non-code difference between this game and the previous one is that the straw is a separate movie clip. This way the straw can be rotated independently of the fox.

The fox movie clip is also different because it doesn't need the walking animation. The fox is really no more than a piece of background in this game, although it appears on top of the straw.

Writing the Code

Several of the functions for this game are identical to the "Balloon Shoot" game, so there is no need to show those here. They are the "initGame," "newBalloon," "moveBalloons," "checkCollision," and "distance" functions.

One of the new functions is "aimStraw." This function replaces the "moveFox" function. It is called from the "actions" movie clip, which now uses the following code:

```
onClipEvent(load) {
    _root.initGame();
}

onClipEvent(enterFrame) {
    _root.newBalloon();
    _root.moveBalloons();
    _root.aimStraw();
    _root.moveBullets();
}
```

The "aimStraw" function needs to calculate the angle in which the player is aiming, and then set the straw movie clip's rotation. It also stores the angle in a variable called "strawRadians," which is used by the "shootBullet" function.

To calculate an angle from two points, you first find the horizontal and vertical difference between the two points. In this function, these differences are stored in "dx" and "dy." Then you run these two numbers through the *Math.atan2* function to return the angle in radians.

TIP

Angles can be measured in radians or degrees. A radian is a measure in which 6.28 radians (two times pi) makes one complete circle. In degrees, 360° makes a full circle. Flash uses radians in mathematical functions such as *Math.sin* and *Math.cos*, and degrees for movie clip properties such as *_rotation*. Therefore, it is necessary at times to convert between these two types of measurements.

NOTE

The *Math.atan2* function is a great tool for game programmers. An arctangent is a function that converts the slope of a line into an angle. Because you can get the slope of a line from two points, an arctangent can then be used to convert two points to an angle. However, arctangents do not take into account which point is the anchor and which is the pointer in determining an angle. Therefore, it is easy to get angles that are actually the opposite of what you wanted. To fix this, you have to write several *if* statements to take care of various cases. However, the *Math.atan2* function lets Flash handle all those special cases. It just takes the horizontal and vertical difference and returns the angle, plain and simple.

```
function aimStraw() {
    // find x and y differences
    dx = _xmouse - straw._x;
    dy = _ymouse - straw._y;

    // calculate angle
    strawRadians = Math.atan2(dy,dx);

    // convert to degrees and set rotation
    strawDegrees = 360*strawRadians/(2*Math.PI);
    straw._rotation = strawDegrees;
}
```

Now, when a bullet is shot, more information than just its movie clip needs to be recorded in the "bullets" array. For each frame movement, you also need to know the angle at which the bullet was fired.

We'll also add a property called "down" to each bullet object in the "bullets" array for the cumulative effect of gravity on the bullet. This property starts at 0.

To make the bullet start at the tip of the straw, set the bullet's x and y location to the straw's location, plus 20 pixels. Distribute these 20 pixels between x and y by using *Math.sin* and *Math.cos* to separate the horizontal and vertical components of the angle.

NOTE

Math.sin and *Math.cos* can be used to take an angle and determine its horizontal and vertical component. To visualize this, imagine a circle with the center at 0,0, the topmost point at 0,–1, and the rightmost point at 1,0. Run any angle through *Math.sin* and you get the y-coordinate of the point on the circle that is at that angle. The *Math.cos* function gives you the x-coordinate. So, *Math.sin(0)* is –1 and *Math.cos(0)* is 0, corresponding to 0,–1.

More important than understanding this, it is important that you understand that movement can be broken down into two things: speed and angle. Measurements for computer screens are always in horizontal and vertical distances, not diagonal ones. *Math.sin* and *Math.cos* allow you to convert speed and angle into horizontal and vertical distances.

```
function shootBullet() {
    // see whether there has been enough time to reload
    if (getTimer() > nextBulletTime) {

        // create bullet clip
        attachMovie("bullet","bullet"+nextBullet,nextBullet+9999);
        bullet = _root["bullet"+nextBullet];

        // set location
        bullet._x = straw._x + Math.cos(strawRadians)*20;
        bullet._y = straw._y + Math.sin(strawRadians)*20;

        // add to array
        // clip = movie clip name
        // angle = angle of initial force
        // down = effect of gravity so far
        bullets.push({clip: bullet, angle: strawRadians, down: 0});

        //get set for next bullet
        nextBullet++;
        nextBulletTime = getTimer()+1000;
    }
}
```

The "moveBullets" function now uses the "angle" and "down" properties of each bullet to move them the appropriate amount. In addition, the "down" property is increased to show the continuing effect of gravity.

Because what goes up must come down, we check for the bullet to hit the bottom of the Stage before we remove it from the array and destroy the movie clip.

```
function moveBullets() {
    // loop through all bullets
    for(i=bullets.length-1;i>=0;i--) {

        // get clip
        bullet = bullets[i].clip;

        // move clip according to initial force
        bullet._x += Math.cos(bullets[i].angle) * 10;
        bullet._y += Math.sin(bullets[i].angle) * 10;

        // add gravity effect
        bullet._y += bullets[i].down;

        // gravity acceleration
        bullets[i].down += .2;

        // see whether it reached bottom
        if (bullet._y > 400) {
            bullet.removeMovieClip();
            bullets.splice(i,1);

        // see whether it hit a balloon
        } else {
            if (checkCollision(bullet)) {
                bullet.removeMovieClip();
                bullets.splice(i,1);
            }
        }
    }
}
```

Loose Ends

Because the bullets in this game move in all different directions, I changed the bullet movie clip so that it resembles a small dot rather than a short line.

Other Possibilities

Like the previous game in this chapter, you can add many complexities, such as more points for faster and higher balloons. The idea of making this into an anti-aircraft war game works well, because anti-aircraft guns are usually stationary, but can fire at different angles.

Balloon Invaders *Similar to Space invaders*

⊙⟫ **Example file: Ballooninvaders.fla**

The most classic of all video games, Space Invaders, includes a very strange but recognizable movement pattern for the enemy units. They move as a group from side to side, slowly dropping down. If they reach the bottom, then the player loses.

Let's change the first game in this chapter so that the balloons work like space invaders.

Project Goal

The balloon behavior is simple. They start off in a group ten balloons wide by three deep, as shown in Figure 10.5. The balloons move right until the first column of balloons hits the right side of the screen. Then all the balloons reverse direction and drop down slightly.

Figure 10.5
The balloon invaders move in a group.

In the meantime, the fox is below moving from left to right and firing at the balloons. The fox must pop all the balloons before the group reaches the bottom of the screen.

Approach

The fox behavior can remain the same as in the first game of this chapter. But the balloon behavior must be completely replaced. In addition, no new balloons need to be created during gameplay. They all appear at the start of the game.

Preparing the Movie

Like the first game in this chapter, the fox has a "stand" frame and a "walk" animation. The balloon has a normal frame and then an explosion animation. All the balloons start off as gray and are colored in with ActionScript. The bullet is a short line movie clip.

Writing the Code

The "actions" movie clip is similar to the first game in the chapter, except that new balloons are not created each and every frame.

```
onClipEvent(load) {
    _root.initGame();
}


onClipEvent(enterFrame) {
    _root.moveBalloons();
    _root.moveFox();
    _root.moveBullets();
}
```

The "initGame" function calls a "createBalloons" function to make the group of balloons. It doesn't have to set any variables like "nextBalloon" or initialize a "balloons" array because new balloons are not created after the initialization of the game.

```
function initGame() {
    // init balloon variables
    createBalloons();

    // init bullet variables
    nextBulletTime = 0;
    nextBullet = 0;
    bullets = [];

    // init score
    score = 0;
}
```

The "createBalloons" function creates 30 balloons in ten columns of three. Each balloon reference is stored in an array. The color of the balloons is set according to which row they are in. Each balloon is given the initial direction and speed of 3.

```
function createBalloons() {
    balloons = new Array();
    balloonNum = 0;

    // create three rows of 10
    for(var y=0;y<3;y++) {
        for(var x=0;x<10;x++) {

            // create new ballow and set position
            attachMovie("balloon", "balloon"+balloonNum, balloonNum);
            balloonClip = this["balloon"+balloonNum];
            balloonClip._x = x*30+20;
            balloonClip._y = y*30+20;
```

```
        // add to array
        balloons.push(balloonClip);

        // set color according to row
        balloonColor = new Color(balloonClip);
        if (y == 0) {
            balloonColor.setTransform({rb: 255});
        } else if (y == 1) {
            balloonColor.setTransform({gb: 255});
        } else if (y == 2) {
            balloonColor.setTransform({bb: 255});
        }

        balloonNum++;
    }
}

    // set initial direction/speed
    balloonDirection = 3;
}
```

The "moveBalloons" function moves all the balloons in the "balloons" array. If any of these hit the side of the screen, then they all reverse direction. If any hit near the bottom of the screen, then the game ends.

```
function moveBalloons() {
    // assume no change in direction
    var newDirection = false;

    // loop through all balloons
    for(var i=0;i<balloons.length;i++) {

        // move balloon
        balloons[i]._x += balloonDirection;

        // see whether balloon hits side
        if ((balloonDirection > 0) and (balloons[i]._x > 530)) {
            newDirection = true;
        } else if ((balloonDirection < 0) and (balloons[i]._x < 20)) {
            newDirection = true;
        }
    }

    // if a balloon hit side, drop down and reverse
    if (newDirection) {
        balloonDirection *= -1;
```

```
        for(var i=0;i<balloons.length;i++) {
            balloons[i]._y += 3;
        }
    }

    // see whether the last one hit bottom
    if (balloons[i-1]._y > 300) {
        gotoAndStop("game over");
    }
}
```

All the functions for creating and moving the fox and bullets are exactly the same as in the first game of this chapter, so I will not repeat that code here. But the "checkCollision" function is different because it must look for the case where all the balloons have been destroyed and end the game.

```
function checkCollision(bullet) {
    // loop though all balloons
    for(j=balloons.length-1;j>=0;j--) {
        balloon = balloons[j];

        // see whether the bullet is close to the balloon
        if (distance(bullet,balloon) < 10) {

            // remove from array
            balloons.splice(j,1);

            // go to "pop" frame of balloon
            balloon.gotoAndPlay(2);

            // add to score
            score += 1;

            // if no more invaders, then game over
            if (balloons.length == 0) {
                gotoAndStop("game over");
            }

            // return true, because there was a collision
            return(true);
        }
    }

    // return false, because there was a collision
    return(false);
}
```

Loose Ends

Like the original game in this chapter, there are both introductory and "game over" frames. I'm using the same frame for both game over conditions: whether the player wins or loses. You may want to have two separate frames with appropriate text on each.

Other Possibilities

To make the game more challenging, you can speed up the invaders. First try increasing the amount that they drop each time. You can also increase the side-to-side speed.

If you want to add levels to the game, you can make a "startSpeed" variable that starts at 3. Set the "balloonDirection" of each balloon to this speed rather than the hard-coded "3." Then, have players go to a "level over" screen when they get all the balloons. When they press the "play next level" button there, it can increase "startSpeed" and go back to the "play" frame where the balloons are initialized with the new, faster, "balloonDirection."

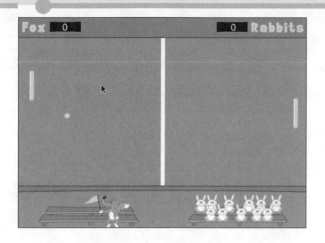

Ball-and-Paddle Games

- Wall Ball
- Paddle Ball
- Paddle Bricks
- 3D Paddle Bricks

The next genre of games dates back to the first video game: *Pong*. This simple game started the arcade revolution in the 70s.

These games all involve a simple ball that bounces off walls and a paddle that the player controls. The player tries to not let the ball get past the paddle.

The first game you will build has a single paddle and a ball. The second game features a second, computer-controlled paddle and an artificially intelligent opponent. The third game in this chapter has the player trying to hit blocks with the ball, like the classic arcade game *Breakout*. The final game moves the paddle and ball concept into the third dimension.

Wall Ball

Example file: Wallball.fla

The first game is called Wall Ball. It features a single, player-controlled paddle and three walls that the ball can bounce off of. The fourth wall is open. The player's task is to not let the ball get past the paddle and through the open wall. Figure 11.1 shows this simple game.

Figure 11.1
The Wall Ball game features a ball, a paddle, and a wall.

Project Goal

The goal is to build a game where a moving ball reflects off walls and a paddle. The paddle should follow the vertical location of the mouse. When the ball gets past the paddle and reaches the edge of the screen, the game should end. Also, when the ball hits the paddle, it should increase in speed slightly.

Approach

The most complex part of this game is getting the ball to accurately reflect off the walls. Many programmers over-simplify this, not taking into account the width of the ball and its speed. As a result, the ball can appear to reflect at a point beyond the wall.

The code needs to look for the situation in which the ball has moved beyond the wall. Then it will determine how far beyond the wall the ball is. Because the ball moves at several pixels per frame, it can easily overshoot the wall by several pixels.

After you know how far past the wall the ball is, you can change its direction, and then place the ball at the appropriate distance from the correct side of the wall. Figure 11.2 shows a diagram of how this works.

Figure 11.2
The diagram explains how the ball is repositioned after a collision with a wall.

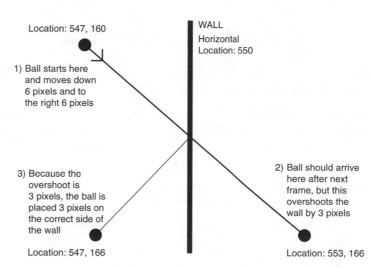

Location: 547, 160

WALL
Horizontal
Location: 550

1) Ball starts here and moves down 6 pixels and to the right 6 pixels

3) Because the overshoot is 3 pixels, the ball is placed 3 pixels on the correct side of the wall

Location: 547, 166

2) Ball should arrive here after next frame, but this overshoots the wall by 3 pixels

Location: 553, 166

Collisions with the paddle are treated just like collisions with a wall. The only difference is that you must make sure the vertical position of the paddle is such that the ball will hit it.

When a ball passes the horizontal location of the paddle, but the paddle is not there, you set a variable flag so that you know the paddle was missed. This way, you won't give the player a second chance to hit the ball as it continues on its journey to the edge of the screen.

Preparing the Movie

The only graphics needed for this game are the ball, the paddle, and the walls. The wall graphics are actually not even used by the code, because the actual game boundaries are in the code as number constants.

Writing the Code

You need only three functions for this game. Check out the example movie, Wallball.fla. All three of these are called from an "actions" movie clip:

```
onClipEvent(load) {
    _root.initGame();
}

onClipEvent(enterFrame) {
    _root.moveBall();
    _root.movePaddle();
}
```

The functions are stored in the main timeline. The first one, "initGame," stores the location of the ball into "x" and "y." It starts "dx" and "dy," which are the horizontal and vertical speeds of the ball, at 5 for each. Then, the function sets a bunch of constants that determine the positions of each wall.

This function also gets the radius of the ball, a value that will be useful in the "moveBall" function. The "passedPaddle" variable is a flag that is set to *true* after the player misses. You should also take this opportunity to turn off the cursor, because it would be a distraction to the player.

```
function initGame() {
    // get start position of the ball
    x = ball._x;
    y = ball._y;

    // set initial speed
    dx = 5;
    dy = 5;

    // set constants
    rightWall = 550;
    leftWall = 0;
    topWall = 0;
    bottomWall = 400;
    ballRadius = ball._width/2;
    passedPaddle = false;

    // hide cursor
    Mouse.hide();
}
```

The "movePaddle" function is the workhorse of this game. It starts by changing "x" and "y" to "dx" and "dy" to get the new location of the ball ①. Then, it checks to see whether the ball has gone past the right wall ②. It adds the radius of the ball to the location of the ball to get the exact position of the right edge of the ball. If the ball has passed the wall, the "movePaddle" function calculates by how much and stores that in "overshoot." The location of the ball is then moved back by twice "overshoot." The direction of the ball is changed by multiplying "dx" by −1. This effectively changes the sign of "dx." So if it was 5 before hitting the wall, it becomes −5.

Next, the code checks to see whether the ball has passed the bottom wall ③. This is similar to the previous segment, except that "y" and "dy" are used instead of "x" and "dx."

When the code checks the top wall, some of the calculations are a little different ④. To determine the location of the top edge of the ball, the radius of the ball is subtracted from the location of the ball. Then, "overshoot" is calculated by subtracting the location of the top edge of the ball from the wall's location.

To detect whether the ball has hit the paddle, the code first calculates the location of the right edge of the paddle ⑤. Then, if the ball is far enough to the left, it calculates the top and bottom of the paddle and determines whether the ball and paddle intersect ⑥.

If the ball hits the paddle, the paddle behaves like any other wall. However, it also increases the speed of the ball by 5% ⑦. If the ball misses the wall, the only action taken at this point is to set "passedPaddle" to *true*.

If "passedPaddle" is *true* and the ball is where the left wall should be, the game is over ⑧. The cursor is set back to normal, and the movie jumps to the "game over" frame.

The "moveBall" function ends by setting the location of the ball movie clip to "x" and "y."

NOTE

The operator "*=" works like "+=," except that it multiplies the original variable by the specified amount. So if "a" is 5, the line "a *= 3" changes "a" to 15. Likewise, if you use "a *= −1", then "a" becomes −5. Using "*= −1" is a quick way to change the sign of a number.

```
       function moveBall() {
①→         // change x and y
           x += dx;
           y += dy;

②→         // check right wall
           if (x+ballRadius > rightWall) {
               overshoot = (x+ballRadius) - rightWall;
               x -= overshoot*2;
               dx *= -1;
           }

③→         // check bottom
           if (y+ballRadius > bottomWall) {
               overshoot = (y+ballRadius) - bottomWall;
```

```
            y -= overshoot*2;
            dy *= -1;
        }

④→     // check top
        if (y-ballRadius < topWall) {
            overshoot = topWall - (y-ballRadius);
            y += overshoot*2;
            dy *= -1;
        }

⑤→     // is it where it should hit the paddle?
        paddleRight = paddle._x+(paddle._width/2);
        if ((x-ballRadius < paddleRight) and !passedPaddle) {

⑥→         // is the paddle there?
            paddleTop = paddle._y-(paddle._height/2);
            paddleBottom = paddle._y+(paddle._height/2);
            if ((y > paddleTop) and (y < paddleBottom)) {

                // hit paddle
                overshoot =  paddleRight - (x-ballRadius);
                x += overshoot*2;
                dx *= -1;

⑦→             // speed up
                dx *= 1.05;
                dy *= 1.05;
            } else {

                // missed paddle, don't check again
                passedPaddle = true;
            }
        }

⑧→     // check left wall
        if ((x-ballRadius < leftWall) and passedPaddle) {
            Mouse.show();
            gotoAndPlay("game over");
        }

        // set ball location
        ball._x = x;
        ball._y = y;
    }
```

Although the "moveBall" function is long and complex, the "movePaddle" function couldn't be any shorter. All it needs to do is set the vertical location of the paddle to the vertical location of the cursor.

```
function movePaddle() {
    // align paddle with cursor
    paddle._y = _ymouse;
}
```

Loose Ends

Be sure the ball movie clip instance is given the name "ball" and the paddle movie clip instance is given the name "paddle." Also, if the walls are not exactly where they are in the example movie, then be sure to set the constants in the "initGame" function to match them.

The main game frame also needs a *stop()* on it so that the main timeline stops, although the "actions" movie clip will continue to loop and call functions.

Other Possibilities

One improvement that can be made to this game is to give players a certain number of balls that they can lose. Then, instead of the game ending as soon as the first ball is lost, it can continue.

You can do this by setting a variable, such as "ballNum," to a particular number at the start of the game. Then, instead of going to a "game over" frame, you can go to a "ball lost" frame if "ballNum" is greater than 0. The player can press a button and play again, but with a "ballNum" of one less.

Paddle Ball

Example file: Paddleball.fla

Although the previous game is fun, it lacks a serious challenge. There is no real way to "win" the game. Instead, you play for as long as you can until you lose.

A more interesting game would allow the player to control one paddle, while the computer would control the other. The player tries not to let a ball get past and hopes the computer misses.

Figure 11.3 shows what the example movie, Paddleball.fla, looks like. The player controls the left paddle and the computer controls the right paddle.

Project Goal

The goal for this game is to create an artificially intelligent opponent for the player to compete against. The left paddle is to be controlled by the player, whereas the right paddle uses logic to try to mimic what a human opponent might do.

Figure 11.3
In Paddle Ball, the player volleys back and forth with the computer.

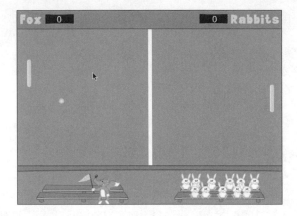

The ball bounces off the top and bottom of the screen, but it is up to the human player and the computer player to make sure it does not leave the screen from the sides.

When a ball gets past either player, the game pauses until the player hits a "serve" button. Then the ball launches itself from the middle of the screen. The game keeps score and ends when either player gets seven points.

Approach

There are many ways to make the artificial intelligence for this game. One would be to have the paddle follow the ball. This would be too perfect, however, because it would be impossible for the computer to miss.

A better way would be to have the computer's paddle move slowly toward the position of the ball. If the ball is moving too fast, the computer might not be able to make it to the correct position quickly enough. Also, the paddle moves only when the ball is moving toward the computer's side.

TIP

Artificial intelligence sounds mysterious and complex. For games, however, it isn't so important that the opponent be smart. The computer opponent merely needs to facilitate fun game play. In many cases, like in this game, it would be easy to make an opponent that is flawless. However, that would make an impossible-to-win game that is no fun. The goal is to make an opponent that presents enough of a challenge so that the game is not easy, but not so much of a challenge that you can't win.

Keeping score just requires a couple of variables. However, pausing the game between serves can be tricky, so the game needs two frames: one in which the program waits for the player to press the "serve" button, and one in which the game action takes place. This second frame starts by setting a random initial direction for the ball.

Preparing the Movie

This movie is basically the same as the previous one. Instead of three frames, you need four: a "start game" frame, a "start level" frame, a "play" frame, and a "game over" frame. The "start level" frame is seen before every ball is served. The "game over" frame is seen only after the last ball has been lost.

There needs to be one paddle movie clip named "paddle" (like in the previous game), and one named "computerPaddle." This second paddle is controlled by your ActionScript. Because the computer paddle is on the right, the right wall needs to be removed. The top and bottom walls should stay.

Writing the Code

Starting with the previous movie, you need to make some changes to the existing functions, and add an important new function. Here is the "actions" movie clip script, which adds a call to this new function, "moveComputerPaddle":

```
onClipEvent(load) {
    _root.startLevel();
}


onClipEvent(enterFrame) {
    _root.moveBall();
    _root.movePaddle();
    _root.moveComputerPaddle();
}
```

Instead of a "startGame" function, this game has a "startLevel" function that does all the same things as the preceding "startGame" function, but also sets the ball moving in a random direction. It does this by sending the ball up 50% of the time, down 50% of the time, as well as left 50% of the time and right 50% of the time. This gives you four possible diagonal directions.

```
function startLevel() {

    // get start position of the ball
    x = ball._x;
    y = ball._y;

    // set initial speed, one of four random diagonals
    dx = 5;
    dy = 5;
    if (Math.random() < .5) dx *= -1;
    if (Math.random() < .5) dy *= -1;
```

```
    // hide cursor
    Mouse.hide();

    // set constants

    rightWall = 550;
    leftWall = 0
    topWall = 0;
    bottomWall = 400;
    ballRadius = ball._width/2;
    passedPaddle = false;
}
```

The "moveBall" function now includes code to detect when the ball has passed the computer's paddle on the right ⑩. This is similar to the code that handles the player's paddle on the left ⑨, which is the same as in the preceding game.

When the ball is lost on either the left side ⑪ or the right side ⑫, the game is usually sent back to the "start level" frame. However, if there are no more balls left, it is sent to the "game over" frame. Depending on who lost the ball, a point is awarded to either "computerScore" or "playerScore."

```
function moveBall() {
    // change x and y
    x += dx;
    y += dy;

    // check bottom
    if (y+ballRadius > bottomWall) {
        overshoot = (y+ballRadius) - bottomWall;
        y -= overShoot*2;
        dy *= -1;
    }

    // check top
    if (y-ballRadius < topWall) {
        overshoot = topWall - (y-ballRadius);
        y += overShoot*2;
        dy *= -1;
    }

    // is it where it should hit the paddle?
    paddleRight = paddle._x+(paddle._width/2);
    if ((x-ballRadius < paddleRight) and !passedPaddle) {

        // is the paddle there?
        paddleTop = paddle._y-(paddle._height/2);
```

⑨→ (marker at "// is it where it should hit the paddle?")

```
            paddleBottom = paddle._y+(paddle._height/2);
            if ((y > paddleTop) and (y < paddleBottom)) {

                // hit paddle
                overshoot =  paddleRight - (x-ballRadius);
                x += overShoot*2;
                dx *= -1;

                // speed up
                dx *= 1.05;
                dy *= 1.05;
            } else {

                // missed paddle, don't check again
                passedPaddle = true;
            }
        }
```

⑩➤
```
        // is it where it should hit the computer's paddle?
        paddleLeft = computerPaddle._x-(computerPaddle._width/2);
        if ((x+ballRadius > paddleLeft) and !passedPaddle) {

            // is the paddle there?
            paddleTop = computerPaddle._y-(computerPaddle._height/2);
            paddleBottom = computerPaddle._y+(computerPaddle._height/2);
            if ((y > paddleTop) and (y < paddleBottom)) {

                // hit paddle
                overshoot =  (x+ballRadius) - paddleLeft;
                x -= overShoot*2;
                dx *= -1;

                // speed up
                dx *= 1.05;
                dy *= 1.05;
            } else {

                // missed paddle, don't check again
                passedPaddle = true;
            }
        }
```

⑪➤
```
        // check left wall
        if ((x-ballRadius < leftWall) and passedPaddle) {
            Mouse.show();
```

```
        computerScore++;
        if (numBalls == 0) {
            gotoAndPlay("game over");
        } else {
            numBalls--;
            gotoAndPlay("start level");
        }
    }
```

```
    // check right wall
    if ((x+ballRadius > rightWall) and passedPaddle) {
        Mouse.show();
        playerScore++;
        if (numBalls == 0) {
            gotoAndPlay("game over");
        } else {
            numBalls--;
            gotoAndPlay("start level");
        }
    }

    // set ball location
    ball._x = x;
    ball._y = y;
}
```

The "movePaddle" function is identical to the one in the preceding game. However, you need to add the "moveComputerPaddle" function that controls the right paddle. This function moves the paddle only if the ball is headed to the right. Then, it moves the paddle up if the ball is above the height of the paddle, and down if it is below.

The speed at which it moves is set at the start of the function. The higher you make this value, the longer the paddle will be able to keep up with the ball.

```
function moveComputerPaddle() {
    // set speed of paddle
    moveAmount = 8;

    // see whether ball is moving in this direction
    if (dx > 0) {

        // move paddle up
        if (y < computerPaddle._y-moveAmount) {
            computerPaddle._y -= moveAmount;
```

```
        // move paddle down
        } else if (y > computerPaddle._y+moveAmount) {
            computerPaddle._y += moveAmount;
        }
    }
}
```

One additional piece of code that you need for this movie is something in the "start game" frame to initialize the number of balls and the score. This number can't be put into the "startLevel" function because it should only be set at the start of the game, not before each ball is served.

```
numBalls = 7;
computerScore = 0;
playerScore = 0;
stop();
```

Loose Ends

You also need to create the "playerScore" and "computerScore" text areas and place them on the Stage. They have been placed in all but the "start game" frame so that they are visible between serves and at the end of the game.

Other Possibilities

It is easy to change the number of balls by just changing "numBalls" in the "start game" frame. However, you can also change other things about the game to make it longer or more difficult. You can increase the speed of the computer's paddle by changing one value in the "moveComputerPaddle" function.

You can also make the computer smarter. For instance, you can write code to predict the destination of the ball and have the computer paddle move there rather than just follow the ball. The ball bounces off the top or bottom wall only once while crossing the screen, so this prediction can be done with just a bit of simple math if you are up for it.

Paddle Bricks

Example file: Paddlebricks.fla

The next game uses the three primary elements of the previous two games—a ball, a paddle, and walls—to build a game far more advanced. This is another classic arcade game, first called *Breakout*, and then cloned under various names.

Figure 11.4 shows the example movie. In addition to a ball and paddle, you can see five rows of bricks at the top of the screen. The object of the game is to bounce the ball off these bricks, which makes them disappear. Get rid of all the bricks and the next level is even faster.

Figure 11.4
The "Paddle Bricks" game features rows of bricks that the player must hit with the ball.

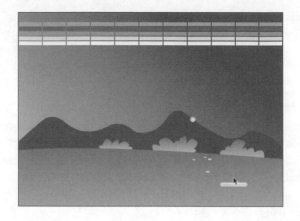

Project Goal

The goal is to build a classic paddle and brick arcade game. The paddle moves horizontally along with the mouse. The ball bounces off the top and sides, but is lost if it gets past the paddle on the bottom.

When a brick is hit by the ball, the ball bounces back, but the brick disappears. After all the bricks have been removed, the level ends. The next level has the same bricks, but a faster ball. If the player loses three balls, the game is over. Check out the movie, Paddlebricks.fla, to see how the game plays.

Another change from the previous ball and paddle games is that the direction of the ball is affected by where the ball hits the paddle. If the ball strikes the left side of the paddle, the ball goes left, if it hits the right side, it goes right. The angle is determined by how far from the center of the paddle the impact occurs.

Approach

The code to detect whether the ball hits the paddle or the walls is similar to the previous two games. One difference is to allow the ball to bounce back from the paddle at any point, not just the top side of the paddle. This makes it a little easier to hit the ball because the player can whack it with the side of the paddle.

When the ball intersects a brick, it reverses the vertical direction. The brick is repositioned off the screen.

Rather than use *hitTest* to determine when the ball hits a brick, you need to examine all four sides of the ball against all four sides of the brick. If the ball and brick overlap at all, it's counted as a hit. With *hitTest*, you can only detect when the center of the ball is inside the rectangle of the brick. That's not accurate enough for this game.

When the ball hits the paddle, you need to calculate the distance from the center of the ball to the center of the paddle. The paddle is 50 pixels long, so the distance can be a little more than 25 pixels, either positive or negative. Divide this number by 4 to get a value between about −7 and 7. This is used as the new value of "dx," which will be the horizontal speed.

This means that the player can direct the ball. If the player hits the ball on the left corner, for instance, the ball is sent sharply to the left. If it is hit in the middle, it should go straight up.

Preparing the Movie

This movie requires five frames, more than any other game so far. The first frame is the "start game" frame. It appears only at the start of a brand new game. Pressing the "Play" button takes the player directly to the "play" frame and the game starts.

The second frame is the "start level" frame. It is shown when the player starts level 2, or any level after that. The "Play" button here also takes the player to the "play" frame in which the new level starts.

The third frame is the "start ball" frame. This frame is shown when the player loses a ball and needs to be served another one. Looking at the example movie, you can see that the bricks exist on both frames three and four, which is the "play" frame. This enables the brick movie clips to remain in place while the movie travels from the "play" frame to the "start ball" frame. Otherwise, the bricks would be reset to their original positions.

The last frame is the "game over" frame. Pressing the "Play" button on this frame takes you back to the "start game" frame where some important variables are reset.

In addition to the frame arrangement, the bricks for frames three and four need to be created. In the example movie, these are 48 pixels wide by 8 pixels high. They are spaced 50×10 pixels in the example movie, which makes 11 bricks across by 5 down for a total of 55 bricks.

TIP

To avoid having to name 55 bricks on the Stage, consider starting with no bricks on the Stage at all, and using *attachMovie* to add each brick with code. Although this technique is not used here, you can see it in action in the next game in this chapter.

Unfortunately, each brick must be individually named for the code to recognize it. They are named "a1" to "a55" in the example movie. The ball clip is named "ball" and the paddle clip is named "paddle."

Writing the Code

Before the game frame is reached, two important variables need to be set in the "start game" frame of the movie. These represent the initial vertical speed of the ball and the number of balls to be served:

```
dy = 3;
numBalls = 3;
stop();
```

When the "play" frame is reached, the usual "actions" movie clip is used to trigger functions on a regular basis. In this game, all the wall and paddle collision detection has been placed in the "moveBall" function, but a separate function—"checkCollisions"—was made for the bricks.

```
onClipEvent(load) {
    _root.startBall();
}

onClipEvent(enterFrame) {
    _root.moveBall();
    _root.movePaddle();
    _root.checkCollisions();
}
```

When the "play" frame begins, the ball is served. The location of the ball is determined by where it happens to be sitting on the Stage before the code takes over. The horizontal speed of the ball is always 3 to the right. The vertical speed was set in the first frame, when "dy" was given a value of 3. However, this will be changed before the next level begins.

In addition to the ball settings, take this opportunity to set some values that will never change during the course of play:

```
function startBall() {
    // get starting point of ball
    x = ball._x;
    y = ball._y;

    // set starting x speed
    dx = 3;

    // hide cursor
    Mouse.hide();

    // set constants
    rightWall = 550;
    leftWall = 0
```

```
    topWall = 0;
    bottomWall - 400;
    ballRadius = ball._width/2;
    paddleTop = paddle._y-paddle._height/2;
    paddleBottom = paddle._y+paddle._height/2;
}
```

The next function controls the paddle by aligning it horizontally with the mouse:

```
// paddle follows cursor
function movePaddle() {
    paddle._x = _xmouse;
}
```

You will recognize the next function because it looks a lot like the "moveBall" function in the other games of this chapter. There are some differences, however.

To determine whether the ball hits the paddle, the code checks to see whether the sides of the ball and the sides of the paddle are overlapping at all ⑬ . Then, when there is a hit, the horizontal speed of the ball is determined based on where the ball hit the paddle ⑭ . In addition, the code to determine when the ball has been missed is simpler because it just checks to see whether the ball has passed the bottom ⑮ .

```
function moveBall() {
    // change x and y
    x += dx;
    y += dy;

    // check right
    if (x+ballRadius > rightWall) {
        overshoot = (x+ballRadius) - rightWall;
        x -= overShoot*2;
        dx *= -1;
    }

    // check left
    if (x-ballRadius < leftWall) {
        overshoot = leftWall - (x-ballRadius);
        x += overShoot*2;
        dx *= -1;
    }

    // check top
    if (y-ballRadius < topWall) {
        overshoot = topWall - (y-ballRadius);
        y += overShoot*2;
        dy *= -1;
    }
```

```
⑬→      // is it where it should hit the paddle?
        if ((y+ballRadius > paddleTop) and (y-ballRadius < paddleBottom)) {

            // is the paddle there?
            paddleLeft = paddle._x-(paddle._width/2);
            paddleRight = paddle._x+(paddle._width/2);
            if ((x+ballRadius > paddleLeft) and (x-ballRadius < paddleRight)) {

                // hit paddle
                overshoot =  paddleTop - (y+ballRadius);
                y += overShoot*2;
                dy *= -1;

⑭→              // set horizontal speed of ball
                // depending on where the paddle
                // and ball connected
                dx = (ball._x - paddle._x)/4;

            } else {

                // missed paddle, don't check again
                passedPaddle = true;
            }
        }

        // check bottom
⑮→      if (y > bottomWall){
            Mouse.show();
            if (numBalls == 0) {

                // no more balls, game over
                gotoAndPlay("game over");
            } else {

                // one less ball
                numBalls--;
                gotoAndPlay("start ball");
            }
        }

        // set ball
        ball._x = x;
        ball._y = y;
    }
```

To determine whether the ball has hit a brick, the code loops through all 55 bricks. A brick at the horizontal location –1000 has already been hit, so it is ignored. Otherwise, the "brickHit" function is called to see whether a brick and the ball overlap. If they do, the brick is removed and the ball bounces.

Notice variable "leveldone." It starts off as *true*, but is changed to *false* as soon as a brick is encountered that is in play and is not being hit by the ball. If the "leveldone" variable remains *true* after all balls have been hit, then the player has succeeded in removing all the bricks. The game now goes to the "start level" frame, but not before the vertical speed of the ball, "dy," has been increased.

TIP

Notice that you must check to see whether the vertical speed of the ball is greater than 7, and set it back to 7 if it is. The bricks are all 8 pixels high. A speed of 8 or higher could cause the ball to skip over bricks without hitting them. Fortunately, a speed of 7 is fast enough that even a good player should not be able to keep up for long.

```
function checkCollisions() {
    // get sides of ball
    ballTop = ball._y - ball._height/2;
    ballBottom = ball._y + ball._height/2;
    ballLeft = ball._x - ball._width/2;
    ballRight = ball._x + ball._width/2;

    // assume level is done
    leveldone = true;

    // loop through bricks to see whether any were hit
    for(i=1;i<=55;i++) {
        brick = _root["a"+i];

        // see whether brick is still around
        if (brick._x <> -1000) {
            if (brickHit(brick)) {

                // brick hit, so take away
                brick._x = -1000;

                // reverse direction of ball
                dy *= -1;

            } else {

                // brick stays, so level is not over
                leveldone = false;
```

```
            }
        }
    }

    // see whether all bricks gone
    if (leveldone) {

        // start new level
        Mouse.show();
        gotoAndPlay("start level");

        // increase vertical speed
        dy += 1;
        if (dy > 7) dy = 7;
    }
}
```

The "hitBrick" function checks all four sides of the ball against all four sides of the brick to see whether there is any overlap. It returns a *true* or *false*.

TIP

Notice that the "hitBrick" function contains four nested *if* statements. You might wonder why a string of four tests with *and* between each one is not used. The reason is speed. With four nested *if* statements, Flash can find one of these conditions to be *false* and never have to check the others. This significantly reduces the amount of work that Flash has to do, and increases the speed of the game. With *and* operators, Flash would have to check all four conditions, even if the first one were *false* to begin with.

```
function brickHit(brick) {
    // perform tests on all four sides
    if (ballTop <= brick._y + brick._height/2) {
        if (ballBottom >= brick._y - brick._height/2) {
            if (ballRight >= brick._x - brick._width/2) {
                if (ballLeft <= brick._x + brick._width/2) {

                    // all four tests true, so brick is hit
                    return(true);
                }
            }
        }
    }

    // brick not hit
    return(false);
}
```

Loose Ends

A lot of elements need to be set perfectly for the code to work. Check out the example movie, Paddlebricks.fla, to see a working version of this game in action. To make your own version, you have to remember to name all the movie clips and place *stop* commands in each frame. You also need to remember the little pieces of code in the buttons and the first frame.

The rows of bricks were colored in using the "Tint" effect to make the game more visually interesting. The colors have nothing at all to do with the game's functionality.

Other Possibilities

To make this a real game, you should add scoring. I didn't want to further complicate the code in the example here. Just add a "score" text area and link it to the "score" variable. Then, add a point every time the player gets a brick.

You might also want to add text areas to tell players what level they are on and how many balls they have left. Sound effects would be a nice and easy addition too.

3D Paddle Bricks

Example File: 3Dpaddlebricks.fla

So far in this chapter you've seen the ball move horizontally and vertically. What if the ball were to move in the third dimension: depth?

Figure 11.5 shows what this might look like. The paddle is a semi-transparent square in the "front" of the game. Four side walls lead to a back wall that is some distance "in" to the screen. The ball appears to shrink as it gets farther from the paddle. The object is to knock out all the bricks in the back wall.

Figure 11.5
The object of this game is familiar, but the perspective view adds a new twist.

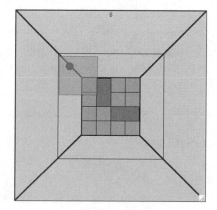

Project Goal

The goal of this game is to create an illusion. Computer screens are hopelessly stuck in two dimensions. But by changing the size of the ball and using perspective lines to make the ball move toward the center of the screen as it gets farther away, you can create the illusion that the ball is moving into the screen.

The goal is to knock out all 16 bricks in the back wall. You do this by hitting each brick once. When the ball reaches the level of the paddle, the paddle must be in position to hit the ball. The spot on the paddle that is hit determines the new angle of the ball. When all 16 bricks have been removed, the level is over. The next level is the same, but the ball moves faster.

Approach

Three variables are necessary to keep track of the position of the ball. You can use "x" and "y" to keep track of the horizontal and vertical position of the ball. A third variable, "z," keeps track of the depth of the ball—how far into the screen it is.

These three variables determine the ball's position inside the imaginary box of the game. This box is 400 units in size horizontally, 400 vertically, and 140 deep. To translate this to screen coordinates is a little tricky. If you look at Figure 11.5 again, you can see that two box shapes are visible. The outer box, which shares a border with the whole screen, is at the level of the paddle. It is 400×400. The inner box, which represents the back wall, is 120×120.

Figure 11.6 shows these two boxes again, but this time marked with x, y, and z coordinates. The upper-left corner of both boxes has an x value of 0 and a y value of 0. However, the outer corner has a z value of 0 whereas the inner corner has a z value of 140. All the other corners are labeled as well.

If the ball is at x and y location 0,0 and moves from 0 to 140 z, then it follows the edge line shown in Figure 11.6. If the ball is at the center of the screen, at 200,200, and moves from 0 to 140 z, it does not appear to move left or right at all. If the ball is at an odd position, like 50,65, and moves from 0 to 140 z, then it must follow its own perspective line so that it appears in the same relative position at the front and back.

The other part of the illusion is to scale the size of the ball down as it moves farther away.

Preparing the Movie

The example movie includes four frames. The second one is where all the action takes place. The background on all frames is the box shown in Figure 11.5. The outer border is 400×400, filling the Stage. The inner border, representing the back of the box, is 120×120 and is at the exact center.

Figure 11.6
The x, y, and z values of each corner of the game area are labeled.

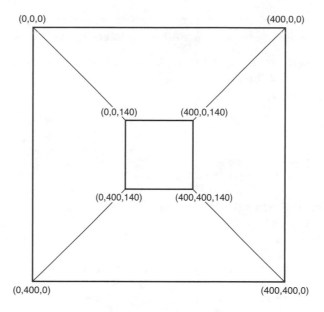

(0,0,0) (400,0,0)

(0,0,140) (400,0,140)

(0,400,140) (400,400,140)

(0,400,0) (400,400,0)

Three other movie clips are also on the screen. The first is the paddle, a 70×70 box named "paddle" and set to have an alpha value of 50% so that it is semi-transparent. The ball is a circle that is 30 units in diameter and is named "ball." There is also an "action" movie clip off to the side.

In the Library, there is another movie clip named "brick." This clip is set to export with the movie. It's used to create the bricks that cover the back wall.

If you look closely at Figure 11.5, you can see that in addition to the thick lines of the inner and outer box, there is also a thin-lined box somewhere in the middle. This set of lines moves with the ball along the edges of the screen. It is there to help the player judge where the ball is located. Test the example movie to see how it works. You need a 400×400 box movie clip to make these lines. The instance name of this movie clip is "ring."

Writing the Code

The code consists mostly of functions placed on the second frame. This first one initializes the game. Instead of individual variables to store the x, y and z values of the ball, we use a single variable object, "ballpos," that has three properties. So, "ballpos.x" refers to the ball's x position. We do the same for "ballvel," which stores the x, y, and z speed of the ball.

The "ballpos" is set so that the ball starts at the center of the back wall. The "ballvel" is set so that the ball starts by coming straight back at the paddle at a speed equal to the game level plus one. So the game starts with the ball having a speed of 2.

The next portion of the "initGame" function creates 16 brick movie clips from the "brick" Library symbol. They are arranged to cover the back wall evenly.

Finally, "initGame" changes the depth of the ball and paddle to make sure that they appear in front of the bricks that were just created.

```
function initGame() {
    // set ball position
    ballpos = {x:200, y:200, z:140};

    // set ball speed
    ballvel = {x:0, y:0, z:-(1+gameLevel)};

    // create back wall bricks
    bricks = new Array();
    for(var x=0;x<4;x++) {
        for(var y=0;y<4;y++) {
            brick = attachMovie("brick","brick"+x+y,x+y*4);
            brick._x = 155+30*x;
            brick._y = 155+30*y;
            bricks.push(brick);
        }
    }

    // ball and paddle in front of bricks
    paddle.swapDepths(101);
    ball.swapDepths(100);
}
```

The job of the "actions" movie clip is to call two functions every frame.

```
onClipEvent(enterFrame) {
    _root.movePaddle();
    _root.moveBall();
}
```

The first of these functions, "movePaddle," is very simple. It just keeps the paddle in line with the cursor.

```
function movePaddle() {
    // paddle position matches cursor
    paddle._x = _root._xmouse;
    paddle._y = _root._ymouse;
}
```

The "moveBall" function, on the other hand, does a lot of work. It starts by changing "ballpos" by "ballvel," thus moving the ball one step ⑯ .

Next, the ball position on the screen is calculated ⑰ . The x position is determined by starting with "ballpos.x" and then adjusting it according to "ballpos.z." The farther away the ball is, the more of an adjustment is made. The other part of the adjustment is determined by how far the ball is from the side. If a ball is 50% between the side and the center (ballpos.x equals 100 or −100), then ballpos.z times 50% is added or subtracted from the x screen location. If you are not quite sure about this calculation, try making up some "ballpos" values to see how they work out.

The next piece of code adjusts the scale of the ball according to the "ballpos.z" value ⑱ . Because "ballpos.z" can go to only 140, then the minimum value for the scale is (200–140)/2, or 35%.

The next piece of the code moves the "ring" movie clip by setting its scale properties ⑲ . The ring acts as a guide so players can tell how far back the ball is located. Many players may not even notice the ring, but their brains will be using it to help them win.

If the ball hits one of the sides of the 3D box ⑳ , then the ball must reverse direction along that plane. All four walls are checked.

The back wall collision ㉑ is a little more complex. The z direction is reversed. In addition, the brick movie clips are examined to see whether the ball hit any of them. A brick that is hit is removed and the player's score is increased by 1.

There is no forward wall, but the user's paddle is at that position instead. If the ball hits a z depth of 0, then the paddle is tested to see whether it is in the way ㉒ . The paddle is 70×70, which means that the ball must be 35 pixels from the center of the paddle in x and y. If the ball hits the paddle, then the new x and y speed is decided by the distance from the collision to the center of the paddle ㉓ . A hit in the exact center means that the ball moves straight ahead, whereas a hit on the left side sends the ball off to the left, and so on.

When the ball hits the paddle, the paddle's _alpha property is increased for the current frame ㉔ . It is then set back to its normal amount in the next frame ㉖ . This temporary increase in intensity offers nice feedback to the user.

If the ball misses the paddle, the game is over ㉕ . On the other hand, if all the bricks are gone ㉗ , the level is complete.

```
     function moveBall() {
⑯►       // move ball in 3 dimensions
         ballpos.x += ballvel.x;
         ballpos.y += ballvel.y;
         ballpos.z += ballvel.z;

⑰►       // position ball on screen
         ball._x = ballpos.x + ballpos.z*(200-ballpos.x)/200;
         ball._y = ballpos.y + ballpos.z*(200-ballpos.y)/200;
```

⑱➤
```
// adjust size of ball
ball._xscale = (200-ballpos.z)/2;
ball._yscale = (200-ballpos.z)/2;
```

⑲➤
```
// adjust wall lines
ring._xscale = (200-ballpos.z)/2;
ring._yscale = (200-ballpos.z)/2;
```

⑳➤
```
// check side collisions
if (ballpos.x > 400) ballvel.x *= -1;
if (ballpos.x < 0) ballvel.x *= -1;
if (ballpos.y > 400) ballvel.y *= -1;
if (ballpos.y < 0) ballvel.y *= -1;
```

㉑➤
```
// back wall collisions
if (ballpos.z > 140) {

    // reverse direction
    ballvel.z *= -1;

    // remove any bricks that have been hit
    for(var i=bricks.length-1;i>=0;i--) {
        if (bricks[i].hitTest(ball._x,ball._y)) {
            bricks[i].removeMovieClip();
            bricks.splice(i,1);
            score++;
        }
    }
}
```

㉒➤
```
// paddle collision
if (ballpos.z < 0) {

    // calc how close ball is to paddle
    px = ballpos.x-paddle._x;
    py = ballpos.y-paddle._y;

    // collision if within 35 pixels
    if ((Math.abs(px) < 35) and (Math.abs(py) < 35)) {
```

㉓➤
```
        // x and y speed according to distance from center
        ballvel.x = px/7;
        ballvel.y = py/7;
```

㉔➤
```
        // paddle brightens to show hit
        paddle._alpha = 90;
```

```
        } else {

            // missed ball
            removeBallAndPaddle();
            gotoAndStop("game over");
        }

        // reverse ball direction
        ballvel.z *= -1;

    } else {

        // return paddle to normal
        paddle._alpha = 50;
    }

    // see whether all bricks are gone
    if (bricks.length < 1) {
        gameLevel++;
        removeBallAndPaddle();
        gotoAndStop("level over");
    }

}
```

Two more utility handlers are in the script. This first one removes the ball and paddle movie clips. If this is not done, they will hang around on the "level over" and "game over" frame.

```
function removeBallAndPaddle() {
    paddle.removeMovieClip();
    ball.removeMovieClip();
}
```

The "removeBricks" function removes all the bricks. It is used by the buttons on the "level over" and "game over" frames.

```
function removeBricks() {
    for(var i=0;i<bricks.length;i++) {
        bricks[i].removeMovieClip();
    }
}
```

The first frame of the movie, the "start" frame, sets the "gameLevel" to 1 and pauses the movie on that frame.

```
gameLevel = 1;
stop();
```

The button on that frame advances to the next frame.

```
on (press) {
    gotoAndStop("Play");
}
```

On the "play" frame are all the functions shown previously. In addition, a single command calls the "initGame" function to get things rolling.

When a level is complete, the game goes to the "level over" frame. The "actions" movie clip is not on this frame, so the ball stops moving automatically. When the user presses the button on this frame, the bricks are removed so that they can be replaced when the "initGame" function is called again.

```
on (press) {
    removeBricks();
    gotoAndStop("Play");
}
```

When the button on the "game over" frame is pressed, the bricks are also removed, but the movie goes to the "start" frame rather than back to "play."

```
on (press) {
    removeBricks();
    gotoAndStop("Start");
}
```

Loose Ends

This game mostly fakes it as far as the 3D math goes. For instance, if the ball is to fly off the paddle at an angle, then the z speed of the ball should be changing so that the overall x, y, and z velocity is always the same. But these little shortcuts make for much simpler code while not compromising game play too much.

You will also probably want to hide the cursor at the start of the game with *Mouse.hide()*, just as you did in the other three games of this chapter. Remember to unhide it when the game is over with *Mouse.show()*.

Other Possibilities

One easy change to this game is to place a picture behind the bricks on the back wall. This can be done without any ActionScript at all. When the bricks are removed, the picture is revealed. You can even place a movie clip with a different picture on each frame. Every time the level is increased, this movie clip advances one frame. So as players clear the bricks on each level, they get a new image. You can use this to tell a story, picture-by-picture. The player must advance through the levels to reveal the story.

Quizzes and Word Puzzles

- Flash Quiz
- Flash Trivia
- Hangman
- Cryptogram

Let's get away from arcade games for a while and look at a series of games that involves words, not actions. Two different types of word games are covered in this chapter. The first is a type of game that asks questions and then determines whether the player answered correctly. The second type of game makes the player figure out a word or phrase by guessing one letter at a time.

Flash Quiz

Example file: Flashquiz.fla

The first two games you will build in this chapter involve questions and answers. The first is a quiz game in which 10 questions are presented, each with 4 possible answers. After the player selects an answer for each, he can see how well he has done.

Figure 12.1 shows the main game frame. The question is near the top, and the four possible answers are below it. The user must click the buttons to the left of each answer.

Figure 12.1

The main game frame shows a question and four answers.

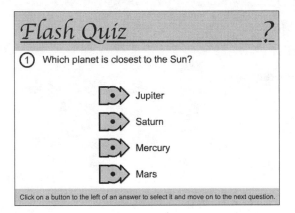

Project Goal

The goal for this project is to make a game that can read a set of questions from an external text file. Then the game displays the questions one by one for the player to answer. Four possible answers are shown. A sound that plays when the player chooses her answer signifies whether she got it right or wrong.

When all 10 questions have been asked, the game is over. A final score is displayed. Go to the example movie Flashquiz.fla on the CD-ROM and play a few rounds to get the idea of how it works.

Approach

The first task is to get the questions and answers from a text file. You can use *loadVars* for this; it grabs a local text file and takes the questions and answers from there.

Unfortunately, *loadVars* can't handle arrays or objects, which is what you need to store a set of questions and answers efficiently. However, you can read in a single piece of text and use *split* to break it into parts to store in an array. This is how you can get 10 questions, 4 answers for each question, and the number of the correct answer, all from one block of text.

After the questions are in an array, the rest is simple. The text from each question and the answers are placed in the appropriate text areas. The number of the correct answer is stored in a variable. Then the program waits for the player to click a button.

Each button calls a function, telling it which answer it represents. If the correct button is clicked, a good sound plays and the number of questions correctly answered is incremented. If the wrong button is clicked, the bad sound is played. Either way, the next question is asked.

When all 10 questions have been asked, the game advances to a "game over" frame where the final score is displayed.

The only extra feature of this game is a neat special effect that causes the text to fly in from the right when each question is first asked.

Preparing the Movie

A lot of things need to be set up before the coding can begin. The first frame, shown in Figure 12.2, shows the "loading" frame. Because the questions are loaded from an external text file, the movie has to wait to make sure that the questions are all there before it can proceed.

Figure 12.2
The "loading" frame stays on the screen until the questions have been loaded.

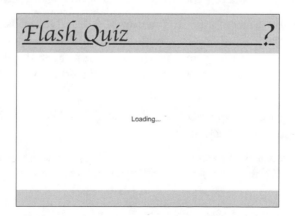

After the questions have been loaded, some ActionScript moves the game along to the second frame, labeled "start game." This frame features some instructions and a button, as shown in Figure 12.3.

Figure 12.3
The "start game"
frame waits until
the user is ready for
the first question.

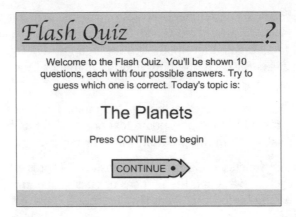

The game frame itself, shown earlier in Figure 12.1, is the most complex. It features a text area for the question, four text areas for the answers, and even a small text area with the question number. There are also four buttons, one to the left of each answer.

The five main text areas are not all they seem in Figure 12.1. Each is actually a text area named "text" inside a movie clip. These five movie clips are called "question" and "answer0" to "answer3." This was done instead of using plain text areas so the clips can be moved on the Stage to create a certain effect to be discussed later.

Writing the Code

There isn't much code in this game, but it is scattered in a few places. The first frame has code in the main timeline that loads the questions from an external text file.

The code starts by creating a *LoadVars* object. A *LoadVars* object is just like a small variable object, except that you can use it to perform some specific tasks with the *LoadVars* object's properties. Specifically, you can request that the object's properties be sent to the server, or that new properties be loaded from the server.

Because you want to request properties from the server, there is no need to set any properties of the *LoadVars* object ahead of time. You'll learn how to send properties in Chapter 17, "Advanced Techniques."

The *load* command, when used on a *LoadVars* object, calls the server and requests some text.

NOTE

The *load* command of the *LoadVars* object attempts to grab a text file from a URL. It then reads in the text file as if the contents of the file were property assignments. For instance, a text file that contained "myVariable=Hello" would set the property "myVariable" in the object to "Hello." Because things do not load instantly on the Web, this might happen several seconds after the *load* command has been issued.

The script starts by creating a *LoadVars* object named "loadQuestions." It then calls the *load* command with the local URL "flashquiz.txt."

The *onLoad* property of a *LoadVars* object defines a function that will be called when the loading is complete. In this case, the function "initQuestions" will be called.

After a *LoadVars.load* is done, then any properties that are sent by the text file will be available to you in ActionScript. For instance, if the property "myProperty" is set to "myValue," then you can ask for "loadQuestions.myProperty" and get "myValue" in return.

```
stop();

// get the questions
loadQuestions = new LoadVars();
loadQuestions.load("flashquiz.txt");

// call initQuestions when loading is complete
loadQuestions.onLoad = initQuestions;
```

The "initQuestions" function takes a long string of text and converts it into an array with questions, answers, and the number of the correct answer for each question.

Here is what the first part of the Flashquiz.txt file looks like. The first line assigns the text "The Planets" to the property "topic." The code will take this property, addressed as "loadQuestions.topic," and assign its value to the root level "topic" variable so that it appears in a dynamic text field.

```
topic=The Planets&questions=Which planet is closest to the Sun?:
➥Jupiter;Saturn;Mercury;Mars:2:
```

In the text file, the property assignment ends with the "&" character. Then the program starts setting the variable "questions." This text is several lines long. Each line is a single question. Each question is broken into three parts: the question text, the answers, and the number of the correct answer. A colon is used to divide these three elements. Furthermore, a semicolon is used to divide the four answers.

```
Which planet is tilted on its axis the most?:Earth;Venus;Mars;Uranus:3:
Which planet is the largest?:Jupiter;Earth;Neptune;Pluto:0:
Which planet has exactly two moons?:Venus;Mars;Saturn;Uranus:1:
```

TIP

An extra colon was used at the end of each line so that when the line is broken into parts by the code, any extra characters at the end of the line are placed in a fourth, unused, part. What extra elements would there be? Well, if you use some Windows text editors, an extra invisible character is placed at the end of every line of text. If you let this extra character be a part of the number of the correct answer, it prevents Flash from converting that number to something it can use. Thus, the extra colon places this extra character harmlessly in an unused fourth element of each line.

WARNING

Be careful not to place an unwanted blank line at the end of the text file. It is easy to press Return or Enter at the end of the last question to create this line. If a blank line is added to the end of the text file, the code uses that as an eleventh question.

This text is broken into array elements by using the *split* command several times. First it is used to separate questions from each other. Then, it is used to separate the parts of the questions. Finally, it is used to separate the answers. The result is a nested array with all the information you need.

```
function initQuestions(questions) {
    // set the topic text
    topic = loadQuestions.topic;

    // break into questions using returns
    // NOTE: character 10 may work better in some cases than character 13
    qArray = loadQuestions.questions.split(String.fromCharCode(13));

    // break each question into question, answers, and correct answer
    for(i=0;i<qArray.length;i++) {
        qArray[i] = qArray[i].split(":");

        // break the answers apart
        qArray[i][1] = qArray[i][1].split(";");
    }

    // start the game
    _root.gotoAndPlay("start game");
}
```

WARNING

I used *String.fromCharCode(13)* to get the carriage return character that is used to break up the lines of a text file. Why didn't I use the ActionScript Constant *newline*? Because *newline* is different between the Mac and Windows version of Flash. On the Mac, it returns character number 13, but on Windows it returns character number 10. Furthermore, some text editors place a character 10 after a line rather than a 13. Some even place both! So if you can't seem to get the game to recognize more than the first question, you may want to change the 13 to a 10 to see whether it fixes the problem.

NOTE

The *split* function takes a string and breaks it into an array of strings. The one parameter it takes is the character used to divide the items. In the previous example, both a colon and a semicolon are used to split strings into arrays.

When the game goes to the "play" frame, the ActionScript in the main timeline immediately calls "initGame." This sets the "questionNum" and "numRight" to 0. It calls "displayQuestion" to show the first question.

```
function initGame() {
    // set variables
    questionNum = 0;
    numRight = 0;

    // ask the first question
    displayQuestion();
}
```

The "displayQuestion" function determines whether the game is over, displays the final score if necessary, and jumps to the "game over" frame if the game is over. Otherwise, it takes the question and each answer and places them in the text areas inside the appropriate movie clips. It places the number of the correct answer in "correctAnswer."

```
function displayQuestion() {
    // see whether all the questions have been asked
    if (questionNum >= qArray.length) {

        // show final score and end the game
        finalScore = numRight + " out of " + qArray.length;
        gotoAndPlay("game over");

    } else {

        // place the question and answers on the screen
        question.text = qArray[questionNum][0];
        answer0.text = qArray[questionNum][1][0];
        answer1.text = qArray[questionNum][1][1];
        answer2.text = qArray[questionNum][1][2];
        answer3.text = qArray[questionNum][1][3];

        // show the question number
        questionNumDisplay = questionNum+1;
```

```
        // remember which one is correct
        correctAnswer = int(qArray[questionNum][2]);

        // make the text slide in
        animateIn();
    }
}
```

NOTE

When you have an array inside another array, you can refer to a specific item by using multiple bracket sets. For instance, "myArray[3][8]" refers to the eighth item in the third array in the "myArray" variable. "myArray" is made up of four or more arrays and the third one has at least nine items.

The "animateIn" function is just a special effect, and does not really affect game play. It sets the position of each text movie clip off the Stage to the right. It then sets a variable called "xstop" for each of these movie clips to the x position where the movie clip should be. Code assigned to each of these clips then acts to move the clips to the left until they line up with "xstop."

```
function animateIn() {
    // set the location of each piece of text
    // and set where each movie clip should stop
    question.xstop = 300;
    question._x = 800;

    answer0.xstop = 400;
    answer0._x = 1000;

    answer1.xstop = 400;
    answer1._x = 1200;

    answer2.xstop = 400;
    answer2._x = 1400;

    answer3.xstop = 400;
    answer3._x = 1600;
}
```

When the user clicks one of the four buttons, the button calls "selectAnswer" with the number of the answer, from 0 to 3. If this matches "correctAnswer," a good sound is played, and "numRight" is increased. If not, a bad sound is played. Either way, the "questionNum" is incremented and the next question is displayed.

```
function selectAnswer(n) {
    // add to count if correct
    if (n == correctAnswer) {
        triggerSound("right");
        numRight++;
    } else {
        triggerSound("wrong");
    }

    // ask next question
    questionNum++;
    displayQuestion();
}
```

A simple function that comes in handy in a number of game situations is "triggerSound." It simply plays a sound with the proper link name.

```
function triggerSound(soundName) {
        // simply play a sound
        soundfx.stop();
        soundfx = new Sound();
        soundfx.attachSound(soundName);
        soundfx.start();
}
```

That's it for the main timeline script. However, two important small scripts are assigned to other elements on the Stage. The first is the script assigned to each text movie clip. It checks to see whether the clip's position is to the right of "xstop" and moves it more to the left if it is. The result is that the movie clip keeps moving left until it hits "xstop." Therefore, when the position of the clip is set offscreen to the right by the "animateIn" function, the question slides in from the right.

```
onClipEvent(enterFrame) {
    if (_x != xstop) _x -= 20;
}
```

Each button also has a short script attached to it. It calls the "selectAnswer" function with a number from 0 to 3. So the first button has this script:

```
on (release) {
    selectAnswer(0);
}
```

Other buttons use a 1, 2, or a 3 in place of the 0.

Loose Ends

You'll need two sounds, one linked with the name "correct" and one with the name "wrong". You'll also need a "continue" button of some sort, such as the one shown in Figure 12.3 earlier. Check out the Flashquiz.fla movie on the CD-ROM if you have any questions about how this all fits together.

Other Possibilities

Although the goal of this program is to present 10 questions to the player, nothing in the code restricts the game to 10 questions. You can ask more or fewer than 10 questions by changing the Flashquiz.txt file.

Also, in addition to showing the player that he got "8 out of 10" correct, you can give the player a ranking. So "8 out of 10" might earn a "You know your planets!" message, although only 2 out of 10 might produce the message "Go back to school."

Flash Trivia

Example file: Flashtrivia.fla

Now that you have a working quiz game, you can build on that to create a trivia game. There are really only a few differences between the quiz game and the trivia game. You'll add more advanced scoring, giving players a chance to score more points if they are quick, and also allowing them to guess more than once while losing points for each wrong guess.

Another feature is randomness. The answers are scrambled so they don't always appear in the same order for everyone. This makes it easier to build the question list, because the first answer in the data file can always be the correct one, but it will not usually be presented as the first answer that the player sees.

Figure 12.4 shows the main play frame of the example movie, Flashtrivia.fla.

Figure 12.4
The trivia game looks a lot like the quiz game, but scoring takes time into account.

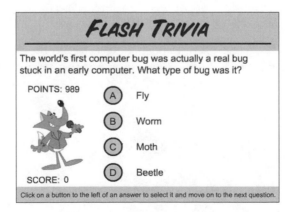

Project Goal

Your goal for this movie is to create a basic trivia game that builds on the previous game. Instead of the answers always appearing in the same order, they appear in a random order each time.

When a question first appears, it is worth 1,000 potential points. As the player tries to determine the correct answer, the number of potential points rapidly decreases. If the player makes an incorrect guess, she loses even more potential points. When the player finally gets the correct answer, the number of potential points remaining is added to her score.

Approach

Like the previous movie, the questions and answers are loaded from an external text file. However, this text file is a little different. In the previous game, the answers were presented in a set order, and an additional item pointed out which answer was the correct one. This time, the correct answer is always first, and is followed by three incorrect answers. You can do this because the answers are shuffled anyway. Here are a few lines from the "flashtrivia.txt" file:

```
questions=The world's first computer bug was actually a real bug stuck in an
early computer. What type of bug was it?:Moth;Beetle;Fly;Worm:
Which is the world's largest Island?:Greenland;Iceland;Australia;New Zealand:
Besides humans, what other animal also has individual fingerprints?:Koala
Bears;Apes;Snakes;Frogs:
```

WARNING

Just as with the previous project, be careful not to place an unwanted blank line at the end of the text file. It is easy to press Return or Enter at the end of the last question to create this line. If a blank line is added to the end of the text file, the code uses that as an eleventh question.

Before each question is asked, the four answers are randomly shuffled into a new array. The correct answer can appear in any of the four spots. Its value is stored in a variable to use later to determine whether the user picked the correct answer.

You can use the same animation as in the previous game, but it should be sped up a little. The question appears right away, with no animation, but the answers fly in quickly from the right. The number of potential points only starts to decrease after all four answers are in place.

When a player picks a wrong answer, not only are points deducted from the number of potential points, but the answer he selected also disappears.

Preparing the Movie

This movie has four frames. The first loads the questions and answers and places them in an array. The second frame explains the game to the player.

The action takes place in the third frame. This frame shows the question, four answers, and a button next to each answer. It also shows the number of potential points and the score, which are both dynamic text areas, the first linked to the variable "potentialPoints" and the second linked to the variable "score."

Remember that the four answers are actually movie clips with text areas inside them. The text areas are all set to represent a variable called "text." The four movie clips, however, are named "answer0" to "answer3."

The last frame of the game is the "game over" frame. This shows the final score and allows the player to click a button to play again.

Writing the Code

The first piece of code is attached to the "loading" movie clip on frame 1. It is basically the same code used in the previous game to load the questions from the text file. When the questions arrive, it calls "initQuestions," which is in the main timeline.

```
stop();

// get the questions
loadQuestions = new LoadVars();
loadQuestions.load("flashtrivia.txt");

loadQuestions.onLoad = initQuestions;
```

The "initQuestions" function breaks the string into questions with two parts. The first part is the question, and the second part is the answers. Then it breaks the answers into individual answers. This is all stored in the "qArray" array.

```
function initQuestions() {
    // break into questions using returns
    // NOTE: character 10 may work better in some cases than character 13
    qArray = loadQuestions.questions.split(String.fromCharCode(13));

    // break each question into question and answers
    for(i=0;i<qArray.length;i++) {
        qArray[i] = qArray[i].split(":");

        // break the answers apart
        qArray[i][1] = qArray[i][1].split(";");
    }
```

```
    // start the game
    _root.gotoAndPlay("start game");
}
```

Most of the code is in the "play" frame. This is where the questions get asked and the player has to react. When the frame begins, the "initGame" function sets the score to 0 and displays the first question.

```
function initGame() {
    // set variables
    questionNum = 0;
    score = 0;

    // ask the first question
    displayQuestion();
}
```

The "displayQuestion" function takes the next question and places the question and answer text in the proper text areas. It also sets the number of potential points for this question to 1,000.

```
function displayQuestion() {
    // see whether all the questions have been asked
    if (questionNum >= qArray.length) {

        // show final score and end the game
        gotoAndPlay("game over");

    } else {
        // rearrange
        answers = shuffleArray(qArray[questionNum][1].slice(0));

        // place the question and answers on the screen
        question.text = qArray[questionNum][0];
        answer0.text = answers[0];
        answer1.text = answers[1];
        answer2.text = answers[2];
        answer3.text = answers[3];

        // show the question number
        questionNumDisplay = questionNum+1;

        // remember which one is correct
        correctAnswer = qArray[questionNum][1][0];
```

```
        // make the text slide in
        animateIn();

        // start potential points at 1000
        potentialPoints = 1000;
    }
}
```

The "scoreCount" function is called once per frame by the "actions" movie clip. It subtracts one point from the number of potential points, making sure that it never drops below 0.

```
// every frame that goes by subtracts one point
function scoreCount() {

    // make sure that last answer has arrived
    if (answer3._x == 400) {

        // subtract point
        potentialPoints -= 1;
        if (potentialPoints < 0) potentialPoints = 0;
    }
}
```

The "shuffleArray" function is used by "displayQuestion" to re-order the answers randomly. It works by creating a new array and then adding one element at a time from the old array to the new array.

```
// take array1 and shuffle into array 2
function shuffleArray(array1) {
    // create new, empty array
    array2 = new Array();

    // loop through array
    do {
        // select a random item
        r = int(Math.random()*array1.length);
        // add item to new array
        array2.push(array1[r]);
        // remove item from old array
        array1.splice(r,1);
    } while (array1.length > 0);

    // send back the new array
    return(array2);
}
```

The "animateIn" function sets the location of the four answers off the Stage to the right. It also notes that each of these movie clips should stop moving left when it gets to the horizontal location 400. A script attached to each movie clip moves the clip quickly to the left until that happens.

```
function animateIn() {
    // set the location of each answer
    // and set where each should stop
    answer0.xstop = 400;
    answer0._x = 800;

    answer1.xstop = 400;
    answer1._x = 1000;

    answer2.xstop = 400;
    answer2._x = 1200;

    answer3.xstop = 400;
    answer3._x = 1400;
}
```

When the player clicks a button, the answer she selected is compared to the "correctAnswer" variable, which was assigned in "displayQuestion." If she got it correct, she gets the potential points, and the next question is displayed. If not, then 200 points are deducted from the number of potential points, and the answer is removed from the screen.

```
function selectAnswer(n) {
    // correct
    if (answers[n] == correctAnswer) {
        triggerSound("right");

        // add score
        score += potentialPoints;

        // ask next question
        questionNum++;
        displayQuestion();

    } else {
        // wrong
        triggerSound("wrong");

        // subtract from potential points
        potentialPoints -= 200;
        if (potentialPoints < 0) potentialPoints = 0;
```

```
        // remove the answer
        _root["answer"+n].text = "";
    }
}
```

The "triggerSound" utility function is the same one used earlier in this chapter. It simplifies adding quick sounds to the rest of the code.

```
function triggerSound(soundName) {
        // simply play a sound
        soundfx.stop();
        soundfx = new Sound();
        soundfx.attachSound(soundName);
        soundfx.start();
}
```

The other pieces of code on the "play" frame include the bit of code on the "actions" movie clip that calls "scoreCount."

```
onClipEvent(enterFrame) {
    _root.scoreCount();
}
```

The code found on each of the four answer movie clips is also used (here is the code for one of the clips). Notice that it moves the movie clip twice as fast as in the quiz game.

```
onClipEvent(enterFrame) {
    if (_x != xstop) _x -= 40;
}
```

Each of the four buttons includes a script that triggers "selectAnswer." Not only do these buttons react to mouse clicks, but each button is assigned a keyboard key as well. For instance, the first button, which you can see is labeled "A" in Figure 12.4 (shown previously), also reacts to the key "A."

```
on (release, keyPress "A") {
    selectAnswer(0);
}
```

Loose Ends

Browse through each element in the example movie Flashtrivia.fla on the CD-ROM. There are many named text areas, including the question, the four answers, the potential points, and the score. Each button is the same movie clip, but a static letter has been placed on top of it. These letters don't do anything except remind the user that he can press a key on the keyboard rather than click the button itself.

Other Possibilities

Like the quiz game, you can place as many questions in the text file as you want. If you know server-side CGI programming, you could even write a server program to generate the Flashtrivia.txt information from a database of questions.

You can easily change the number of potential points with which a question starts, and change the number of points deducted for a wrong answer.

Hangman

▷‹Example file: Hangman.fla

This next game should be familiar to all. The classic pencil-and-paper game, hangman, asks the player to guess which letters are used in a phrase. If the letter she guesses is in the phrase, that letter is revealed in every position where it is located. If the letter is not in the phrase at all, a piece of a drawing of a man getting hanged is added. If the drawing is complete before the phrase has been guessed, the player loses.

Project Goal

The goal here is to re-create the classic hangman game in Flash. The player can use the keyboard to make guesses. Flash takes care of showing the letters and drawing the hanging man, or in this case, the fox.

Figure 12.5 shows the main game frame with the fox fully drawn and some letters showing. In this case, the game has just been lost.

Figure 12.5

This hangman game has been lost.

Approach

This game requires a lot of string manipulation. The phrase to be guessed is a string. From that, you build a string that uses underscore characters in place of letters. This is what the player sees.

When the player makes a guess, that letter is compared to *every* letter in the original phrase. If the letter matches one in the phrase, that letter is shown in that position on the screen.

If the player guesses wrong, the fox movie clip is advanced to the next frame, which adds a part of the fox. If this is the last frame of the fox movie clip, the game is over.

Preparing the Movie

The main element is the text area on the screen. The text area starts with all underscores and spaces, which are replaced gradually with letters as letters are correctly guessed.

The text area has to be set up as Dynamic Text and linked to the variable "display." You also need to set the field to Multiline. This can all be done in the Properties panel when the field is selected.

The display text uses the "Monaco" font, which is a monospaced font found on every Mac. If you are building your movie in Windows, you might have to use another monospaced font such as "Courier New" instead.

TIP

Monospaced font is necessary for this game so that the words wrap around from line to line exactly the same as game play continues. If the letters were different widths, the addition of new letters that were smaller or larger than the underscore would force Flash to rewrap the text.

This game also needs an "actions" movie clip that accepts keyboard input and passes it on to the main timeline script.

Writing the Code

The main parts of the code lie in the main timeline. There are only three functions. The first sets up the phrase at the start of the game.

The first function loops through all the letters in the phrase and creates a "display" string that contains underscores in place of letters. This is what the player sees at the start of the game.

```
function initGame() {
    // get phrase
    phrase = "Imagination is more important than knowledge";

    // build display
    display = "";
    for(i=0;i<phrase.length;i++) {
        // place spaces in the correct spots
```

```
        if (phrase.charAt(i) == " ") {
            display = display + " ";

        } else {
            // place underscores in place of letters
            display = display + "_";
        }
    }
}
```

Each time the player presses a key, the "actions" movie clip sends the character code for that letter to the "makeGuess" function. The first thing this function does is convert the code to a letter.

The "letter" variable is tested by the utility function "isAlpha" to see whether it is a letter. This means that other keys, such as the spacebar or a number, are ignored. You'll learn more about the "isAlpha" function later.

Then, the function loops through each letter of the phrase looking for matches. While it is doing this, the function is rebuilding the "display" variable. Every match found is placed in "display," as well as each letter that was guessed previously.

The variable "gotOne" is set to *false* before all this happens. If any match is found, "gotOne" is set to *true*. If it remains *false* at the end of the loop, the player guessed wrong, and the fox movie clip is advanced to the next frame.

```
function makeGuess(code) {
    // get the character that corresponds to the key pressed
    letter = String.fromCharCode(code);

    // check to see whether it is a letter
    if (isAlpha(letter)) {

        // assume that the letter will not be found
        gotOne = false;

        // start building new display
        newDisplay = "";
        for(i=0;i<phrase.length;i++) {

            // see whether letters match
            if (phrase.charAt(i).toUpperCase() == letter.toUpperCase()) {

                // place letter in display text
                newDisplay = newDisplay + letter.toUpperCase();

                // note that at least one match has been found
                gotOne = true;

            } else {

                // not found, so display same character
                newDisplay = newDisplay + display.charAt(i) ;
            }
        }

        // show new display
        display = newDisplay;

        // if no match found, then add more to fox
        if (!gotOne) {
            fox.nextFrame();

            // see whether the fox is done
            if (fox._currentFrame == 8) {
                gotoAndPlay("lose");
            }

        } else if (display == phrase.toUpperCase()) {
            // the display matches the original, game over
```

```
                    gotoAndPlay("win");
            }
        }
    }
```

The "isAlpha" function is a good utility function that takes any character string and tests to see whether the first character is a letter. It uses *charCodeAt* to get the code of the first letter. Because the code numbers for lowercase letters are 32 higher than uppercase, you can subtract 32 from any code greater than 90 to look for uppercase and lowercase letters with one test.

NOTE

The *charCodeAt* function returns the code of any character in a string. The one argument it takes is the position of the character. So you can use it to look at the first character with *charCodeAt(0)*.

```
// utility to test whether a character is in A-Z
function isAlpha(letter) {
    // get character code
    n = letter.charCodeAt(0);

    // convert lowercase to uppercase
    if (n > 90) n -= 32;

    // see whether it is in A-Z
    return ((n >= 65) and (n <= 90));
}
```

The other piece of code needed here is attached to the "actions" movie clip. It takes any keypress and sends it along to the "makeGuess" function.

NOTE

The *Key.getAscii()* function returns the character code of the key pressed. It can be used inside an *onClipEvent(keyUp)* function attached to a movie clip.

```
onClipEvent (keyUp) {
    _root.makeGuess(Key.getAscii());
}
```

Loose Ends

The final movie needs a "win" and "lose" frame to jump to when the game is over. The example movie, Hangman.fla, keeps these frames simple, but you can insert animation for each of these. For instance, the "win" animation can show the fox being set free, whereas the "lose" animation can show something more gruesome.

Other Possibilities

The phrase in this example is hard-coded into the "initGame" function. However, you can use what you learned about loading external text from the two other games in this chapter to make it easier to change the phrase. You could even include a list of phrases to be shown one after the other.

If you want to include punctuation in the game, you can modify the code to look for other things, in addition to spaces, that will be automatically revealed at the start of the game. In fact, you could use *isAlpha* to test whether it is a letter, and display it at the start of the game if not.

Cryptogram

Example movie: Cryptogram.fla

Cryptograms are a fairly common type of word puzzle that offer more of a challenge than the hangman-like games. If you have never seen one, check your local newspaper's puzzle page. Chances are good that you'll find one near the daily crossword.

In a cryptogram, a sentence or phrase is encrypted with the simplest technique: Each letter of the alphabet is replaced with another letter. For instance, "Hello" might be "JQXXE ", where J stands for H, Q for E, X for L, and E for O. Because X replaces L, it must do so for all instances of L in the phrase.

> **NOTE**
> The odd thing about cryptograms is that they get easier to solve as they get longer. A common way to start solving them is to look for single-letter words, which must be either "a" or "I," and then two-letter words, which are usually "is," "it," "in," "of," or "on." If a three-letter word starts the phrase, it is usually "The."

Project Goal

Cryptograms are usually done with paper and pencil (or pen for those who want a challenge). A computer version can actually make the puzzle solving easier. In the paper version of the game, if the player identifies that Z is E, he or she must then look for other instances of Z and change them to E. If the player changes his or her mind, then all the Es must be erased.

This game takes care of this automatically. When the player indicates that a Z is an E, all Zs in the puzzle are immediately mapped to E. If the player then wants to change that decision he or she can easily make all of the Zs represent As.

Approach

This game uses two letter maps. The first letter map maps each letter of the alphabet to its encoded counterpart. For instance, look at this letter map:

```
SLGKWPZRMCYINEQFHXAVBOUDJT
```

In this letter map, the first letter of the alphabet, A, is encoded as S. The second letter, B, is encoded as L, and so on. Using this letter map, the word "Hello" is encoded as "RWIIQ."

The second letter map is the one the user is using to decode the puzzle. It starts off as this:

```
ABCDEFGHIJKLMNOPQRSTUVWXYZ
```

As the user maps encoded letters to what he or she thinks they decode to, the user's letter map changes. For instance, if the user decides that R maps to H, then the user's map changes to this:

```
ABCDEFGHIJKLMNOPQHSTUVWXYZ
```

By taking a phrase and using the first letter map, you get an encoded phrase that can be used in the cryptogram. Then, when the encoded phrase is passed through the user's letter map, the phrase is decoded back into its original state, provided that the user has created the correct letter map.

In this game, the player can move forward and backward through the letters of the puzzle with the arrow keys. When a user presses a letter key, the letter map changes to map the currently selected letter to the key pressed.

Figure 12.6 shows the game in progress. The upper letters are the ones that the player has already mapped. Letters that are not mapped are shown with an asterisk. The lower letters are the encrypted phrase. Only the upper letters change as the player solves the puzzle.

Figure 12.6

In the cryptogram puzzle, the lower letters are the encoded message, whereas the upper letters change according to the player's choices. The last letter in the first line is bold because it is the currently selected letter.

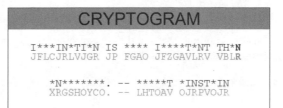

Preparing the Movie

The only active elements on the screen are two nearly-identical dynamic text fields. The first, named "decryptedText" and linked to the variable "decrypted," is slightly higher than the second, named "encyrptedText" and linked to the variable "encrypted." The font color of the second field is a bit lighter as well.

Both text fields use Courier New as a font, so that the letters are monospaced as they are in the hangman game.

Writing the Code

An unusual thing about this movie is that all the code is in the one frame script. All of it. There's not even a single button or movie clip. The Library for this movie is, in fact, empty.

The frame script starts off by calling "initGame." This sets the phrase and initializes the letter maps. The user map is actually set to all asterisks. This maps every letter to an asterisk. The result is that all letters display as asterisks in the decrypted text field.

The encryption map, called "letterMap," is set by a call to "createLetterMap," which is covered next. You can also see the yet-to-be-written functions "showPhase" and "showCursor." The first updates the text fields on the screen using the latest version of the letter maps. The second makes the currently-selected letter in the phrase bold. The "charpos" variable represents which letter is selected.

The "initGame" function ends by creating a keyboard listener, which makes sure that the function "getLetter" is triggered each time the user presses a key on the keyboard.

NOTE

Listeners are a great new addition to Flash MX. A listener tells Flash to recognize when an event occurs and to trigger a set of commands or a function when it does. The code can create a listener by first defining a standard object. The event to be listened for, in this case "onKeyUp," is set to link to a function. Then the *addListener* command attaches this object to a Flash object, in this case the *Key* object. Only certain Flash objects can have listeners attached and they can only be used for specific events relative to the object. For instance, *Key* listeners can hear only *onKeyUp* and *onKeyDown* events.

```
initGame();
stop();

function initGame() {
    // phrase to use
    phrase="Imagination is more important than knowledge. -- Albert Einstein";
```

```
    // init all variables
    createLetterMap();
    userMap = "**************************";
    charpos = 0;

    // show phrase and cursor
    showPhrase();
    showCursor();

    // listen for key presses
    keyListener = new Object();
    keyListener.onKeyUp = getLetter;
    Key.addListener(keyListener);
}
```

To create a random letter map, it seems that all you need to do is loop through all the letters and assign a new, random letter to each letter of the alphabet. However, it is not that simple. You need to be sure that not just any letter is picked, but only a letter not yet used. For instance, you don't want to assign R to both A and B.

The second layer of complexity appears when you realize that you don't want to assign a letter to itself. So, for instance, if G is assigned to G, then you want to throw out the letter map and make a new one.

The "createLetterMap" function loops until it finds a valid letter map. This usually happens on the first or second try.

```
// create random string of letters
function createLetterMap() {
    do { // loop until valid map created
        letterMap = "";
        for (var i=0;i<26;i++) {
            do { // loop until unqiue letter chosen
                r = Math.floor(Math.random()*26); // random number
                c = String.fromCharCode(r+65); // convert to letter
            } while (letterMap.indexOf(c) > -1);
            letterMap += c;
        }

        // check to make sure map is good
        bad = false;
        for(var i=0;i<26;i++) {
            if (letterMap.charCodeAt(i) == i+65) {
                bad = true; // letter at solved location
                break;
            }
```

```
        }
    } while (bad);
}
```

The "showPhrase" function loops through the letters of the phrase. It runs each letter though the "letterMap" to get the encrypted value. It then runs each encrypted letter through the "userMap" to get the current value according to the user. If a character is not a letter, but is a space or punctuation mark, then the character is shown without encryption.

```
function showPhrase() {
    encrypted = "";
    decrypted = "";
    for (var i = 0; i<phrase.length; i++) {

        // get real letter at this location
        c = phrase.toUpperCase().charAt(i);

        if ((" .-,'").indexOf(c)>-1) {
            // so white space as is
            encrypted += c;
            decrypted += c;
        } else {

            // use map to find encrypted character
            encryptedChar = letterMap.charAt(c.charCodeAt(0)-65);
            encrypted += encryptedChar;

            // use second map to find decrypted character
            decryptedCharacter = userMap.charAt(encryptedChar.charCodeAt(0)-65);
            decrypted += decryptedCharacter;
        }
    }
}
```

When the user presses a key, the *Key* object listener calls the function "getLetter." The key pressed is placed into two variables: "ascii" for the ASCII key code, and "code" for the keyboard code. The "ascii" value is used to identify letters, and the "code" value is used to identify the arrow keys.

If the arrow keys are being pressed, then the "charpos" is updated. At the end of this function, the "showCursor" function is called so that the correct letter in the phrase is made bold.

If a letter is pressed, then the "userMap" is updated to reflect the fact that the user wants to map the current encrypted letter to the key pressed. The text fields are updated with "showPhrase." Then the decrypted phrase is compared to the original phrase to see whether they match.

```
function getLetter() {
    // get ascii code and keyboard code
    var ascii = Key.getAscii();
    var code = Key.getCode();

    // move cursor with arrow keys
    if (code == Key.LEFT) {
        charpos--;
        if (charpos < 0) charpos = 0;
    } else if (code == Key.RIGHT) {
        charpos++;
        if (charpos > phrase.length-1) charpos = phrase.length-1;

    } else {
        // get upper case letter pressed
        var keyChar = String.fromCharCode(ascii);
        keyChar = keyChar.toUpperCase();

        // make sure it is a letter
        if ((keyChar >= "A") and (keyChar <= "Z")) {

            // get letter in phrase
            phraseChar = phrase.toUpperCase().charCodeAt(charpos)-65;

            // if the character is a letter
            if ((phraseChar >= 0) and (phraseChar < 26)) {

                // get character code in map
                letterNum = letterMap.charCodeAt(phraseChar)-65;

                // replace the character in the second map
                userMap = replaceChar(userMap,letterNum,keyChar);

                // update phrase
                showPhrase();

                // check for game over
                if (phrase.toUpperCase() == decrypted) {
                    gotoAndStop("game over");
                }
            }
        }
    }
}
```

```
    // update cursor
    showCursor();
}
```

Unfortunately, there is no ActionScript command to allow you to easily change a single character in a string to another character. So you need to make your own function to do that. This function takes the characters before the change and appends them to the characters after the change, with the new character in the middle.

```
// replace a character in a string
function replaceChar(mainString, num, newchar) {
    newString = mainString.substring(0,num)+newchar+
    ➥mainString.substring(num+1,mainString.length);
    return(newString);
}
```

To show the user to which letter the "charpos" variable is pointing, that letter is bolded in both the encrypted and decrypted fields. Using the new Flash MX TextFormat object is the way to do that. *TextFormat* objects have a ton of properties. When you apply a text format to a field, only those properties that have been specifically set in the object are changed in the field.

The "plainFormat" *TextFormat* object only specifies that *bold* be false. So when it is applied to the text fields "decryptedText" and "encryptedText," any bold characters are changed to plain. The "cursorFormat" object is the opposite. All characters to which it is applied are bolded. The code sets the text format of only the one character in the fields that match "charpos."

```
function showCursor() {
    // set both fields to plain
    plainFormat = new TextFormat();
    plainFormat.bold = false;
    decryptedText.setTextFormat(plainFormat);
    encryptedText.setTextFormat(plainFormat);

    // set one character in both fields to bold
    cursorFormat = new TextFormat();
    cursorFormat.bold = true;
    decryptedText.setTextFormat(charpos,cursorFormat);
    encryptedText.setTextFormat(charpos,cursorFormat);
}
```

Loose Ends

The example movie contains a "game over" frame. This is where the movie jumps when the puzzle is solved. You can also use the *removeListener* if you want to force the movie to stop responding to key presses.

Other Possibilities

As the user moves through the phrase with the arrow keys, the cursor is sometimes over spaces and other inactive characters. You can add more code to test cursor movement segments to recognize when the cursor is over white space and continue to move it forward or backward until it hits a letter.

Although the example movie has a phrase that is embedded into the code, you can also read the phrase in with a *LoadVariables* or *LoadVars* command. This enables you to change the phrase without having to recompile the .swf.

Picture Puzzles

- Jigsaw Puzzle
- Sliding Puzzle
- Matching Game
- Find the Picture

Games that use images as the central playing pieces are very versatile. The images can be anything from any topic. Therefore, you can use them on just about any kind of Web site.

This chapter looks at four different types of picture puzzles. The first is a simple jigsaw puzzle, in which the player assembles pieces of a picture. The second game asks the player to slide square puzzle pieces along a grid until he or she has put the picture together. In the third game, the player turns over puzzle pieces two at a time to try to find matches. The final game asks the player to match a small picture segment to a larger picture while a clock is ticking.

Jigsaw Puzzle

Example file: Jigsawpuzzle.fla

Jigsaw puzzles consist of a number of similar-sized pieces that interlock to create a complete picture. They are usually made of cardboard and require the player to use a large surface area, such as a dining room table, to solve them. Something like this does not translate well into a computer game because a typical computer screen is pretty small in comparison.

However, you can easily make a similar game that will provide light entertainment on a Web site. Figure 13.1 shows the example movie, Jigsawpuzzle.fla. It consists of 24 puzzle pieces and an empty grid where they are to be placed.

Figure 13.1
This jigsaw puzzle game is nearly complete.

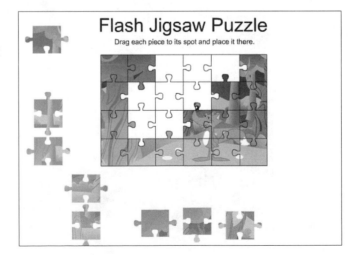

Project Goal

The goal for this game is to be a simple, yet usable, jigsaw puzzle game. The player can drag the pieces from the edge of the Stage onto the grid. When the correct piece is placed near the correct spot, it locks into place.

Approach

The way to accomplish this goal is with a short movie clip script attached to an "actions" movie clip off the Stage. When the user clicks the Stage, this script determines which piece is under the cursor. It then enables standard Flash dragging for this piece.

When the mouse button is lifted, the code determines whether the piece is now near its correct spot. If the piece is there, then it locks the piece to that exact spot.

We'll start with all the piece movie clips at 75% alpha to make them slightly lighter. Then, when the player sets a piece in its spot, it changes to 100% alpha. This provides some feedback to the player that the piece is now at rest. It's also important to be sure that a piece is not at 100% when the user clicks to drag, so that any pieces already properly placed can't be dragged again.

You can know whether a piece is in the correct spot because all the pieces are made so that their centers are at the center of the entire picture. For instance, the piece for the upper-left corner has a center far to the right and below the piece, as shown in Figure 13.2.

Figure 13.2

The center of this piece corresponds to the center of the image.

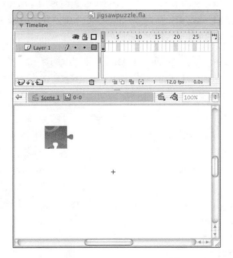

Now imagine every piece built like this. The center point remains at the center of the picture no matter where in the picture the piece falls. If you are unsure of what I mean, stop and take a look at the example movie, Jigsawpuzzle.fla, right now. Examine several of the puzzle-piece movie clips and you can see how this center point remains constant.

This simplifies the code a great deal. Each piece now needs to be in exactly the same location as the puzzle outline to fit properly. So you don't have to figure out what the location of each piece should be; they are all exactly the same.

Preparing the Movie

So how did I make the 24 puzzle pieces in this game? That, indeed, was the hardest part. However, there is no magic trick to it; it just took a lot of hard work. For the benefit of those who must know, I'll try to explain. This is not the only way to make puzzle pieces from a Flash graphic, however; I'm sure there are others, some possibly easier.

First, I started with the image, which was a bunch of ungrouped lines and fills on a single layer. I converted all the lines to fills, so I had only filled areas making up the entire picture.

Then, I assembled the puzzle frame. This was a collection of lines that looks like the outline shown earlier in Figure 13.1. I drew only a few parts of it along Flash's grid, and then copied and pasted it enough times to make the whole outline.

Next, I filled each area of the grid with red. I then selected all these filled areas except the one representing the puzzle piece in the upper-left corner. I copied these filled areas and then pasted them on top of my picture. I then selected and removed the entire red area, which left just that one puzzle piece.

Because many of these actions destroyed previous steps, I kept copies of the outline and the picture in other layers. I was then able to redo half of these steps to get the next piece. I did that 24 times to get all 24 pieces.

When this was all done I had 24 movie clips. I still had to use the grid to realign them so that the center point was where I wanted. It took me about 20 minutes to complete the process after I figured it out. However, you might be able to come up with an even faster method.

After I had all the pieces, I placed each movie clip on the Stage and gave it an instance name to match its movie clip name. The 24 pieces are named "0-0" to "5-3" to match the horizontal and vertical position of the piece. However, I placed each piece randomly around the edge of the Stage. I also set each movie clip to use the "alpha" effect at 75%. Then I placed a movie clip of the outline of the puzzle in the center and named it "outline."

Writing the Code

All the code is attached to a simple "actions" movie clip just off the Stage. It starts with an *onClipEvent(mouseDown)*, which reacts to the user clicking somewhere on the Stage.

This code just loops through each of the puzzle pieces and finds out whether one is under the cursor. It also makes sure that this piece is not at 100% alpha, which would indicate that it has already been placed.

If a piece is found, Flash is told to drag that piece with the *startDrag* command. The nested loops are then abandoned.

NOTE
The *startDrag* command is a basic action that allows the user to drag a single movie clip. It isn't as versatile as drag methods used earlier in this book, but it works in this simple case. A *stopDrag* command turns off the dragging.

```
onClipEvent(mouseDown) {
    // get mouse location
    mx = _root._xmouse;
    my = _root._ymouse;

    // loop through pieces looking for hit
    for(x=0;x<6;x++) {
        for(y=0;y<4;y++) {
            piece = _root[x+"-"+y];

            // see whether the piece is under the cursor
            // and if it has not yet been placed
            if (piece.hitTest(mx,my) and (piece._alpha < 100)) {
                // this is the piece clicked
                piece.startDrag();

                // break out of all loops
                x = 6;
                y = 4;
                break;
            }
        }
    }
}
```

When the player lifts up the mouse button, the piece is set down. The code checks the distance of the center of the piece from the center of the outline. If they are closer than 10 pixels, the piece is moved to the exact position where it belongs. The alpha effect is then set to 100% for the player to see and for the code to recognize that the piece can no longer be dragged.

```
onClipEvent(mouseUp) {
    // stop piece from moving
    stopDrag();

    // get distance from center of piece
    // to center of outline
```

```
        dx = _root.outline._x - piece._x;
        dy = _root.outline._y - piece._y;
        dist = Math.sqrt(dx*dx+dy*dy);

        // if close enough, then set it in place
        if (dist < 10 ) {
            piece._x = _root.outline._x;
            piece._y = _root.outline._y;

            // set to full color
            piece._alpha = 100;
        }
    }
}
```

Other Possibilities

This game is about as simple as jigsaw puzzle programs can get. There are a few small changes that can be made without much trouble. For instance, you could store the original position of each piece when dragging starts, and then have it snap back to that position if the player does not place it in the proper spot.

You could also write a function that checks to see whether all the pieces have been placed. Then you could go to another frame that contains some sort of payoff. You could also go further than the 24 large pieces here and have more, smaller pieces.

Each piece could be randomly rotated 90, 180, or 270 degrees. The player could press the spacebar to rotate the pieces around while dragging. A piece then fits in place only if it's rotated properly.

Of course, there are more difficult variations, such as puzzles that don't have a fixed outline. Players could combine any two or more pieces anywhere on the screen until they assembled the whole picture. However, this sort of game would take much more programming. Instead, let's move on to another type of picture puzzle.

Sliding Puzzle

☞ Example file: Slidingpuzzle.fla

Although jigsaw puzzles can make an incomplete transition to the computer screen, sliding puzzles work better as computer games than they do as physical games. Sliding puzzles usually consist of 15 square puzzle pieces that slide around on a grid made for 16 pieces. The empty space provides the extra area needed for sliding pieces around.

Figure 13.3 shows the game, a 15-piece sliding puzzle of the fox. You can play it in the example movie, Slidingpuzzle.fla. Any of the 4 pieces adjacent to the empty space can be clicked to slide that piece into the empty space. The object of the game is to arrange the picture properly, with the empty space at the bottom right.

Figure 13.3

The sliding puzzle game features 15 pieces and 1 empty slot.

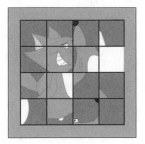

Project Goal

The goal of this project is to create a simple, easy-to-play sliding puzzle game. The only player interaction involves clicking a single piece at a time. If a piece is adjacent to the empty spot, it moves there.

An important part of this game is the setup. The Flash movie features the puzzle pieces all in the right spots. To create more of a challenge, the program starts by making 100 random moves. This sufficiently shuffles the pieces, making the puzzle challenging but solvable.

Approach

Most of the code in this game is used to shuffle the pieces at the start. First, a piece is picked at random. Next, the four spaces around it are examined to see whether any of them are the empty space. If one is, then the piece is moved there. If not, another piece is selected until one is found that is adjacent to the empty space. This process is repeated 100 times.

When the shuffle is over, it's up to the player to move the pieces. When the player clicks a piece, the piece is examined to see whether an empty space is adjacent. If so, the piece is moved there.

Preparing the Movie

You can use any method you like to create the pieces. I selected squares from a graphic to get the 15 pieces. Unlike the jigsaw puzzle pieces, they don't need any special positioning. The center of each movie clip can be the center of each piece. This makes these pieces easy to create.

After you have all the pieces, place them on the Stage as they should be when the puzzle has been solved. I made the puzzle pieces 54×54 pixels. This means that they need to be spaced 54 pixels apart both horizontally and vertically. Because Flash is not always precise when you manually place movie clips, even with the grid turned on, it's a good idea to use ActionScript to align all the pieces exactly before starting the game.

For now, it's just important to get the pieces close to their starting spots and name them. I gave them the names "tile1" through "tile15" so that the code can find them.

Writing the Code

Most of the code is on the main timeline. It starts by aligning the pieces at exactly 54 pixel distances. Then, it loops 100 times, making 100 random moves.

```
function initGame () {
    // set the horizontal and vertical distance
    // between tiles
    tileDist = 54;

    // set all tiles in exactly the correct spot
    for (x=1;x<=4;x++) {
        for (y=0;y<=3;y++) {
            tile = x+y*4;
            _root["tile"+tile]._x = x*tileDist;
            _root["tile"+tile]._y = y*tileDist+tileDist;
        }
    }

    // make 100 random but valid moves
    for(tilenum=0;tilenum<100;tilenum++) {
        do {
            // pick a random tile
            tile = "tile"+(random(15)+1);
            // see whether there is an empty space near it
            emptySpace = findEmpty(tile);
        // keep looping until a tile is found that
        // has an empty space near it
        } while ( emptySpace == "none" );

        // move this tile to the empty space
        moveTile(tile,findEmpty(tile));
    }
}
```

When a random tile is selected, the "findEmpty" function is used to determine whether any of the four adjacent spots is the empty one. Note that the code needs to make sure that the space is not beyond the edge of the playing area before testing for a piece.

```
// given a tile, see whether the empty space is near it
function findEmpty (tile) {
    // get location of tile
    tilex = _root[tile]._x;
    tiley = _root[tile]._y;

    // see whether there is a tile to the left
    if (tilex > tileDist) {
        if (!tileThere(tilex-tileDist, tiley)) {
```

```
                return("left");
            }
        }

        // see whether there is a tile to the right
        if (tilex < tileDist*4) {
            if (!tileThere(tilex+tileDist, tiley)) {
                return("right");
            }
        }

        // see whether there is a tile above
        if (tiley > tileDist) {
            if (!tileThere(tilex, tiley-tileDist)) {
                return("above");
            }
        }

        // see whether there is a tile below
        if (tiley < tileDist*4) {
            if (!tileThere(tilex, tiley+tileDist)) {
                return("below");
            }
        }

        // tiles are in all directions
        return("none");
}
```

NOTE

Placing an exclamation point in front of a condition reverses it. That is, it turns a *true* into a *false* and a *false* into a *true*. It is known as a "not" operation. For instance, in the preceding code, instead of checking for "tileThere," the code is checking for "not tileThere."

The "findEmpty" function uses "tileThere" to see whether any piece is at a certain location. The function calls "tileThere" for the location to the left, right, above, and below.

```
// check to see whether there is a tile at a certain location
function tileThere (thisx, thisy) {
    // loop through tiles
    for (i=1;i<=15;i++) {
        // see if x matches
        if (_root["tile"+i]._x == thisx) {
            // se if y matches
```

```
            if (_root["tile"+i]._y == thisy) {
                return true;
            }
        }
    }

    // no tile there
    return false;
}
```

After a move has been decided on, the "moveTile" function is used to make the move. This same function is used to allow the player to make moves as well.

```
// move a tile in a certain direction
function moveTile (tile, direction) {
    if (direction == "above") {
        _root[tile]._y -= tileDist;
    } else if (direction == "below") {
        _root[tile]._y += tileDist;
    } else if (direction == "left") {
        _root[tile]._x -= tileDist;
    } else if (direction == "right") {
        _root[tile]._x += tileDist;
    }
}
```

After the player is in control, the "tileUnderMouse" utility function is used to determine which piece has been clicked.

```
// utility function to see on which tile the
// player clicked
function tileUnderMouse () {
    for (i=1; i<=15; i++) {
        if (_root["Tile"+i].hitTest(_xmouse, _ymouse)) {
            return (i);
        }
    }
}
```

The main timeline script ends by calling "initGame" and kicking off the shuffle.

```
initGame();
stop();
```

The player interacts with the puzzle through a small "actions" movie clip just off the Stage. The movie clip grabs mouse clicks, figures out what was clicked, and makes the move.

```
onClipEvent(mouseDown) {
    // get tile clicked
    tileClicked = _root.tileUnderMouse();

    // see whether there is an empty space nearby
    emptySpace = _root.findEmpty("tile"+tileClicked);

    // move the piece to the empty space
    _root.moveTile("tile"+tileClicked,emptySpace);
}
```

Loose Ends

The code relies on the fact that the puzzle pieces are exactly 54 pixels apart, and the playing area is a 4×4 grid. If you want to change any of this, you need to check the code carefully and make changes.

Other Possibilities

One desirable addition to this game would be for it to recognize when the puzzle is complete and go to some sort of payoff frame. You could do this by recording the pieces' original positions in an array and comparing their positions after each move. When the positions all match, the puzzle has been solved.

Matching Game

Example file: Matching.fla

This next game is probably the most common computer game on the Web. I've seen it in Shockwave, Flash, Java, JavaScript, and even as plain HTML with a CGI backend. It is simple to build, addictive to play, and easy to customize for any site or situation.

A matching game, or memory game as it is sometimes called, involves a grid of cards, all face down. There are two of every type of card. The player gets to turn two cards face up at a time. If they match, the cards are removed. If not, they are both turned back over. The player tries to remember where each card is located to make it easier to find matches.

Figure 13.4 shows a screenshot of the game on the CD-ROM named Matching.fla with a 36-card grid, in which 4 cards have been removed so far and 2 cards have just been turned over. Those 2 cards do not match, so they are turned face down again as soon as the player selects another card.

Figure 13.4
The object of the matching game is to remove all the cards and reveal any picture behind them.

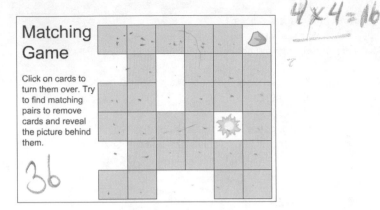

Project Goal

The goal of this project is to create a simple, yet versatile, matching game. The player can pick one card, and then a second card. Each card turns over to reveal its picture when clicked. If the cards match, they are both removed. If not, they both turn back over when the user selects another card.

Approach

There are actually only two library elements for this entire game. The first is a movie clip that contains a frame representing the cards turned face down. All the rest of the frames show each picture. Because there are 18 different pictures, the movie clip has a total of 19 frames. If you want the clip to show the back of a card, send it to frame 1. If you want the clip to show a picture, send it to a frame from 2 to 19.

The second library element is a button that is inside the "cards" movie clip. It is used to react to user clicks.

The game starts off by creating the 36 movie clips, arranged in a grid on the Stage. Each movie clip shows the back of a card, but it remembers what picture it is supposed to show when the card is turned face up. There are two clips with each picture, making 18 pairs of cards.

When the player selects the first card, the card shows its picture. Then, when the player selects the second card, it also turns over and compares itself to the other card. If they match, both are removed. If not, nothing happens until the next card is clicked. When that occurs, the two old cards turn back over, and a new card is revealed.

Preparing the Movie

In the example movie, Matching.fla, you can see the "Cards" movie clip. The timeline of this movie clip shows 19 frames. Figure 13.5 shows this timeline. The first frame represents the card face down, and thus with no picture on it. The other 18 frames each have their own, different pictures.

Figure 13.5

The timeline of the "Cards" movie clip shows 19 frames, the first with no picture and the other 18 with different pictures.

The card button is simply a rectangle the same size as the cards. The card button is placed in the third layer of the "Cards" movie clip, as you can see in Figure 13.5. This places it under the background. The button will not be seen, but it will react to mouse clicks just the same.

The "Cards" movie clip also includes a background. The first frame, representing the back of a card, has a gray background. The other frames, all of which have a picture to show, have white backgrounds.

Writing the Code

Almost all the code for this game is in the main timeline. The movie starts off by calling the "initGame" function. This function creates a list of 18 pairs of cards, picks random cards from this first list, and then places them in the second list to shuffle the deck.

Next, it creates 36 cards, all along a 6x6 grid. Each movie clip automatically starts face down, but a custom property of the movie clip, "picture," is set to the number of the picture it should represent.

```
initGame();
stop();

function initGame() {
    // make sorted list of cards
    cardsListOrdered = [];
    for(i=1;i<=18;i++) {
        cardsListOrdered.push(i,i);
    }

    // shuffle list
    cardsListSorted = [];
    while (cardsListOrdered.length > 0) {
        r = int(Math.random()*cardsListOrdered:length);
        cardsListSorted.push(cardsListOrdered[r]);
        cardsListOrdered.splice(r,1);
    }
```

```
// create card clips and assign their location and picture
x = 0;
y = 0;
for(i=0;i<36;i++) {
    attachMovie("Card","Card"+i,i);
    _root["Card"+i].picture = cardsListSorted[i];
    _root["Card"+i]._x = x*60+200;
    _root["Card"+i]._y = y*60+50;

    // move to next card spot
    x++;
    if (x > 5) {
        x = 0;
        y++;
    }
}

firstclip = 0;
}
```

NOTE

Notice that the *push* command can be used to add more than one item to an array at a time. For instance, "myArray.push(7,12)" adds a 7 and then a 12 to the array "myArray."

The "initGame" function ends by setting "firstclip" to 0. This is the variable that will hold a reference to the first card clicked. When a movie clip is clicked, the button inside the movie clip reacts to the click by sending a message, which includes a reference to the movie clip, up to the main timeline through the "clickCard" function.

The "clickCard" function can take one of three actions. If "firstclip" is 0, then it sets "firstclip" to the movie clip that was clicked, and turns that card over by telling it to go to the frame that has the appropriate picture on it.

If "firstclip" is set to a movie clip reference, then one card is already showing. In that case, the program turns a second card over, sets "secondclip" to that movie clip, and compares the two movie clips. If they match, both clips are immediately removed.

A third condition, which is actually checked before the other two options, occurs if the player clicks the same card twice. In this case, "clip" will equal "firstclip." The card is simply turned back over and "firstclip" is set to 0.

Before the "clickCard" function checks any of these three conditions, it checks to see whether two cards are already turned over. If so, that means the player just completed selecting two cards and did not get a match. Before the next card is turned over, these two cards are set to face down. *or turned back over*

```
function clickCard(clip) {
    // see whether two cards are showing
    if (secondclip != 0) {

        // turn those two cards back over
        firstclip.gotoAndStop(1);
        secondclip.gotoAndStop(1);
        firstClip = 0;
        secondClip = 0;
    }

    // see whether same card was clicked
    if (firstclip == clip) {

        // turn card back over
        firstclip.gotoAndStop(1);
        firstClip = 0;

    // see whether no cards are showing
    } else if (firstclip == 0) {

        // turn first card over
        clip.gotoAndStop(clip.picture+1);
        firstclip = clip;

    // must be one card showing
    } else {

        // turn second card over
        clip.gotoAndStop(clip.picture+1);
        secondClip = clip;

        // see whether two cards match
        if (firstclip.picture == secondClip.picture) {

            // remove both cards
            firstClip.removeMovieClip();
            secondClip.removeMovieClip();
            firstClip = 0;
            secondClip = 0;
        }
    }

}
```

add in show dialog box if match is complete

That's all there is to the game. The button inside the "Cards" movie clip has just one line of code in it that sends the message that the movie clip was clicked on back to the main timeline.

```
on (press) {
    // send click info to main timeline
    _root.clickCard(this);
}
```

Loose Ends

Remember to place a *stop()* command in the first frame of the "Cards" movie clip. Otherwise, all the cards will start by animating through all the pictures.

This game can easily be customized by changing the background image to appear behind the cards. The example movie doesn't have any image in the background, but it would be easy to add one. The pictures on the cards can match the theme of that picture. You can pick almost any theme. You can also add a picture to the first frame of the "Cards" movie clip to represent the backs of the cards. *(where the gray bkgd is)*

Other Possibilities

Although the example here has 36 cards, you can easily expand or shrink that number. Just remember to adjust the grid size as well as the array lengths at the start of the game. If the number of cards doesn't fit into a square grid, you will have to adjust the code, or write new code, to determine the layout of the cards.

Another possibility is to have four of each card, rather than two. This will make it easier to find the first match.

If you want to have the game recognize when all the cards have been removed, you can include a counter that increments every time a match is found. In the case of the example movie, when the counter hits 18, the game is over. You can then go to a "you win" frame.

Find the Picture

Example movie: Findthepicture.fla

Here's a rather unusual game that is more commonly found in puzzle books than on computers. Making a Flash version of this game demonstrates several useful techniques.

In the Find the Picture game, the player is not looking for a picture, but a segment of a picture. The complete image is shown on the right while an enlarged segment is shown on the left. The object is to quickly find the location of the segment in the larger picture.

Figure 13.6 shows the game. The segment on the left is chosen at random and enlarged by a factor of three. The user must click on the matching portion of the full picture. Bonus points are awarded depending on how fast the segment is found.

Figure 13.6

In this game, you try to find the location of the small image on the left inside the larger image to the right.

Project Goal

To make this game, your ActionScript must be able to take a random segment of a larger picture and display it next to the full picture. This requires a trick involving masking. The ActionScript must also be able to match the segment with a corresponding area on the full picture.

In addition to the image manipulation, a timer must be built in to this game. The timer starts at a large number and counts down. When players discover the segment in the picture, they are awarded points based on the timer.

Approach

The way the picture segment is shown on the screen relies on a trick with Flash layers. In a movie clip, the picture is at one layer and a small square acts as a mask to that layer. Only the part of the picture under the square is visible when the movie clip is displayed on the screen.

The picture is 400×300. The square is 36×36. When the picture is moved around under the mask square, only the 36×36 portion under the square is visible. Although the picture movement is done with ActionScript, the masking is all done in the movie clip's timeline during the movie's preparation.

When the user spots the location of the picture segment in the full picture, he or she will want to click on it. It would be natural to place an invisible button at that location, except that a button would give itself away because the user's cursor would change to a hand. Instead, place a normal movie clip there and use *hitTest* to determine when it has been clicked on.

This movie uses Flash MX listeners to place all the code in the main timeline. This means that the reaction to the mouse click and the servicing of the ever-changing timer is part of the main timeline script, not any "actions" movie clip.

> **TIP**
>
> With Flash MX and the Flash 6 player, it is possible to do almost anything with just one script in the main timeline. The trick is to register events, such as *onMouseUp* and *onEnterFrame*, to functions. These can replace the equivalent *onClipEvent* handlers in "actions" movie clips. But because this technique is not backward compatible with Flash 5, it may take a while for it to become widely used.

This game features not one, but three pictures. The player's total score is the sum of the time bonuses after all three picture segments have been located. Play the game now to familiarize yourself with the game play.

Preparing the Movie

The base movie clip is the one in the Library named "picture." It contains three bitmap pictures, one on each frame. There is a *stop()* command on the first frame. The pictures are aligned so that the upper left corner of each picture is at the center point of the movie clip.

This "picture" movie clip is never on the Stage by itself, but is instead inside two other movie clips: "fullPicture" and "maskedPicture."

In the "fullPicture" movie clip, the "picture" movie clip is on one layer and a small square movie clip named "button" is on top of it in another layer.

In the "maskedPicture" movie clip, the "picture" movie clip is also on one layer and the "button" movie clip is on another. However, the button's layer is a mask layer, masking the picture layer. This means that only the section of the picture under the square is visible when the "maskedPicture" movie clip is placed on the Stage.

On the Stage, the "fullPicture" and "maskedPicture" movie clips are placed side by side. The "maskedPicture" movie clip is a bit difficult to move around because when you are dragging it around, it shows its full boundaries, which are quite large and cover the whole Stage. I've also scaled this movie clip to 300% on the Stage, which makes it even bigger.

The main timeline contains four frames. The first is the instructions page. Then comes the "play" frame. When the user is finished with one picture, the movie goes to the "next" frame to give the player a chance to pause before the next picture. The last frame is the "game over" frame.

There are two dynamic text fields used in the movie. The first, "displayBonus" is used in the "play" frame. The "displayScore" field is used in the "next" and "game over" frames.

Writing the Code

When the movie starts, the "roundNum" and "score" are set. The "roundNum" variable keeps track of which picture should appear.

```
// start at picture 1
roundNum = 1;
score = 0;
stop();
```

When the user presses the button on the first frame, the game begins. All the code is in the main timeline, in the first layer. The "setUpRound" function is what the button triggers.

After the function takes the movie to the "Play" frame, it then proceeds to set up the two movie clips. The "picture" movie clip instance inside each is advanced according to "roundNum."

Then a random spot in the picture is chosen. This spot takes into account the fact that the segment square is 36×36, so any random location should be at least 18 pixels from the edge of the image.

In the "maskedPicture" movie clip, the picture is repositioned so that the spot is located directly under position 0,0, which is where the mask square is located. So if the random spot is at 100, 150, the picture should be moved −100 horizontally and −150 vertically to get it there.

In the "fullPicture" movie clip, the picture remains still while the "button" movie clip moves to position itself at the correct location. This movie clip is set to have an _alpha property of 0, making the button invisible.

TIP

Rather than setting the _alpha of the movie clip to 0, try setting it to 25 when testing. This enables you to see it more quickly and confirm that your game is working.

```
function setUpRound(pictureNum) {
    // go to game frame
    gotoAndStop("Play");

    // set picture in both movie clips
    fullPicture.picture.gotoAndStop(pictureNum);
    maskedPicture.picture.gotoAndStop(pictureNum);

    // get random location in picture
    w = fullPicture._width;
    h = fullPicture._height;
```

```
x =   Math.random()*(w-36)+18;
y =   Math.random()*(h-36)+18;

// set masked picture to show correct portion
maskedPicture.picture._x = -x;
maskedPicture.picture._y = -y;

// place button in the corrent spot
fullPicture.button._x = x;
fullPicture.button._y = y;

// hide the button
fullPicture.button._alpha = 0;

// start bonus timer
startTime = getTimer();
}
```

The "setUpRound" function ends by initializing the variable "startTime" with the current time. This time is used by the next piece of code, which recalculates the bonus amount each frame. It takes the current time, subtracts "startTime," and then subtracts this total from 30,000 milliseconds. The result is that the bonus timer starts at 30,000 milliseconds and counts down to 0.

Instead of placing this in an "actions" movie clip, I've simply assigned a function to the *onEnterFrame* event, which is new to Flash MX.

```
// recalculate bonus every frame
_root.onEnterFrame = function() {
    // bonus is 30000 minus time
    bonus = 30000-Math.floor(getTimer() - startTime);
    if (bonus < 0) bonus = 0;
    displayBonus = "BONUS: "+bonus;
}
```

Another event that must be tracked is the *onMouseDown* event. When this happens, *hitTest* is used to determine whether the user has clicked on the hidden button. If he has, then the button is made more visible and the movie jumps to another frame. The bonus amount is added to the score and the score is displayed.

```
// set up mouse listener
_root.onMouseDown = function() {

    // see whether user clicked the button
    if (fullPicture.button.hitTest(_root._xmouse,_root._ymouse)) {
```

```
        // see whether button is hidden
        if (fullPicture.button._alpha < 50) {

            // show button
            fullPicture.button._alpha = 50;

            // add bonus to score
            score += bonus;
            displayScore = "SCORE: "+score;

            if (roundNum < 3) {
                // if this is not the last one, show next screen
                gotoAndStop("next");

            } else {
                // if this is the last one, end the game
                gotoAndStop("game over");
            }
        }
    }
}
```

Loose Ends

The "maskedPicture" movie clip, in addition to the picture and the mask, has a border layer that matches the mask. This helps it stand out on the screen. There are also static text pieces for every frame explaining to the player what is going on.

You can custom set each bitmap's properties to determine the level of compression and smoothing. You may want to play with this setting until you get results you like.

Other Possibilities

It should be easy for you to add pictures to this game. You can have as many as you want. Just remember to set the code to recognize which is the last picture in the *onMouseDown* handler.

You can also adjust the "button" movie clip size to be larger than 36×36. Remember to adjust the "setUpRound" function so that it positions the button farther than 18 pixels from each edge.

Instead of bitmaps, you can also use vector images. This makes an easier game, but that would make it more suitable for young children. With a face-lift and an animated introduction, this game could be a good one for very young children who don't even know how to read.

Brain Puzzles

- Memory Game
- Deduction
- Pegs
- Recursive Blocks

The sliding puzzle and the matching game from the last chapter are both thinking puzzles. The player is not timed, but is given every opportunity to examine the problem at hand and solve the puzzle. Let's look at some more of these brain puzzles.

This chapter shows you four classics. In the first game, the player is asked to memorize a sequence and repeat it. In the next game, the player must deduce the items in a short sequence, given hints after each guess. Then, in the third game, the player jumps pegs to eliminate them until he has only one peg left. In the last game, the player eliminates groups of blocks of the same color in a grid.

Memory Game

Example file: Memory.fla

The memory game is sometimes called *Simon* after a popular electronic toy. The game described here, like that toy, has four different elements that play in a random sequence. You can see it in the example movie, Memory.fla. An element is a colored light that lights up and a sound that plays at the same time. In this game, the elements are represented on the screen by four birds sitting on a branch (see Figure 14.1).

Figure 14.1
The memory game features four birds that chirp in a random sequence.

The game has two main phases. In the first phase the birds chirp in a sequence. In the second phase the user tries to re-create that sequence in the same order. Then the phases repeat, adding a new chirp to the sequence. Pretty soon, the sequence gets so long that the player cannot re-create it and the game is over.

Approach

The sequence of chirps is stored in an array. Every turn, a new, random number from 1 to 4 is added to the array. The number determines which bird chirps at that part of the sequence.

The first part of the game consists of the birds singing. That frame is controlled by an "actions" movie clip, which moves through the numbers in the sequence and tells the birds when to chirp.

The next part of the game waits for the player to click the birds. When the player does, this part of the game checks to see whether the correct bird was clicked. It follows the player through the sequence of chirps, waiting for the player to mess up. If the player doesn't mess up, it adds a new chirp to the sequence and starts over again.

Preparing the Movie

This movie has six frames. You can see them all in Figure 14.2. The two key frames are frames 3 and 4: the "play" and "repeat" frames. The "play" frame is where the birds chirp automatically, and the "repeat" frame is where the player clicks the birds.

Figure 14.2

The six frames of the memory game are "start," "wait," "play," "repeat," "correct," and "wrong."

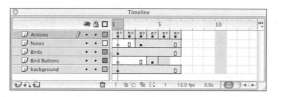

Each bird has three parts. The first part is a movie clip with the bird. The first frame has the bird as a still image. The second frame and the rest of the movie clip are an animation of the bird opening its mouth to chirp. The movie starts with each bird stopped on the first frame.

The second part of each bird is a button. The same button is used for each bird, but different code is attached to it. The button is behind each bird and is invisible.

TIP

If you look closely at the "Bird Button" library element in the example movie, you can see that the "Up," "Over," and "Down" frames of the button are blank, but the "Hit" frame contains the shape of the bird. This means that no image is displayed for the button on the Stage, but the valid hit area of the button matches the shape in the "Hit" frame of the button. This is a different technique for making an invisible button from simply creating a button and setting its alpha effect to 0.

The third part of each bird is a simple animation that shows a note flying out of the bird's mouth. This is a single movie clip used once for each bird. Each instance of this note animation and each bird is named to match. For instance, the first bird and note are named "bird1" and "note1." The note animation has a blank first frame, where it is stopped. The second frame has a short animation that loops back to the first frame. The note is triggered to fly out of the bird's mouth at the appropriate time.

If you examine the "bird" animations, you can see that a sound is included with each one. This sound automatically plays when the bird animates. Each sound is slightly different.

The different parts of the birds appear in different frames. The bird movie clips themselves appear in all six frames. However, the buttons appear only in the "repeat" frame because that is the only place where the player should be able to click the birds. The note animations appear only on frames 3–6 because they aren't needed in frames 1 and 2.

The movie also has specific instructions on each frame about what the user should be doing. A "scoreDisplay" text area is in the upper-right corner of all frames except the first.

Writing the Code

The code for this movie is divided into two parts. The first part is a bunch of functions placed in the first frame of the movie. The second part is in a "playback actions" movie clip that controls the playback of the chirps in the "play" frame. Many other places also have short pieces of code.

The functions used in this movie can all be found in the first frame of the main timeline. They are used to set up the game, react to user clicks, and help play back the chirps.

Calling "initGame" to set up all the variables is the first thing that happens in this game. This happens when the game first runs, and when the game is over, the player chooses to play again, and the game gets sent back to frame 1.

The "initGame" function clears the "notes" array and then calls "addNextNote" to place a random number in that array. It also sets the score display to 0.

```
initGame();
stop();

function initGame(n) {
    // start notes array
    notes = new Array();
    scoreDisplay = "Score: 0";

    // add first note
    addNewNote();
}
```

The "addNextNote" function picks a number frame 1 to 4 and places it in the "notes" array.

```
function addNewNote() {
    // pick a number from 1 to 4
    r = int(Math.Random()*4+1);

    // add number to list
    notes.push(r);
}
```

The other functions in the main timeline deal with different stages of the game. This next function, "startRepeat" is called when the player has heard the birds chirp and it's now the player's turn to click the birds to make them chirp.

The variable "repeatNum" used to keep track of which note the player should be clicking. It starts at 0 and counts along as the player clicks each bird.

```
function startRepeat() {
    // mark which note the user should play next
    repeatNum = 0;

    // go to the frame where buttons are active
    gotoAndPlay("repeat");
}
```

The "clickBird" function is called from the buttons hidden behind the birds. It sends along the number of the note clicked. The first thing the function does with the number is to trigger the bird animation and the matching note animation. Then it compares the note against the next note in the list of notes. If they match, the player got it right. The "repeatNum" variable increments. If this is the last note, the game jumps to the "correct" frame. If not, it waits for another note. If the note does not match, then the game jumps to the "wrong" frame and the game is over.

```
function clickBird(note) {
    // make the bird play the note
    _root["bird"+note].gotoAndPlay(2);

    // also trigger the note animation
    _root["note"+note].gotoAndPlay(2);

    // see whether it was the right note
    if (note == notes[repeatNum]) {

        // expect the next note
        repeatNum++;

        // if no more notes, then he got it correct
        if (repeatNum > notes.length-1) {
            scoreDisplay = "Score: " + notes.length;
```

```
            gotoAndPlay("correct");
        }
    } else {

        // he got one wrong
        gotoAndPlay("wrong");
    }
}
```

The "play" frame plays back each note in the sequence through a script attached to a "playback actions" movie clip. The script starts off by setting two variables. The "noteNum" variable keeps track of which note to play next, and the "nextTime" variable keeps track of when to play the next note.

```
onClipEvent(load) {
    // start with note 0
    noteNum = 0;
    nextTime = 0;
}
```

In each step of the movie that passes while the movie sits on the "play" frame, the current time is compared to the value of "nextTime." If the current time is greater, the next note plays.

The bird and note animation are triggered just as they will be when the player clicks them. Then, "noteNum" and "nextTime" are changed to prepare for the next note. The "nextTime" is increased by 1000, so the next note plays 1 second later.

When all the notes have been played, the game calls the "startRepeat" function previously discussed. This sends the game to the "repeat" frame to await the player's attempt at re-creating the sequence.

```
onClipEvent(enterFrame) {
    // if it is time to play the next note
    if (getTimer() > nextTime) {

        // get the note
        note = _root.notes[noteNum];

        // make the bird sing and note animate
        _root["bird"+note].gotoAndPlay(2);
        _root["note"+note].gotoAndPlay(2);

        // wait 1 second until next note
        nextTime = getTimer() + 1000;
        noteNum++;
```

```
        // if no more notes, then continue to next step
        if (noteNum > _root.notes.length) {
            _root.startRepeat();
        }
    }
}
```

Each button on the Stage in the "repeat" frame must call "clickBird" when clicked. Each of the four scripts is slightly different because they must send a different number to "clickBird." Here is the script for the first one:

```
on (press) {
    clickBird(1);
}
```

Loose Ends

All six of the frames in this movie should have a *stop()* command placed on them. In frames 2 to 6, that is the only command on those frames.

There are also buttons on the "wait," "correct," and "wrong" frames. The "wait" frame has a button that takes the game to the "play" frame, where the sequence is played. The "correct" frame button takes the player back to the "play" frame. However, it must also call "addNewNote" to add a note to the sequence.

```
on (press) {
    addNewNote();
    gotoAndPlay("play");
}
```

The button on the "wrong" frame sends the game back to the "start" frame where the game is reinitialized so another game can begin.

Also, remember to include a text area that is linked to the variable "scoreDisplay," so players will know how well they have done.

Other Possibilities

You can customize this game to fit all sorts of different themes by changing the background and the four elements. You can also have more or fewer than four elements to change the difficulty level of the game.

Deduction

Example file: Deduction.fla

This next game is played completely by using logic. You might have seen it as a computer game before, or you might recognize it as the two-player, store-bought game called *Mastermind*.

The object of the game is to guess a random sequence of five colors. The player starts off with a wild guess. Then, the computer responds by telling the player how he did. The player gets the number of colors correctly placed, and the number of colors that are correct, but in the wrong spot. Based on this information, the player makes another guess. This continues for a set number of turns or until the player gets the sequence correct.

Figure 14.3 shows the deduction game as it looks in the example movie Deduction.fla. The playing area is a log and the colors are rocks. The player can choose any of five colored rocks, or no rock at all, to fill a space. The computer responds with a white rock for every correct color and a black rock for every correct color in the wrong spot.

Figure 14.3
The deduction game allows the player to build a sequence of rocks and then grades the results with white and black rocks.

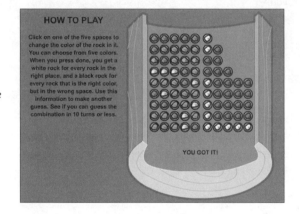

Project Goal

The goal of this movie is to create the simple game called Deduction. The player gets 10 chances to guess the correct sequence. The player is given feedback after every guess.

Approach

The game starts by creating a random sequence of five colors. This sequence is kept a secret by the computer until the end of the game.

Each turn starts by presenting five new empty spaces for the player to set. In addition to these five spaces, a "Done" button appears to the right. Figure 14.4 shows what the game looks like when the player starts.

The player can click any of the five spaces to change its color. The spaces actually rotate through six possibilities: five colors and an empty space.

Figure 14.4
The game starts by presenting five empty spaces and a "Done" button.

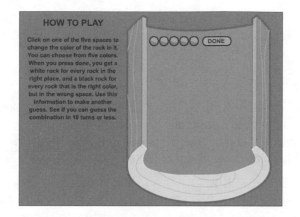

After the player has set the five spaces to her satisfaction, then she can press the "done" button to have it graded. A white stone represents a correctly placed color, and a black stone represents a color that is correct if used elsewhere.

The next five empty spaces are then shown below the previous row, along with a new "done" button. Figure 14.5 shows what the game play looks like after several moves.

Figure 14.5
The deduction game looks like this after several moves.

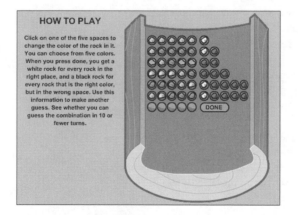

Preparing the Movie

The "rock" movie clip contains eight frames. The first frame shows an empty space. Frames 2–6 show the five colors from which the player has to choose. Frames 7 and 8 show the white and black stones, and are labeled "white" and "black" so the code can refer to them easily.

Only the background and instructions need to be placed on the Stage. The rocks and "done" button are created by the code. You need to set the "linkage" property of the "rock" to "rock." A small button is also created to go inside each rock. The "done" button is easily created, but because you want to manipulate its existence and location, you need to place it inside a movie clip and set the linkage on that as well.

Writing the Code

The code for the game is all in the first frame of the main timeline. It starts by setting a whole bunch of constants. These numbers determine the location of various elements on the Stage as the script creates them. Instead of having these constants spread throughout the code, I have gathered them at the start of the program so they will be easy to find and change.

The solution sequence is created from five random numbers and is stored in "solution." The "row" variable is used to store the turn number. The "createRow" function is called to start the game.

```
initGame();
stop();

function initGame() {
    // define locations and spacing
    // of the elements
    topRowLoc = 60;
    leftColLoc = 280;
    rightColLoc = 390;
    horizSpace = 21;
    vertSpace = 23;
    solutionx = 336;
    solutiony = 320;

    // create a random solution
    solution = new Array();
    for(i=0;i<5;i++) {
        solution.push(int(Math.Random()*5));
    }

    // init variables
    rows = new Array();
    row = 0;

    // set up first row
    createRow();
}
```

At the start of every turn, "createRow" makes five new movie clips and sets their locations. In addition, a new "done" movie clip is set to be just to the right of that. The result looks like Figure 14.4 (shown previously).

```
function createRow() {
    // create a new row of 5 empty spaces
    for(i=0;i<5;i++) {
        attachMovie("rock","rock"+row+"-"+i,row*10+i);
        clip = _root["rock"+row+"-"+i];
        clip._x = leftColLoc + i*horizSpace;
        clip._y = topRowLoc + row*vertSpace;
        clip.active = true;
    }

    // create the "done" button
    attachMovie("done","done",1000);
    _root.done._x = rightColLoc+20;
    _root.done._y = topRowLoc + row*vertSpace;
}
```

When the player clicks the "done" button, "doneGuess" is called. "doneGuess" starts by making the five buttons in the current row inactive. In "createRow," a custom property of each movie clip called "active" was set to *true*. Now, this property is set to *false* ①. The code attached to each button uses this value to determine whether it can be clicked or not.

The array "temp" is used to store the number of each color that appears in the sequence ②. For instance, if there are two of color 1, one of color 4, and two of color 5, the array is "[2,0,0,1,2]."

The next loop checks to see how many colors match the solution perfectly ③. As matches are found, the numbers in the "temp" array are reduced. This means that the values in "temp" now represent all the colors still left to be matched.

The next loop checks each of the unmatched colors in the player's sequence and determines which of those are in "temp" ④. By counting these, you can get the number of colors that are useful, but in the wrong spots.

The next two loops create white and black rocks to represent the number of colors that are correct, and the number of colors that are correct but in the wrong spots ⑤.

The "done" button is removed so that it does not remain in each column ⑥. A new "done" button will be created when the next turn begins.

Finally, the function ends by checking to see whether all five colors are correct ⑦. If so, the movie jumps to the "win" frame. If not, the code checks to see whether this was the 10th turn. If it was, the movie jumps to the "lose" frame. If not, "createRow" is called to start the next turn.

```
function doneGuess() {
    numRightSpot = 0;
    numRightColor = 0;
```

①➤
```
// make all five button inactive
for (i=0;i<5;i++) {
    _root["rock"+row+"-"+i].active = false;
}
```

②➤
```
// determine how many of each color there are
temp = [0,0,0,0,0];
for (i=0;i<5;i++) {
    temp[solution[i]]++;
}
```

③➤
```
// see how many are correct
for (i=0;i<5;i++) {
    thisColor = _root["rock"+row+"-"+i]._currentFrame - 2;
    if (thisColor == solution[i]) {
        numRightSpot++;
        temp[thisColor]--;
    }
}
```

④➤
```
// see how many are correct color, but wrong spot
for (i=0;i<5;i++) {
    thisColor= _root["rock"+row+"-"+i]._currentFrame - 2;
    if (thisColor!= solution[i]) {
        if (temp[thisColor] > 0) {
            numRightColor++;
            temp[thisColor]--;
        }
    }
}
```

⑤➤
```
// create white rocks
level = row*10+5;
x = rightColLoc;
for(i=0;i<numRightSpot;i++) {
    attachMovie("rock","white rock"+level,level);
    clip = _root["white rock"+level];
    clip.gotoAndStop("white");
    clip._x = x;
    clip._y = topRowLoc + row*vertSpace;
    level++
    x+=horizSpace;
}

// create black rocks
for(i=0;i<numRightColor;i++) {
```

```
            attachMovie("rock","black rock"+level,level);
            clip = _root["black rock"+level];
            clip.gotoAndStop("black");
            clip._x = x;
            clip._y = topRowLoc + row*vertSpace;
            level++
            x+=horizSpace;
        }
```

⑥➤
```
        // remove "done" button
        done.removeMovieClip();
```

⑦➤
```
        // see whether the player wins
        if (numRightSpot == 5) {
            gotoAndPlay("win");
        } else {
            row++;

            // see whether the player loses
            if (row >= 10) {
                showSolution();
                gotoAndPlay("lose");
            } else {
                createRow();
            }
        }
    }
```

When the player loses the game, the "showSolution" function creates five new movie clip instances and uses them to display the actual solution. In the example movie, this is placed at the bottom of the playing area.

```
function showSolution() {
    // place solution at bottom of screen
    for(i=0;i<5;i++) {
        attachMovie("rock","solution"+i,1001+i);
        clip = _root["solution"+i];
        clip._x = solutionx + i*horizSpace;
        clip._y = solutiony;
        clip.gotoAndStop(solution[i]+2);
    }
}
```

Figure 14.6 shows a game that has been lost. The "showSolution" function has placed the actual solution at the bottom of the screen.

Figure 14.6
This game has been lost, and the code has placed the actual solution at the bottom.

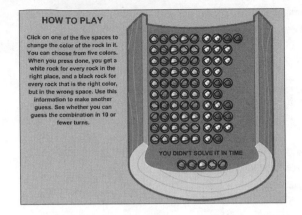

The only piece of code that remains is the little bit that is attached to the button in every "rock" movie clip. Its job is to advance the color by one, looping back to the first frame, an empty space, if clicked enough times. This code also checks the "active" property to make sure this is the current row.

```
on (press) {
    if (active) {
        f = _currentFrame+1;
        if (f > 6) f = 1;
        gotoAndStop(f);
    }
}
```

Loose Ends

Remember to label the last two frames of the "rock" movie clip "black" and "white." Also, remember to include the "done" button inside a "done" movie clip, which is then linked as "done." Unfortunately, this is necessary because buttons by themselves cannot be created dynamically by ActionScript. Think of the "done" movie clip as a wrapper around the "done" button.

Other Possibilities

The important thing to remember if you modify this game is that the constants at the beginning of the code need to be adjusted to match any change to your background. If you keep that in mind, you can do just about anything with this game.

To change the difficulty of the game, try increasing the number of guesses allowed. You can also increase or decrease the number of colors and spaces.

Pegs

The classic game of pegs has probably been around for thousands of years. Recent versions are made of cheap plastic, or as Web-based games like this one.

The game consists of a grid of peg holes, like the one in Figure 14.7. Pegs are in every hole except one. The player has to take a peg and jump another peg, landing in an empty hole. The peg that was jumped is then removed. Play continues until no more moves are possible.

Figure 14.7

This is the most common of many pegboard configurations. You can make up your own as well.

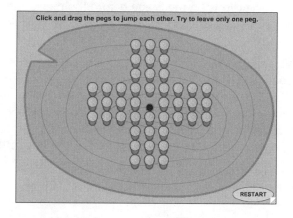

A good player can "win" the game by getting down to a single peg. A quick game, without much thought put into the moves, can leave 8 or 12 pegs.

Project Goal

The goal of this project is to make a "pegs" game using the most common configuration, shown previously in Figure 14.7. The player clicks and drags to move pegs. An invalid move is not allowed, and a valid move automatically removes the piece jumped.

Approach

This entire game takes place in a single frame and starts without a single game element on the Stage.

The holes and pegs are separate movie clips. The code places them both on the Stage, which spares you the tedious task of placing each movie clip and naming it. Instead, the code does the work.

When the player drags a peg to a new hole, a lot of code is needed to determine whether the move is valid. First, the move has to be to an empty hole, two spaces away from the current hole. Then the hole that was jumped must have a peg in it. If these conditions are met, the move is allowed. The jumped peg is removed from the board.

Preparing the Movie

Only a "peg" and "hole" movie clip are needed. The "peg" movie clip also has a button placed inside it that sends a message to the main timeline when the button is clicked and when it is released.

Because neither movie clip is on the Stage before the movie runs, they both have to be linked. The code refers to them with the names "peg" and "hole."

Writing the Code

Almost all the code is in the only frame of the main timeline. The code starts off by creating the "hole" and "peg" movie clip instances and arranging them on the Stage. It uses an *if* statement that you can see commented in the following code to rule out any holes that are not on the grid shown earlier in Figure 14.7. The code also checks to make sure that pegs are added to every hole, except the one in the center.

The function ends by storing the total number of holes in the variable "maxHole." This will be useful in future functions that need to loop through each movie clip to check for certain conditions.

```
initGame();
stop();

function initGame() {
    // location constants
    holeSpace = 30;
    puzzleLeft = 160;
    puzzleTop = 80;

    // loop through and create pegs
    i = 0;
    for(y=0;y<9;y++) {
        for(x=0;x<9;x++) {

            // check to see whether peg should not be created
            // this will create the + pattern
            if (((y < 3) or (y > 5)) and ((x < 3) or (x > 5))) continue;

            // add new hole and place it
            attachMovie("hole","hole"+i,i);
```

```
            _root["hole"+i]._x = x*holeSpace + puzzleLeft;
            _root["hole"+i]._y = y*holeSpace + puzzleTop;

            // do not add peg to center hole
            if ((x != 4) or (y != 4)) {

                // add new peg and place it
                attachMovie("peg","peg"+i,100+i);
                _root["peg"+i]._x = x*holeSpace + puzzleLeft;
                _root["peg"+i]._y = y*holeSpace + puzzleTop;
            }

            i++;
        }
    }

    // remember how many holes/pegs
    maxHole = i;
}
```

When the player clicks a peg, she is actually clicking a button inside that movie clip. Both the "press" and "release" action are passed on to the functions in the main timeline. The "dragPeg" function is called by the "press" action. The "dragPeg" function records the position of the peg in "pegx" and "pegy" and then allows the peg to be dragged. It also uses *swapDepths* to bring the peg in front of all others.

```
function dragPeg(peg) {
    // remember the original location
    pegx = peg._x;
    pegy = peg._y;

    // move this peg on top of all others
    peg.swapDepths(2000);

    // allow Flash to drag the movie clip
    startDrag(peg, true);
}
```

The "dropPeg" function is called when the player releases the mouse button while dragging. It starts by releasing the movie clip from being dragged ⑧ . Then "dropPeg" loops through all the holes to see whether any are under the mouse location ⑨ .

If the mouse is over a hole, the next step is to determine whether the hole is currently empty ⑩ . Next, the code looks in all four directions to see which of the four possible directions the user could be moving. It uses "dx" and "dy" to define the relative location of the hole ⑪ . For instance, if the player jumps to the right, then "dx" is set to 1, "dy" to 0. If the player jumps up, then "dx" is 0, "dy" is −1. If the hole that the player jumps to is not one that is two spaces to the right, left, above, or below the starting hole, then both "dx" and "dy" are 0 ⑫ .

Even if the player moves two spaces to an empty hole, the move is valid only if she jumped another peg. This next section of code checks for that middle peg ⑬ . If the code finds a middle peg there, it removes the peg and sets the peg doing the jumping to its new location.

If any of these conditions fail, the move is not a valid one. The "placed" variable remains *false* and is detected at the end of the function ⑭ . The peg is then moved back to its starting position.

```
    function dropPeg(peg) {
⑧→      // release control of peg clip
        stopDrag();

        // assume this is not a valid move
        placed = false;
        overHole = false;

⑨→      // find over which hole, if any, the peg was released
        for(i=0;i<maxHole;i++) {
            hole = _root["hole"+i];
            if (hole.hitTest(_xmouse,_ymouse)) {
                overHole = true;
                break;
            }
        }

⑩→      // see whether the hole is empty
        if (!pegThere(hole._x,hole._y)) {

⑪→          // find out difference between starting location
            // and destination
            dx = 0;
            dy = 0;
            if ((pegx == hole._x) and (pegy-holeSpace*2 == hole._y)) {
                // above
                dy = -1;
            } else if ((pegx == hole._x) and (pegy+holeSpace*2 == hole._y)) {
                // below
                dy = 1;
            } else if ((pegy == hole._y) and (pegx-holeSpace*2 == hole._x)) {
                // left
                dx = -1;
```

```
            } else if ((pegy == hole._y) and (pegx+holeSpace*2 == hole._x)) {
                // right
                dx = 1;
            }
```

⑫➤
```
            // dx and dy will both be 0 unless the destination
            // was a valid distance away
            if ((dx != 0) or (dy != 0)) {
```

⑬➤
```
                // find the peg in the middle
                midThere = false;
                for(i=0;i<maxHole;i++) {
                    mid = _root["peg"+i];
                    if ((mid._x == pegx + dx*holeSpace) and (mid._y == pegy +
                    ➥dy*holeSpace)) {

                        // because there is a peg in the middle,
                        // this move is valid
                        // set the new location of the peg
                        peg._x = hole._x;
                        peg._y = hole._y;

                        // remove the middle peg
                        mid.removeMovieClip();

                        // remember that the move was successful
                        placed = true;
                        break;
                    }
                }
            }
        }
```

⑭➤
```
        // check to see whether the move was successful and
        // reset the peg location if not
        if (!placed) {
            peg._x = pegx;
            peg._y = pegy;
        }
    }
```

"dropPeg" uses the "pegThere" utility function to take a location and return *true* if a "peg" movie clip is found at *exactly* that location.

```
function pegThere(x,y) {
    // loop through all pegs to see whether any is in this location
    for(i=0;i<maxHole;i++) {
```

```
            peg = _root["peg"+i];
            if ((peg._x == x) and (peg._y == y)) {
                return true;
            }
        }
    }
    return false;
}
```

During the game, a "Restart Game" button is always at the bottom of the screen. This allows the player to restart when she runs out of moves, or when she realizes that she has started the game off badly. The button needs to do more than just call "initGame." It first needs to clear out any remaining "peg" clips and all the "hole" clips.

```
function restartGame() {
    // remove all movie clips
    for(i=0;i<maxHole;i++) {
        _root["peg"+i].removeMovieClip();
        _root["hole"+i].removeMovieClip();
    }

    // start new game
    initGame();
}
```

The code attached to the button inside the "peg" movie clip is simple. All it does is pass on the press and release to other functions.

```
on (press) {
    _root.dragPeg(this);
}

on (release) {
    _root.dropPeg(this);
}
```

Other Possibilities

The main way you can vary this game is to create other game boards. I've seen pages of combinations in old game books like the ones you find in the "Games" section of a large bookstore. Many grids involve diagonal jumps instead of horizontal and vertical ones. This requires some reworking of the code.

Another variation would be to have a single peg that is a different color from all the rest. The extra-hard challenge to the player would be to leave only that specific peg.

Recursive Blocks

▷⟨Example movie: Blocks.fla

I've seen this game implemented in many variations under many names. The basic idea is that the screen is filled with a large grid of colored blocks. The player can click on a block to remove it from the grid. But in order for the block to be removable, it must have a neighbor, either next to it or above or below it, that is of the same color.

When the player clicks on an eligible block, the block is removed. In addition, its neighbor of the same color is also removed. In return, any neighbors of that block of the same color are removed. So the result is that a connected area of blocks of the same color can be removed by clicking on any block in the area.

After a group of blocks is removed, the blocks above the empty spaces collapse down to fill the gap. Then if any columns of blocks are completely empty, the grid collapses to the left to fill gaps.

Figure 14.8 shows the game when it first starts. In addition to the block being one of four different colors, I've also placed a small graphic in each block, according to color. This makes it easier to see in the black and white figure. The only way to really understand the game is to try it out, so you should do that now before proceeding.

Figure 14.8
The Recursive Blocks game starts with a random grid of colored blocks.

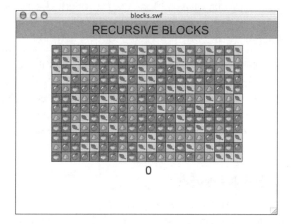

Project Goal

The goal of this project is to make a game that provides only basic game play. In addition to the general rules already discussed, a simple scoring system will be added. However, no attempt will be made to determine when a game ends. Suggestions on how to do this are given at the end of the chapter.

Approach

The grid is a series of movie clips created by ActionScript. When the user clicks on a block, it is removed from the grid at first, after its color has been noted. Then, each of its four neighbors are tested to see whether they are the same color. If none are, then the block clicked is restored to its original color.

The method for removing blocks is recursive. Each neighbor of the clicked block is tested to see whether it is the same color. If it is, then each neighbor of that block is tested, and so on. This recursive method eventually finds blocks that have no neighbors of the same color, and so the recursion ends.

If you are not quite sure you understand how this recursion works, walk through it with an example. For instance, the user clicks on a red block. Of its four neighbors, the block above and the block to the right are red. Take the block above. None of its neighbors are red. Take the block to the right. The block below that one is red. Take this third red block. None of its neighbors are red. So the block clicked is removed. The block above it is removed, the block to the right is removed and the block below the block to the right is removed.

Although this game won't detect the case where there are no more possible moves, it will keep score. The best way to keep score in a game like this is to use an exponential scoring system. So if a group of two blocks is removed, the player scores 4 points: 2 times 2. If a group of three blocks is removed, the player scores 3 times 3, or 9 points. If a group of 4 blocks is removed, the player scores 4 times 4, or 16 points.

This type of scoring system rewards the player who finds large groups of blocks. For instance, removing 10 groups of 2 blocks will get the user 40 points (2 times 2 is 4, 4 times 10 is 40). But removing one group of 20 blocks gets the user 400 points (20 times 20). Not only should the player look for larger groups of blocks, but he or she should try to create larger groups of blocks by pulling out small groups so that large groups become linked together into an even larger group.

Preparing the Movie

The movie has very little in it except a movie clip in the Library to represent the blocks. This clip has four frames, each representing a color. There is also a small picture for each frame. The fifth frame is blank and represents an empty space on the grid. The first four blocks have a button on them so they can be clicked. This movie clip must be set to export with the movie in its Linkage properties because it is not initially on the Stage.

The main timeline of the movie includes two frames, the first containing the instructions and a Play button. The second is the "Play" frame.

Writing the Code

Creating the blocks happens in the "startGame" function. The function loops through 20 horizontal columns and 12 vertical rows to create 240 blocks. Each block is a new instance of the "block" movie clip created with *attachMovie*. In addition to being placed at the correct location on the Stage, each block is given the properties "x" and "y" so it can identify its position later.

A random number from 1 to 4 is chosen and the block's movie clip goes to that frame.

```
function startGame() {
    // go the game frame
    gotoAndStop("Play");
    score = 0;

    // create grid of blocks
    level = 0;
    for(var x=0;x<20;x++) {
        for(var y=0;y<12;y++) {
            mc = _root.attachMovie("block","block "+x+" "+y,level);
            mc._x = 20*x + 85;
            mc._y = 20*y + 60;
            mc.x = x;
            mc.y = y;

            // random color
            mc.gotoAndStop(Math.ceil(Math.random()*4));
            level++;
        }
    }
}
```

When the user clicks on a block to select it, a short script sends the "x" and "y" properties of the block to a function so that the program can begin to decide what action should be taken.

```
on(release) {
    _root.clickBlock(x,y);
}
```

The "clickBlock" function examines the color of the block and stores it in "c." It then removes the block. The "testNeighbor" function is called four times: one for each neighbor. The function returns the number of matching neighbors found in that direction. So if the neighbor above is the same color, and three more of its neighbors are also the same color, then a 4 is returned. By adding that number to "n," you get a complete count of how many blocks are in the group.

NOTE

Notice the keyword *var* in front of the assignment for "c." This makes "c" a local variable, only existing in the "clickBlock" function. Any use of "c" outside of the "clickBlock" function will refer to a separate variable. When using recursive techniques where one function is calling itself or similar functions, it is best to use local variables so the variables don't step on each other as the program moves from function to function.

If more than one block is found to be in the group, then the "collapseDown" and "collapseAcross" functions are called to collapse the remaining blocks. Otherwise, the block clicked is returned to its previous color so it appears that nothing has happened.

```
// block sends clicks here
function clickBlock(x,y) {

    // get color of this block
    var c = _root["block "+x+" "+y]._currentframe;

    // remove the block
    _root["block "+x+" "+y].gotoAndStop(5);

    // test all four neighbors
    var n = 1;
    n += testNeighbor(x-1,y,c);
    n += testNeighbor(x+1,y,c);
    n += testNeighbor(x,y-1,c);
    n += testNeighbor(x,y+1,c);

    // if any neighbors matched
    if (n > 1) {
        // collapse grid
        collapseDown();
        collapseAcross();

        // add to score
        score += n*n;

    } else {
        // put the block back
        _root["block "+x+" "+y].gotoAndStop(c);
    }
}
```

The "testNeighbor" function tests a new block against a color. If the color matches, then the block is removed. The function then calls itself for each of the four neighbors surrounding it. It keeps track of "n," which is the number of neighbors that match.

If the current block does not match the color, then 0 is returned rather than "n," to show that no matching neighbors were found in this direction.

```
function testNeighbor(x,y,c) {
    if (_root["block "+x+" "+y]._currentframe == c) {

        // remove neighbor
        _root["block "+x+" "+y].gotoAndStop(5);
        var n = 1;

        // test all of these neighbors
        n += testNeighbor(x-1,y,c);
        n += testNeighbor(x+1,y,c);
        n += testNeighbor(x,y-1,c);
        n += testNeighbor(x,y+1,c);

        // return number of matches found
        return(n);

    } else {
        // no match found
        return(0);
    }
}
```

After the block is clicked and all its same-color neighbors have been removed, the next step is to let any remaining blocks fall vertically into any empty spots. This is done by looping through all the columns with the variable "x". Then, "y" loops through all the blocks in that column from bottom to top. If a block is empty, then the first non-empty block above it is moved down.

```
function collapseDown() {

    // loop through all columns
    for(var x=0;x<20;x++) {

        // loop through all block in column from bottom to top
        for(var y=11;y>0;y--) {

            // see whether block is empty
            thisColor = _root["block "+x+" "+y]._currentFrame;
            if (thisColor == 5) {

                // loop through all blocks above this one
                for(var i=y-1;i>=0;i--) {
```

```
                         // if this is a non-blank
                         aboveColor = _root["block "+x+" "+i]._currentframe;
                         if (aboveColor != 5) {

                             // move down
                             _root["block "+x+" "+y].gotoAndStop(aboveColor);
                             _root["block "+x+" "+i].gotoAndStop(5);
                             break;
                         }
                     }
                 }
             }
         }
     }
 }
```

After all the blocks have fallen, there is a chance that some columns may be completely empty. When this happens, all the columns to the right of the empty one should be moved to the left to fill the gap.

To do this, the "collapseAcross" function moves through all the columns from left to right. If an empty column is found with a non-empty column next to it, then the non-empty column is moved one column to the left.

This process is repeated over and over until no cases of empty columns can be found. Then the loop ends and the function is done.

```
function collapseAcross() {

    // continue to loop until no more columns are open
    do {
        n = 0;

        // check all columns
        for(var x=0;x<19;x++) {

            // if this column is empty
            if (_root["block "+x+" 11"]._currentframe == 5) {

                // if the next column is occupied
                if (_root["block "+(x+1)+" 11"]._currentframe != 5) {
                    n++;

                    // move all blocks in column over one
                    for(var y=0;y<12;y++) {
                        c = _rcot["block "+(x+1)+" "+y]._currentframe;
                        _root["block "+x+" "+y].gotoAndStop(c);
```

```
                        _root["block "+(x+1)+" "+y].gotoAndStop(5);
                    }
                }
            }
        }

        // loop ends when no columns were moved
    } while (n > 0);
}
```

Loose Ends

In the game there is a "score" field placed under the play area. This keeps track of the variable "score," which is increased in the "clickBlock" function.

Other Possibilities

One thing missing from this game is a way for it to recognize when the game is over. As it stands, you can place an "I'm Done!" button on the frame and let the player decide when a game is over.

ActionScript can be used, however, to determine the two possible ways for a game to end. The first way is when all of the blocks are removed. This is rare; most games leave several blocks that can't be removed. But when it happens, you can detect it by looking for the bottom left block to be empty after the "collapseDown" function has run.

```
if (_root["block 0 11"]._currentFrame == 5) {
    gotoAndStop("game over");
}
```

Most games end with a few blocks left, none of which touch another block of the same color. Checking for this can be more difficult.

The best way to do it is to loop through all the blocks, skip over ones that are empty, and test the non-empty ones to see whether they have any neighbors of the same color. If one is found, then the game is not over.

Casino and Card Games

- Slot Machine
- Video Poker
- Simple Blackjack
- Pyramid Solitaire

Gambling games have always been a popular genre of computer games. The Web is full of casino and card games in Flash, Shockwave, and Java. Most are just for fun, but some allow you to bet real money.

In this chapter, you'll look at four just-for-fun casino games. The first is a pure game of chance: a slot machine. Next, you'll see how to make a video poker game. Then, you'll look at a game that requires a little more skill for the player: blackjack. The final game is one of my favorites: pyramid solitaire, the most fun of all the solitaire games.

TIP

I'd like to warn developers about the difference between a just-for-fun casino game and a real one. Real casino games that involve real money or prizes require complex security programming to make sure the player can't cheat by hacking at the data on his computer or the data sent over the network. A developer who accepts a project to build a real casino game should be an expert in computer and network security, not just a Flash expert. Even if you are an expert at both, proceed with great caution in accepting such a project: It will be difficult and probably cause you many headaches.

Slot Machine

Example file: Slotmachine.fla

A slot machine is a simple type of game, but with a somewhat complex interface. The player simply clicks the slot machine's lever to pull it, and then waits for the result. The slot machine does the rest of the work.

Figure 15.1 shows the example movie slot machine. The lever to the right is the only part with which the player interacts. The three windows each present a different item when the slot machine is done.

Figure 15.1

A simple slot machine with a lever and three windows.

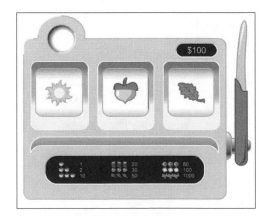

Project Goal

Although some slot machines have many strange and interesting ways to bet and win, this one is simple. The player clicks to pull the lever. Then the wheels in the three windows appear to spin. One by one, they stop on a random item.

When all three wheels stop, the three items showing determine the outcome of the turn. The amount won is equivalent to the amounts shown at the bottom of the machine in Figure 15.1.

Approach

The only difficult part in this game is the spinning. One way to do it would be to have different items move from bottom to top through the window. The problem with this approach is that they would have to move very fast to appear to be spinning as fast as real slot machine wheels spin. Flash just can't animate things at that speed on most computers.

Instead, you can use a blurry spin animation. This animation is a few frames of blurred color in a movie clip. Figure 15.2 shows a few of these frames.

Figure 15.2
These frames of animation create the effect of a spinning wheel when played rapidly.

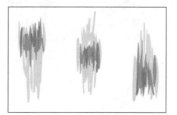

Each of the three windows has a copy of the "spin" movie clip. When it's time for the wheels to spin, all three of these movie clips are told to play, and told precisely how many times to loop. They are given different numbers so that the wheels stop spinning at different times.

Check out the example movie Slotmachine.fla to see how the wheels spin and stop at different times.

Preparing the Movie

There are three key library elements in this movie. All the rest are just background elements. The first element is the lever. The first frame has a button on it that the player can click. The rest of this movie clip is an animation of the lever being pulled.

The "spin" movie clip starts with a blank frame where the "spin" movie clip waits until the player pulls the lever. The frame is transparent so that the "symbols" movie clip can show through.

The rest of the frames in the "spin" movie clip contain the blur animation shown earlier in Figure 15.2. Behind these images is an opaque white field that covers the "symbols" clip while the wheels are spinning.

The "symbols" movie clip contains seven frames, each with a different symbol on it. In the example movie, the symbols include an acorn, apple, leaf, log, moon, sun, and fox.

Writing the Code

Most of the code for this game creates functions in the main timeline. However, let's start by looking at all the pieces of code found in the movie clips.

In the example movie, if you move the lever from its current spot, you will see a button under it. Attached to this button is a simple script that calls the "pull" function in the main timeline:

```
on (release) {
    pull();
}
```

The "spin" movie clip has two short scripts in it. A plain *stop()* command appears on the first frame. A script that reduces a counter called "numTimes" by one appears on the last frame. If this counter is 0, it returns the movie clip to the first frame and notifies a function in the main timeline. Otherwise, it causes the movie clip to loop back to frame 2.

```
numTimes--;
if (numTimes <= 0) {
    gotoAndStop(1);
    _root.spinDone(_name);
} else {
    gotoAndPlay(2);
}
```

Much of the code in the main timeline deals with determining how much money, if any, the player won on the spin.

The code starts, however, by setting each of the three symbols to a random frame, and giving the player $100 in "cash":

```
initGame();
stop();

function initGame() {
    // start three symbols out randomly
    for(i=1;i<4;i++) {
        _root["symbol"+i].gotoAndStop(randomSymbol());
    }
```

```
        // start cash at $100
        cash = 100;
        showCash();
    }
```

Rather than display the player's cash as a plain number, the next function places a dollar sign, followed by the "cash" variable into "displayCash." This variable is linked to a text area on the Stage.

```
    // display cash with $
    function showCash() {
        cashDisplay = "$"+cash;
    }
```

When the user clicks on the lever button, several things happen. First, $1 is subtracted from the player's cash. Next, the "arm" movie clip is sent to frame 2 so it can animate the lever going down. Then, all three "spin" movie clips begin animating. Each clip starts with a different "numTimes" setting—8, 6, and 4—to make the first animation loop 8 times, the second 6, and the third 4.

The result of each spin is also determined at this time. The "symbol" movie clips are set, although they are hidden behind the opaque "spin" animations until they are done.

```
    // pull the handle
    function pull() {

        // deduct $1 per pull
        cash--;
        showCash();

        // play arm animation
        _root["arm"].gotoAndPlay(2);

        // tell spin animations to go
        for(i=1;i<4;i++) {
            // tell spin animations how many times
            _root["spin"+i].numTimes = 8-i*2;
            _root["spin"+i].gotoAndPlay(2);
        }

        // pick a random result for each symbol
        for(i=1;i<4;i++) {
            _root["symbol"+i].gotoAndStop(randomSymbol());
        }
    }
```

The way a random symbol is picked is not simple. If each of the seven symbols had an even chance of appearing, then each matching outcome would have the same chance of happening. In other words, three acorns would appear as often as three foxes. This would mean that having different payouts for different matching sets wouldn't make sense.

TIP

Actual slot machines have a surprisingly complex method for picking the symbols that end up in the windows. These methods involve complex mathematical formulas so that the casino can control exactly how much of a chance the player has of winning.

Instead, each symbol needs to have a different chance of appearing. A log symbol, for instance, appears 29% of the time. A fox symbol, on the other hand, appears only 6% of the time.

The way this is done is by placing the relative chance of a symbol appearing into a list. Then, a random number is picked. If this random number falls within the percentage chance of the first symbol, then the first symbol is picked. If not, then the code proceeds to the next number in the list. This is done until a symbol is picked. Walk yourself through the following code to see how it works:

```
// choose a random symbol based on probability calculations
function randomSymbol() {
    // get chances of each symbol appearing
    chances = [29,21,16,12,9,7,6];

    // determine total count of chances
    totalChances = 0;
    for(j=0;j<chances.length;j++) {
        totalChances += chances[j];
    }

    // pick a random number
    r = int(Math.random()*totalChances);

    // determine which symbol the number represents
    for(j=0;j<chances.length;j++) {
        if (r < chances[j]) {
            return(j+1);
        } else {
            r -= chances[j];
        }
    }
}
```

When a "spin" movie clip is done animating, it calls the "spinDone" function with the name of the movie clip instance. Movie clip "spin1" is singled out as the last animation in the sequence. When this one is done, the "calcWin" function is called to determine the winnings.

```
// called by each spin animation
function spinDone(name) {

    // see whether this is the last symbol to stop spinning
    if (name == "spin1") {

        // calculate winnings
        win = calcWin();
        cash += win;
        showCash();
    }

}
```

The "calcWin" function determines whether all three symbols match. It also counts the number of acorns in the sequence. If all three match, then the amount won is determined by which symbol it is. If there is no match, the player can still win a little with one or two acorns present.

```
// determine how much the player won
function calcWin() {

    // how many acorns
    numAcorns = 0;
    for(i=1;i<4;i++) {
        if (_root["symbol"+i]._currentFrame == 2) numAcorns++;
    }

    // is it three matching symbols?
    firstSymbol = _root["symbol1"]._currentFrame;
    threeOfAKind = true;
    for(i=2;i<4;i++) {
        if (_root["symbol"+i]._currentFrame != firstSymbol) threeOfAKind=false;
    }

    // determine payout of three matches
    if (threeOfAKind) {
        if (firstSymbol == 1) {
            win = 20;
        } else if (firstSymbol == 2) {
            win = 10;
        } else if (firstSymbol == 3) {
            win = 30;
```

```
        } else if (firstSymbol == 4) {
            win = 50;
        } else if (firstSymbol == 5) {
            win = 80;
        } else if (firstSymbol == 6) {
            win = 100;
        } else if (firstSymbol == 7) {
            win = 1000;
        }

    // two acorns
    } else if (numAcorns == 2) {
        win = 2;

    // one acorn
    } else if (numAcorns == 1) {
        win = 1;

    // nothing
    } else {
        win = 0;
    }

    return(win);
}
```

Loose Ends

If you look at the example movie, you will see that the slot machine background is actually in the foreground. The three windows are holes in this image where the symbols and spin animations show through.

You might also want to decide what to do when a player reaches $0. You can check for this condition and then branch to another frame when it happens. You can tell players that the game is over, or that they have been given another $100 to play with.

Other Possibilities

More complex slot machines could include multiple symbols in a window. Some machines show three symbols, stacked vertically, and the player can win by matching symbols across three horizontal lines and two diagonal lines between the windows. Sometimes the player can choose to insert from one to five coins to enable potential wins along different lines.

Because this Flash movie is not for gambling, but just for fun, it is more important to see the potential for changing the graphics to match different Web site themes. For instance, you could have candy symbols for a kid's site. The appearance of the machine and the type of symbols chosen can make a slot machine movie a good addition to many Web sites.

Video Poker

Example file: Videopoker.fla

In casinos, the video poker machines are right next to the slot machines. They are essentially the same thing: You insert a coin and take a chance that you might win. The only difference is that you get to interact with the machine in the middle of the game to affect the outcome.

Make no mistake: The house always wins in the end. However, because the player gets to replace some cards in the middle of the game, video poker makes the player feel like he has a better chance. This will also make it more difficult for us to build.

Project Goal

Video poker is played in three steps. The first step is the game waiting for the player to ask that cards be dealt. Then, the player looks at the five cards and assesses them. The second step is when the player decides which cards to keep and which to discard. The last step is when new cards have been dealt and the final value of the hand is decided. This immediately leads back to the first step.

The game needs to present the player with a set of five cards randomly chosen from a shuffled deck. Figure 15.3 shows the screen with five cards.

Figure 15.3
The video poker game shows the player five cards.

The player can choose to replace any or all the cards. After that is done, the program must examine the final five cards and determine what they are worth.

Approach

The first thing the program needs is a shuffled deck of cards. This is an array of strings such as "h7," which represents the seven of hearts. The four suits are represented by "c," "d," "h," and "s." An ace is a 1, as in "c1" for the ace of clubs, and the jack, queen, and king are "11," "12," and "13."

Creating an ordered deck of cards is easy; however, a random deck is another matter. To create a shuffled deck, you start with an ordered array and then pick random items from it, one by one, and place them in a new array.

The first five cards from the array are then displayed on the screen. A button is placed under each card. One click changes the card to the image of the back of a card. A second click returns the card in case the player changes her mind.

After the player is satisfied with her choices, she hits the "Draw" button. Then any cards tagged for replacement are replaced by the next cards in the shuffled deck.

The trickiest bit of programming comes at the end of the game. An array of the five final cards must be evaluated for its poker value. Here is a list of possible values:

- **Low pair**—A pair of cards, 10 or lower.
- **High pair**—A pair of jacks, queens, kings, or aces.
- **Three-of-a-kind**—Any three cards of the same value.
- **Straight**—Five cards with consecutive values such as 8, 9, 10, jack, and queen. An ace can be either before a 2 or after a king.
- **Flush**—Five cards of the same suit.
- **Full house**—A pair and three-of-a-kind.
- **Four-of-a-kind**—Four cards of the same value.
- **Straight flush**—Five cards with consecutive values, all the same suit.
- **Royal flush**—A straight flush with a 10, jack, queen, king, and ace.

To determine whether the final hand meets any of the previously listed criteria, you have to analyze the array of cards in several ways.

After the hand's value has been determined, the final step is to match that value to a win amount and give the player the cash.

Preparing the Movie

The main library element in this game is the deck of cards, which is a 54-frame movie clip. The first frame shows the blank outline of a card. The second frame shows the back of any card. Frames 3 to 54 each show a different card in the deck. Each frame is named with the same name the code uses to identify cards. For instance, "c1" is the ace of clubs and "h11" is the jack of hearts.

If you look at the example movie, Videopoker.fla, you will see that the "deck" movie clip is complemented by a whole library folder filled with graphics. This makes it easier to reuse elements from card to card.

The movie is set up with five instances of the "deck" movie clip. They are named "card0" to "card4." The first frame needs only a "deal" button, as does the third frame. The middle frame should have a "draw" button instead, as well as a "hold/replace" button under each card.

Writing the Code   *change cash to points*

The first frame of the main timeline contains most of the code. It starts by setting the player's "cash" to 100.   *start @ 0*

```
startGame();
stop();

// init cash
function startGame() {
    cash = 100;
}
```
change this to setting points

As in the slot machine, use a function to display the player's cash with a "$" before it:

```
// display cash with $
function showCash() {
    cashDisplay = "$"+cash;
}
```
Keep take out don't want to show points yet

A hand starts with the player paying $1. Each hand is dealt from a fresh new deck of 52 cards. The "firstDraw" function picks the first five cards and the "showCards" function sets the movie clips on the Stage to those cards.   *alter to fit 25 cards*

```
// start a hand
function startDeal() {
    // deduct from cash
    cash--;
    showCash();

    // shuffle and deal
    createDeck();
    firstDraw();
    showCards();
}
```
use this — show points · *leave out change to show Points* · *do this*

Creating a completely random deck involves two steps. The first is to create an ordered deck. This is done by looping through all the suits and values and adding a card to an array for each combination.

Next, the program takes random cards from this ordered deck and places them in another array. When that array is full and the previous array is empty, you have a shuffled deck.

```
// create a shuffled deck
function createDeck() {
    // creat an ordered deck
    suits = ["c","d","s","h"];
    temp = new Array();
    for(suit=0;suit<4;suit++) {
        for(num=1;num<14;num++) {
            temp.push(suits[suit]+num);
        }
    }

    // pick random cards until deck has been shuffled
    deck = new Array();
    while (temp.length > 0) {
        r = int(Math.random()*temp.length);
        deck.push(temp[r]);
        temp.splice(r,1);
    }
}
```

The "firstDraw" function takes five cards from the deck and pushes them into the "cards" array. It also initializes a small array called "hold," which remembers which cards the player wants to keep.

```
// deal first five cards
function firstDraw() {
    cards = new Array();
    for(i=0;i<5;i++) {
        cards.push(deck.pop());
    }

    // set hold array to all held
    hold = [true,true,true,true,true];

    showCards();
}
```

To translate the array of cards in the player's hand to something that the player can see, the "showCards" handler sets the frame for each of the five movie clip instances on the Stage to match the strings in the "hand" array:

```
// set card movie clips to the player's hand
function showCards() {
    for(i=0;i<5;i++) {
```

```
        _root["card"+i].gotoAndStop(cards[i]);
    }
}
```

(handwritten margin note: change to if Hold none other code)

After all the cards have been shown to the player, he must decide what to do next. The "Hold/Draw" button under each card calls the "holdDraw" function with a number from 0 to 4. The first time a button is clicked, the code changes the movie clip instance to show the back of a card. If the player clicks the button again, the code replaces the card. The player can toggle back and forth as many times as he wants before clicking the "Draw" button.

The "hold" array will have a *true* in any position to represent that the player wants to keep the card, and a *false* if the player wants to replace it:

```
// toggle a card between hold and draw
function holdDraw(cardNum) {

    // card being held, turn it over
    if (hold[cardNum]) {
        _root["card"+cardNum].gotoAndStop("back");
        hold[cardNum] = false;

    // card turned over, hold it instead
    } else {
        _root["card"+cardNum].gotoAndStop(cards[cardNum]);
        hold[cardNum] = true;
    }
}
```

When the player clicks the "Draw" button, the "secondDraw" function replaces any cards that are marked by a *false* in the "hold" array. The function calls "showCards" to display the changes.

The code then immediately uses the function "handValue" to determine what the player has. This value is passed into "winnings" to determine how much cash, if any, should be added to the player's cash. Also, the variable "resultsDisplay" is used to display both of these values on the screen.

```
// replace cards not held and decide on winnings
function secondDraw() {

    // replace cards not held
    for(i=0;i<5;i++) {
        if (!hold[i]) {
            cards[i] = deck.pop();
        }
    }
    showCards();
```

```
    // figure out what player has
    handVal = handValue(cards);

    // determine the amount won
    winAmt = winnings(handVal);
    resultsDisplay = handVal + ": " + winAmt;

    // add winnings
    cash += winAmt;
    showCash();

    gotoAndPlay("done");
}
```

Before you get into the critical "handValue" function, you need to create a utility function called "compareHands." The function "handValue" needs to sort the cards in the player's hand so that the lowest values are first. Flash doesn't know anything in particular about a deck of playing cards, so you have to teach it.

The "compareHands" function takes two cards and compares them. It isolates characters 1 and 2 from each card, which means that it ignores character 0. This means that "c7" becomes 7 and "c13" becomes 13.

It then returns one of three responses: -1 means card a is numerically before card b, 0 means card a is the same value as card b, and 1 means card a comes numerically after card b.

This function is required by the *sort* command that will be used in the "handValue" function. If *sort* didn't have this specialized function, it would attempt to sort the "hand" array in alphabetical order, which would place all clubs in front of all diamonds because one starts with a "c" and the other a "d." Instead, you want the cards to be sorted in numerical order.

```
// this function is used by the sort command to
// decide which cards come first
function compareHands(a,b) {

    // get number value of cards
    numa = Number(a.substr(1,2));
    numb = Number(b.substr(1,2));

    // return -1, 0, or 1 depending on comparison
    if (numa < numb) return(-1);
    if (numa == numb) return(0);
    if (numa > numb) return(1);
}
```

The "handValue" function, which is coming up next, starts by making a copy of the "cards" array and storing it in the "hand" array. It then sorts this array using the "compareHands" function ①.

For instance, if the player's hand is ["h4," "d5," "c2," "s3," "h6"], then the array after the sort will be ["c2," "s3," "h4," "d5," "h6"]. This makes it easier for the code to determine whether the array has a set of cards that are in consecutive order, called a "straight."

A "straight" is determined by looking at each card and seeing whether it is one value higher than the card before it ②. If this condition holds throughout the array, then it is a straight.

This technique won't find one type of straight: when a straight starts with a 10, goes up to a king and then wraps back around to an ace. This is a special type of straight recognized in poker and you can perform a simple test to determine whether it has occurred ③.

TIP

Some people think that straights can wrap around the end of a deck, with the ace acting as the first and last card. For instance: a queen, king, ace, two, and three. This is not a valid poker straight, but merely an odd variation used in some friendly amateur games. An ace can be used as the first card of the straight (ace, two, three, four, five), or the last card of a straight (ten, jack, queen, king, ace), but not both for wrap-around sequences. The rules of poker are detailed in many sources, such as the popular *Hoyle* series of books.

Next, you check to see whether all the cards have the same suit ④. This is done by comparing all cards, except the first one, with the first card. If all cards match the suit of the first card, then they must all match.

The next step is to make an array called "counts" and store the number of cards of each value in it ⑤. This array has 14 values, each representing the number of cards in the hand of that value. The first item in the array is not used because there is no card of "0" value.

For example, if a hand has an ace, two threes, a four, and a jack, the array would be [0,1,0,2,1,0,0,0,0,0,0,1,0,0].

Finally, the code can start the task of determining what type of hand the player has. The "counts" array is looped through and any 2, 3, or 4 is noted ⑥. A single appearance of a 2 means that the player has a pair. A single appearance of a 3 means the player has three-of-a-kind. A single appearance of a 4 means the player has four-of-a-kind. It is also possible to find a second appearance of a 2, or both a 2 and a 3 in the hand. The first is two-pair, and the second is a full house.

Next, a test is made to determine whether there are any pairs that are jacks or higher ⑦ . Video poker typically rewards only pairs that are jacks or higher and gives nothing for pairs that are 10 or lower.

Another test checks to see whether the player has an ace in the hand ⑧ . This is used in case the player has a straight flush. If the player has a straight flush and one card is an ace, then it means the player has the highest sort of straight flush: a royal flush.

Now the function has a whole series of true or false values: "straight," "flush," "hasKingAndAce," "fourOfAKind," "threeOfAKind," "twoPair," "pair," "fullHouse," and "jackOrHigher." With these true or false values, the actual value of the hand can be determined and returned as a string ⑨ .

```
// determine what the player has
function handValue() {

    // make a copy of the player's cards and sort them
    hand = cards.slice();
    hand.sort(compareHands);

    // make arrays with suits and numbers for easy access
    suits = new Array();
    nums = new Array();
    for(i=0;i<5;i++) {
        suits.push(hand[i].substr(0,1));
        nums.push(Number(hand[i].substr(1,2)));
    }

    // see whether they are in perfect order
    straight = true;
    for(i=0;i<4;i++) {
        if (nums[i] + 1 != nums[i+1]) straight = false;
    }

    // look for 10, J, Q, K and Ace
    if ((nums[0] == 1) and (nums[1] == 10) and (nums[2] == 11)
        and (nums[3] == 12) and (nums[4] == 13))  straight = true;

    // see whether they are all the same suit
    flush = true;
    for(i=1;i<5;i++) {
        if (suits[i] != suits[0]) flush = false;
    }

    // make array of how much of each number is in hand
    counts = new Array();
```

① → (points to `hand.sort(compareHands);`)

② → (points to `// see whether they are in perfect order`)

③ → (points to `// look for 10, J, Q, K and Ace`)

④ → (points to `// see whether they are all the same suit`)

⑤ → (points to `// make array of how much of each number is in hand`)

```
        for(i=0;i<14;i++) {
            counts.push(0);
        }
        for(i=0;i<5;i++) {
            counts[nums[i]]++;
        }
```

⑥→
```
        // use counts array to find matches
        pair = false;
        twoPair = false;
        threeOfAKind = false;
        fourOfAKind = false;
        for(i=1;i<14;i++) {
            // pair found
            if (counts[i] == 2) {
                // second pair found
                if (pair) {
                    twoPair = true;
                // first pair found
                } else {
                    pair = true;
                }
            // three-of-a-kind
            } else if (counts[i] == 3) {
                threeOfAKind = true;
            // four-of-a-kind
            } else if (counts[i] == 4) {
                fourOfAKind = true;
            }
        }
```

⑦→
```
        // see whether any matches are jacks or higher
        jackOrHigher = false;
        for(i=1;i<14;i++) {
            if (((i == 1) or (i > 10)) and (counts[i] >= 2)) {
                jackOrHigher = true;
            }
        }
```

⑧→
```
    // see whether hand has both king and ace
        hasKingAndAce = false;
        if ((counts[1]==1) and (counts[13]==1)) hasKingAndAce = true;
```

⑨→
```
        // return the type of hand the player has
        if (straight and flush and hasKingAndAce) {
            return("Royal Flush");
        } else if (straight and flush) {
```

For MX2004
A.S in Fr. 2 on main time l>
Line1– start Deal();
   2– stop();

A.S. in Fr. 3 on main
Stop();

```
       return("Straight Flush");
   } else if (fourOfAKind) {
       return("Four-Of-A-Kind");
   } else if (pair and threeOfAKind) {
       return("Full House");
   } else if (flush) {
       return("Flush");
   } else if (straight) {
       return("Straight");
   } else if (threeOfAKind) {
       return("Three-Of-A-Kind");
   } else if (twoPair) {
       return("Two Pair");
   } else if (pair and jackOrHigher) {
       return("High Pair");
   } else if (pair) {
       return("Low Pair");
   } else {
       return("Nothing");
   }
}
```

The only function left is the "winnings" function, which takes a string generated by "handValue" and finds the appropriate amount won:

```
// take the type of hand and return the amount won
function winnings(handVal) {
    if (handVal == "Royal Flush") return(800);
    if (handVal == "Straight Flush") return(50);
    if (handVal == "Four-Of-A-Kind") return(25);
    if (handVal == "Full House") return(8);
    if (handVal == "Flush") return(5);
    if (handVal == "Straight") return(4);
    if (handVal == "Three-Of-A-Kind") return(3);
    if (handVal == "Two Pair") return(2);
    if (handVal == "High Pair") return(1);
    if (handVal == "Low Pair") return(0);
    if (handVal == "Nothing") return(0);
}
```

Loose Ends

Each "hold/draw" button contains a slightly different piece of code. The first one looks like this:

```
on (press) {
    holdDraw(0);
}
```

The "0" tells the "holdDraw" function that the request is about card 0. The other four buttons have the number 1 to 4 there instead.

Although the first frame of the movie immediately calls "startGame," as you can see from the code in the "Writing the Code" section, the second frame must call "startDeal." Check out the example movie to see it yourself.

Other Possibilities

I picked the amounts specified in "winnings" using common sense. However, you might want to pick different numbers depending on how much you want the game to favor the house or the player.

You will also want to handle the case where the player runs out of money. Send her to a "game over" frame, for instance.

Another variation on this game would be to allow players to bet from $1 to $5 per turn. This allows players to bet less when they feel unlucky and more at other times.

Simple Blackjack

Example file: Blackjack.fla

Blackjack is another popular casino card game that translates well to the computer screen. After all, the dealer in blackjack follows a precise set of rules. Therefore, you can write a program to imitate the dealer's behavior.

Project Goal

The goal here is not to create a full-featured blackjack game, but rather a basic one. There are several rules in blackjack that are rarely used, such as doubling down, insurance, and splitting. These are seldom used by the player, and they complicate the code to the point of making it super-advanced. So instead of dealing with those rules and making this section of the book useful to only a few, those rules have been omitted so this section is easier to understand.

Figure 15.4 shows the example movie in action. You can see that the player has drawn five cards for a total of 18. The dealer drew three cards to get 21.

This simple blackjack game deals two cards to the player and dealer. The dealer's first card is facedown until the player has finished drawing. The player can draw until he gets 21 or more. Then, the computer draws for the dealer until the dealer has at least 17.

If the player gets 21 in his first two cards, he immediately wins the bet, plus 50%. If the dealer gets 21, the hand ends immediately. After that, whoever gets the higher amount without passing 21, wins.

The player also can control how much he bets, from $5 to $25, in increments of $5.

Figure 15.4
The Flash Blackjack game shows a hand just completed where the dealer beat the player 21 to 18.

Approach

As in the video poker game, there is a "deck" array that stores a shuffled deck of cards. The difference here is that there are actually six decks of cards shuffled into the same "deck" array. In blackjack, this is called a "shoe."

Both the player and the dealer have an array representing the cards in their hands. You have to make a special consideration for the dealer's first card, because it shouldn't be shown until the player is finished drawing.

Unlike video poker, determining the value of a hand is simple in blackjack. The only twist is that an ace can be worth 1 or 11. However, because two aces worth 11 would total 22, there is no point in ever making a second ace worth 11. So, all you need to do is to recognize that if a hand has an ace in it, count it as 1, and then add 10 to the hand if that 10 won't put the hand over 21. So a hand with a 3, 9, and an ace equals 13, because making the ace worth 11 makes the hand worth 23.

Preparing the Movie

Unlike video poker, there can be anywhere from 2 to 11 cards in a hand. So for each hand, 11 movie clip instances are placed named "player0" to "player10" and "dealer0" to "dealer10." Instead of having a blank card outline for the first frame of the "deck" movie clip, nothing is placed in that frame. Therefore, when you place them on the Stage, all you see is Flash's default movie clip marker. You can see all 22 of them in Figure 15.5.

This movie has a complex timeline. Each labeled marker in the timeline represents a different point in the game. Figure 15.6 shows this complex timeline and you can see most of the labels.

Figure 15.5

All the cards appear as little circles—Flash's movie clip marker for when there is nothing else visible for that movie clip.

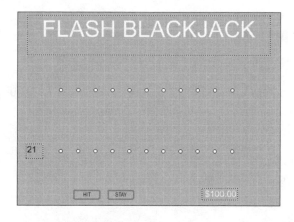

Figure 15.6

The complex timeline of the blackjack game has a labeled frame for each step. Frame 4's label is the only one obscured. It reads "shuffle."

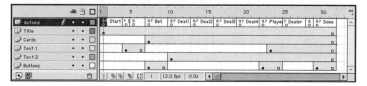

As the game progresses, so does the playback head along the timeline. Each keyframe calls a different function in the code. The code itself appears in the first keyframe.

Because of the nature of Flash timelines, it is important to take a look at the example movie, Blackjack.fla, on the CD-ROM to see for yourself where all the keyframes are and what code they call.

Writing the Code

The first frame calls "initGame," but there is no *stop()* command right after it. The timeline should continue and move directly to the "shuffle" frame.

```
initGame();
```

The "initGame" function sets up the player's "cash":

```
function initGame() {
    cash = 100;
    showCash();
}
```

The "createDeck" function is similar to the one used in video poker, but it actually adds each card six times to create a show of six decks.

One of the drawbacks of the six decks is that it can take some time to shuffle in Flash. Therefore, the "shuffle" frame appears just one frame before the keyframe where the "createDeck" function is called. This ensures that the word "shuffle" appears in the screen before the code starts working on the assignment. Therefore, the player doesn't have to wonder if her computer froze.

```
// create a shuffled deck
function createDeck() {
    // create an ordered deck
    suits = ["c","d","s","h"];
    temp = new Array();
    for(i=0;i<6;i++) {
        for(suit=0;suit<4;suit++) {
            for(num=1;num<14;num++) {
                temp.push(suits[suit]+num);
            }
        }
    }

    // pick random cards until deck has been shuffled
    deck = new Array();
    while (temp.length > 0) {
        r = int(Math.random()*temp.length);
        deck.push(temp[r]);
        temp.splice(r,1);
    }
}
```

deals with 6 decks

The "initHand" function sets up the "playerHand" and "dealerHand" arrays. It also sets the flag "showDealerFirstCard" to *false* and sets the bet to the default $5.

```
// init hand arrays and bet
function initHand() {
    playerHand = new Array();
    dealerHand = new Array();
    showDealerFirstCard = false;

    bet = 5;
    showBet();
}
```

The "addToBet" function responds to the player clicking the "Add to bet" button. It adds $5 to the bet, but doesn't allow the player to go above $25.

```
// allow the player to increase her bet up to $25
function addToBet() {
    bet += 5;
    if (bet > 25) bet = 25;
    showBet();
}
```

When the player hits the "Deal" button, "makeBet" is called to transfer the bet amount out of the player's cash pool. The movie then flows forward through the four frames: "Deal1" to "Deal4."

```
// take the money away from the player
function makeBet() {
    cash -= bet;
    showCash();
}
```

Each of the four "Deal" frames calls "dealCard." Twice this function is called with "playerHand" and twice with "DealerHand." The function deals two cards to the player and two to the dealer. The function "showCards" is also called in each of these frames.

```
// take one card from the deck and give it to the player
function dealCard(hand) {
    hand.push(deck.pop());
}
```

The "showBet" and "showCash" functions display the current bet and the player's cash with a "$" in front of them. Remember to create the appropriate text areas for each of these.

```
// display cash with $
function showCash() {
    cashDisplay = "$"+cash;
}
```

```
// display bet with $
function showBet() {
    betDisplay = "$"+bet;
}
```

The "showCards" function loops through each of the cards in both the player's and dealer's hands and sets the movie clips on the Stage to represent them. It uses the flag "showDealerFirstCard" to determine whether the first card in the dealer's hand is shown or the back of a card is shown instead.

```
// show all cards in both hands
function showCards() {
    // only show the dealer's first card when player is finished
```

```
    if (showDealerFirstCard) {
        _root["dealer0"].gotoAndStop(dealerHand[0]);
    } else {
        _root["dealer0"].gotoAndStop(2);
    }

    // show the rest of the dealer's cards
    for(i=1;i<dealerHand.length;i++) {
        _root["dealer"+i].gotoAndStop(dealerHand[i]);
    }

    // show all of the player's cards
    for(i=0;i<playerHand.length;i++) {
        _root["player"+i].gotoAndStop(playerHand[i]);
    }

    // show the numerical value of both hands
    playerValue = handValue(playerHand);
    dealerValue = handValue(dealerHand);
}
```

After the initial deal of two cards each, there is the chance that either player has black-jack. If the player does, then she immediately wins her bet, plus 50% more. If the dealer does, then the player loses right away.

```
// check to see whether either has blackjack
function checkForBlackjack() {

    // if player has blackjack
    if ((playerHand.length == 2) and (playerValue == 21)) {
        // award 150% winnings
        cash += bet*2.5;
        showCash();
        result = "Blackjack!";
        gotoAndPlay("Done");

    // if dealer has blackjack, instant loss
    } else if ((dealerHand.length == 2) and (dealerHand == 21)) {
        result = "Dealer has blackjack!";
        gotoAndPlay("Done");
    }
}
```

After the initial four cards are dealt, the movie comes to a rest on the "Player" frame. This frame has a "Hit" and a "Stay" button. The player can use the "Hit" button to request another card. The "hit" function is called. If the new card puts the player at 21 or more, then the game automatically moves forward.

```
// player draws another card
function hit() {
    dealCard(playerHand);
    showCards();
    playerValue = handValue(playerHand);

    // if player gets 21 or busts, go to dealer
    if (playerValue >= 21) startDealer();
}
```

When the player is finished drawing, the dealer gets to go. The "startDealer" function kicks off this stage of the game by setting the "showDealerFirstCard" to *true* and displaying it through an extra call to "showCards." Then the game advances to the "Dealer" frame.

```
// show dealer's first card and let dealer draw
function startDealer() {
    showDealerFirstCard = true;
    showCards();
    gotoAndPlay("Dealer");
}
```

The "Dealer" frame loops over and over, calling "dealerMove" each time. In each case, the dealer's hand is examined to see whether it's worth 17 or more. The house rules for this game are that the dealer must hit on 16 or lower and stand on everything else. When the dealer stands, the "decideWinner" function is called.

```
// dealer draws if < 17
function dealerMove() {
    if (handValue(dealerHand) < 17) {
        dealCard(dealerHand);
        showCards();
        gotoAndPlay("Dealer");

    // dealer is done
    } else {
        decideWinner();
    }
}
```

The "handValue" function is used in many of the functions shown in the previous code to calculate the numerical value of a hand. The value of each card is added to the total, with aces representing 1. If an ace is found and the addition of 10 will not bust the hand, then 10 is added to the total.

```
// calculate hand value
function handValue(hand) {
    total = 0;
    ace = false;

    for(i=0;i<hand.length;i++) {
        // add value of card
        val = Number(hand[i].substr(1,2));

        // jack, queen, and king = 10
        if (val > 10) val = 10;
        total += val;

        // remember whether an ace is found
        if (val == 1) ace = true;
    }

    // ace can = 11 if it doesn't bust player
    if ((ace) and (total <= 11)) total += 10;

    return(total);
}
```

The following function uses a series of conditions to determine who won. Not only is the "cash" adjusted if the player wins, but each case also sets the "result" variable, which is then displayed on the Stage in the "Done" frame.

```
// see who won, or whether there is a tie
function decideWinner() {
    showCash();
    if (playerValue > 21) {
        result = "You Busted!";
    } else if (dealerValue > 21) {
        cash += bet*2;
        result = "Dealer Busts. You Win!";
    } else if (dealerValue > playerValue) {
        result = "You Lose!";
    } else if (dealerValue == playerValue) {
        cash += bet;
        result = "Tie!";
    } else if (dealerValue < playerValue) {
        cash += bet*2;
        result = "You Win!";
    }
    showCash();
    gotoAndPlay("Done");
}
```

The "Done" frame contains a "Next Hand" button that calls the following function. This function checks to make sure that there are more than 26 cards left in the deck. If not, another shuffle is performed. If there are enough cards left, then "initHand" is called and the game returns to the "Bet" frame.

Either way, the "resetCards" function is used to set all the "deck" movie clips on the Stage back to the first frame so that the cards don't persist on the screen.

```
// start next hand
function newDeal() {
    resetCards();

    // if deck has less than 26 cards, reshuffle
    if (deck.length < 26) {
        gotoAndPlay("shuffle");
    } else {
        initHand();
        gotoAndPlay("Bet");
    }
}

// remove cards from table
function resetCards() {
    for(i=0;i<dealerHand.length;i++) {
        _root["dealer"+i].gotoAndStop(1);
    }
    for(i=0;i<playerHand.length;i++) {
        _root["player"+i].gotoAndStop(1);
    }
}
```

Loose Ends

The main timeline for this movie is the most complex of any game in this book. Therefore, it is important to check out the example movie on the CD-ROM to get a good sense of where everything goes.

You'll also need to create various text areas to display the value of each hand, the bet amount, the cash amount, and the result.

Other Possibilities

Although this game is a good one from which to learn a little ActionScripting, it will disappoint avid blackjack players. Therefore, for the benefit of advanced ActionScript programmers, here's a bit about how to add some of the missing features to the game.

Doubling down is the easiest feature to add. All you need to do is create another button on the "Player" frame called "Double." When the player clicks it, he is dealt one new card, his bet is subtracted once again from his cash, and the play passes to the dealer. However, you have to make sure that the player has not already drawn any cards because doubling can happen only when the player has just his initial two cards.

Insurance is a little harder to do because it creates another branch in the flow of the game. Insurance happens when the dealer is showing an ace. In that case, the player can choose to take out insurance, which is basically a bet against the dealer having 21. If insurance is accepted, and the dealer has 21, then the hand immediately ends. Although the player loses his original bet, he wins the insurance bet.

Splitting is a difficult addition to this game. If the player has two cards of equal value, such as two 9s, then she should be allowed to split the hand into two hands, each starting with a single 9. This means that you cannot store the player's hand in a single array, "playerHand," but you must make it an array of arrays. In most cases, this "playerHands" array contains a single array representing the only hand. If the player splits, then it will contain two arrays. The player might be able to split more than once, giving you three, four, or more arrays inside the "playerHands" array. Then each hand must be played out. You can see how this complicates every part of the game. Even at the end of the game, the player could potentially win, lose, and tie some or all hands.

Pyramid Solitaire

Example movie: Pyramid.fla

Pyramid solitaire is not as popular as standard solitaire nor as complex; however, it is easier to learn and very addictive. Figure 15.7 shows the basic game setup.

Figure 15.7

Pyramid solitaire is played with a pyramid of 28 cards and the remaining deck.

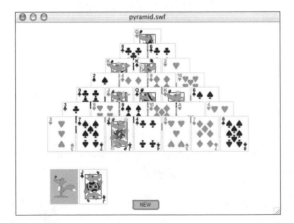

Any card that is completely uncovered is playable. If another card in the pyramid covers part of a card, it cannot be played until the covering cards are removed. To remove a card, the player must match it up with another card so that the total value of both cards equals 13. For instance, a 10 and a 3, or a 6 and a 7, can be paired up. An ace has a value of 1, a jack a value of 11, a queen is a 12 and a king is a 13. This means that the king is the only card that can be selected by itself, without a second card.

The object, of course, is to remove all the cards in the pyramid. To help with this, the remaining 24 cards in the deck are placed under the pyramid and cards can be turned over one at a time. Whichever card is face-up can be combined with a card in the pyramid to total 13.

Take a moment to play the example movie. You may want to put the book down because you might end up playing for a while.

Project Goal

The goal of this project is to make a complete pyramid solitaire game. It will even recognize the rare case when a player "wins" by removing all the cards in the pyramid. When players feel that they are at an impasse, or that the hand dealt is not likely to be fruitful, they can hit a button to re-deal at any time.

Approach

We use the same deck of cards from the blackjack game. The game starts by shuffling the deck and dealing out the pyramid. The rest of the cards are placed in a face-down pile at the bottom of the screen. The player can click on this stack and the card is shown in a face-up stack next to it, which starts out empty. Every click on the face-down stack deals a new card to the face-up pile.

The player can select any uncovered card in the pyramid or the card in the face-up pile. A border in the form of a movie clip highlights the card selected.

When the player clicks another card, it is compared to the first card to see whether it totals 13. If so, then both cards are removed. If one of these cards is in the face-up stack, then the card under it is revealed.

The way to determine whether a card in the pyramid is uncovered is to loop through all the cards in the pyramid to see whether either of the two cards that are supposed to cover it are still there. For instance, the second card in the third row should be covered by the second and third cards in the fourth row and the third card in the fourth row. If either is still there, then the card cannot be selected.

When a card is removed from the face-up stack, the previously visible card must be revealed. This means that you need to keep track of the cards in the face-up stack by placing them into an array as they are turned over.

Kings are a special case. If a king is selected, then it is immediately removed from either the face-up stack or the pyramid, providing it is not covered.

Preparing the Movie

The movie uses the same "deck" movie clip in the Library as the blackjack game. It needs to have its Linkage property set to export with the movie. There is also an "outline" movie clip that is also set to export.

The only frames needed are the "Play" frame and a "Game Over" frame. The latter would be used only in the rare case of a win. Both frames should have a "New" button placed on them that re-deal the game whenever the user wants.

Writing the Code

Almost all the code appears in the main timeline. It starts with the function "startGame." After a new, shuffled deck of cards is created, seven rows of cards are also created ⑩. The first row has one card in it, the second row has two cards, and so on.

Each card is placed according to its row and position in the row ⑪. In addition, the scale of each card is reduced to 50% because the deck used in the blackjack game is about twice the size of what you want for this game ⑫.

The value of the card is taken from the "deck" array ⑬. This corresponds to the frame label inside the "deck" movie clip. This value is stored in the "value" property of the movie clip and goes to the correct frame. The movie clip properties "row" and "col" store the movie clip's position in the pyramid ⑭.

You then create the face-down and face-up stacks by making a movie clip for each ⑮. The face-down stack is sent to the frame "back" to show the image of the back of a card. The other stack remains on frame one, which is blank.

The variable "firstcard" is set to *undefined* ⑯. This variable holds the value of the first card in a pair to be selected by the user. The "stack" array is used to keep track of the cards in the face-up stack. This way when a card in that stack is used, the value of the previous card can be dug out.

Finally, the outline movie clip is created from the Library symbol ⑰. It is moved off-screen for now.

```
    startGame();
    stop();

    function startGame() {

        // shuffle deck
        createDeck();

        // place pyramid cards
        level = 0;
        for(row=0;row<7;row++) {
            for(i=0;i<=row;i++) {
```

⑩→

```
                // make new movie clip
                mc = _root.attachMovie("Deck","card"+level,level);

(11)            // position clip
                mc._x = i*60-row*30 + 275;
                mc._y = row*30 + 50;

(12)            // reduce size from standard deck
                mc._xscale = 50;
                mc._yscale = 50;

(13)            // set value of card
                mc.value = deck.pop();
                mc.gotoAndStop(mc.value);

(14)            // remember its position
                mc.row = row;
                mc.col = i;
                level++;
            }
        }

(15)    // place face-down and face-up stacks
        for(i=0;i<2;i++) {
            mc = _root.attachMovie("Deck","stack"+i,level);
            mc._x = i*60 + 100;
            mc._y = 340;
            mc._xscale = 50;
            mc._yscale = 50;
            level++;
        }

        // show back of card for face-down stack
        _root["stack0"].gotoAndStop("back");

(16)    // set up selection and face-up stack
        firstCard = undefined;
        stack = new Array();

(17)    // set up outline for use
        outline = _root.attachMovie("outline","outline",1000);
        outline._xscale = 50;
        outline._yscale = 50;
        outline._x = -1000;
    }
```

The "createDeck" function is similar to the one in the blackjack game. However, this time you're sorting only one deck of cards. The result ends up in the global variable "deck."

```
// create a shuffled deck
function createDeck() {
    // create an ordered deck
    suits = ["c","d","s","h"];
    temp = new Array();
    for(suit=0;suit<4;suit++) {
        for(num=1;num<14;num++) {
            temp.push(suits[suit]+num);
        }
    }

    // pick random cards until deck has been shuffled
    deck = new Array();
    while (temp.length > 0) {
        r = int(Math.random()*temp.length);
        deck.push(temp[r]);
        temp.splice(r,1);
    }
}
```

Instead of using a movie clip script or button to detect mouse clicks, I'll register this function to handle them.

First, it loops through all the cards in the pyramid and determines whether any are the victim of the click ⑱ . The loop starts at 28 and counts down. This way cards on top are considered before the cards under them.

If a pyramid card has been clicked, then the code tries to determine whether a card is on top of it ⑲ . It does this by calling "cardPresent" with the row and column of the two cards that could possibly be covering the one clicked.

If the local variable "card" is still undefined, then no card has been chosen. One last check is made to see whether the player has clicked the face-up card stack, which is the movie clip "stack1" ⑳ .

If a card has been selected, and the global variable "firstcard" is still undefined, then no other card is currently selected. A reference to this card is placed in "firstcard" ㉑ .

If another card is already selected, then the value of the new card and the old card are totaled. The utility function "cardValue" is used to get the numerical value of the cards ㉒ . If the total is 13, then both cards are removed with another utility function, "removeCard."

If, on the other hand, the "firstcard" has a value of 13 by itself, then it must be a king and is removed by itself ㉓ .

If the "stack0" movie clip has been clicked, then it means that the user has decided to take a card from the face-down deck and flip it over to the face-up deck. The last value in the "deck" array is taken and used to change the frame of the movie clip "stack1" ㉔ . The "stack" array is used to keep track of cards that are flipped between these stacks.

To highlight the card selected, the "outline" movie clip is moved to the same position as the selected card ㉕ .

Finally, the first card in the pyramid is tested ㉖ . If it is missing, then the user must have removed the top card of the pyramid and won the game.

```
_root.onMouseDown = function() {
    var card = undefined;

    // see whether one of the pyramid cards was clicked
    for(var i=27;i>=0;i--) {
        if (_root["card"+i].hitTest(_xmouse,_ymouse)) {
            var card = _root["card"+i];
            break;
        }
    }

    // if a pyramid card, is it uncovered?
    if (card != undefined) {
        if (cardPresent(card.row+1,card.col) or
        ➡cardPresent(card.row+1,card.col+1)) {
            card = undefined;
        }
    }

    // perhaps it was the face-up stack?
    if (card == undefined) {
        if (stack1.hitTest(_xmouse,_ymouse)) {
            card = stack1;
        }
    }

    // got a card, so check it
    if (card != undefined) {

        // first card clicked
        if (firstCard == undefined) {
            firstCard = card;

        // ignore second click on same card
```

```
            } else if (firstCard == card) {

            // if second card clicked and both total 13
            } else if (cardValue(firstCard) + cardValue(card) == 13) {

                // remove both cards
                removeCard(card);
                removeCard(firstCard);
                firstCard = undefined;

            // otherwise, make this the first card
            } else {
                firstCard = card;
            }
        }

        // if only one card selected, but it is a king
        if (cardValue(firstCard) == 13) {
            removeCard(firstcard);
            firstCard = undefined;
        }

        // if face-down stack clicked, deal card
        if (stack0.hitTest(_xmouse,_ymouse)) {
            stack1.value = deck.pop();
            stack1.gotoAndStop(stack1.value);
            stack.push(stack1.value);

            // if no more cards in stack, remove face-down stack
            if (deck.length == 0) {
                stack0.removeMovieClip();
            }
        }

        // place outline over selected card
        if (firstCard != undefined) {
            outline._x = firstCard._x;
            outline._y = firstCard._y;
        } else {
            outline._x = -1000;
        }

        // if top card of pyramid is gone, player won
        if (_root["card0"] == undefined) {
            gotoAndStop("game over");
```

```
        }
    }
```

All that's left is a bunch of utility functions. The first one, "removeCard," takes away a card from either the face-up stack or the pyramid. To remove a card from the face-up stack, it must simply reset the "stack1" movie clip to the frame that represents the previously-shown card. This is where the array "stack" comes in handy. Each card placed on the face-up stack is added to "stack." To get a card back, you just need to *pop* the last one off the "stack" and then examine the last item of "stack."

If the card is from the pyramid, then the reaction is much simpler. The movie clip is removed.

```
function removeCard(thisCard) {
    if (thisCard == stack1) {
        // remove card from stack
        stack1.gotoAndStop(1);
        stack.pop();
        stack1.value = stack[stack.length-1];
        stack1.gotoAndStop(stack1.value);
    } else {
        // remove card from pyramid
        thisCard.removeMovieClip();
    }
}
```

The next utility routine, "cardPresent," loops through the cards to determine whether any card that still exists has a matching "row" and "col" property.

```
function cardPresent(row, col) {
    // loop through pyramid to see whether this card is there
    for(var i=0;i<28;i++) {
        thisCard = _root["card"+i];
        if ((thisCard.row == row) and(thisCard.col == col)) {
            return (true);
        }
    }
    return(false);
}
```

The "cardValue" function takes the "value" property of a card movie clip, strips the first character, and returns the numerical value. For instance, if the "value" of the card is "c9," then a 9 is returned.

```
function cardValue(card) {
    // strip first letter from name of card to get its value
    n = card.value;
    n = parseInt(n.substr(1,2));
```

```
        return(n);
    }
```

The last utility function loops through all the pyramid cards and removes any that are left. It also removes "stack0" and "stack1." This clears the Stage in preparation for another round.

```
function clearGame() {
    // remove pyramid cards
    for(var i=0;i<28;i++) {
        _root["card"+i].removeMovieClip();
    }

    // remove stack
    stack0.removeMovieClip();
    stack1.removeMovieClip();
}
```

Loose Ends

The New button on the screen has a simple script that first calls "clearGame" and then "startGame." This resets the game any time the player wishes.

```
on (press) {
    clearGame();
    startGame();
}
```

Other Possibilities

The game can be made considerably easier if you allow players to turn over the face-up deck and go through the cards as many times as they like. You can do this by recognizing when the "deck" is empty and putting each card from "stack" back on to "deck."

There are many other solitaire games you can build. My collection of game research includes more than 200 variations. Most require that cards be dragged around and moved from stack to stack. This makes the ActionScript far more complex, but not impossible for a skilled programmer.

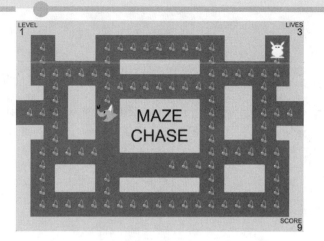

## 16

Arcade Games

- Space Combat
- Space Rocks
- Maze Chase
- Moon Lander
- Platform Scroller

When most people think of computer games, they think of classic computer arcade games, such as *Space Invaders*, *Asteroids*, *Pac-Man*, *Centipede*, and *Lunar Lander*. In this chapter, you will create games in this genre.

The first game you'll build is a generic space combat game in which you shoot at objects coming at your ship. Then, you'll look at a similar game played from a different perspective called Space Rocks. Next, you'll build a maze chase game, and then a game called Moon Lander. We'll end with a slightly more advanced arcade game called a platform scroller.

Space Combat

Example file: Spacecombat.fla

Arcade games are sometimes also called "twitch" games because the only skill needed to do well is a fast reflex. This is very true of the first game, called Space Combat.

Figure 16.1 shows the example movie from the CD-ROM site, Spacecombat.fla. You can see that you are inside a spaceship with some nasty-looking asteroids coming your way.

Figure 16.1
The Space Combat game makes you the pilot of a spaceship trying to make it through an asteroid field.

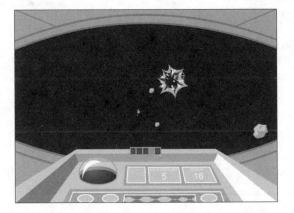

Project Goal

This game allows the player to fire little bullets at the oncoming asteroids. If the bullets hit the asteroids, they explode harmlessly. However, if an asteroid makes it past the bullets, it might hit the player's ship, causing damage.

The game keeps track of the number of asteroids the player hits, as well as the number of asteroids that hit the player's ship. Some asteroids might pass above, below, or to the sides of the ship without causing any damage. The game ends after the player sustains 20 impacts.

Approach

The two active pieces of this game are the asteroids and the bullets. The asteroids originate from a spot near the center of the screen and move toward a spot in an area larger than the screen. If the asteroid winds up outside the screen area, it is assumed that it missed the ship. If it finishes inside the screen area, it hits the ship, causing damage. As the asteroid travels, its scale increases, creating the illusion of 3D space.

The bullets come from both the bottom-left and bottom-right corners of the screen. They travel toward a spot indicated by the position of the mouse at the time of the firing. When they reach that final spot, any asteroid at that location is destroyed.

Destroying an asteroid not only scores points, but prevents that asteroid from hitting the ship. Thus, the player should concentrate her fire on asteroids that look like they are coming toward the ship.

Preparing the Movie

There isn't too much to the library elements in this movie. The "foreground" is the top and the bottom pieces in Figure 16.1 that represent the interior of your ship. All the foreground elements, including the score and damage text near the bottom of the screen, are in the "foreground" movie clip. This way, you can easily move this single movie clip all the way in front of all the asteroids and bullets.

The asteroids are in a three-part movie clip called "rock." The first part is a static frame with an image of the rock as it appears to move closer to the ship. The second part consists of several frames of animation showing the rock exploding when it is hit by a bullet. This sequence is labeled "explode red." The final part is another sequence labeled "explode blue." Check the example movie on the CD-ROM to see how this movie clip has been put together. Figure 16.2 shows this clip.

Figure 16.2

The Flash main windows shows the "rock" movie clip. You can see part of the asteroid exploding.

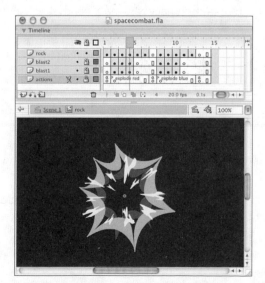

There is also a "point" movie clip that is used to create the bullets, and a "cursor" movie clip that is used to replace the normal cursor with crosshairs.

The movie has three frames: "start," "play," and "game over." All the action takes place on the "play" frame.

Writing the Code

All the code is triggered by an action placed on a small "actions" movie clip just off the Stage and a "button" button just below it. The "actions" movie clip calls one function when the play begins, and four others every frame.

```
onClipEvent (load) {
    // set up game
    _root.initGame();
}

onClipEvent (enterFrame) {
    // move crosshairs
    _root.moveCursor();

    // move all bullets
    _root.moveBullets();

    // 5% chance of a new rock
    if (Math.random() < .05) _root.createRock();

    // move all rocks
    _root.moveRocks();
}
```

The "button" button captures the spacebar and uses that to call a function in the main timeline:

```
on (keyPress "<Space>") {
    // spacebar = fire bullets
    fire();
}
```

You'll find all the functions in the main timeline. The "initGame" function creates arrays to hold information about the asteroids and bullets. It moves the "foreground" and "cursor" movie clips to the front so that any rocks and bullets appear under them, which makes it appear as if they are outside the spaceship.

The "damage" and "hits" variables are reset. The "level" variable does not pertain to the level of play, but instead the current movie clip level used to create new clips. Each time a new movie clip is created to represent a bullet or an asteroid, a fresh new level starts.

The *Mouse.hide()* command is issued to make the normal computer mouse go away. You'll track the cursor with a movie clip instead.

```
function initGame() {
    // create arrays for bullets and rocks
    bullets = new Array();
    rocks = new Array();

    // move foreground crosshairs to front
    _root["foreground"].swapDepths(9999999)
    _root["cursor"].swapDepths(9999998)

    // set up game variables
    level = 0;
    damage = 0;
    hits = 0;


    // hide the mouse, use crosshairs instead
    Mouse.hide();
}
```

The "actions" movie clip calls the "moveCursor" function every frame. The function positions the "cursor" movie clip at the location of the cursor. The player uses this cursor to aim.

```
function moveCursor() {
    // move cursor to the mouse position
    cursor._x = _xmouse;
    cursor._y = _ymouse;
}
```

The "button" button passes info about spacebar presses to the "fire" function. This records the location of the cursor, creates a pair of new "point" movie clips to represent the bullet, and adds items to the "bullets" array representing the starting points, ending points, distance traveled, and movie clip for each bullet.

```
function fire() {
    // get location of the mouse
    x = _xmouse;
    y = _ymouse;

    // add left bullet
    level++;
    attachMovie("point","bullet"+level,level);
    bullets.push({startx: 50, starty: 350, destx: x, desty: y,
    ➥dist: 1.0, clip: "bullet"+level});
```

```
// add right bullet
level++;
attachMovie("point","bullet"+level,level);
bullets.push({startx: 500, starty: 350, destx: x, desty: y,
➥dist: 1.0, clip: "bullet"+level});
}
```

After a bullet has been fired, it is moved each and every frame by the "moveBullets" function. This function uses the "bullets" array to track each existing bullet. The "dist" property is decreased each frame to 40% of its previous value. The bullet is drawn at a location between its starting and ending points, determined by "dist." A value of 1.0 for "dist" would mean that it is drawn at its starting point, whereas a value of 0.0 would mean it is drawn at its ending point.

However, when the bullet reaches a "dist" of 0.01, it is considered close enough to the end of its journey. At that instant, the "checkForHit" function is called to determine whether it hit anything. Regardless, the bullet is removed from the movie and the array.

This game does not pretend to model a real 3D reality or real physics. Instead, it is creating an illusion that works as an arcade game.

```
function moveBullets() {

    // loop through all bullets
    for(i=bullets.length-1;i>=0;i--) {

        // increase distance traveled by 40%
        bullets[i].dist *= .4;

        // if bullet is too far away, remove it
        if (bullets[i].dist < .01) {
            checkForHit(bullets[i].destx,bullets[i].desty);
            _root[bullets[i].clip].removeMovieClip();
            bullets.splice(i,1);

        // reposition bullet closer to destination
        } else {
            bullets[i].x = bullets[i].dist*bullets[i].startx +
            ➥(1.0-bullets[i].dist)*bullets[i].destx;
            bullets[i].y = bullets[i].dist*bullets[i].starty +
            ➥(1.0-bullets[i].dist)*bullets[i].desty;
            _root[bullets[i].clip]._x = bullets[i].x;
            _root[bullets[i].clip]._y = bullets[i].y;
        }


    }

}
```

An asteroid is created in a similar way to a bullet. However, a random starting and ending spot is chosen. The starting point is some point within 25 pixels horizontally and vertically from the center of the screen. The ending point is 550 horizontal pixels and 400 vertical pixels away from the center. This is exactly twice the size of the Stage. The result means that the asteroid always starts near the center, but can finish anywhere from dead center to way off the screen.

```
function createRock() {
    // create a random origin for the rock
    startx = Math.random()*50+250;
    starty = Math.random()*50+175;

    // create a random destination for the rock
    destx = Math.random()*1100-275;
    desty = Math.random()*800-200;

    // add the rock movie clip
    level++;
    attachMovie("rock","rock"+level,level++);
    rocks.push({startx: startx, starty: starty, destx: destx,
    ➥desty: desty, dist: .01, clip: "rock"+level});
}
```

Like the "moveBullets" function, "moveRocks" uses the "dist" property of each asteroid to move it. However, this time the rock is getting closer to the screen, so "dist" starts at 0.01 and increases by 10% each frame. Not only is the location set according to the "dist" property, but the _xscale and _yscale is also set, which makes the asteroid appear to get larger as it approaches the ship.

If the asteroid makes it to a "dist" greater than 1.0, then it has reached the ship. If the asteroid is still on the Stage, then it has hit the ship. The asteroid explodes and "damage" is increased. If "damage" is greater than or equal to 20, then the game is over.

```
function moveRocks() {

    // loop through all rocks
    for(i=rocks.length-1;i>=0;i--) {

        // decrease distance by 10%
        rocks[i].dist *= 1.1;

        // see whether rock is close enough to hit or pass ship
        if (rocks[i].dist > 1.0) {

            // see whether it hit ship
            if (rocks[i].destx > 0 and rocks[i].destx < 550 and
            ➥rocks[i].desty > 0 and rocks[i].desty < 400) {
```

```
            // explode and add to damage
            _root[rocks[i].clip].gotoAndPlay("explode blue");
            damage++;
            foreground.displayDamage = damage;

            // see whether there is too much damage
            if (damage >= 20) {
                removeAllRocks();
                Mouse.show();
                gotoAndStop("game over");
            }

        // harmlessly passed
        } else {
            _root[rocks[i].clip].removeMovieClip();
        }

        // either way, remove from array
        rocks.splice(i,1);

    // reposition rock
    } else {
        rocks[i].x = (1.0-rocks[i].dist)*rocks[i].startx +
        ➥rocks[i].dist*rocks[i].destx;
        rocks[i].y = (1.0-rocks[i].dist)*rocks[i].starty +
        ➥rocks[i].dist*rocks[i].desty;
        _root[rocks[i].clip]._x = rocks[i].x;
        _root[rocks[i].clip]._y = rocks[i].y;

        // resize rock to appear closer
        _root[rocks[i].clip]._xscale = 100*rocks[i].dist;
        _root[rocks[i].clip]._yscale = 100*rocks[i].dist;
    }


    }
}
```

The "checkHit" function is called by each bullet as it reaches its destination. This function loops through each rock and checks to see whether the bullet has hit it. If so, then the rock explodes and is removed from the array. The "hits" variable is increased.

```
function checkForHit(x,y) {

    // loop through all rocks
    for(j=rocks.length-1;j>=0;j--) {
```

```
        // see whether rock will be hit by bullets at this location
        if (_root[rocks[j].clip].hitTest(x,y)) {

            // if hit, explode red and remove from array
            hits++;
            foreground.displayHits = hits;
            _root[rocks[j].clip].gotoAndPlay("explode red");
            rocks.splice(j,1);
        }
    }
}
```

At the end of each explosion animation, as seen earlier in Figure 16.2, a short script calls "killRock." This function removes the very movie clip that calls it. By doing this, you can remove each rock from the array at the exact moment when it is destroyed, but keep the movie clip around for a few more frames as it explodes.

```
function killRock(clip) {
    // when rock finishes exploding, it calls this to remove itself
    clip.removeMovieClip();
}
```

When the game is over, the "removeAllRocks" function is called so that bullets and asteroids don't hang around on the "game over" frame.

```
function removeAllRocks() {

    // loop through all rocks and take them out
    for(i=rocks.length-1;i>=0;i--) {
        _root[rocks[i].clip].removeMovieClip();
    }
}
```

Loose Ends

The "foreground" movie clip contains the text areas linked to the "hits" and "damage" variables. Unfortunately, because they are down one level inside this movie clip, they don't react to changes in "hits" and "damage," which reside on the main timeline. So, these text areas need to be set with commands such as "_root.displayDamage = damage;". I have called these text areas "displayDamage" and "displayHits" to avoid any confusion.

Other Possibilities

You might want to play with this movie and create your own variations. One idea would be to always have the bullets fire to the same point on the screen. Then, allow the player to use the arrow keys to steer the ship. For instance, if the player moves left, you can foster that illusion by moving all the rocks to the right a bit.

You can also improve the existing game by creating levels and improving how "damage" is displayed. For instance, you could have a damage meter of some sort. When the player is getting close to the maximum amount of damage, a red alert light could even flash.

Space Rocks

Example file: Spacerocks.fla

Now let's re-create the previous game from a different perspective. This time, the ship is viewed as a small graphic at the center of the screen. The asteroids are "space rocks" moving in various directions. This game is like many classic arcade games of the '70s and '80s. Figure 16.3 shows a screenshot of the example movie, Spacerocks.fla. This sort of game should be familiar to most readers.

Figure 16.3
The Space Rocks game features a small ship and rocks of various sizes.

Project Goal

This game is more involved than most and features game levels and limited player lives. The player can be hit by a rock three times. If the player destroys all the rocks, he moves on to the next level where rocks are faster and more numerous.

The player can spin the ship left or right, fire a thruster that pushes the ship in the direction it is facing, and fire bullets. After the thruster has been used, the ship continues to move a little bit each frame. As the player spins the ship and uses the thrusters, the velocity of the ship changes using simple momentum. The player can stop the ship by pressing the down arrow.

The bullets are little movie clips that start at the same location as the ship, and move in the same direction the ship was facing when the bullet was fired. Instead of allowing the player to fire a constant stream of bullets, the player can fire after only a short recharge time.

The rocks start off as movie clips at 100% scale with a random direction and speed. When they are first hit by a bullet, they break into two rocks at 50% scale with a new random direction. These rocks, in turn, can break into two smaller rocks at 25% of the scale of the original rock. Beyond that, the rocks just disintegrate. When all the rocks are gone, the level is complete. However, if a rock collides with the ship, the player loses a life.

Preparing the Movie

The library for this movie isn't complex. There are three types of rocks, called "rock1," "rock2," and "rock3." Each time a rock is created, it is chosen from one of the three movie clips at random to give the game some graphic variety.

The "ship" movie clip has a static first frame, but a short animation that starts on the second frame and shows the thruster firing. The first frame of this animation is called "thrust." Instead of using *attachMovie* to put the ship on the Stage, you place the ship in the middle manually, which saves the trouble of creating the instance and setting the location in the code.

There is also a "bullet" movie clip to be used to create the bullets. An "actions" movie clip and a "button" button are used to hold code for the game. A "Play" button is used as the only real button element on the screen.

The movie will have a "start" frame, "play" frame, "ship hit" frame, "level over" frame, and "game over" frame. Each has the appropriate text. All but the "play" frame have a copy of the "Play" button on the screen, but with different code for each instance. Check out the example movie, Spacerocks.fla, to see where all these elements are and what code is attached to each one.

Writing the Code

Like the Space Combat adventure, there will be an "actions" movie clip and a "button" button just off the Stage that have scripts attached to them. The "actions" movie clip contains calls to one function to start a level, and then several functions that move the elements on the screen a little each frame.

```
onClipEvent(load) {
    // set up everything for game
    _root.startLevel();
}

onClipEvent(enterFrame) {
    // move the ship a step
    _root.shipMove();
```

```
    // move all bullets a step
    _root.bulletsMove();

    // move all rocks a step
    _root.rocksMove();

    // see whether there are any collisions
    _root.checkHits();
}
```

The "buttons" button has a set of *on* definitions that map different keys on the keyboard to various user actions:

```
on (keyPress "<Space>") {
    // fire one bullet
    shipFire();
}

on (keyPress "<Right>") {
    // turn 30 degrees to right
    shipTurn(30);
}

on (keyPress "<Left>") {
    // turn 30 degrees to left
    shipTurn(-30);
}

on (keyPress "<Up>") {
    // move forward
    shipThrust();
}

on (keyPress "<Down>") {
    // stop ship
    shipBreak();
}
```

On the "start" frame, you can take the opportunity to set a few variables when the player presses the "Play" button to start the game. The score is reset to 0, the game level to 1, and the player gets 3 lives.

```
on (press) {
    gameLevel = 1;
    lives = 3;
    score = 0;
    gotoAndPlay("play");
}
```

The functions are all inside the main timeline script for the "play" frame. The first one deals with setting up the game at the start of a level, or just after a player loses a life.

The "ship" referred to in the code is the movie clip instance on the Stage called "ship." In addition to built-in properties of the movie clip such as _x and _y, you'll make up some new properties. The "dx" and "dy" properties represent the amount that the ship moves horizontally and vertically.

The "startLevel" function also creates the "bullets" and "rocks" arrays to hold lists of movie clips that represent these elements.

The "level" variable deals with the movie clip levels, not the game level, used in the *attachMovie* command. You'll use "gameLevel" for that.

The next step is to create the large rocks to start the level. Two rocks are created for the first level, three for the second level, and so on.

The "timeOfLastFire" variable is used in the "shipFire" function later to be sure that the player cannot fire too rapidly:

```
function startLevel() {
    // ship stationary
    ship.dx = 0.0;
    ship.dy = 0.0;

    // new arrays
    bullets = new Array();
    rocks = new Array();

    // start using movie clip level 0
    level = 0;

    // add new rocks = number of level + 1
    for(i=0;i<gameLevel+1;i++) {
        newRock(100,0,0);
    }

    // all to fire right away
    timeOfLastFire = 0;
}
```

The next set of functions are reactions to keypresses. They all control the ship in some way. The first one rotates the ship a certain number of degrees. If you look back at the two calls to this handler made by the "button" button, you'll see that it is called with the value of 30 in one case and −30 in the other. Those calls rotate the ship 30° in one direction or another.

```
function shipTurn(amt) {
    // rotate the ship
    ship._rotation += amt;
}
```

The next function activates the thrusters. It uses *Math.cos* and *Math.sin* to translate the rotation of the ship into a horizontal and vertical component. Unfortunately, the *_rotation* property of a movie clip is in degrees, but the two math functions require radians. To convert, you need to multiply the degrees by 2 × pi, and divide by 360. In addition, you need to subtract 90° so that 0° points straight up rather than to the right.

```
function shipThrust() {
    // thrust ship in direction it faces
    ship.dx += Math.cos(2.0*Math.PI*(ship._rotation-90)/360.0);
    ship.dy += Math.sin(2.0*Math.PI*(ship._rotation-90)/360.0);

    // show engines firing
    ship.gotoAndPlay("thrust");
}
```

On the other hand, if the player presses the down-arrow key, you can easily stop the ship at its current location by setting the "dx" and "dy" properties of the movie clip to 0.

```
function shipBreak() {
    // stop ship
    ship.dx = 0;
    ship.dy = 0;
}
```

When the player presses the spacebar, the ship should fire a bullet. However, it first checks to see whether enough milliseconds have passed since the last bullet was fired.

A bullet is created from the movie clip "bullet," and the "dx" and "dy" properties of this movie clip are created and set just as they are for the ship. In addition, a pointer to the movie clip is added to the "bullets" array so that the bullet can be referenced later.

```
function shipFire() {

    // make sure enough time has passed since last fire
    if (timeOfLastFire+200 < getTimer()) {


        // remember time of this fire
        timeOfLastFire = getTimer();

        // create bullet
        level++;
        attachMovie("bullet","bullet"+level,level);
```

```
        // set bullet location and direction
        clip = _root["bullet"+level];
        clip._x = ship._x;
        clip._y = ship._y;
        clip.dx = 10.0*Math.cos(2.0*Math.PI*(ship._rotation-90)/360.0);
        clip.dy = 10.0*Math.sin(2.0*Math.PI*(ship._rotation-90)/360.0);

        // add to bullets array
        bullets.push(clip);
    }
}
```

The ship is moved one step per frame by increasing its _x and _y properties by its "dx" and "dy" properties. If the ship moves too far to the right, beyond the 550-pixel limit of the Stage, then 550 pixels are subtracted to make it wrap around to the other side. The same goes for the left, top, and bottom of the screen.

```
function shipMove() {
    // move ship horizontally and wrap
    ship._x += ship.dx;
    if (ship._x > 550) ship._x -= 550;
    if (ship._x < 0) ship._x += 550;

    // move ship vertically and wrap
    ship._y += ship.dy;
    if (ship._y > 400) ship._y -= 400;
    if (ship._y < 0) ship._y += 400;
}
```

Bullets move like the ship does. However, you need to loop through the "bullets" array to move all the bullets. Also, when the bullets reach the edge of the screen, they are removed rather than allowed to wrap around.

```
function bulletsMove() {
    // loop through all bullets
    for(i=bullets.length-1;i>=0;i--) {

        // move ship horizontally and vertically
        bullets[i]._x += bullets[i].dx;
        bullets[i]._y += bullets[i].dy;

        // see whether the bullet is off the edge of the screen
        if ((bullets[i]._x > 550) or (bullets[i]._x < 0) or
        ➥(bullets[i]._y > 400)or (bullets[i]._y < 0)) {

            // remove clip and array item
            bullets[i].removeMovieClip();
```

```
        bullets.splice(i,1);
    }


  }
}
```

Rocks are added to the game through calls to the "newRock" function. Like the "fire" function, this adds a movie clip to the game. However, the function chooses from one of three movie clips named "rock1," "rock2," and "rock3."

The rock is created at a location passed into the function as a parameter, and is also assigned a scale by another parameter. The direction of the rock is decided by random numbers, with the possibility for faster and faster rocks as the game level increases.

The rocks also spin a random amount, either positive or negative.

Pointers to all rocks are added to the "rocks" array so they can be referenced later:

```
function newRock(size,x,y) {
    // create rock clip
    level++;
    rockNum = int(Math.random()*3+1);
    attachMovie("rock"+rockNum,"rock"+level,level);

    // set rock location and size
    clip = _root["rock"+level];
    clip._x = x;
    clip._y = y;
    clip._xscale = size;
    clip._yscale = size;

    // set rock speed and direction
    clip.dx = Math.Random()*gameLevel+.5;
    if (Math.random() < .5) clip.dx *= -1;

    clip.dy = Math.Random()*gameLevel+.5;
    if (Math.random() < .5) clip.dy *= -1;

    // set rock spin
    clip.spin = Math.random()*6-3;

    // add rock to rocks array
    rocks.push(clip);
}
```

To make the rocks move, you use code similar to the code that determines how the ship and bullets move. The rocks wrap around on the screen just as the ship does. In addition, remember to rotate the rocks each step according to their "spin" property that you created.

```
function rocksMove() {

    // loop through all rocks
    for(i=rocks.length-1;i>=0;i--) {
        clip = rocks[i].clip;

        // move rock horizontally and wrap
        rocks[i]._x += rocks[i].dx;
        if (rocks[i]._x > 550) rocks[i]._x -= 550;
        if (rocks[i]._x < 0) rocks[i]._x += 550;

        // move rock vertically and wrap
        rocks[i]._y += rocks[i].dy;
        if (rocks[i]._y > 400) rocks[i]._y -= 400;
        if (rocks[i]._y < 0) rocks[i]._y += 400;

        // spin rock
        rocks[i]._rotation += rocks[i].spin;
    }
}
```

To simplify things, all the collision detection code has been placed into one function. This function loops through the rocks and the bullets, and uses *hitTest* to determine whether there are any collisions.

When a bullet hits a rock, the location and scale of the rock are recorded and then the rock is removed. If the scale of the rock is above 25%, then two new rocks are created in the same spot. Each of these rocks is half the size of the previous one. Each rock obtains a new random direction and spin.

The "checkHits" function also determines whether any rock is colliding with the ship. If a rock collides with the ship, the player loses a life and goes to the "ship hit" frame. If there are no more lives left, the player goes to the "game over" frame.

One final check that "checkHits" does is to determine whether the "rocks" array has dwindled down to 0. If so, the player has destroyed all the rocks and the movie advances to the "level over" frame.

```
function checkHits() {

    // loop through all rocks
    for(i=rocks.length-1;i>=0;i--) {

        // loop through all bullets
        for(j=bullets.length-1;j>=0;j--) {
```

```
        // see whether bullet hit rock
        if (rocks[i].hitTest(bullets[j]._x,bullets[j]._y,true)) {

            // remove bullet
            bullets[j].removeMovieClip();
            bullets.splice(j,1);

            // get size and location of new rocks
            newsize = rocks[i]._xscale / 2;
            x = rocks[i]._x;
            y = rocks[i]._y;

            // remove rock
            rocks[i].removeMovieClip();
            rocks.splice(i,1);

            // create two new rocks in its place
            if (newsize >= 25)  {
                newRock(newsize,x,y);
                newRock(newsize,x,y);
            }

            // increase score
            score++;

            // no need to keep checking bullets against this rock
            break;
        }
    }

    // see whether rock hits ship
    if (rocks[i].hitTest(ship._x,ship._y,true)) {

        // see whether there are not more lives
        if (lives < 1) {
            removeAll();
            gotoAndPlay("game over");

        // life left, deduct life
        } else {
            removeAll();
            lives--;
            gotoAndPlay("ship hit");
        }
    }
}
```

```
    // see whether there are no more rocks
    if (rocks.length == 0) {
        removeAll();
        gotoAndPlay("level over");
        gameLevel++;
    }
}
```

The "removeAll" function is used just before the "checkHits" function, which causes the movie to jump to a new frame. It removes all the rocks and bullets from the screen so they don't overlap the text on those frames.

```
function removeAll() {
    // remove all bullets
    for(i=0;i<bullets.length;i++) {
        bullets[i].removeMovieClip();
    }

    // remove all rocks
    for(i=0;i<rocks.length;i++) {
        rocks[i].removeMovieClip();
    }
}
```

Loose Ends

As always, be sure the linkage properties for each movie clip in the library are set so that Flash knows to include the clip in the final file. All the rocks and the bullets need to be linked like this because they are not on the Stage anywhere before the game starts.

I've also created three text areas to represent the "gameLevel," "lives," and "score" variables. I've placed them in separate corners with additional text as labels above each.

Other Possibilities

There are many other features that games such as Space Rocks sometimes have. Occasionally, little "UFOs" float around, awarding you bonus points if you hit them. Often, the ship is equipped with a shield that can be used to protect it from collisions a limited number of times. A "hyperspace" feature zaps the ship to a random spot on the screen and a "smart bomb" feature destroys any rocks within a certain distance from the ship.

This is definitely an excellent game with which a budding ActionScript expert can stretch her wings by adding more and more features—the more challenging the feature is to implement, the better.

Maze Chase

◉ ▷ **Example file: Mazechase.fla**

This next game is also a common genre of classic arcade games that I call maze chase games. *Pac-Man* and its sequels are probably the best-known examples of this genre, but there are many others.

In the example game, shown in Figure 16.4, the fox runs around a preset maze trying to eat the berries. An evil bunny is also running around the maze. The fox must avoid the bunny while getting to all the berries.

Figure 16.4

The fox tries to eat the berries while the bunny tries to get the fox.

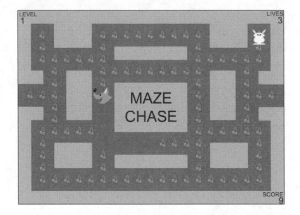

Project Goal

The example game tries to re-create some of the classic features of the maze-chase genre. The berries on the screen disappear as the fox passes over them. The fox can jump from one side of the screen to the other by passing through the tunnel on either side. If the bunny catches the fox, the player loses a life.

Preparing the Movie

If you look at the Mazechase.fla example movie, you will see only a few library items. The main ones are the background, the fox, the bunny, and the berry.

Creating the background is simple, but must be done carefully. Imagine the screen as a grid of squares 25 pixels wide by 25 pixels high. The berries appear at intersections of this grid—at all intersections, that is, except for ones that are covered by the background image.

Check out Figure 16.5. This is the "background" movie clip with Flash's grid turned on and set to 25×25. You can control the grid by choosing View, Grid, Edit Grid.

Figure 16.5
With the Flash grid turned on, you can clearly see the intersections where berries will appear.

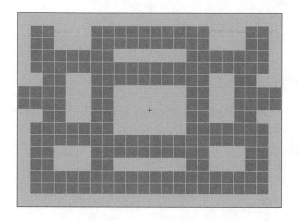

The background is built with the rectangle drawing tool. By using the grid, you can create it quickly. Not only are the areas of the grid filled in to create the background, but a line border is present around the filled-in areas. This helps ensure that the background walls overlap the edges of the gridlines a little bit. When the program adds the berries at grid intersections, it doesn't add berries to intersections that are along the edge of a wall.

The "fox" movie clip has a normal static frame as the first frame, but a short biting animation for the rest. When the fox is supposed to eat a berry, you send this movie clip to the second frame. This shows the fox biting down, and then returns the fox to the first, static frame.

The "berry" movie clips have two frames. The first has a berry and the second is blank. You move each clip to the second frame as the berries get eaten. This way, the movie clips remain on the Stage at all times to guide the fox and bunny, but they are visible only before the berry is eaten.

The "bunny" movie clip is a constant animation. The bunny always moves, so there is no need for a static frame.

All these movie clips, except "background," aren't present until the movie runs and the code creates them with *attachMovie*.

This movie has pretty much the same set of five frames that the "Space Rocks" movie did: "start," "play," "lose life," "level over," and "game over."

Writing the Code

The first frame contains a copy of the Play button that starts a new game. Its script not only goes to the "play" frame, but also initializes a few variables:

```
on(press) {
    lives = 3;
    score = 0;
```

```
    gameLevel = 1;
    gotoAndPlay("play");
}
```

There is an "actions" movie clip on the "play" frame that has a script attached to it. This script's job is to initialize everything at the start of the game, after a life is lost, and when a new level should begin. The script also calls the "move" and "moveBunny" functions to keep the game going.

```
onClipEvent(load) {
    // set everything at the beginning
    _root.startLevel();
}

onClipEvent(enterFrame) {
    // move the fox
    _root.move();

    // move the bunny
    _root.moveBunny();
}
```

All the functions for this game can be found in the main timeline script for the "play" frame. This starts with the "startLevel" function.

The main job of the "startLevel" function is to create the berries. The function does this by looping through 15 vertical positions and 21 horizontal positions, seeking out points on the grid that do not have the "background" movie clip covering them.

The "berry" movie clip is placed at all the proper locations, and a pointer to each movie clip is placed in the "berries" array.

This function also creates the "fox" and "bunny" movie clip instance. It creates and sets several new properties for each clip, including the "dest" or destination for each clip.

TIP

Notice that the "dest" property of the "fox" and "bunny" is set to a small object, such as {x:275, y:275}. This makes it easy to refer to these values. For instance, you could refer to the horizontal destination as "fox.dest.x."

```
function startLevel() {
    level = 0;

    // create berries
    berries = new Array();
```

```
// loop through grid of locations
for(y=1;y<16;y++) {
    for(x=1;x<22;x++) {

        // see whether the background covers location
        if (!(background.hitTest(x*25,y*25,true))) {

            // create a berry and place it there
            attachMovie("berry","berry"+level,level);
            clip = _root["berry"+level];
            clip._x = x*25;
            clip._y = y*25;

            // add to array of berries
            berries.push(clip);
            level++;
        }
    }
}


// create the fox and set his location
attachMovie("fox","fox",level++);
fox._x = 275;
fox._y = 275;

// also add movement and destination properties
fox.move = {x:0, y:0};
fox.dest = {x:275, y:275};
fox.nextmove = 0;

// create the bunny and set his location
attachMovie("bunny","bunny",level++);
bunny._x = 275;
bunny._y = 125;

// also add movement, destination, and remember previous location
bunny.move = {x:1, y:0};
bunny.dest = {x:300, y:125};
bunny.nextmove = 0;
bunny.last = {x:275, y:125};

}
```

The "move" function is called every frame and moves the location of the fox according
to the "move" object. It has a special provision in the function to recognize whether the
fox is about to move off the left or right side of the screen, and wraps the fox around if

it does. This makes it possible for the fox to travel through the tunnel on either side of the screen.

The fox or bunny's destination is always the next berry. Even if there is no longer a visible berry there, the movie clip is always there. When the fox reaches this berry, marked by the "dest" object of the fox, then the "eatBerry" function is called so that the berry can be removed if it is still visible. The "nextMove" function is called to determine the next destination.

Note that the fox moves 5 pixels at a time. This works out well because all the berries are 25 pixels apart. Therefore, it takes exactly five steps to reach the next berry. The speed at which these steps are taken is determined by the amount added to the "nextMove" property. In this case, 50 milliseconds are added, which means there will be at least 50 milliseconds between moves.

```
function move() {
    // see whether it is time for another move
    if (getTimer() > fox.nextmove) {

        // don't allow another move for 50ms
        fox.nextmove = getTimer() + 50;

        // move fox
        fox._x += fox.move.x*5;
        fox._y += fox.move.y*5;

        // see whether the fox went though the tunnel
        if (fox._x > 550) fox._x = 0;
        if (fox._x < 0) fox._x = 550;

        // see whether the fox reached his destination
        if ((fox._x == fox.dest.x) and (fox._y == fox.dest.y)) {
            eatBerry();
            nextMove();
        }
    }
}
```

To eat a berry, you loop through all the berries and look for one that matches the location of the fox. That berry is sent to the second frame so that it disappears. In addition, the score is increased.

As the array of berries is searched for a matching berry, you'll also note any berries that have not been eaten. As long as one berry is found that has not yet been eaten, the level is not yet over.

```
function eatBerry() {
    // assume all berries are gone
    allGone = true;

    // loop through all berries
    for(i=0;i<berries.length;i++) {

        // see whether this berry is where fox is
        if ((berries[i]._currentFrame == 1) and (berries[i]._x == fox._x) and
        ➥(berries[i]._y == fox._y)) {

            // remove berry
            berries[i].gotoAndStop("nothing");

            // open fox mouth
            fox.gotoAndPlay("eat");

            // add to score
            score++;

        // if a berry is found that has not been eaten, then level is not over
        } else if (berries[i]._currentFrame == 1) {
            allGone = false;
        }
    }

    // if all berries eaten, then end level
    if (allGone) {
        gotoAndPlay("level over");
        gameLevel++
    }
}
```

When the fox reaches a berry, the code needs to determine the next destination, if any. The *Key* object is used to test all four arrow keys. If any are pressed, then the "move" object of the fox is set. However, this does not mean that the move is valid.

For a move to be valid, there needs to be another berry in that direction exactly 25 pixels away. If that is not the case, then the "move" object is set back to zeros.

```
function nextMove() {
    // assume no movement
    fox.move.x = 0;
    fox.move.y = 0;

    // check arrow keys and set potential movement
    // also flip fox left or right if needed
```

```
    if (Key.isDown(Key.LEFT)) {
        fox.move.x = -1;
        fox._xscale = Math.abs(fox._xscale);
    } else if (Key.isDown(Key.RIGHT)) {
        fox.move.x = 1;
        fox._xscale = -Math.abs(fox._xscale);
    } else if (Key.isDown(Key.UP)) {
        fox.move.y = -1;
    } else if (Key.isDown(Key.DOWN)) {
        fox.move.y = 1;
    }

    // predict new destination
    newx = fox._x + fox.move.x*25;
    newy = fox._y + fox.move.y*25;
    okToMove = false;

    // loop through berries to see whether any match destination
    for(i=0;i<berries.length;i++) {

        // found a match, set new destination
        if ((berries[i]._x == newx) and (berries[i]._y == newy)) {
            fox.dest.x = newx;
            fox.dest.y = newy;
            okToMove = true;
        }
    }

    // special settings for going through tunnel
    if (newx == 550) {
        okToMove = true;
        fox.dest.x = 25;
    } if (newx == 0) {
        okToMove = true;
        fox.dest.x = 525;
    }

    // if destination doesn't match berry, then don't move
    if (!okToMove) {
        fox.move.x = 0;
        fox.move.y = 0;
    }
}
```

The bunny moves in an unpredictable manner. When it reaches a berry spot, the following code loops through all the berries to find the ones that are adjacent to the current bunny location. Then, one of these possibilities is picked at random to be the next destination for the bunny. The one qualification needed is that the new destination not be the same as the previous location. In other words, the bunny cannot suddenly move back the way it came. This forces the bunny down long corridors without any back-and-forth stuttering. However, if the bunny reaches a corner and has only the option of going back the way it came, it is allowed.

The last thing the "moveBunny" function does is to check to see whether the bunny is close to the fox. If it is, then the bunny caught the fox and the player loses a life.

```
function moveBunny() {

    // see whether it is time for next bunny move
    if (getTimer() > bunny.nextmove) {

        // don't allow another bunny move for a while
        bunny.nextmove = getTimer() + 60 - gameLevel*10;

        // move bunny
        bunny._x += bunny.move.x*5;
        bunny._y += bunny.move.y*5;

        // see whether bunny reached destination
        if (bunny._x == bunny.dest.x and bunny._y == bunny.dest.y) {

            // create an array of possible next locations
            possibilities = new Array;
            for(i=0;i<berries.length;i++) {

                // calculate distance from present location to berry
                xdiff = Math.abs(berries[i]._x - bunny._x);
                ydiff = Math.abs(berries[i]._y - bunny._y);

                // see whether this is an adjacent berry
                if ((xdiff == 25 and ydiff == 0) or
                ➥(xdiff == 0 and ydiff == 25)) {

                    // then this is a possibility
                    possibilities.push(berries[i]);
                }
            }

            // pick a random possibility
            do {
                r = int(Math.random()*possibilities.length);
```

```
            // get new destination and movement
            bunny.dest.x = possibilities[r]._x;
            bunny.dest.y = possibilities[r]._y;
            bunny.move.x = (possibilities[r]._x - bunny._x)/25;
            bunny.move.y = (possibilities[r]._y - bunny._y)/25;

        // use this possibility only if it is not
        //going back to the last spot
        // or if this is the only choice
        } while ((bunny.dest.x == lastx and bunny.dest.y == lasty) and
        ➥(possibilities.length > 1));

        // remember the previous location
        lastx = bunny._x;
        lasty = bunny._y;
    }

}

// see whether bunny is close to fox
if (Math.abs(bunny._x - fox._x)<=10 and Math.abs(bunny._y - fox._y)<=10) {
    if (lives < 1) {
        gotoAndStop("game over");
    } else {
        lives--;
        gotoAndStop("lost life");
    }
}
}
```

Loose Ends

Remember that the fox, bunny, and berry movie clips need to be linked with the appropriate name. You'll need *stop()* commands for each frame, as well as some frames of the
smaller movie clips.

Other Possibilities

There are plenty of features that you can add to this game. You could have more than
one bunny, or special berries that allow the fox to chase the bunnies for a short time.
You could also have a center "cage" area from which the bunnies come out one at a
time, and bonus points that pop up throughout the maze.

Other ideas include having the bunny be a little smarter and actually chase the fox, having the bunny compete with the fox by eating the berries, and awarding bonus points at
the end of each level based on how fast the level was completed.

Moon Lander

⟩⟨Example file: Moonlander.fla

This next game is a Flash version of a classic arcade game. *Lunar Lander* was possibly the second computer game *ever* created. The first incarnation of this game ran on University mainframe computers and was purely text based. Each second that went by, the computer would spit out a line of text telling you where your lander was, and how fast it was going. You could make adjustments as you came down.

Since then, the game has been created in various graphical formats, most of them featuring the side view used here. Figure 16.6 shows a game in progress.

Figure 16.6
The moon lander descends, trying to make it to one of the landing pads.

Project Goal

The goal is to create a standard lander-style game. The ship starts at the top of the screen. The player controls a powerful vertical thruster under the ship, as well as weaker thrusters on each side of the ship.

As time goes on, gravity pulls the ship down. The player uses the thrusters for a limited amount of time as fuel is consumed every time they are fired.

The player's goal is to land the ship safely on one of the landing pads. Missing the pads, or touching any part of the surface other than the pads, results in the lander exploding.

This game has multiple levels. In the example movie, there are three levels, all featuring a different surface.

Preparing the Movie

In examining the movie clips needed for this movie, first look at the "ship" movie clip. Figure 16.7 shows the full Flash window with the ship movie clip selected. You can see that there are several labeled frames. The first frame is "normal," followed by "up," "left," "right," and "explode."

Figure 16.7
The "ship" movie clip includes the frames "normal," "up," "left," "right," and "explode."

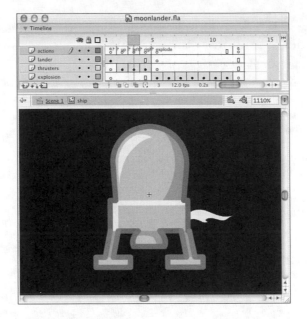

The first frame represents the ship with no thrusters firing. The second has the main thruster firing, moving the ship up. The third and fourth frames show each of the side thrusters. The bottom portion of Figure 16.7 shows the "left" frame. Note that the word "left" refers to the fact that the ship should be moving to the left. The flame of the thruster is, in fact, shooting to the right.

The "explode" frame is the beginning of a short animation showing the ship being blown to bits. This animation is used if the player misses the landing pad.

In addition to a "background" movie clip that does not interact with the code at all, three other movie clips represent the hillsides of the three levels of the game. These clips are named "Ground - level 1" to "Ground - level 3."

The "pad" movie clip is just a simple yellow rectangle that is used to detect when the lander's two feet make a safe touchdown.

The main timeline for this movie is actually quite complex. Table 16.1 shows each frame and what it contains.

Table 16.1   Frames in the Main Timeline

Frame	Contains
start	Contains an introduction to the movie and a "Play" button to start the game.
start level	Warns the player that the first level is about to begin.

Frame	Contains
level1	The player plays through the first level on this frame. If he doesn't crash, he continues to the next frame.
level1 done	When the player lands safely on level 1, he gets a congratulatory message and a "Play" button that lets him play the second level.
level2	The player plays through the second level on this frame. If he doesn't crash, he continues to the next frame.
level2 done	When the player lands safely on level 2, he gets a congratulatory message and a "Play" button that lets him play the third level.
level3	The player plays through the third level on this frame. If he doesn't crash, he continues to the next frame.
game over	The player is congratulated for making all three landings successfully. A "Play" button lets the player try again.
lost ship	If the player crashes on any level, he is sent to this frame and the game is over. A "Play" button lets him try again.

You'll also have two very simple movie clips, "fuel gauge" and "fuel meter," which both consist of a rectangle outline and a solid rectangle. The "meter" is placed inside the "gauge." You'll use code to shrink the "meter" so that it fills less of the "gauge" rectangle as fuel runs out.

Writing the Code

You'll have "actions" movie clips on the three frames "level1," "level2," and "level3." These movie clips contain the calls to the functions needed for the game. Only one function is called when the level begins, and one function is called continuously as the level progresses.

```
onClipEvent(load) {
    _root.startLevel();
}

onClipEvent(enterFrame) {
    _root.moveShip();
}
```

Both of these functions can be found in the main timeline on the first frame. This script actually starts with a "startGame" function that is called when the player clicks the "Play" button on the first frame. It sets the variable "gameLevel," which appears as a text area in the upper-right corner of the game. It then calls "startLevel" to begin level 1.

```
function startGame() {
    gameLevel = 1;
    startLevel();
}
```

The "startLevel" function performs a variety of tasks. First, it moves the movie to the correct frame according to the "gameLevel" variable. Then it sets the ship to the top center of the screen. The speed of the ship, which is stored in "dx" and "dy" properties of the "ship" movie clip instance, are set to 0. The variable "gravity" is used to accelerate the ship downward toward the group.

The "hitPoints" and "footPoints" arrays contain various points relative to the center of the ship. You'll check all the "hitPoints" to determine whether the ship has collided with the group. The two "footPoints" are used to determine whether both feet have been placed on a landing pad.

The "pads" array is used to store the names of the three landing pad movie clips on the screen. One of the levels has only two landing pads, but Flash ActionScript is forgiving about such things.

```
function startLevel() {
    gotoAndStop("level"+gameLevel);

    // start ship still
    ship._x = 275;
    ship._y = 25;

    // start ship still
    ship.dx = 0;
    ship.dy = 0;

    // init gravity
    gravity = .1;

    // init fuel
    fuel = 100;
    showFuel();

    // set collision points
    hitPoints = new Array();
    hitPoints.push({x:-9,y:13});
    hitPoints.push({x:9,y:13});
    hitPoints.push({x:0,y:-10});
    hitPoints.push({x:-8,y:-7});
    hitPoints.push({x:8,y:-7});

    // set landing points
    footPoints = new Array();
    footPoints.push({x:-9,y:13});
    footPoints.push({x:9,y:13});
```

```
    // make array from pad clips
    pads = new Array();
    for(i=0;i<3;i++) {
        pads.push(_root["pad"+i]);
    }
}
```

The function "moveShip" is called every frame by the "actions" movie clip. This function is used to call a variety of smaller functions that control the ship. It is usually better to break up a long piece of code into such smaller functions.

```
function moveShip() {
    shipThrusters();
    shipMovement();
    checkForLand();
    checkForCrash();
}
```

The "shipThrusters" function checks to see whether any fuel is left. If not, the "ship" movie clip is sent to the "normal" frame. Otherwise, if the player is holding down either the up-, left-, or right-arrow keys, then one of the thrusters is on. The "ship" is sent to the proper frame, and "dx" or "dy" are changed to reflect the effect of the thruster. Fuel is also deducted.

```
function shipThrusters() {
    // check thrusters and adjust speed
    if (fuel < 0) {
        ship.gotoAndStop("normal");
    } else if (Key.isDown(Key.UP)) {
        ship.dy -= .4;
        ship.gotoAndStop("up");
        fuel -= 2;
        showFuel();
    } else if (Key.isDown(Key.LEFT)) {
        ship.dx -= .2;
        ship.gotoAndStop("left");
        fuel -= 1;
        showFuel();
    } else if (Key.isDown(Key.RIGHT)) {
        ship.dx += .2;
        ship.gotoAndStop("right");
        fuel -= 1;
        showFuel();
    } else {
```

```
            // no thruster at all
            ship.gotoAndStop("normal");
        }
    }
```

The next function, "shipMovement" adds the pull of gravity. The position of the ship is then modified by the speed of the ship.

```
function shipMovement() {
    // gravity pulls ship down
    ship.dy += gravity;

    // move ship
    ship._x += ship.dx;
    ship._y += ship.dy;
}
```

The "checkForLand" function loops through the "footPoints" and checks whether each foot is inside a "pad" movie clip. If one or the other is not, then the "landed" variable is set to *false*. This is also the case if the speed of the ship is greater than 3, which is too fast for the ship to be traveling for a landing.

If the "landed" variable remains *true* through these tests, then the ship has touched down. All that is needed is to go to the next frame in the main timeline and increment the "gameLevel" variable.

```
function checkForLand() {
    // check to see whether both feet are on a pad
    // loop through both feet
    landed = true;
    for(i=0;i<footPoints.length;i++) {

        // loop through all pads
        footDown = false;
        for(j=0;j<pads.length;j++) {

            // see whether foot is on a pad
            if (pads[j].hitTest(ship._x+footPoints[i].x,
            ➥ship._y+footPoints[i].y,true)) {
                footDown = true;
                break;
            }
        }

        // if a foot in not down, then the ship has not landed
        if (!footDown) {
            landed = false;
```

```
            break;
        }
    }


    // see whether the ship is going too fast
    if (ship.dy > 3.0) landed = false;

    if (landed) {
        // made it
        gotoAndPlay(_currentFrame+1);
        gameLevel++;
    }
}
```

On the other hand, you also need to see whether the lander crashed. The "hitPoints" array contains a list of points around the ship, including the two feet, the middle of each side, the top, and the bottom center. Because there is no way to detect whether one full object intersects another, you test just these points and use them to determine whether there is a crash. If any of these points is inside the "activeground" movie clip instance, then the ship has crashed. The "activeground" is the "Ground - levelX" movie clip's instance name on each level.

```
function checkForCrash() {
    // not landed, so check for crash
    if (!landed) {

        // loop through all hit points
        for(i=0;i<hitPoints.length;i++) {

            // check hit point against the ground
            if (activeground.hitTest(ship._x+hitPoints[i].x,
            ➥ship._y+hitPoints[i].y,true)) {
                ship.gotoAndPlay("explode");

                // lost life, or game over
                gotoAndPlay("lost ship");
                break;
            }
        }
    }
}
```

One utility function used by this movie is the "showFuel" function, which takes the "meter" movie clip inside the "gauge" movie clip and sets its _xscale property to the "fuel" variable. Because the "fuel" variable starts at 100 and goes down to 0, it easily translates to be used in the *_xscale* property. If the fuel range were different, then you would need to massage the numbers a bit to make it fit into a 0 to 100 range before applying it to the *_xscale*.

```
function showFuel() {
    gauge.meter._xscale = fuel;
}
```

TIP

Note that to get the "meter" movie clip to shrink from the right to the left, the center of the clip had to be placed so that the rectangle extended from the center to the right. If the center had been left at the center of the graphic, then changing the *_xscale* would have shrunk the graphic into the center, rather than from right to left.

Loose Ends

Each "play" button in this movie has a small, one-line script attached to it. Check each one out to see which frame it takes the movie to or what function it calls.

Note that the same "thrust animation" was used for each of the three types of thrust in the "ship" movie clip. For the left and right thrusters, the clip was rotated 90° and –90°. The animation for the two side thrusters was shrunk because these are not supposed to be as powerful as the main thruster.

Other Possibilities

As this game stands, there is no scoring. You could award points for each successful landing, possibly with more points for tougher-to-reach landing pads. You could also give a speed bonus and an unused-fuel bonus. Expanding the game with more levels is as easy as drawing the hillsides. When you run out of ideas, you could always alter the code so that higher levels use the same graphics, but with less fuel available at the start or with higher gravity.

Platform Scroller

Example movie: Platform.fla

After the initial wave of basic arcade games ended in the early '80s, the next big thing in computer games was the platform scrolling game. This started with the famous Mario Bros series by Nintendo. By the end of the '80s, platform scrollers were the most common type of console game. They are still produced today.

The idea of a platform scroller is that the character moves back and forth through a 2D side-view world. The character can jump off the ground and walk on higher "platforms." Typically, the goal was to grab objects to acquire points and to avoid other creatures that move around the world.

Figure 16.8 shows the fox in a simple platform scroller. The fox can move back and forth and jump. The acorns can be taken to get points, but the bunnies must be avoided.

Figure 16.8
This Flash platform scroller contains the most basic elements of the genre.

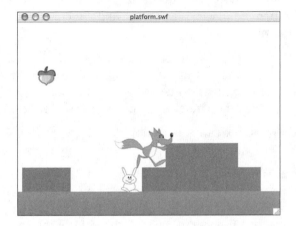

Project Goal

Platform scrollers can grow to become quite complex. Enemies, like the bunnies in this game, can be attacked by jumping on them. Some objects can give the player special abilities, like a speed increase, or power over otherwise undefeatable creatures.

We'll keep it as simple as possible here and concentrate on the basics. The fox will move left and right and be able to jump. Platforms, which are made up of blocks, will prevent the player from moving horizontally. The player must jump on them and walk over them instead.

Walking in this game means that the entire world scrolls to the left or right. The fox remains fixed in the middle of the screen. The illusion of movement comes from the fact that everything else is moving, not the fox.

Acorns represent 100 points in the game. The fox must come close to them to take them. Bunnies, on the other hand, are the enemy and the fox must avoid them by jumping over them.

The design of the world—where the platforms, acorns, and bunnies go—is easy to adjust. So after completing this example movie, you can create you own world for the fox to run around in.

Approach

The game world is represented by an array of small objects. These objects have a "type" property, matching the movie clip, that should be used. The movie clip also has an "x" and "y" property to determine its position in the world. An example of an object would be "{type:"box",x:100,y:0}".

The player starts off at position 0, 0. As the player moves to the right, the "x" position of the player increases. So if a box starts off at an "x" of 100, and the player is at an "x" of 0, then the box should be 100 pixels to the right of the player. If the player moves over 10, then the player is at 10 "x" and the box should now be drawn 90 pixels to the right of the player.

The player's character, the fox, never moves horizontally on the screen. It will always remain at the center of the screen. All the objects are drawn according to how far away from the fox they are supposed to be. When I talk about the fox moving, I mean that the fox is moving within the virtual world of the game, not on the screen.

Determining when the fox can and cannot move is the most important part of this game. If the fox runs into a box, it should stop moving in that direction.

The way that this is handled is that the position of the fox is compared to that of all the other boxes in the world. If a box is closer to the player than any other box in that direction, then its location is considered the farthest point in that direction that the fox can move. For instance, if a box is 200 units to the right of the fox, then the fox cannot move any further than 200 units to the right. If, in checking through all the objects, another box is discovered to be only 100 pixels from the fox, then 100 becomes the new maximum distance that the fox can move in that direction.

The same happens for vertical movement. When the fox jumps, it is given a vertical velocity that moves the fox upward. With each frame, this vertical velocity is tempered by gravity, so the fox slows down and eventually falls. All the objects in the world are examined to determine the highest and lowest point the fox can reach. When the fox "lands" at the lowest point, the vertical movement stops. This is usually the ground. But the lowest point may also be a platform box that is under the fox.

Preparing the Movie

There are only four movie clips in the movie. The "fox" movie clip contains several frames. The first is an image of the fox standing still. Following that is an animation of the fox running in one direction. Following that is a short animation of the fox jumping from a standstill. The instance of this movie clip placed on the Stage is named "fox" and is scaled to 25%.

The "box" movie clip is a simple 50×50 brown box. Only one frame is needed.

The "acorn" movie clip starts off with a static image of an acorn. There is a *stop()* on this frame. However, the rest of this movie clip is a short animation showing a number "100" growing out of nothing. This is the animation that will play when the player gets the acorn and scores 100 points.

The "bunny" movie clip is a two-frame clip that animates the bunny shuffling its feet. This animation works no matter what direction the bunny moves.

The "box," "acorn," and "bunny" movie clips must all be set to export with the movie in the movie clip Linkage properties.

The main timeline has three frames. The first contains the instructions and a "Play" button. The last frame contains a "Game Over" message. The middle frame is the "Play" frame and contains the fox and a background image of the ground. No other elements are present because they will all be created by ActionScript when the game runs.

Writing the Code

With a few minor exceptions, all the code in this game is in the main timeline on the "Play" frame. It starts with the "startGame" function. This sets some constants, such as the speed of the fox and the bunny, initializes the fox so it starts in the correct spot, and calls two other functions, "createWorld" and "createObjects," which are responsible for creating all the elements in the world.

```
startGame();
stop();

function startGame() {
    // establish constants
    floor = 350;
    foxSpeed = 10;
    bunnySpeed = 2;
    jumpPower = 60;

    // initialize fox
    foxPos = {x:0,y:0};
    fallSpeed = 0;
    falling = false;
    fox.swapDepths(999);

    // moveFox should be called every frame
    _root.onEnterFrame = moveFox;

    // create the objects in the world
    createWorld();
    createObjects();
}
```

The "createWorld" function creates the array "objects" and populates it with the positions of all of the boxes, acorns, and bunnies in the world. It also sets the "worldEnd" global variable, which is the right limit of the world. The left limit is assumed to be 0.

```
function createWorld() {
    objects = new Array();
    objects.push({type:"box", x:250, y:0});
    objects.push({type:"box", x:300, y:0});
```

```
objects.push({type:"box", x:500, y:0});
objects.push({type:"box", x:550, y:0});
objects.push({type:"box", x:600, y:0});
objects.push({type:"box", x:650, y:0});
objects.push({type:"box", x:700, y:0});
objects.push({type:"box", x:550, y:50});
objects.push({type:"box", x:600, y:50});
objects.push({type:"box", x:650, y:50});

objects.push({type:"box", x:850, y:0});
objects.push({type:"box", x:900, y:0});
objects.push({type:"box", x:1050, y:100});
objects.push({type:"box", x:1100, y:100});
objects.push({type:"box", x:1150, y:100});

objects.push({type:"acorn", x:150, y:0});
objects.push({type:"acorn", x:275, y:200});
objects.push({type:"acorn", x:1100, y:250});
objects.push({type:"bunny", x:400, y:0});
objects.push({type:"bunny", x:1200, y:0});

worldEnd = 1400;
}
```

TIP

If you plan to make a larger world for the fox to run around in, or perhaps multiple levels, you will probably want to change the "createWorld" function so that it reads data from an external text file instead of producing each element with a line of code. This external text file can specify the type and position of each element in an separate item, the same way that the quiz and trivia games in Chapter 12, "Quizzes and Word Puzzles," read their questions in from an external file.

After the "objects" array is ready, the "createObjects" function loops through it to make all the movie clips.

```
function createObjects() {
    for(var i=0;i<objects.length;i++) {
        _root.attachMovie(objects[i].type,"object "+i,i);
    }
}
```

The "moveFox" function is the central engine driving the entire game. It is a series of checks that watch for certain events to take place in the game.

It starts by calling "determineBounds" with the position of the fox ①. This function returns a maximum left, right, up, and down amount that the fox can move without hitting a box.

Next, "moveFox" checks to see whether there is room below the fox for it to fall, yet the fox is not falling, as signified by the "falling" variable ②. If this is the case, then the fox begins to fall.

If "falling" is true, then "checkFall" is called to handle the vertical movement ③.

Next, both the left and right arrow keys are checked to see whether they are pressed ④. If one is, then either "foxBounds.left" or "foxBounds.right" is checked to make sure there is room to move. The world bounds, 0 and "worldEnd," are also checked to make sure that the fox doesn't move too far left or right. The "moving" variable is set to true only if an arrow key is pressed. This variable is used to determine which part of the "fox" movie clip should be shown.

When the spacebar is hit, the fox should jump ⑤. A jump is the opposite of a fall, so the "fallSpeed" is set to a positive number. When the fox is falling, it is a negative number. If the fox is standing still at the moment that the spacebar is pressed, then the jump animation of the fox movie clip should be shown. If the fox is moving, however, then the fox movie clip remains in mid-stride.

The next piece of code takes care of the fox animation ⑥. If the fox is moving, and it is not falling (or jumping), then the fox movie clip moves to the next frame. This keeps the legs moving. If the fox is neither moving nor falling, then the fox movie clip goes to the standing-fox image on frame 1.

Although the horizontal position of the fox stays at the center of the screen, its vertical position does change. The "foxPos.y" property is its actual position, with the ground being position 0. So to get the _y property of the movie clip, you need to subtract "foxPos.y" from "floor" ⑦.

The "moveFox" function ends by calling three other functions. The "moveBunnies" function take cares of the bunnies. The "drawObjects" function draws all the boxes, bunnies, and acorns according to the new world position of the fox. The "getAcorns" function checks to see whether the fox has captured any acorns.

```
      function moveFox() {
①→        // get movement bounds for fox
          foxBounds = determineBounds(foxPos);

②→        // if no ground under fox, then start falling
          if ((foxBounds.bottom > 0) and (!falling)) falling = true;

③→        // fall
          if (falling) checkFall();
```

④➤
```
        // left arrow, move left if no boundary hit
        if (Key.isDown(Key.LEFT)) {
            if (foxSpeed < foxBounds.left) {
                foxPos.x -= foxSpeed;
            }
            if (foxPos.x < 0) foxPos.x = 0;
            fox._xscale = 25;
            moving = true;

        // right arrow, move right if no boundary hit
        } else if (Key.isDown(Key.RIGHT)) {
            if (foxSpeed < foxBounds.right) {
                foxPos.x += foxSpeed;
            }
            if (foxPos.x > worldEnd) foxPos.x = worldEnd;
            fox._xscale = -25;
            moving = true;

        // must not be moving
        } else {
            moving = false;
        }
```

⑤➤
```
        // if on the ground and spacebar hit, then jump
        if (Key.isDown(Key.SPACE) and (!falling)) {
            fallSpeed = jumpPower; // jump = fall up
            falling = true;
            if (!moving) { // use jump animation only if not moving
                fox.gotoAndPlay("jump");
            }
        }
```

⑥➤
```
        // if moving and not falling, animate
        if (moving and !falling) {
            fox.nextFrame();

        // if not moving or falling, then show stand frame
        } else if (!moving and !falling) {
            fox.gotoAndStop(1);
        }
```

⑦➤
```
        // position fox movie clip vertically
        fox._y = floor - foxPos.y;

        // bunnies get their turn to move
        moveBunnies();
```

```
    // draw all objects according to new positions
    drawObjects();

    // see whether any acorns are hit
    getAcorns();
}
```

The "getBounds" function looks complex, but it is actually quite simple. It starts by assuming that there is nothing within 100 units of the fox, whether to the left, right, or above the fox. It assumes that there is nothing below the floor, which is the current height of the fox above the floor, "pos.y".

It then loops through all the objects. It cares about only "box" objects, so it rules out any others. Then it calculates the distance from the fox to the object and records it in "dx" and "dy."

If the box shares the same vertical space as the fox (in other words, it is about the same distance off the ground), then the function sees whether the box is to the left or right. It then sees whether the box is closer to the left or right of the fox than any other box so far. It does the same thing for the vertical distance.

After all the boxes have been examined, the "bounds" object contains the horizontal and vertical boundaries of the fox in its current position. For instance, if "bounds.left" is 20, that means that the closest box to the left is 20 units away.

The "determineBounds" function is generic enough so that it can be used by both the fox and the bunnies. The function is called with "pos," which can be either "foxPos" or an item in the "objects" array, such as a bunny.

```
function determineBounds(pos) {
    // assume distance bounds, ground is bottom
    var bounds = {left:1000,right:1000,top:1000,bottom:pos.y};

    // loop through all objects
    for(var i=0;i<objects.length;i++) {

        // only look at boxes
        if (objects[i].type == "box") {
            var dx = objects[i].x - pos.x;
            var dy = objects[i].y - pos.y;

            // if box is in same vertical space
            if ((dy >= 0) and (dy <= 50)) {

                // if box to the to left, see whether it is closest so far
                if ((dx+50 <= 0) and (Math.abs(dx+50) < bounds.left)) {
                    bounds.left = Math.abs(dx+50);
```

```
                    // if box is to the right, see whether it is closest so far
                } else if ((dx >= 0) and (dx < bounds.right)) {
                        bounds.right = dx-50;
                }
            }

            // box is in same horizontal space
            if ((dx >= -50) and (dx <= 50)) {

                    // if box is below, see whether it is closest so far
                    if ((dy+50 <= 0) and (Math.abs(dy+50) <= bounds.bottom)) {
                        bounds.bottom = Math.abs(dy+50);

                    // if box is above, see whether it is closest so far
                    } else if ((dy-50 >= 0) and (dy-50 < bounds.top)) {
                        bounds.top = dy-50;
                    }
                }
            }
        }

    return(bounds);
}
```

If the fox is in the air, whether it is jumping up or falling down, it is considered falling. The "checkFall" function takes care of the vertical movement. When the player jumps, "fallSpeed" is set to the value of "jumpPower" which is 60. So the fox starts by wanting to move 60 vertical pixels. For each frame that the jump/fall occurs, the "fallSpeed" is dampened by 10, which is the effect of gravity pulling down. Eventually "fallSpeed" will reach 0, at the top of the jump, and then "fallSpeed" will become negative and the fox will accelerate to the ground.

If the velocity of the fall is not enough so that the fox reaches the ground just yet, then the fall is allowed to continue. However, if the ground is hit or passed, then the fall ends and the fox's vertical position is fixed to the ground once again.

The "checkFall" function also looks at "foxBounds.top" to see whether there is a box above the fox. If the fox hits its head, then the upward thrust of the jump is immediately removed by setting "fallSpeed" to 0. The jump/fall continues, but it is only a fall now.

```
function checkFall() {
    // accelerate due to gravity
    fallSpeed -= 10;

    // room to fall at full speed
    if (fallSpeed > -foxBounds.bottom) {
        foxPos.y += fallSpeed;
```

```
    // complete distance to ground and stop falling
    } else {
        foxPos.y -= foxBounds.bottom;
        fallSpeed = 0;
        falling = false;
        fox.gotoAndStop(1); // stand
    }

    // see whether fox hits head on box above
    if (foxPos.y > foxBounds.top) {
        foxPos.y = foxBounds.top;
        fallSpeed = 0;
    }
}
```

The "drawObjects" function is what makes the fox appear to move. All the objects are repositioned so that they appear in the correct positions relative to the fox.

```
function drawObjects() {
    // loop through all objects
    for(var i=0;i<objects.length;i++) {

        // set horizontal position according to where fox is
        _root["object "+i]._x = x = 275 + objects[i].x  - foxPos.x;

        // set vertical position according to floor
        _root["object "+i]._y = floor - objects[i].y;
    }
}
```

The "getAcorns" function loops though the objects looking for acorns. Any that it finds are tested to see whether they are close enough to the fox for the fox to grab them.

After an acorn is taken, its "type" is set to "used." It will now be ignored in all the functions of the game because none look for "used" objects.

```
function getAcorns() {
    // loop through all objects looking for points
    for(var i=objects.length-1;i>=0;i--) {
        if (objects[i].type == "acorn") {

            // if within 30 pixels, player got it
            if (distance(_root["object "+i],fox) < 30) {
                _root["object "+i].play();
                objects[i].type = "used";
                score += 100;
            }
```

```
            }
        }
    }
```

The "getAcorns" function calls on "distance" to determine how close the fox and acorn are. This utility function will be used by the "moveBunnies" function later on as well.

```
// utility function to determine actual distance between movie clips
function distance(mc1,mc2) {
    d = Math.sqrt(Math.pow(mc1._x-mc2._x,2)+Math.pow(mc1._y-mc2._y,2));
    return d;
}
```

The "moveBunnies" function controls all the bunnies. However, there is no point controlling bunnies that are not visible on the screen at the moment, so only bunnies closer than 275 horizontal pixels are moved.

Those that are moved first call the "determineBounds" function to see how far to the left and right they can move. If they are able to, they move toward the player's position. If the fox is foolish enough to get too close to the bunny, the game ends.

```
function moveBunnies() {
    // loop through all objects looking for bunnies
    for(var i=objects.length-1;i>=0;i--) {
        if (objects[i].type == "bunny") {

            // move only bunnies on screen
            if (Math.abs(objects[i].x-foxPos.x) < 275) {

                // move toward fox
                if (foxPos.x < objects[i].x) {
                    var dx = -bunnySpeed;
                } else if (foxPos.x > objects[i].x) {
                    var dx = bunnySpeed;
                }

                // determine bounds for this bunny
                bunnyBounds = determineBounds(objects[i]);

                // move only as far as bounds
                if ((dx < 0) and (bunnyBounds.left > Math.abs(dx))) {
                    objects[i].x += dx;
                } else if ((dx > 0) and (bunnyBounds.right > Math.abs(dx))) {
                    objects[i].x += dx;
                }

                // see whether bunny is close enough to fox
                if (distance(_root["object "+i],fox) < 30) {
```

```
                       root.onEnterFrame = undefined;
                    trace("got ya");
               }
            }
         }
      }
   }
```

Loose Ends

The fox movie clip contains three sections: "stand," "run," and "jump." A *stop()* command is on the first frame. On the last frame of the "run" animation is a "gotoAndPlay("run")" command. This keeps the animation looping.

The acorn movie clip also needs a *stop()* on the first frame.

Another loose end is the registration points of the movie clips. Each has its registration point set so that the point is at the bottom of the movie clip, horizontally centered. Figure 16.9 shows the "box" movie clip with a registration point.

Figure 16.9

All the movie clips are set up so their registration points are at the bottom center of the graphic.

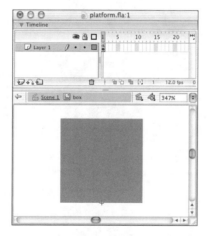

Other Possibilities

This game is pretty much the simplest platform scroller possible. It is so simple it doesn't even have an end. There are several ways to add an ending.

First, you could make reaching the rightmost point the end of the game or level. This world is relatively small, but if it were several times larger, just getting to the other side would be an accomplishment.

Another way to end the game would be to make the player get all the acorns. Again, you'd have to make the world much larger.

Most platform scrollers offer some way to get rid of the bad guys. Typically, this is done by jumping on them. Right now, if you jump on a bunny, the game ends just as if you had run horizontally into a bunny. But if you can detect that the player's vertical movement is "falling" at the time of impact, then you can have the fox win the battle, remove the bunny, and score more points.

Platform scrollers can get quite complex. It would be easy to continue for hundreds of pages and add more and more features to the game. But you now have the basics. Combined with the skills you have learned in other chapters, you should be able to expand the game as you wish.

Advanced Techniques

- Performance and Optimization
- Loader Screens
- Copy Protection
- High Score Boards
- Testing Flash Player Versions

17

Although the previous chapters demonstrated hundreds of ActionScript techniques, some useful techniques that apply to games haven't been covered yet. Instead of including these concepts in a particular game, this chapter features these techniques by themselves.

In this chapter, you'll look at such diverse topics as optimization, loading animations, high score boards, and copy protection. At the end, you'll get an idea of what other advanced techniques exist.

Performance and Optimization

When using Flash to create games, the issue of speed comes up constantly. Versions of Flash previous to Flash 5 did not have a robust enough scripting language to allow you to create many games. Even so, Flash 5 was very slow. Too slow, in fact, for many fast-paced arcade games. However, Flash MX has improved the speed of Flash movies considerably. Flash MX can be used to make games that Flash 5 was too slow for. Even games created with Flash 5 show a lot of improvement when played back with the Flash 6 player. Whether you are using Flash 5 or MX, optimization techniques can help any game run faster.

Using Alternatives

The basic concept behind optimization is that there is more than one way to accomplish any task in Flash. For the most part, this is true. For instance, if you want to move a graphic from one side of the Stage to the other, you can do it with animation tweening or with ActionScript.

There are two ways to think about the alternatives available when you are creating something in Flash. The first type of alternative involves finding another way to accomplish exactly the same task. For instance, moving a graphic with tweening or with ActionScript could produce exactly the same result.

The other alternative involves making a change in the program so that it produces a similar, yet somehow different, result. For instance, if the graphic moves across the screen too slowly, you can shrink the graphic to make it smaller, but theoretically faster.

The key to optimization is realizing when there are alternatives and weighing the advantages against the disadvantages. To see the advantages of an alternative, you can use a technique called benchmarking.

Benchmarking

If you want to compare two alternatives for speed, you need a way to measure that speed. Sure, you could just go by whether something *looks* faster, but that's not very accurate. Benchmarks allow you to test to determine which alternative is faster and just how much faster it is.

A typical benchmark compares two or more alternatives to performing the same or a similar task. In each case, the time is marked just before the task begins, and then again when the task ends. The result is the time it took for the task to complete. With a little math, this can be converted into a measurement such as frames per second (fps).

Take the example of a graphic character running across the Stage. Figure 17.1 shows a full-sized fox in the middle of the screen in the process of running from the right to the left.

Figure 17.1

This test has a large fox racing from right to left in 30 frames.

In Figure 17.1, you can see that the speed of the movie is 35fps. The movie is actually set to run at 120fps. However, because the Flash player has to do so much work to show the animation, the movie will actually run at 35fps.

You must use a little bit of code to get the "35fps" to show up in the upper-right corner. This simple line was placed on the first frame of the movie to keep track of the time when the animation started:

```
startTime = getTimer();
```

On the last frame of the animation, frame 30, a few more lines of code use the starting time and the current time to calculate how many milliseconds it took for the animation to complete. It then places this in the text area.

```
totalTime = getTimer() - startTime;
totalFrames = 30;
fps = totalFrames/(totalTime/1000);
readout = int(fps) + " fps";
```

You can see all this in the example movie Benchmark1.fla on the CD-ROM in the folder for this chapter. When I run this movie by pressing [Cmd]+Return on my Macintosh PowerBook running OS 10.1.3, I get results ranging from 33 to 35fps.

Example file: Benchmark1.fla

> **TIP**
>
> It's important to remember to set your frame rate up to 120fps, the maximum that Flash MX will go in cases like this. If you set it to, say, 12fps, the Flash MX default, then the animation will never rise above 12fps. So, even though one technique might be much faster than the other, as long as they both run at 12fps, you won't see any difference.

So Figure 17.1 was made by Testing the movie inside Flash MX. What about if you run the final .swf file in the Flash 6 standalone player, completely outside of Flash? You get even better results with an average of about 42fps. So the Flash player is faster than the Flash application preview window. Flash in the browser (Internet Explorer 5.1 for Mac OS X) was slower, at about 22fps.

Of course, these numbers only make sense relative to each other. When these tests were run on other computers, some Macs and some Windows, the results were different. Some were slower; some were faster. You can't even be sure that the speed will be the same on another computer of the same make and model. One computer could have different system extensions on it, be involved in more network activity, or have more disk fragmentation. Benchmark tests are only valid when they are performed on the same computer under the same conditions.

Choosing the Best Alternative

Looking further at the previous example, suppose that the resulting 22–42fps is not good enough for you. For instance, the purpose of the animation could be for the fox to zip quickly from one side of the screen to the other. At 22fps, or even 42fps, this doesn't quite have the effect you wanted.

One alternative might be to shrink the number of frames in the animation from 30 to 15. This should double the speed of the sequence, but lessen the smoothness of the animation. Also, because the fox movie clip controls the speed of the fox's stride, the fox will appear to take half the number of steps to move the same distance.

If that is not an option, then perhaps size is. What if the fox was half the size? One theory could be that because the same amount of vectors are in the fox, no matter what the scale, Flash should take just as long to draw it. Another theory is that because the fox is half the scale, fewer pixels need to be drawn every step, therefore increasing the speed of the fox.

These theories can be tested with the benchmarking script. Using the same movie, but scaling both keyframes of the fox to 50%, you get the same animation but with a smaller fox. The benchmark script tells you whether the frame rate changed. This movie can be found on the CD-ROM as Benchmark2.fla. You can see the result in Figure 17.2.

Example file: Benchmark2.fla

Figure 17.2
The half-sized fox is much faster than the full-sized one.

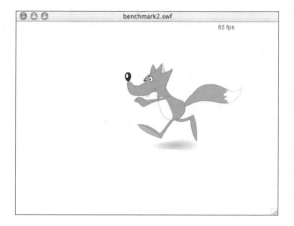

The smaller fox is much faster than the full-sized one. In the Flash player on my Powerbook, I measured 60–70fps, about twice the speed of the previous test. This confirms the theory that smaller graphics draw faster.

Now the only question is whether this half-sized fox fulfills your design needs. If it is better to have a fast half-sized fox than a larger, slower fox, then you have your answer.

Benchmarking ActionScript

You can also use benchmark tests to determine whether ActionScript alternatives can make a speed difference. The technique is the same: Measure the time it takes for a task to complete and compare that time against its alternatives.

For instance, suppose you notice that in your code, you use comparisons like this:

```
if (myVariable == true) {
```

You realize that you could have simply stated it this way:

```
if (myVariable) {
```

The first is sometimes easier to read, but you wonder whether the second offers any speed advantage. After all, you could be using hundreds or thousands of such comparisons inside loops and such.

Chances are that either of these comparisons takes less than a millisecond to perform. So, comparing one against the other will show too small of a time difference, if any, to measure in milliseconds. As a result, you need to compare thousands of them instead.

The following piece of code is built to compare true/false comparison types. It begins by creating a large array filled with 5,000 true and false values. The creation of this array will not be timed. However, after the array is set, the timing begins. The timed code is a loop that looks at each item in the array and counts the number of items that are *true*. It determines which are true by comparing them using the == comparison operator. When the code is done, it spits out the total time it took to do the 10,000 comparisons.

```
function benchMark1() {
    // create a new array
    testArray = new Array;

    // fill the array with alternating true and false
    temp = false;
    for(i=0;i<10000;i++) {
        testArray.push(temp);
        if (temp == false) {
            temp = true;
        } else if (temp == true) {
            temp = false;
        }
    }

    // get the start time
    startTime = getTimer();

    // count how many trues there are
    count = 0;
    for(i=0;i<testArray.length;i++) {
        if (testArray[i] == true) {
            count++;
        }
    }

    // get the end time
    totalTime = getTimer() - startTime;

    // show results
    trace("Benchmark Test: using ==")
    trace("Total Time: " + totalTime + "ms");
}
```

By itself, the result of this program means nothing. However, you will also create a "benchmark2" function that replaces the line if (testArray[i] == true) { with if (testArray[i]) {. This is the only difference between the two functions. Therefore, if there is a speed difference between the functions, it must be due to the one line that is different.

The results show that the second option is faster. On my computer, it took 978 milliseconds to complete the timed code in "benchmark1" and only 958 milliseconds to complete the code in "benchmark2." This shows that using the == comparison on a true or false value is slower than just using the value itself. You can try this code in the example movie Benchmark3.fla on the CD-ROM.

⊙⊳◌Example movie: Benchmark3.fla

This sort of benchmark test is the type of thing that professional programmers do all the time, regardless of what programming language they are using. If you program in ActionScript a lot, it is useful to develop a constant curiosity about which methods are faster than others. The resulting knowledge from tests like this will allow you to optimize your Flash games.

Loader Screens

Although you should always try to keep the file size of your Flash movies as small as possible, it is inevitable that you will have movies that take longer than a few seconds for modem users to download. As a matter of fact, it might take several minutes for some users to download a game that is several hundred kilobytes in size.

It has become customary for Flash and Shockwave developers to create "loader screens" for these large movies. The loader screen is usually the first frame or scene of a movie and is thus streamed to the user's browser first. It then presents a message such as "Loading Game…" to users so they know what is going on.

You can provide even more information to the user while the movie is loading. By using ActionScript, you can show the user just how much of the movie has been downloaded so far, or how much there is to go.

Building a Loader

⊙⊳◌Example file: Loader1.fla

Figure 17.3 shows the first frame of the example movie Loader1.fla on the CD-ROM. This frame appears to the user after only a few kilobytes of the movie have been downloaded. It then keeps the user informed of the status of the download, complete with a moving progress bar in the middle of the screen.

The code to do this is actually quite simple. By using the ActionScript functions *getBytesTotal()*, you can determine how many kilobytes any movie clip contains. If you use _root with *getBytesTotal()*, you can find out how many kilobytes are in the entire movie. Similarly, you can use *getBytesLoaded()* to determine how much of the movie has been loaded so far.

Figure 17.3
Both a progress bar and a text area keep the user informed as the movie loads.

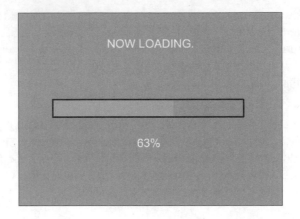

In Loader1.fla, there is a movie clip instance of a simple rectangle called "Progress Bar Fill" on the Stage. It was created so that the center of the movie clip is at the upper-left corner of the rectangle. This is exactly how the fuel gauge in the "Moon Lander" game in Chapter 16, "Arcade Games," was created. Because the center of the movie clip is at the left side of the rectangle, you can set *_xscale* to any number from 0 to 100 and the width of the movie clip will change to fill an area to the right of its center.

You attach a short script to this movie clip instance that will read the *getBytesLoaded()* of the main timeline and set the rectangle accordingly. In addition, it passes on some text to the "loadingMessage" text area in the main timeline. When the entire movie has been loaded, it forces the main timeline to move to the "complete" frame. You can see this frame in Figure 17.4. It announces that the loading is complete, and then waits for the player to click a button to continue. This is a good practice because the user might have taken her eyes off the screen during a long download, and you wouldn't want her to miss the beginning of any animation you might have.

Figure 17.4
The "complete" frame waits for the player before continuing to the content in the movie.

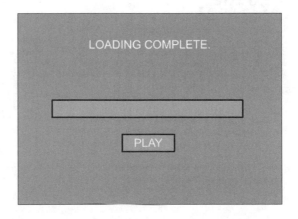

```
onClipEvent(load) {
    // get complete file size
    totalFileSize = _root.getBytesTotal();

    // hide progress bar
    this._xscale = 0;
}

onClipEvent(enterFrame) {

    // see how much has been loaded so far
    bytesLoaded = _root.getBytesLoaded();

    // convert to a value from 0 to 1
    amountLoaded = bytesLoaded/totalFileSize;

    // convert to a value from 0 to 100
    percentLoaded = int(100*amountLoaded);

    // set the scale of the progress bar
    this._xscale = percentLoaded;

    // set the text area in the main timeline
    _root.loadingMessage = percentLoaded + "%";

    // see whether that is everything
    if (amountLoaded >= 1.0) {
        _root.gotoAndStop("complete");
    }
}
```

Check out Loader1.fla on the CD-ROM to see how it all fits together. The loader is actually scene 1, whereas the rest of the content is in scene 2. A *play()* command is used to continue the movie from the "complete" frame when the user hits the "Play" button.

Note that you won't see much if you try to run the ".swf" file from the CD-ROM or if you try to preview it in Flash. The movie loads quickly from your local hard drive—too quickly for you to see any loading. You'll have to upload the file to your Web site and then try it out in your browser to see the movie in action.

TIP

Flash MX has a great way to preview how a movie will play over a slow connection. Rather than choose Control, Test Movie, choose Control, Debug Movie. This brings up the Debug window with the movie in it. Before pressing the Play button in the Debug window, choose View, Show Streaming. Now the movie loads artificially slowly, rather than being completely available instantly.

A More Advanced Loader

Example file: Loader2.fla

In the earlier Figure 17.3, you can see that the text area reads "63%." Instead of this type of measurement, you can also provide the user with the amount of bytes loaded and the total amount of bytes. You can do this by changing the "loadingmessage" assignment line in the code to this:

```
_root.loadingMessage = int(bytesLoaded/1000) + "kb/" +
➥int(totalFileSize/1000) + "kb";
```

Then, instead of "63%," you would see "90kb/143kb," which I like much better.

You can also tell the user how fast the download is proceeding by doing a little math. You can set variables to remember the time when the code starts tracking the load and the amount loaded at that first measurement. Then, you can determine how fast the load is occurring by taking how many bytes have been loaded so far divided by how much time it took. Using this number, you can predict how long it will take for the load to complete, as well.

The following code can be found in the Loader2.fla movie on the CD-ROM. This is similar to the previous loader code, but includes all the extra text readouts, such as speed and time left.

```
onClipEvent(load) {
    // get starting information
    totalFileSize = _root.getBytesTotal();
    startTime = getTimer();
    startBytes = _root.getBytesLoaded();

    // hide progress bar
    this._xscale = 0;
}

onClipEvent(enterFrame) {

    // see how much has been loaded so far
    bytesLoaded = _root.getBytesLoaded();

    // convert to a value from 0 to 1
    amountLoaded = bytesLoaded/totalFileSize;

    // convert to a value from 0 to 100
    percentLoaded = int(100*amountLoaded);

    // set the scale of the progress bar
    this._xscale = percentLoaded;
```

```
// get the speed
timeSoFar = getTimer() - startTime;
speed = bytesLoaded/timeSoFar;

// get the time left
bytesLeft = totalFileSize - bytesLoaded;
timeLeft = (bytesLeft/1000)*(speed/1000);

// convert to a number with one decimal place
speed = int(10*speed)/10;

// set the text areas
_root.bytesMessage = int(bytesLoaded/1000) + "kb/" +
➥int(totalFileSize/1000) + "kb";
_root.speedMessage = speed + "k/sec";
_root.timeMessage = int(timeLeft) + " seconds remaining";

// see whether that is everything
if (amountLoaded >= 1.0) {
    _root.gotoAndStop("complete");
}
}
```

Other Types of Loaders

Although the previous two loaders are standard, there are many other possibilities. On the simpler side, you could just have a static frame that reads "Loading, Please Wait…" and goes to the next frame when loading is done.

You can make it a bit more complex by placing a movie clip or graphic with a looping animation on that frame.

Still more complex would be a whole scene where each frame represents a different stage of the loading procedure. For instance, each frame could show a character building something. The structure becomes more and more complete as the rest of the movie loads.

To do these types of loaders, it might not be necessary to use *getBytesTotal()* and *getBytesLoaded()* at all. You could instead use *ifFrameLoaded()* to determine whether all the graphics for a specific frame in the movie have been loaded. This could be useful if you want the player to start playing some aspect of your game, but don't want him to continue beyond a certain point until the proper frames are ready.

My favorite suggestion for a loader, however, is to make the time spent for the player more useful. Place the instructions for the game on the loading frame. That gives players something to do rather than just sit and watch the progress bar grow.

Copy Protection

So you've read this book and you decide to make your own game. You spend months on it. When you're finished, you have the ultimate Flash game. It's great and you're convinced that it will become super popular and make you famous.

You post the game on the Web and sit and wait. After a few weeks, you find that hundreds of people have played the game. You also find that another Web site, the home page of some kid from Nebraska, has a similar game on it.

Wait a minute! That's your game! It's on this kid's home page and he claims that he made it! What's worse is that he is getting millions of hits on his homepage. He's taking credit for the game you made.

There are several ways to prevent this. First, let's look at how this happens.

How and Why Games Are Stolen

I've been making Web-based games in Shockwave and Flash for more than six years. I've found my creations used without permission on various Web sites, from personal home pages to legitimate business pages.

The first thing to realize is that in 90% of these cases, the thief meant no harm. To many people, the Internet has become a huge, free playground. They get tons of content free and never have to think about who owns that content, the cost to create it, copyright issues, or intellectual property issues. It doesn't matter because most of the content is free.

Then, when someone starts to create his own Web site, whether it's just a home page or the start of an online business, he doesn't think about these issues. Instead, he figures that if he can view something free, he can use it on his Web site free. If he sees a cool layout on a Web page, he views the source and copies the HTML. If he sees a neat animated GIF on another site, he right-clicks and saves it to his computer to use on his site. Then, when he sees your game, he takes that too, and places it on his site.

Then there are the people who know it's wrong, but don't understand the harm it does. They feel it is no worse than driving 56mph in a 55mph zone. To them, the Internet is one large multi-billion dollar corporation, and they couldn't possibly be doing any harm by putting one little game up on their sites.

I've heard it all over the years: people who claim I gave them permission to place the games on their sites even though I never spoke to them before; people who claim that because they bought one of my books, anything on my Web site could be placed on theirs; people who claim that "content must be free" and that they are allowed to steal the games.

The methods that people use to get to your Flash content are surprisingly simple. One way is for the thief to view the HTML source of the page where your movie resides, get the name and path of the movie from the "src" parameter in the OBJECT or EMBED tag, and then point her browser directly at the .swf file. After the .swf is the top-level content in the browser, she can choose File, Save As, to save the .swf to her local hard drive.

Even if you come up with some clever way to hide the HTML source for the user, he can always look into his browser's cache files and pick out the .swf of the appropriate time stamp and size.

Preventing Your Game from Running Elsewhere
Example file: Copyprotection1.fla

So how do you prevent someone from stealing your game? You can't. But you can prevent them from running your game on another Web site, thus making the stolen game useless.

The key is the _url property. This property returns a string with the full path of your .swf file. For instance, if the movie is at `http://www.garyrosenzweig.com/flash5book/ copyprotection1.swf`, that string is what _url returns.

After you have this string, you can break it down to discover the root domain name at its heart. For instance, the above address has the root domain `garyrosenzweig.com`. Here is some code from the example movie Copyprotection1.fla on the CD-ROM:

```
// show the full path
urlText = "This game is being loaded from: " + _url;

// get everything between the "://" and the next "/"
c1 = _url.indexOf("://")+3;
c2 = _url.indexOf("/", c1);
domain = _url.substring(c1,c2);

// throw away any prefixes before the second to last "."
c3 = domain.lastIndexOf(".")-1;
c4 = domain.lastIndexOf(".",c3)+1;
domain = domain.substring(c4,domain.length);

// show the root domain
domainText = "The root domain is: " + domain;
```

The usefulness of having the root domain is that you can check it against what the domain of your site should return. The root domain is used because the path to your game might look different to different people. For instance, `http://garyrosenzweig.com` and `http://www.garyrosenzweig.com` take you to the same place but return different _url results. Also, some sites have more than just a "www." before their domains, such as `www.games.garyrosenzweig.com`.

If the root domain is not what the program expects, then the game has been stolen. Instead of the movie then continuing on to play the game, it can go to another frame entirely, preferably with a nasty message.

 WARNING

You might not want to make the message too nasty. There have been plenty of times when I have given a client a licensed copy of one of my games to be placed on her site and forgotten to adjust the code to allow the game to run on her site. In that case, she'll see your "nasty" message and might have a different opinion of you if it is over the top.

Example file: Copyprotection2.fla

Here is some code that will check the _url against the domain where the game is supposed to be. You can find this code in Copyprotection2.fla.

```
// get everything between the "://" and the next "/"
c1 = _url.indexOf("://")+3;
c2 = _url.indexOf("/", c1);
domain = _url.substring(c1,c2);

// throw away any prefixes before the second to last "."
c3 = domain.lastIndexOf(".")-1;
c4 = domain.lastIndexOf(".",c3)+1;
domain = domain.substring(c4,domain.length);

// go to the proper page
if (domain != "garyrosenzweig.com") {
    gotoAndPlay("stolen");
} else {
    gotoAndPlay("start");
}
```

Instead of having the movie go to a different frame, you could have it call *getURL()* with the address of an HTML page that will have a message on it. This way, you don't have to place that message frame into each movie you make.

How to Get Around Copy Protection

This plan for copy protection is not flawless. There is one simple way for a thief to get around it. He could leave the game on your server, and create his own HTML page where the "src" parameter of the OBJECT and EMBED tags points to the .swf file on your site. He serves the HTML, and you serve the .swf. The _url property correctly reports that the game is on your site, so the copy protection never kicks in.

This is a far better way to have your game stolen, however. For one thing, the .swf is still completely in your control. You could always change its name or move it to another location. If you find that someone has stolen your game this way, you could really play with him by changing the location of the game on your site, updating your own HTML to point to the proper place, and then replacing the old .swf with one that contains a nasty message to the visitors of the thief's site.

More Methods of Protecting Yourself

If you find that someone has stolen your game, either because you left it unprotected or because the thief found a way around the protection, there are still steps you can take.

The first thing you should do is email the person. After all, most people don't mean any harm and will apologize immediately and take the game down, lesson learned.

If the person doesn't respond, or can't be reached, try emailing his Internet service provider. If the person's site is something like `http://www.biginternethomepagecompany.com/~joethief/` then you can pretty easily find the `http://www.biginternethomepagecompany.com` and find an address there. If he has his own domain, use one of the many "whois" services you can find on the Internet to find out more about the owner. When you do a "whois" search, the results usually also list the network service provider for the site, whom you can e-mail after you find his main page.

Although Joe Thief might not email you back or might refuse to take down the game, his ISP is sure to want to take action to avoid a potential lawsuit.

High Score Boards

Most Flash games are played on the Internet. Not only does this offer great access to the games, but it can also offer a level of connectivity and community. A simple way to take advantage of the connectivity is to include a high score board. People can post scores to the server, and then view the best scores of all the people playing the game.

Adding a high score board to your game is no trivial task, however. It requires more than just Flash skills, because a program must be written for the Internet server to receive, record, and organize the scores.

How High Score Boards Work

High score boards can actually be built many ways. One way is to write a Java-based XML Socket program that your Flash game can communicate with via the XML object. Another way is to have your Flash game send and receive scores through JavaScript on the Web page, which then communicates with the server.

The most straightforward approach is to use a server-side Perl script to handle the scores, which is what you'll do here. Unfortunately, this means you'll have to learn about Perl and CGI scripts.

CGI (Common Gateway Interface) scripts are programs that run on Web servers. Perl is a programming language like ActionScript, but it is made to run on Web servers. A Perl program usually ends with a ".pl" or a ".cgi" extension rather than the ".html" extension used for a standard Web page. When the user browses to a Perl program, rather than the text of the program being served as an ".html" page would, the commands of the program are interpreted by the server as Perl commands. If the Perl program contains any output, that output is returned to the Web browser, or, in this case, to the Flash movie.

TIP

Perl is a subject big enough to deserve its own book. In fact, many books have been published on Perl, far more than have been published on Flash. If you want more information about Perl, go to your local bookstore and pick one out.

This example uses two Perl programs to maintain the high scores. The first is Submitscore.pl and it takes care of receiving a new score from the Flash movie. The second is Getscores.pl and it returns a list of the top 10 scores to the Flash movie.

Both these programs need to access a small database of scores. CGI programs usually use a server database, such as SQL, to store data. However, this example uses something a little simpler: a plain text file.

Each line of this text file contains a different submitted score. The three parts to this score are the name of the player, the score, and the time it was submitted. The Flash movie submits the name and score to the Submitscore.pl program, which adds the time stamp to it.

The Getscores.pl program looks at the text file with all the scores and performs two functions. First, it examines each score and rewrites the text file from scratch, excluding any old scores. This keeps the high score list fresh with only recent scores. The other function that Getscores.pl performs is to return to the Flash movie the 10 highest scores in order. This list is displayed for the players to see.

TIP

I like the idea of throwing away scores from the database when they get too old. This prevents one or more extreme scores from dominating the database over the period of years. It also encourages good players to return to the game often to reclaim their bragging rights.

The Perl Programs

The two Perl programs are on the CD-ROM as Submitscore.pl and Getscores.pl. To get these programs working on your server, you'll need to upload the files and set their permissions. If you have never done this before, ask your network administrator or Internet service provider about how to do this. Not all servers are configured to run CGI programs. If you are on a low-end or free Internet service that provides Web space to its users, you can probably assume that it doesn't allow CGI programs.

Although this section isn't a "Beginners Guide to Perl," the complete Perl programs with brief explanations of what each section does are shown here. If you aren't familiar with CGI programs, team up with someone who is.

Comments in Perl start with a # character. The Submitscore.pl program starts with a comment, but one that is actually used by the Web server to determine the path of the program that interprets Perl scripts. The path given here is a common path and might work on your server. If not, contact your Internet service provider.

```
#!/usr/bin/perl
```

The first real line of code starts by sending some output back to the Flash movie. This particular piece of output is the text "Content-type: text/html" followed by two line breaks. The first line of any file sent from a Web server tells the browser, or Flash movie in this case, what type of data is coming. In this case, the answer is plain text data.

```
# create header for text document to return
print "Content-type: text/html\n\n";
```

Next, the data is passed to the script from the Flash movie and temporarily stored in the variable "$get_data":

```
# get data passed in
$get_data = $ENV{'QUERY_STRING'};
```

When data arrives over a Web connection, it's usually encoded so that special characters arrive safely. Letters such as A, B, and C are not encoded, but spaces are encoded as "+", and nonalphanumeric characters are encoded as strings, such as "%0A." To reverse this encoding, you use the next two odd-looking lines of code:

```
# convert escape characters
$get_data =~ s/%([\dA-Fa-f][\dA-Fa-f])/pack ("C",hex($1))/eg;
$get_data =~ tr/\+/ /;
```

Next, you get the current time, in Unix server seconds. You'll use this as the time the score was posted. This is better than using the Flash movie time, because people are in different time zones, and some people don't even have their clocks set correctly on their computers.

```
# get the server time in seconds
$server_time = time();
```

Next is a loop that takes the "$get_data" string and breaks it into parts. It starts out as something like "name=Gary&score=967." This is broken into two items by dividing it at the "&", and then each item is broken into a key and a value by dividing it at the "=".

```
# take post data and create an array of data
@split_data = split("&",$get_data);
foreach $data_item (@split_data)
   {
   ($key, $value) = split("=",$data_item);
   $info{$key} = $value;
   }
```

The text database for your high scores is Highscore.txt. To start this file, upload a blank text file of that name and set its permissions so it can be written to by the Perl programs. The next lines of code open this file so that text can be appended to it:

```
# set filename for highscore database
$filename = "highscore.txt";

# open the database
open(OUTFILE,">>$filename") || exit;
```

After the file has been opened, the program writes a single line of text to it that contains the score, name, and time, and looks something like "967&Gary&978887513."

```
# append the data to the database
print OUTFILE "$info{'score'}&$info{'name'}&$server_time\n";
```

Finally, the Submitscore.pl program ends by closing the text file and returning some information to Flash. In this case, the "resultText" variable is set to the string "OK."

```
# close the database
close(OUTFILE);

# signify data written ok
print "resultText=OK\n";

# end this script
exit;
```

The Getscores.pl program is slightly more complex than Submitscore.pl. It has the task of reading the database, removing any old scores, and then returning a list of the top 10 scores.

It starts the same way as Submitscore.pl. Then the file opens the database and reads all the contents in an array variable called "@score_text."

```
#!/usr/bin/perl

# create header for text document to return
print "Content-type: text/html\n\n";
```

```
# set filename for highscore database
$filename = "highscore.txt";

# read high score data
open(DATABASE,$filename) || exit;
@score_text = <DATABASE>;
close(DATABASE);
```

Next, the program calculates what time it was, in Unix server seconds, exactly seven days ago.

```
# get the server time
$server_time = time();

# how long to keep the scores
# (7 days * 24 hours * 60 minutes * 60 seconds)
$keep_time = 7*(24*60*60);
```

The database is now opened again, but for writing. This new data overwrites the old file.

```
# open database file for writing
open(DATABASE,">" . $filename) || exit;
```

The following loop examines each score and determines whether it is too old. If it is, then it isn't rewritten to the new file.

```
# loop through each score
foreach $score_line (@score_text) {
  # get score data
  @score_item = split(/&/,$score_line);
  # get score time
  $score_time = $score_item[2];
  # if the score is not old, write it back out again
  if ($score_time > ($server_time-$keep_time)) {
    print DATABASE "$score_line";
  }
}

#close database
close(DATABASE);
```

Next, the Perl program sorts the scores. Because the score is the first thing in each item of the score database, the items are sorted by score, in this case from highest to lowest.

```
# sort scores
@score_text = sort { $b <=> $a } @score_text;
```

The next loop takes the first 10 scores and returns them as output. Each item of each line is specially formatted. A line looks something like " 1. Gary 967." The number of the line is followed by a period. Then, the name is included, padded out to 18 spaces if it is shorter. Then the score is included, padded to the left to 9 spaces in case it is shorter.

```
# determine number of scores to send
$num_scores = 10;
$score_count = 1;


# loop through first scores and send the data
print "highScoresText=";
foreach $score_line (@score_text) {

    # take post data and create an array of data
    @split_data = split("&",$score_line);
    # output the line number plus a period
    printf("%2i. ", $score_count);
    #output the player's name, left justified, padded to 18 spaces
    printf("%-18s ",$split_data[1]);
    #output the score, right justified, padded to 9 spaces
    printf("%9i\n",$split_data[0]);
    $score_count++;
    if ($score_count > $num_scores) { last; }
}


#exit script
exit;
```

All this Perl programming can be confusing if you have never seen Perl before or if you have only programmed in Flash. Take comfort in the fact that this sort of project is usually a team effort between a Flash programmer and a Perl programmer. Seek one out if you can.

Demonstration High Score Movie
✏Example file: Highscores.fla

Two programs on the CD-ROM use the high score scripts. The first is a demonstration movie that shows how a score is written to the database, and how scores are then retrieved from the database.

This movie, Highscores.fla, looks like Figure 17.5. The area to the bottom left allows you to submit a new score, and the area to the right allows you to view all high scores.

Figure 17.5

The high score demonstration movie allows you to test your Perl scripts.

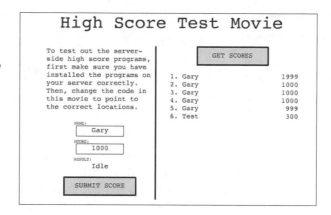

All the code in the Highscores.fla movie is located in the two buttons you can see in Figure 17.5.

The "Submit Score" section shows the player's name and score in editable text areas. When you run this program, you can type in a name and a score, and then click the Submit Score button. This is the code attached to that button.

```
on (press) {

    // location of the "submitscore.pl" program
    url = "submitscore.pl";

    // build LoadVars object
    myLoadVars = new LoadVars();
    myLoadVars.name = name;
    myLoadVars.score = score;

    // send
    returnedVars = new LoadVars();
    myLoadVars.sendAndLoad(url,returnedVars,"GET");
    resultText = "Sending...";

    // get result
    returnedVars.onLoad = function() {
```

```
        resultText = "Done."
    }
 }
```

You used the *LoadVars* object in Chapter 12, "Quizzes and Word Puzzles," for the quiz and trivia games. In those cases, you didn't send any variables to the server; you just requested a text file. In this case, you are calling a Perl program to send information to the server.

The "GET" at the end of the *sendAndLoad* command tells Flash that the GET protocol will be used to send the variables. This is one of two choices. The other is the POST protocol. Both of these correspond to the two ways that HTML pages can send data to the server with forms.

The values sent are the two properties of the "myLoadVars" object: "name" and "score." When the operation is done, the function defined for *onLoad* is executed. In this case, it just puts a message into the "resultText" text field.

The "Get Scores" button has a similar piece of code attached to it, but it doesn't need to send any variables:

```
on (press) {
    // location of the "getscores.pl" program
    url = "getscores.pl";

    // request data
    myLoadVars = new LoadVars();
    myLoadVars.load(url);
    highScoresText = "Getting High Scores...";

    // operation done
    myLoadVars.onLoad = function() {
        highscoresText = myLoadVars.highscoresText;
    }
 }
```

The text returned by the Getscores.pl program starts with a "highScoresText=." This places the remaining text into the variable of that name. The *onLoad* function takes this property value of "myLoadVars" and places it in the text field linked to a global variable of the same name. So as soon as the text arrives, it is shown there.

Implementing High Scores in a Game
Example file: Whackafoxwithscores.fla

A second high scores example file on the CD-ROM is called Whackafoxwithscores.fla. This is the same "Whack-A-Fox" game from Chapter 8, "Hunt and Click Games," but with a high score board added.

This is an easy movie to add high scores to because it was broken into three scenes. The "Start" scene has been changed to show the high score board when the game loads. In addition to the plain *stop()* command at the start of the first frame in this scene, you'll add the code needed to get the high scores:

```
// location of the "getscores.pl" program
url = "getscores.pl";

// request data
loadVariables (url,this);

// feedback to know that the button was pressed
highScoresText = "Getting High Scores...";

stop();
```

A text area named "highScoresText" has also been added to the middle of the screen. It looks like Figure 17.6.

Figure 17.6

The Whack-A-Fox game now displays high scores when it starts.

At the end of the game, in the "End" scene, there is a movie clip with some text areas and a "Submit Score" button. The score of the game must be set inside this movie clip. The game itself is run by an "actions" movie clip in the "Play" scene. Therefore, the "score" variable is a property of that movie clip, not of the main timeline. With the line "_root.score = score;" added to the script, the main timeline now also has a variable called "score" with the score in it.

When the "End" scene starts, the first frame places this score into the "sendscores" movie clip. It also resets the "name" variable in that movie clip to a blank string.

```
sendscores.name = "";
sendscores.score = score;
stop();
```

Figure 17.7 shows this "End" frame. You can see that text fields contain the player's score, a text input area for the player to enter his name, and the "Submit Score" button.

Figure 17.7
The last frame of the new Whack-A-Fox game allows the player to submit his score.

The player types his name into the first text area, but the text area containing the score is not available to him. After the player is satisfied with his name, he can click Submit Score, which runs this script:

```
on (press) {

    // location of the "submitscore.pl" program
    url = "submitscore.pl";

    // send variables
    myLoadVars = new LoadVars();
    myLoadVars.name = name;
    myLoadVars.score = score;
    returnVars = new LoadVars();
    myLoadVars.sendAndLoad(url,returnVars,"GET");

    // remove button so it can't be clicked again
    submitButton._visible = false;
}
```

The score is sent to the server in the same way that it is done in the Highscores.fla demonstration movie. However, the button's *_visible* property is also set to false. This prevents the player from pressing the button more than once and entering several scores.

High Score Board Issues

High score boards seem an obvious improvement to any game. But they bring about some more complex issues that you might not have considered.

By letting players type in anything they want as their names, you are essentially letting them publish something on your Web site. Sure, most players will just type a name or alias, but some will decide that profanity is what goes in the "name" box.

So why not check for curse words in the Flash game or the Perl script? You can do that, but there are many ways to get around it. People will use alternative spellings of words, or put spaces or dashes in between them. Others will use perfectly normal words to say something inappropriate. There's no way to prevent it completely.

Large professional sites usually require that players register before posting scores. But building a registration scoring system is far more complex than what this chapter can cover. Doing this requires a complete database system with security measures to boot.

Another issue is cheating. After a high score board is in place, players will find ways to cheat. It is actually quite easy to do. Methods range from finding ways to pause the Flash game at critical points so the player can catch her breath to using cheater programs that peek and poke at the memory in the player's computer. This can easily turn 42 points into 42 million points.

You can also use other programming languages to create high score boards. PHP is a Perl-like language that is very popular. Older languages such as C and C++ can be used to make CGI programs as well.

Testing Flash Player Versions

Example movie: Version.fla

Flash 4 and 5 ActionScript were so different from each other that it was unlikely that a Flash 5 movie with complex ActionScript would work at all if the user had the Flash 4 player. However, Flash 5 and MX are similar enough that a movie with Flash MX ActionScript code will often work with the Flash 5 player.

This creates an interesting problem. It would be easy to make a Flash MX game that works for some people using Flash 5—up to a point. When a piece of code is hit that requires the Flash 6 player, the game will stop working or perform unpredictably.

Getting the Player Version

The way to handle this is to make sure that the user has Flash 6 before you let them play the game. Thanks to the *getVersion()* function, you can do that.

The *getVersion()* function returns a simple string like "MAC 6,0,21,0". The first word is an abbreviation for the platform, usually MAC or WIN. The second part is the version of the Flash player currently running on the user's machine.

Each part of the version number is separated by commas. This makes it hard to compare the version number to a requirement. For instance, how do you determine whether "MAC 6,0,21,0" is greater than or equal to version 6?

With some string manipulation, you can convert the value returned by *getVersion()* to something more useful. The following function breaks the string down using the space and commas as points of reference. It creates a variable object that you can more easily address.

```
function getVersionNumber() {
    // get space and comma locations
    spacePos = getVersion().indexOf(" ");
    firstComma = getVersion().indexOf(",");
    secondComma = getVersion().indexOf(",",firstComma+1);
    thirdComma = getVersion().indexOf(",",secondComma+1);
    lastChar = getVersion().length;

    // build version object
    version = new Object();
    version.platform = getVersion().substring(0,spacePos);
    version.n1 = getVersion().substring(spacePos+1,firstComma);
    version.n2 = getVersion().substring(firstComma+1,secondComma);
    version.n3 = getVersion().substring(secondComma+1,thirdComma);
    version.n4 = getVersion().substring(thirdComma+1,lastChar);

    return(version);
}
```

The result of "getVersionNumber" will look something like this:

```
{platform: MAC, n1: 6, n2: 0, n3: 21, n4: 0}
```

So if you want to get the major version number of Flash, you can simply use "getVersionNumber().n1".

Requiring Versions

Typically, you will want to compare the version number against a minimum requirement that you need for your game. For instance, you might want to require that the user have at least version 6.0.21.0 to play your game.

Here is a function that takes a full version number and compares it to the actual version of the Flash player running. It returns true only if the version is greater than or equal to the requirement.

```
function requiredVersion(required) {
    version = getVersionNumber();

    // false if version number is less than what is required
    if (version.n1 < required.n1) return(false);
```

```
    // true if version number is greater than what is required
    if (voroion.n1 > required.n1) return(true);

    // version numbers are equal, so go to minor version numbers
    // and repeat the previous tests
    if (version.n2 < required.n2) return (false);
    if (version.n2 > required.n2) return (true);

    if (version.n3 < required.n3) return (false);
    if (version.n3 > required.n3) return (true);

    if (version.n4 < required.n4) return (false);
    if (version.n4 >= required.n4) return (true);
}
```

You can use this function like this:

```
if (requiredVersion({n1:6,n2:0,n3:21,n4:0})) {
    gotoAndPlay("start");
} else {
    gotoAndStop("version problem");
}
```

If the user's version is less than 6.0.21.0, then the movie goes to a frame that explains that she needs to upgrade before using the game.

NOTE

All the code in "getVersionNumber" and "requiredVersion" will work in both Flash 5 and 6 players. They have to. The code would be worthless if it worked only in version 6. The whole idea is to warn Flash 5 player users of the potential problem.

A common use for this function would be to check for a minor update to the Flash player. For instance, suppose Macromedia releases Flash version 6.0.42.0. This new version has a bug fix that your game needs to operate correctly. You can check to make sure users have this version and warn them if they do not.

It's important that this check return true if the user has the required version, *or newer*. An example of a common mistake that programmers make is to look for a specific version number, like version 6. Then if the player has version 5, or any other version, it warns him that he needs to upgrade. A year later, version 7 comes out, and because version 7 is not version 6, the user gets the same warning! I see this all the time in Flash, Shockwave, and JavaScript programming. The "requiredVersion" function always returns true if the version is newer than the required version.

Flash 6 Player Capabilities

In addition to learning about the Flash player version number, you may also need to find out about other capabilities of the different variations of the player. Flash is being ported to various devices such as handheld PDAs and set-top boxes. Some of these devices are not able to support the full array of features that Flash 6 does on Mac and Windows.

You can test for a specific feature with the *System.capabilities* property. This property returns an object with various properties. Here is a piece of code that loops through all the properties and returns each value.

```
// list all capabilities
capabilitiesDisplay = "";
for(i in System.capabilities) {
    capabilitiesDisplay += i+": "+System.capabilities[i] + newline;
}
```

The returned list looks like this on my Macintosh Powerbook:

```
language: en-US
input: point
manufacturer: Macromedia Macintosh
os: Mac OS 10.1.3
serverString: A=t&MP3=t&AE=t&VE=t&ACC=f&DEB=t&V=MAC%206%2C0%2C21%2C0&M=
Macromedia Macintosh&R=1152x768&DP=72&COL=color&AR=1&I=point&OS=
Mac OS 10.1.3&L=en
isDebugger: true
version: MAC 6,0,21,0
hasAudio: true
hasMP3: true
hasAudioEncoder: true
hasVideoEncoder: true
screenResolutionX: 1152
screenResolutionY: 768
screenDPI: 72
screenColor: color
```

One of the problems with *System.capabilities* is that there is no guarantee that that property names and value types will remain the same from player the player. You'll have to test *System.capabilities* on any system on which you want to play your movies back. Then you'll need to compile a possible list of properties and values that you want to check. For instance, you may notice that "hasMP3" is false on some players, whereas another player doesn't even list a "hasMP3" property. As the Flash 6 Player is ported to other machines, only time will tell how consistent *System.capabilities* is.

One useful way to use *System.capabilities* is to grab the *screenResolutionX* and *screenResolutionY* properties to advise the user if she has her display setting set to something that would be too small to comfortably display your movie. You can also deconstruct the *System.capabilities.os* in the same way that you already saw *getVersion()* deconstructed so that you can check to be sure that the user has a recent-enough OS.

Internet Resources for the Flash Developer

So you've read this whole book, taken every game and built your own from it, and you're still hungry for more information about Flash? Well, there's plenty to be had. The Web is full of sites for Flash developers, by Flash developers.

All these sites are independent of Macromedia and contain a wealth of information. You'll find that most have similar content: articles, tutorials, open-source files, and message boards. The quality of the site largely depends on its contributors, especially when it comes to message boards. Every serious Flash developer should find a site or three from the following list that fits his or her style and become a part of that community.

The author maintains the site http://developerdispatch.com/, which includes a longer list of links to other sites. Visit http://developerdispatch.com/ for news and updated links about Flash MX.

Actionscript.com—http://www.actionscript.com/

Actionscripts.org—http://www.actionscripts.org/

Art's Flash Files—http://www.artswebsite.com/coolstuff/flash.htm

Developer Dispatch—http://www.developerdispatch.com

Flash 4 All—http://www.flash4all.de/ (German and English)

The Flash Academy—http://www.enetserve.com/tutorials/

Flash Geek—http://www.flashgeek.com/

Flash Heaven—http://www.flashheaven.de/ (German and English)

Flash Kit—http://www.flashkit.com/

FlashMaestro—http://www.flashmaestro.fm/ (Spanish)

Flash Magazine—http://www.flashmagazine.com/

Flash Pro—http://www.flashpro.nl/

Flazoom—http://www.flazoom.com/

Kirupa—http://www.kirupa.com/developer/

Colin Moock—http://www.moock.org/webdesign/flash/

Pro Flasher—http://www.proflasher.com/

Warp 9—http://www.warp9.it/ (Italian)

We're Here Forums—http://www.were-here.com/

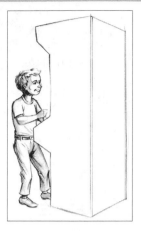

The History of Games

Imagine a world without computer games. It's not that hard considering the first computer game, *Space War*, was created in 1962. Then it wasn't until the 1970s that the general public could play the first video games.

Imagine being the person to create the first computer game. There was little inspiration to draw on. Today, we can look back on countless video games and home computer games. Almost everything we create is a derivative of something out of the past.

That first computer game was totally original. Since then, computers have revolutionized the world of games. Plus, we have a lot of inspiration.

From *Senet* to *Space War*

Games predate written history. It seems that we have always been interested in building little virtual realities where we can compete.

The Evolution of Board Games

The first board games were racing games, much like today's backgammon. One of the oldest game boards in existence is for a game called *Senet*, which was popular in Egypt more than 2,000 years ago.

Figure B.1
Senet was played by the ancient Egyptians.

The game involved two players, each of whom had several pieces. The players threw sticks, because dice had not yet been invented, and moved their pieces along the board. The goal was to get your pieces to the end, which represented heaven.

This same game was adopted by other cultures for more than a thousand years. Each culture changed the playing pieces and what the game's goal represented, but for the most part the game was the same.

NOTE
Senet's goal was actually to get your pieces to the last few spaces, which represented heaven. Many games used this as their goal. Today's game of hopscotch actually has the same goal, even though most people who play it don't know that the last space represents heaven.

In addition to racing games, another early type of game was a variety of *Nine Men's Morris*. This game involved a board with connected points. Each player had nine pieces and could move one piece per move along one connection to another point. If a player got three pieces in a row, he was allowed to remove one of his opponent's pieces.

This type of game evolved into games such as checkers and chess. The goal was to remove your opponent's pieces, while at the same time protecting yours.

Games like this simulated an all too common theme in human history: war. Other cultures developed games like it, such as *Go* in Japan.

The ultimate war game, chess, evolved out of these early simple games. It started in 6th century India, but did not adapt modern features, such as the powerful queen, until the 15th century.

Chess spread throughout the world quickly, and is seen today by many as the ultimate game: easy to learn, but hard to master. In the 20th century, the best chess players in the world are seen as celebrities, and chess tournaments make headlines.

The world of board games changed to what it is today in the late 19th century and early 20th. Companies such as Milton Bradley and Parker Brothers started inventing, mass-producing, and marketing games. New standards such as *Scrabble* and *Monopoly* were born out of old ideas. In addition, older games were codified by people such as Sir Edmund Hoyle, who set their rules in stone.

In America during the 20th century, a closet shelf full of board games became a standard. Games rose and fell in popularity as efforts by game companies to market them succeeded and failed.

War and Role-Playing Games

Board games are a casual experience for the most part. A typical game is easy to learn and can be played in an hour or two. However, some gamers desire a more engaging experience.

War games have existed in some form or another throughout history. However, the first modern war games were played in the 19th century. Military experts used large tables covered with sand and elaborate figures to plan out and test strategies.

The main purpose of the first war games was to plan out real battles. However, they soon came to be used as training tools as well. Military students would reenact battles and make up scenarios. It was, and still is, a valuable tool.

Simplified versions of war games began to be used for recreation. The author H.G. Wells is often cited as the inventor of the first recreational war game. Boards with grids replaced the large tables. Instead of doing complex calculations, players used simple dice rolls and rules to decide the outcome of moves.

In the 1960s and 70s, war games were mass-produced in boxes with booklets that described the rules and large paper grids to play on. Several new games were produced annually, and magazines were even published on the subject.

From the world of war games came the world of role-playing games. The inventors of *Dungeons & Dragons* were out to make an interesting war game scenario that involved soldiers from the middle ages going into an old castle and dungeon. Before they completed the scenario, they ended up with a whole new game complete with a telephone book-sized set of rules. When they published a simplified version of these rules, they created a gaming phenomenon.

Dungeons & Dragons spawned many competitors and also many other types of role-playing games. Just about every type of adventure could be found in a box at your local hobby store: science fiction, espionage, Old West, and even game systems to handle any type of world.

The role-playing games broke down the idea of what a game was and how long of an experience it was. It created a cottage industry of game companies and players that were willing to try new things. This set the stage for the computer age of games.

From *Space War* to *Pong*

The first computer game was created by Steve Russell and other graduate students in 1962 on a PDP-1 mainframe computer at the Massachusetts Institute of Technology. It involved two space ships that floated around in the gravity-free environment of space and shot pixels at each other. The graphics were actually much better than what was to follow. The game even included a mathematically generated star field behind the ships.

This first game was addicting and fun. It was made freely available by the creators, so it soon found itself on just about every PDP-1 computer at every college that had one. However, commercial success was out of the question, as PDP-1 computers were too expensive to make into arcade machines, and no one owned a personal computer yet.

Meanwhile, the computer game evolved. A game called *Lunar Lander* consisted of absolutely no graphics, but could be played on computers that had no screen, only a spool of paper as an output device. A line of text would appear to tell you your position, velocity, and fuel remaining. You made a move, and the new position, velocity, and fuel update were printed. The object was to land before running out of fuel.

Not far behind these games was the classic *Adventure*. This was a precursor to all computer adventure and role playing games. The game was purely text based. It described your location, and you gave commands such as "go north" or "pick up sword."

The computer game first came into the public eye with early arcade games, such as *Pong*. These games were first placed in shopping malls, right next to pinball machines and other coin-operated devices. But they soon took over the arcades.

From *Pong* to *Pac-Man*

The first coin-operated video game was Nolan Bushnell's *Computer Space*. It was like *Space War*, with the user controlling a ship out to destroy an enemy flying saucer. The machine accepted quarters.

Computer Space was not very successful. It turned out that the concept and controls were too advanced for people who had never seen a computer before.

Bushnell took his modest profits, only $500, and created his own company: Atari.

NOTE
Atari is the warning call that players give each other in the Japanese game of *Go*.

Atari's first creation was *Pong*, a game much simpler than *Computer Space*. The game was a success. Atari distributed the game through the same channels as pinball machines.

The next step for Atari was to sell *Pong* into homes. Atari teamed up with Sears to sell a home version of the game in 1975. Then, in 1976, Atari introduced *Breakout*, the first of the more complex video game classics. Not only was *Breakout* notable because it brought video games to a new level, but also because it was designed by Steven Jobs, who later revolutionized the personal computer industry.

In 1979, a Japanese company, Taito, developed *Space Invaders*, the first genuine video game hit. It began to take over the arcades. Atari fought back with its own hit, *Asteroids*.

Also during 1979 and 1980, dozens of other games were invented in which players fought robots and aliens. However, the next big hit came from a simple maze game where the hero was a yellow dot.

Pac-Man was not expected to be a hit. It was seen as too "cute" to be taken seriously. But kids in the arcades loved it. It was also the first arcade game that appealed to girls as well as boys and the first video game to bring in money from merchandising.

In 1982 there were 1.5 million arcade game machines in America in about 24,000 arcades and many miscellaneous locations. At the same time, 20 million home video games were sold, which cut heavily into the amount of television watched at home. In 1982, the video game industry was bringing in twice as much revenue as the American film industry.

The early 1980s saw a constant stream of new video games by competing companies. The video arcade industry peaked around that time, and then fell back to the more stable level that we have today. This decline was caused by several factors, including the modernization of the mall and the advent of home game systems.

Figure B.2
The heyday of video arcade games was in the early 1980s, but the machines still remain popular today.

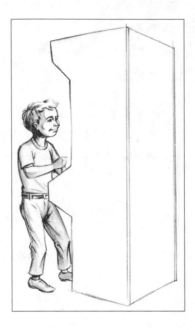

The Video Game Comes Home

In the late 1960s, an electrical engineer named Ralph Baer began creating the first home video game system. His first models didn't even use microchips. However, they did connect directly to a standard television set. This eventually became the Odyssey game system.

The Odyssey included 12 different games printed on circuit cards. In addition, players had to place a transparent screen over their televisions to provide the background. Players also had to keep track of their own scoring by marking little sheets of paper.

The next advancement was provided by the General Instruments Corporation, which developed a microchip that manufacturers could buy for $5 or $6 that allowed more complex home video games to be developed. Coleco used it to develop the Telstar system.

Soon, companies such as Fairchild, RCA, Atari, and Mattel introduced new game systems that could be programmed. This allowed other companies to develop cartridges for them. The Atari Video Computer System eventually dominated the field. It sold more than 12 million units and more than 200 game cartridges were created for it.

The home video game system is still just as popular today, but the players are different. Sony's PlayStation II, Microsoft's Xbox, and Nintendo's GameCube system are the three most popular.

Figure B.3
The home video game system became a household item in the 1980s.

These modern home systems rival both the personal computer and the coin-operated arcade machine. The processors are fast, and the CD media or cartridges contain quite a bit of data.

Games Invade Computers

At the same time, the introduction of the personal computer meant that more complex games could be played as well. A huge library of games existed for computers such as the Apple II. It was easy for any programmer, with almost no money, to develop games for computers and avoid the expensive manufacturing process of the video game console.

In the 1980s, just about every successful video arcade game was translated to a game for the personal computer. Some of these games were legitimate versions made by their original creators, and others were imitations.

In addition, new games sprung up for the personal computer. Because no hardware had to be built to make the games available, it cost less to develop a game for a computer. The only things you needed to actually manufacture were the floppy disks and any printed materials.

This meant that games with a smaller potential audience could be produced. When modems and bulletin board systems became popular in the late 1980s, you could even make a game and distribute it free.

Eventually the CD-ROM drive gave game developers the chance to create games with a multimedia flair. *Myst* set the standard for CD-ROM adventure games that is still followed today. This game has hundreds of detailed still images.

Today's CD-ROM adventure games feature even more detailed images, along with soundtracks and complex interfaces. In the mid-1990s, *Phantasmagoria* used seven CD-ROMs to create an intense environment.

In addition to offering a large potential distribution base, computers also allowed developers to experiment with new techniques. Games such as *Doom* started the "first-person 3D shooter" genre. By the mid-1990s, just about *every* action game on the market fit into this category.

Web-Based Computer Games

Macromedia Flash and Shockwave are part of a new chapter in the history of games. The Web gives people easy access to all sorts of content, and at the same time makes it easy for developers to publish their content.

Although floppy disks and CD-ROMs built the computer game industry, they also made sure that games could only be published by those who had enough money to secure shelf space in software stores. With Web-based games, this is not an obstacle.

The result is that more developers can take their games directly to the people who play them. It also means that companies that would not normally be in the games business are making games. For instance, every major Web portal has a games section featuring its own games.

Web-based games are made in either Flash, Shockwave, or Java. However, some games are made with simple HTML and server-side scripting, and others are made with lesser-known browser plug-ins.

At the start of 2002, Flash MX shows considerable promise at becoming the most used game development environment on the Web. Whether this trend continues depends on the developers and what Macromedia has in store for future versions of Flash.

Further Reading

If you are interested in the history of games and computer games, here are some books that you might want to check out:

Screen Play: The Story of Video games
George Sullivan
Copyright 1983
Publisher: Frederick Warne & Co., Inc., New York, NY

Content: History of computer and video games.

Joystick Nation
by J.C. Herz
1997
Published by Little, Brown & Company Limited

Content: History of computer and video games.

The World of Games
Jack Botermans, Tony Burrett, Pieter van Delft, Carla van Splunteren
1987
Published by Facts on File, Inc., New York and Oxford

Content: History of games. A lot of illustrations.

The Greatest Games of All Time
Mathew J. Costello
1991
John Wiley & Sons, Inc.

Content: Interesting stories about old and new games, the game industry, and video games. Highly recommended.

Game Over: Press Start to Continue
David Sheff
1993
Random House

Content: The history of Nintendo. Highly recommended.

Hackers: Heroes of the Computer Revolution
Steven Levy
1984
Anchor Press

Content: A great account of many computer pioneers, including a lot of information about the gaming industry in the early '80s.

According to Hoyle
Richard L. Frey
1956, 1965, 1970
Fawcett Columbine

Content: Game rules.

The Oxford History of Board Games
David Parlett
1999
Oxford University Press

Content: The history of games.

Family Fun & Games
1992
Sterling Publishing Company

Content: Game rules.

A Brief History of Home Video Games
(An Online Book)
Sam Hart
1996–1999
`http://newton.physics.arizona.edu/~hart/vgh`

Content: Essays about different video game machines.

Index

G

J - K

N

Q - R

S

Hey, you've got enough worries.

Don't let IT training be one of them.

Get on the fast track to IT training at InformIT,
your total Information Technology training network.

  | **www.informit.com** |

■ Hundreds of timely articles on dozens of topics ■ Discounts on IT books from all our publishing partners, including Que Publishing ■ Free, unabridged books from the InformIT Free Library ■ "Expert Q&A"—our live, online chat with IT experts ■ Faster, easier certification and training from our Web- or classroom-based training programs ■ Current IT news ■ Software downloads ■ Career-enhancing resources

Installation Instructions

Windows 95/NT 4

1. Insert the CD-ROM into your CD-ROM drive (See NOTE at Bottom).
2. From the Windows desktop, double-click on the My Computer icon.
3. Double-click on the icon representing your CD-ROM drive.
4. Double-click on the icon titled START.EXE to run the multimedia user interface.

NOTE: If Windows 95/NT 4.0 is installed on your computer, and you have the AutoPlay feature enabled, the Start.exe program starts automatically whenever you insert the disc into your CD-ROM drive.

Read This Before Opening the Software